BESTSELLING
BOOK SERIES

# Machinima For Dummies®

| Table CS-1 | Sims 2 Keyboard Commands |
| --- | --- |
| **Keyboard Shortcut** | **Command** |
| Ctrl+Shift+C | Brings up the cheat window/console. |
| W, S, A, D | Forward, backward, slide left, slide right. |
| <, > | Rotate camera left and right. |
| Q, E | Move camera up, move camera down. |
| Z, X | Zoom in, zoom out. |
| Tab | Enter or leave camera mode. |
| Ctrl+4 through Ctrl+9 | Remember camera position. |
| 4 through 9 | Go to prerecorded camera position. |
| P | Pause game/unpause game. |
| V | Start/stop recording to video file. |

| Table CS-2 | MovieStorm Keyboard Commands |
| --- | --- |
| **Keyboard Shortcut** | **Command** |
| Ctrl+click | Rotate a placed object. |
| Esc | Get out of Demolish mode. |
| Press and hold middle mouse button | Move around. |
| Mousewheel | Crane up and down. |
| Click and hold right mouse button | Pan around. |
| In a camera view, click an object | Switch to Targeted camera. |
| In a camera view, double-click a character | Move to a one-shot on that character. |

# Machinima For Dummies®

## Table CS-3 — Medieval II: Total War CineEd Commands

| Keyboard Shortcut | Command |
| --- | --- |
| Tab in MTW2 window | Switch between camera and free view. |
| P in MTW2 window | Switch to picture-in-picture mode. |
| Shift+right-click on timeline | Set rewind point. |
| Spacebar | Play back/pause camera movement only. |
| Enter | Play back/pause recorded action and camera. |
| <, > | Zoom in and out on timeline. |
| Insert/double-click timeline | Add new keyframe. |

## Table CS-4 — Medieval II: Total War

| Keyboard Shortcut | Command |
| --- | --- |
| NumPad 8 | Move forward quickly. |
| NumPad 5 | Move forward slowly. |
| NumPad 2 | Move backward. |
| NumPad 4, 6 | Slide left and right. |
| NumPad 1, 3 | Turn left and right. |
| NumPad *, / | Move up and down. |
| NumPad -, + | Look down and up. |
| <, > | Reduce or increase tool intensity. |

## Top Ten Machinima Tips

Take a break every so often.

Get other people's opinion on your work.

Don't be too ambitious.

Don't copy other Machinima movies.

Plan before you do anything else.

The script is the most important part of your movie!

Try to use existing art (unless you can't legally).

The sound can tell as much of the story as the visuals.

Your movie's finished only when you've released and publicized it!

Don't be afraid to enter competitions.

## For Dummies: Bestselling Book Series for Beginners

# Machinima

## FOR

## DUMMIES®

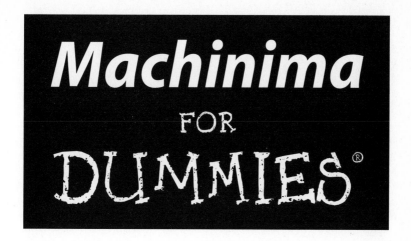

# by Hugh Hancock and Johnnie Ingram

Wiley Publishing, Inc.

**Machinima For Dummies®**

Published by
**Wiley Publishing, Inc.**
111 River Street
Hoboken, NJ 07030-5774
www.wiley.com

WILEY

# About the Authors

**Hugh Hancock,** one of the two people who coined the word *Machinima* in 1999, has worked in the medium for more than a decade running Strange Company (`www.strangecompany.org`), the world's oldest professional Machinima production company. He has lectured on Machinima on three continents, had his work shown on five (we're still waiting for Antarctica), had his films featured in *Entertainment Weekly,* on Suicide Girls (`www.suicide girls.com`), and in *The New York Times,* and produced Machinima films for the BBC, BAFTA, Electronic Arts, and many others. In 2007, he was awarded the first Award for Outstanding Contribution to Machinima by the Online Machinima Film Festival. Most recently, he completed work on BloodSpell (`www.bloodspell.com`), Strange Company's first feature film, and is currently working on Strange Company's next major project. He lives in Edinburgh and is intermittently single.

**Johnnie Ingram** is the former site editor of Machinima.com and holds degrees in both drama and computer science. He lives with his computers in a converted church hall in Scotland. He has previously worked as a theater director, an online journalist, and a drama teacher, as well as once dressing up as a priest in order to sell washing powder. He was first assistant director for *BloodSpell.* He is now a self-employed Web designer and Strange Company's Head Of Beverage Acquisition and Caffeine Development. He is married with one cat.

# Dedication

**Hugh:** This book is dedicated to the Strange Company Volunteer Corps, who have selflessly given many hours' work to help Strange Company make films in computer games, and to the Machinima community, who have been wonderful people to know for a decade, and without whom there'd not be much point in writing this book. That might sound sappy, but I mean it.

**Johnnie:** To Laura, for the obvious reasons, and all the other reasons as well. It's only time. Also for Heidi Burkitt, Richard Killian, Neville Wijeyeratnam, and Mike Caden.

# Authors' Acknowledgments

We'd like to thank Phil "Overman" Rice, our technical reviewer, both for his work on the book and for being, as we say in the UK, a top bloke.

At Wiley, Melody Layne, our acquisitions editor, came up with the idea for the book in the first place, made it happen, and has been a brilliant contact throughout. Kelly Ewing, our project editor, has done a fantastic job polishing our prose and coped admirably with the sudden crash course in geek culture. Chris Morris was great editing the first part of the book, and it was a pleasure working with him.

We'd like to thank our agent, not just because we've always wanted to say that, but also because she did a great and highly professional job guiding two novice authors through the publishing minefield. Thanks, Caitlin.

We'd like to thank all the people we landed on with zero seconds' notice to help proofread our tortured prose: Martin Page, Paul Marino, Matt Kelland, Dave Lloyd, Ben Sanders, Peter Brophy, Friedrich Kirschner, Ezra Fergusson, Stuart Brown, Eric Call, and Jennifer Urban.

Thanks to everybody in the Machinima community for all their help and support.

And finally, we'd like to thank all our other friends who we neglected, missed coffee with, and, in extreme cases, concussed with large piles of paper. Thanks to all of them, and in particular to Alex Nuttgens, Amanda and Gordon McDonald, Paul AJ Hamilton, Steve Wallace, Caroline Dunford and Graham Gibson, Jehane Barbour, Ian Mulliner, Barry Martin, Charlie Stross, Martin Page, Clare Brady, Paul Caden, Eleanor Dickenson, Nicola Freize, Joe Gibson, Rachel Holmes, Keiran Leach, Chris and Mary Ingram, Simon Ingram, JD Smith, Trudy Wijeyeratnam, David Wright, everybody at Edinburgh's Open Roleplaying Community, and the person who we've forgotten and will now be paranoid that we secretly don't like them.

## Publisher's Acknowledgments

We're proud of this book; please send us your comments through our online registration form located at www.dummies.com/register/.

Some of the people who helped bring this book to market include the following:

*Acquisitions, Editorial, and Media Development*

**Project Editor:** Kelly Ewing

**Sr. Acquisitions Editor:** Melody Layne

**Technical Editor:** Phil Rice

**Editorial Manager:** Jodi Jensen

**Media Development and Quality Assurance:** Kate Jenkins

**Media Development Coordinator:** Jenny Swisher

**Media Project Supervisor:** Laura Moss-Hollister

**Editorial Assistant:** Amanda Foxworth

**Sr. Editorial Assistant:** Cherie Case

**Cartoons:** Rich Tennant (www.the5thwave.com)

*Composition Services*

**Project Coordinator:** Adrienne Martinez

**Layout and Graphics:** Carl Byers, Joyce Haughey, Shane Johnson, Stephanie D. Jumper, Heather Ryan, Alicia B. South, Ronald Terry, Christine Williams

**Proofreader:** Aptara

**Indexer:** Potomac Indexing, LLC

**Anniversary Logo Design:** Richard Pacifico

**Publishing and Editorial for Technology Dummies**

**Richard Swadley,** Vice President and Executive Group Publisher

**Andy Cummings,** Vice President and Publisher

**Mary Bednarek,** Executive Acquisitions Director

**Mary C. Corder,** Editorial Director

**Publishing for Consumer Dummies**

**Diane Graves Steele,** Vice President and Publisher

**Joyce Pepple,** Acquisitions Director

**Composition Services**

**Gerry Fahey,** Vice President of Production Services

**Debbie Stailey,** Director of Composition Services

# Contents at a Glance

# Table of Contents

# Introduction

• • • • • • • • • • • • • • • • • • • • • • • • • • • • • • • • • • • • • • • • • • • •

*I*f you ever meet either Hugh or Johnnie, your humble authors (who very much enjoy writing in the third person), there's a simple way to have some fun. Ask them "What is Machinima?" Then watch as they stumble over their words.

Machinima is the maverick film-making process that evolved from hackers messing with the insides of their favorite computer games. At last count, it had attracted the attention of everyone from *The New York Times* to George Lucas and Stephen Spielberg.

It's a philosophy, a fervent belief, a technique, and, last of all, a technology.

As a philosophy, it's about taking advantage of the technologies used in video games and twisting, tweaking, and reusing them to make movies. It's a philosophy that says, "Hey, these virtual worlds look pretty neat. Why not just shoot our movies in them and do things we can't do in the real world?"

As a belief, it holds that everyone, everywhere, should be able to make movies. Not just cute indie movies or things that you can shoot with a camcorder, but any movie you want to make. Starships. Guns. Action. Cast of thousands. Anything.

As a technique, or rather a body of techniques, it's — well, it's this book. It's a whole bunch of tips, hints, and occasionally downright dirty tricks designed to fool software that really was not designed for filmmaking into making darn good movies anyway.

And as a technology? Well . . .

At the risk of showing you the man behind the curtain, the text you're reading now was actually one of the last things we wrote for this book. On the day we wrote this introduction, we'd already written more than 8,000 words for the book. We also shot 25 seconds of movie footage that day. The scene we shot is a huge, dramatic battle sequence. A column of mounted knights rides down a hill, through cannon fire, past a column of war elephants, and plunges into the back of a pack of fleeing peasants. It's about seven shots that would have taken days — and tens, if not hundreds, of thousands of dollars — to shoot in conventional video.

We conceived, designed, shot, and wrapped the entire thing in our lunch hour.

*That* is Machinima.

# About This Book

No matter how much we guide you along the way, by far the best way to learn about Machinima is to sit down at your keyboard and make some. Machinima is a hacker's technique at its core, and it's about as hands-on as you can get. We encourage you to experiment; to play with the game engines and tools that we'll talk about; to get your hands dirty; and to have fun.

There's no need to read the book from cover to cover. We certainly wouldn't recommend that as your first task. We're going to be delving deeply into the murky waters of Machinima movie-making. The entire book is probably too much for anyone to swallow in one go. For those who do want to start at the beginning and work diligently through to the very end, we've tried to cover the basics in the early chapters and let you get stuck into making a movie as soon as we can. Later chapters focus on some of the more advanced theory and practice behind movie-making and Machinima.

Above all, though, this book is designed as a reference that you can dip into at random. Machinima is a field containing a huge range of potential subjects. We've tried to cover them all while still producing a tome that you can lift without the aid of heavy machinery.

# Foolish Assumptions

We don't know you (although we're sure that you're very nice) and we've no idea how you're planning to approach this book. We don't know if you're an experienced Machinima maker, an interested geek, or a complete newcomer. Wherever you lie on the scale, we hope this book will be useful to you. If you'll forgive the presumption, though, we've made a few assumptions about you:

- ✔ **You want to find out how to tell stories using Machinima techniques.** We don't expect you to have any specific ideas yet, just a desire to create.

- ✔ **You're pretty new to all this stuff.** You may already have made some Machinima, but you're still looking for a solid grounding in Machinima techniques, using several different engines.

  Of course, if even the word *Machinima* was new to you before you plucked this book from the shelf, that's fine, too. Welcome to the revolution!

- ✔ **You have access to a computer (probably a PC).** You need a reasonably modern computer to run most of the games that we reference in this book. Although some Machinima-capable games run under Mac OS or Linux, the vast majority require a PC running Microsoft Windows (preferably Windows 2000 or later).

You don't need a bleeding-edge system with all the mod-cons, but if your machine is more than a couple of years old, it'll struggle with some of the more demanding engines. The faster the better, of course — you can never have too much power.

✔ **You have broadband Internet access.** Machinima is a technique that was born on the Internet and still lives happily under its parents' roof to this day. Without a broadband Internet connection, you're going to find bits of this book a little tricky. We recommend Web sites to you, ask you to download the latest game patches, or recommend that you watch the newest Machinima movies over video-sharing sites.

# How This Book Is Organized

This book has four major parts, each covering a meaty chunk of Machinima knowledge, plus the "bonus" fifth, The Part of Tens. If you're looking for something specific, a quite terrifyingly detailed Table of Contents at the start of the book and the Index at the back of book can help you out.

## Part I: Introducing Machinima

In this part, we take you through very basics of how Machinima is created and give you the chance to make your first movie. If you were James Bond, this part would be the bit where M calls you into her office and gives you a potted ten-minute summary of the latest threat to the British Crown.

## Part II: Getting Serious

In our second part, we go deep into film-making and give you everything you need to know to make a very competent movie — even a feature film, if you so desire. We introduce you to The Sims 2, arguably the most popular Machinima engine in the world. We tell you about cinematography and film-making, storytelling, editing, and distribution, show you how to make characters and sets, and give you an overview of all the technologies available to you as a Machinima filmmaker.

# Part III: Advanced Machinima Creation

In Part III, we introduce more advanced topics. We discuss two more Machinima creation engines, the hyper-popular World of Warcraft and the hyper-spectacular Medieval II: Total War, which you can use to make radically different movies to those possible in The Sims 2. We talk about sound editing and sound recording, as well as how to publicize your movie to make yourself a household name. And finally, we cover some of the legal issues that afflict Machinima in the hope that you can avoid becoming a household name in, you know, a bad way.

# Part IV: The Final Frontier: Pro Machinima

This part contains the hard-core material. It's deep. It's serious. It probably had a liberal arts education and can quote Allen Ginsberg from memory.

We look into 3D modeling and how to create 3D objects using the same techniques that are used in top-name animation companies. We discuss becoming a Machinima professional — and whether you should. We take you deep inside the technology: recoding, hacking, and tweaking it for your own ends using programming languages and more. Finally, we come full circle as we reintroduce Moviestorm, the engine we use in Part I, this time as the most fully featured and professional Machinima production tool available.

# Part V: The Part of Tens

In venerable *For Dummies* tradition, we end the book with a list of lists. Ten Machinima movies you must watch, ten Machinima sites you must visit, and ten Machinima mistakes you must avoid.

# Conventions Used in This Book

When we say *conventions,* we don't mean a large meeting in a hotel where someone dresses up as Darth Vader. Just in case you were unsure:

   ✔ **We've written each chapter of this book as a self-contained whole.** If they were plants, they would be those freaky things that live on air alone.

✔ **We don't write code very often,** because Machinima isn't incredibly coding-heavy. When we do, you can distinguish it from text because it looks like this:

```
SET Machinima_For_Dummies = 1337
```

✔ **We quote movie scripts at various points in the book.** When we do quote, we use conventional script format. We discuss script format in more detail in Chapter 4.

# Icons Used in This Book

Every so often, we felt something in this book was especially noteworthy, so we highlight those points with icons:

This icon points out helpful tidbits or pointers — anything that's a quick tip for the topic on hand.

All your base may shortly be overrun by hideous aliens if you fail to heed these warnings! Or at least something may crash or go a bit funny.

As you may expect, it's a good idea not to forget these points.

Coming to you live from the School of Hard Knocks, these are practical points that we've learned through real-world experience. Hopefully, they'll help you avoid or engineer similar circumstances.

This icon marks hard-core techie material. You don't need to know it to understand the rest of the book. If you're as geeky as us, though, you'll probably find it interesting.

This icon shows you when you can find items included on this book's DVD.

# *Where to Go from Here*

Onward! To victory! We few, we lucky few, we band of Machinimators. . . .

You could dive straight in to Chapter 1, if you like. We promise that within 50 pages, you'll have completed your first movie. Or if there's something particularly interesting to you — perhaps you're a World of Warcraft addict (Chapter 11) or really want to get to the big battles in Medieval II: Total War (Chapter 12) — feel free to skip ahead.

But most importantly, try Machinima out for yourself! This book is great (your authors say modestly), but you'll discover more techniques faster by actually diving in and creating movies yourself. Moviestorm is on the cover DVD, so go install, play, create, stick it up on YouTube, get discovered, and make a million bucks! Or, you know, at least get a few hundred views, and a temporary stalker named Boris. Either way, read, make, enjoy. Good luck and welcome to the Machinima revolution.

# Part I
# Introducing Machinima

The 5th Wave — By Rich Tennant

"Wait a minute... This is a movie, not a game?! I thought I was the one making Keanu Reeves jump kick in slow motion."

## In this part . . .

What the heck is this Machinima stuff anyway? It's not as easy an answer as you may think. But, amazingly enough, the obvious next question, "How do I make some?" is actually easier.

In this part, we introduce you to Machinima, explain how it came to have that silly name, and help you make your first movie — all within the space of two chapters!

# Chapter 1

# Getting to Know Machinima

*Y*ou may be a Machinima enthusiast already. If so, you can probably skip this chapter — you already know why Machinima is great, you already know at least roughly how it's made, and you've probably heard Hugh's funny story about how the name came to be.

But if you're just flicking through this book in the bookstore, or you've had it recommended to you, you're probably thinking, Machiniwhat? It's that thing where kids make movies with video games, isn't it? Why would you need an entire book on that?

## The Future Is Here: Machinima Arrives

It's getting hard to find anything that isn't easy to do. Publishing went first, arguably, with the word processor and printer turning any guy with a $400 PC into a publishing house. Hugh remembers "publishing" his first role-playing game at age 12 using a ZX Spectrum.

Next, it was music. Professional recording quality came down in price, until suddenly it was possible to record and mix pro-quality audio in your bedroom. Johnnie has committed some music in his time, but prefers it stricken from the record.

And latest, it's been film. Cheap, digital video cameras and even cheaper hard drives mean that shooting and editing capabilities that would have had Lucasfilm drooling 25 years ago are available on the desktop. And with the rise of video-sharing sites like YouTube, you can even end-run the distribution chains and become a superstar from your own backyard.

Hollywood still holds the high ground, though. Unlike writing or music, many films require more than recording equipment. They need stunts. Effects. Locations. A cast of hundreds. A thousand elephants. And only Hollywood films can shell out the money for that. Hence, if you want to make *Clerks* on your own, you can do that, but to make *The Matrix,* you need Hollywood.

Enter Machinima.

# Shooting in a Virtual World

*Machinima* is the technique of making films inside virtual realities (see Figure 1-1). At its heart, lungs, liver, gall bladder, or other major organ, Machinima is a very simple concept. It's the moment when anyone — and this has happened over and over again — looks at a modern 3D computer game and says, "We could make a film in that!".

Machinima isn't a technology. There's no piece of software called Machinima. It's a technique — the technique of taking a viewpoint on a virtual world, and recording that, editing it, and showing it to other people as a film.

Using Machinima, you can create virtually any locations and any characters you can imagine, all within the same technology that powers 3D computer games. And inside those locations, you can do whatever you want.

**Figure 1-1:** As Strange Company's *BloodSpell* shows, you can do things with Machinima that would cost millions in other media.

Need a firefight? Games engines are good at them. How about a sweeping vista? Not a problem. How about a gigantic battleship swooping from the skies, firing plasma charges from its cannon, crewed by the ghosts of those who died to its guns, whilst below a thousand Vikings battle their way up a mountain pass? No worries, pal. Would you like fries with that?

Of course, you can already do all these things in conventional 3D animation packages. But normal 3D has two problems: It's expensive ($900 minimum for a good 3D package, and much more for most industry-standard tools), and more problematic yet, it's slow. To create a five-minute animated film takes a single animator a year or more. *The Matrix* is well out of sight.

Machinima, by contrast, is fast. It takes about as long to shoot a film in Machinima as it does on Digital Video. And that means you can shoot a short film without giving up your life to it. In fact, it's quite possible for a bunch of dedicated people to produce an epic, *Star Wars*–scale feature film using its technology.

We know because we did it. Hugh and Johnnie originally began working together on the virtual set of *BloodSpell,* Hugh's first feature film (see Figure 1-2). Using Machinima, and with a core crew of five part-time volunteers (plus Hugh), they completed shooting a script that would have cost well over $10 million in conventional filmmaking for a total cost of approximately $5,000, in under three years.

**Figure 1-2:**
*BloodSpell,*
by Strange
Company.

And that was using 2004 technology. Machinima has gotten a lot better since then, which means a feature film should take a lot less time.

Perhaps two years? One year? Go try it and find out.

We did it. We're going to spend the rest of the book showing you how you can do it, too.

# Machiniwhatnow?

Where on earth did that term Machinima come from? To answer that, we'll have to cut back a few years. Boodliboop . . . Boodliboop . . . Boodliboop . . . It's 1999. The dot-com boom is in full flow. And on a small mailing list called *q2demos,* a small group of people dream of global domination for their new filmic medium, which uses computer game technology to make films, and was born about three years before. Only one thing's standing in the way of their triumph: the fact that said artform is currently known as *Quake Movies.*

Machinima grew out of hacks made to the game Quake, which allowed players to edit recordings of their gameplay into real movies. And while most of these movies were the equivalent of hip-hop songs explaining how tough and macho the game player was and how he would slap you down and steal your woman, or, you know, shoot you with an imaginary rocket and then laugh into his Jolt Cola, some filmmakers were using these Quake Movie hacks to make real films.

Among the early advocates of whatever-the-heck-we-were-going-to-call-it was Anthony Bailey, a frighteningly smart mathematics postgrad and the director of arguably the first Machinima hit, *Quake done Quick.* Anthony had been doing some thinking, and he'd come up with an idea. Combining the concepts of *Machine* and *Cinema,* he — very diffidently — proposed to the list that perhaps, maybe, they could call this new artform *Machinema.*

Also on this list was one Hugh Hancock — probably less smart, definitely less diffident (and one of the authors on this book). Hugh thought this new term was a great idea and started using it everywhere — in e-mails, in Web postings, in the name of his new super-site.

Some time later, Anthony contacted him and said he was very pleased with the fact that Hugh had adopted the name and popularized it, and that he really liked the change Hugh had made, in changing the *e* to an *i,* because now it didn't just contain *Machine* and *Cinema,* it also contained *Anima,* life, which Anthony really thought, was the missing element in his original naming concept.

Hugh, meanwhile, hadn't realized he had made a change. He'd just not read Anthony's original message very carefully. He hadn't changed *Machinema* to *Machinima,* so much as misspelled it. And so he did what any decent person would have done — he took a deep breath and said, "Yes. I thought it was an important change, too. Glad you liked it."

And that, ladies, gentlemen, and things of all ages, is how the word *Machinima* was born.

# Using Machinima to Make Films

When film was young, new, and shiny, around the 1900s, its creators thought of it just as a way of recording moving images — as we do today. But the pioneers of filmmaking soon realized that, in fact, what their artform involved was the creation of a new eye — a viewpoint on the world.

It was possible to cause this eye to skip from object to object, to view, and to frame scenes, in ways that a real eye couldn't. A real eye could never cut, or fade, or dissolve. By manipulating, directing, cutting, and altering what that eye saw — and only what that eye saw — they could create a completely new work of art.

Fast-forward almost exactly 100 years. Now, Machinima creators have another artificial eye — the viewpoint that a computer or games console generates onto the virtual world of a computer game. Just like the camera, that viewpoint is all that we ever see of the world. Just like a camera, it can be manipulated — made wider or narrower, fooled or faked by perspective. And just like a camera, with some simple software, it can be recorded and then its "experiences" cut apart and put back together to create what we've come to call a *film* — in this case, a Machinima film.

But this computer game world doesn't physically exist (see Figure 1-3). We can't walk into it. We created it virtually, and that means we can do anything we like inside it, without the limitations of our normal, physical universe. We can create puppets that look like people, and we can control their movements and reactions, through computer game code or with a mouse and keyboard. We can fire off explosions, destroy walls, summon helicopters, and create enormous planet-sized spacecraft.

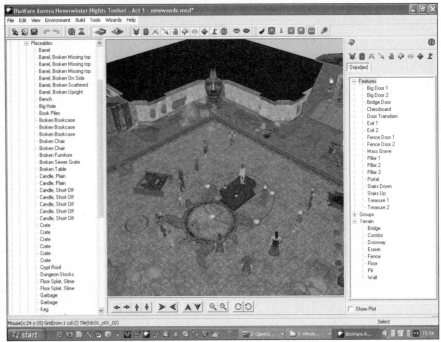

**Figure 1-3:**
A virtual set.

Machinima is, in essence, the simple realization that whenever we look at a computer game or virtual world, what we're seeing is a set, and that we're looking at it through a camera.

To put it another way, Machinima is making films with computer games. Choose the game you like, film what you want to happen, and turn it into a film. It's fast, cheap, fun, and cool.

## What Machinima does well

So, why would you want to make a movie using Machinima instead of using a video camera and real, live, human actors?

✔ **It's cheap.** First and foremost, Machinima is cheap. In fact, it's stupidly cheap. To make Machinima, you need a computer and a computer game. Personal computers are so prevalent that you'll have one already, or at least access to one, so your only real expenditure is the cost of your game of choice. If it's your favorite game, you may already own it as well, so your total costs are a very bank-balance friendly zero. We discuss the current choices for Machinima games in Chapter 5.

Of course, you can spend more money if you want, purchasing separate video-capture solutions, expensive video-editing packages, and the

like. All these things can be useful, but you can make your movie without them.

✔ **It's not limited by scale.** We can (and do) use Machinima to make
movies that would require, a multimillion-dollar Hollywood budget if we
were using any other technology. Huge, dramatic vistas, epic battles,
and breathtaking stunts: Machinima can tackle all of these features without breaking a sweat.

✔ **It's great for learning.** Machinima is a great learning tool for a potential
filmmaker. If you film something that you don't like, you've wasted nothing more than your time. There's no financial cost and no deadline other
than whatever you impose upon yourself. That means that you're free to
try different techniques and approaches and learn from your mistakes.

✔ **It handles action sequences well.** The nature of video games is such
that they tend to lend themselves toward exciting gun battles, or vehicle
racing, or huge magical duels between rival wizards. You can harness
those features for your Machinima: If that's the sort of story you want to
tell, then Machinima is the perfect tool for you.

✔ **It's quick and dirty.** Machinima is fast. You'll still get frustrated by
tedious, fiddly things that you have to correct, but in comparison to
other filmmaking techniques, Machinima is darn speedy. It's faster than
3D-rendered animation (the sort of thing that was used to make *Toy
Story* and *Shrek*). It's far, far faster than traditional hand-drawn animation. Most impressively of all, it's still fast if you're the sole member of
your production team. One person with one computer can produce a
movie faster than entire teams of conventional animators.

## What Machinima does less well

Nothing! We're awesome! Honest. Okay, we'll fess up:

✔ **It's not great on people.** Honestly, there's one big disadvantage of using
Machinima over using live film: Computer-generated characters are
never going to be as convincing in the role of a person as, well, a person.

We've borrowed ideas from Hanna-Barbera, Japanese limited-animation
anime, stop-motion video, '80s cartoons, and pioneers of filmmaking. We
use camera technique, high-quality animation, advanced puppeteering
technology, the latest advances in game characters, brilliant voice
actors, and psychological techniques. There are a lot of tricks you can
use to get around Machinima's limitations.

But, if you're making Machinima, your visual actors aren't going to be
able to carry a shot in the same way that a great human actor can. Working
around that drawback is one of the hallmarks of a great Machinima
director.

Or, as at least one well-known Machinima director has done, you can just tell stories about robots.

✔ **Small isn't beautiful.** Actually, Machinima's great at doing small. If you want to make the next *Bug's Life,* consider making it in Machinima. When we say "small" here, we mean in budgetary terms. If you want to make the next *Dogville* or *Clerks,* Machinima is the wrong choice for you.

If all you want to do is to shoot a film of two guys talking, it will be faster to shoot the film in real life than to use Machinima, and it will look better. There's no point using Machinima when you don't need its unique advantages (see preceding section). If you've already got access to the location you want to use, you've got the actors you want to play the characters, and there's nothing that you can't easily do in real life in your script, then we heartily recommend pulling up the Real Life engine. The resolution on that thing is amazing.

✔ **You're no oil painting.** If you want to compete with Pixar head-to-head, Machinima won't let you do it. Sorry.

Machinima leverages technology that's like nothing the world's ever seen, and it produces amazing visual results. At their best, Machinima visuals are in many ways equivalent to the best Hollywood 3D studios could produce seven or eight years ago.

Note the "seven or eight" bit there. Machinima uses games technology, which tends to look about as good as conventional computer graphics did about five years beforehand. And it takes a year or so before any game is sufficiently well-supported and understood for really good Machinima to be produced in it. Hence, if you're creating Machinima, you're not going to be producing cutting-edge visuals.

But, honestly, seven or eight years ago, computer graphics looked pretty good. And in three years' time, seven years back from then will look even better. So you can produce some slick-looking stuff using Machinima, as films like *Still Seeing Breen* and *The Return* demonstrate. But no matter how you cut it, Machinima isn't likely to have Pixar quaking in its boots.

✔ **Some things aren't cheaper.** Lots and lots of things are cheaper to do in Machinima. But some things aren't. For example, if you want to create entirely new, custom characters, it'll be as hard and as expensive as if you were working on a conventional 3D production. If you want to produce detailed animations of things that aren't in the game, that'll have to be done in conventional animation software, too. Some things are just hard, no matter how you do them.

✔ **You don't have total control.** Hugh sometimes complains that he feels like he spends half his life saying, "Machinima isn't animation! It's puppetry!"

3D animation offers its users total control over everything they see on the screen. Want that head turn a quarter of a second earlier? No problem. Machinima, on the other hand, doesn't offer anything like that degree of control. You're not animating every facet of the characters' movement, you're using puppetry to control as much as you can, quickly and live. Some stuff will go wrong. Some stuff won't be possible. And some stuff will come out differently than how you expected and will look even better.

Machinima filmmaking demands a certain amount of flexibility and forgiveness in its shooting, as well as the ability to be patient about the point you're saying, "Okay, take 17, guys. Let's try and get it right this time."

On *BloodSpell,* individual shots would regularly have to be taken more than ten times to get the result Hugh was looking for. However, even counting that, we managed to shoot more than a minute of highly complex footage a day, with a crew of two or three people — a speed of production that George Lucas would envy.

✔ **You may not be able to make money.** Most *game-licensing agreements* — you know, the things that you click through when you install the game, the ones that contain clauses like "If your computer explodes as a result of this game, it's not Publisher's fault" — prohibit using that game for commercial purposes. That means, practically, that you can't make Machinima and sell it if you're using that game. That's a downer. Having said that, an increasing number of Machinima environments, such as Second Life, IClone, and Moviestorm, do allow you to make money from your creations. So, if you're interested in doing this as a living, just make sure to use one of them.

# Making a Machinima Film

You can make Machinima in dozens of game engines in a whole bunch of different ways. There are tips, tricks, shortcuts, round-about routes, breakthroughs, and holy wars over how it's best to make a Machinima movie.

The basic process for making a Machinima film is much the same regardless of the film.

No matter what movie you're making, you'll go through the following steps:

1. **Write the story.**

   Stop. Seriously, now, stop. Before you go any further, before you press *W* to move your character forward, before you set up your first shot, you really, really need to know what you actually want to film.

   It's amazing how often Machinima creators miss this first step, but it's crucial. For more on storytelling and scriptwriting, see Chapter 4.

For a short film, you'll spend maybe a week writing the script. That week will be the most important factor in whether your movie ends up being good or bad.

Consider what your chosen game engine can do. If you're filming in Battlefield 2, a fantasy epic will probably be a little tricky to achieve. If you're in The Sims 2, it may not be the time to bust out the script for *Star Wars 7 — Return of Return of the Jedi*.

2. **Create your cast.**

Before you do anything else, you'll need your actors. In Machinima, these guys are your puppets. You'll move them around in your virtual world with mouse and keyboard, or with programmed scripts, just as if you were moving them around dangling from strings in a Punch and Judy show.

Some game engines will have a fixed selection of characters, and if you want to create more, you'll need to jump into a 3D modeling package, or at least a image editor. In other game engines, you'll be able to edit and alter characters inside the game itself, lowering their brows and tweaking their noses to your heart's desire. (See Chapter 7 for more information on casting.)

3. **Create your sets.**

Next, you create the locations in which your film takes place. Much like a set designer in the real world, you'll be putting your locations together from simple building blocks; instead of plywood and nails, you'll have polygons, and instead of paint and wallpaper, you'll be using Photoshop or the GIMP.

Some game engines require that you make your locations up from very simple primitives — cubes, pyramids and so on, textured and placed to form the world — while others allow you to place down pre-created "tiles" and decorate them from libraries of existing props. (See Chapter 6 for more on set design.)

4. **Record your actors.**

Yes, actual actors. Because Machinima is often quite limited in terms of how much you can express with your characters, a lot of the work of a Machinima film is done by the voice actors. Whether drama or comedy, a group of good actors are vital to a strong Machinima film.

It's fairly simple to record quality dialogue these days — a $40 microphone, a PC, and a duvet do the job quite well. And a lot of very talented actors in stage schools, amateur dramatics, and student theatre are desperate for the chance to practice their craft. For Strange Company, recording voice actors is one of the most fun and rewarding parts of the entire Machinima production process.

**5. Set your game up for filming.**

Machinima creators record the visuals of their chosen game in many different ways. It's possible, for example, to take the output of your computer's TV connector — the one you usually use to watch your oh-so-entirely-legal downloaded Buffy episodes on your big screen — and hook that up to a camcorder or a video recorder.

You can also download a piece of software, such as the well-known FRAPS (www.fraps.com), that will record whatever's on your screen to a video file on your PC. Or you can buy a *frame grabber* — a moderately expensive piece of hardware that allows you to record from your video card's high-quality computer video output.

Finally, some games and programs, such as The Sims 2 or Moviestorm, have in-built video recorders. These recorders are the simplest and highest-quality way of all to record your Machinima video.

You' also need to make sure that you've got a good "camera" to record from in the game. For *BloodSpell,* for example, we had to write a script to make our RPG character invisible, allowing us to film shots without a big pink dwarf in the way!

**6. Record!**

Here, you work just like a conventional film director. First, you set up your shot, you give instructions to your actors, and then you shout "Action!" and let the cameras roll. (It looks a bit funny shouting "Action" if you're the only guy working on the film, but Hugh likes to do it anyway.)

Depending on your chosen game and how you've decided to work, you'll either be giving instructions to your actors via *scripts* — simple computer programs that anyone can write, or graphical programs that do the same job — or you'll actually be talking to other people and telling them how to control your characters. These approaches have different advantages and disadvantages. It's quicker to explain what you want to a human, but they get it wrong more often, too!

You record the results to either a tape or a PC, and then you have your raw footage.

**7. Edit.**

Machinima films are mostly edited just like real films. Some games offer in-game editing, where you can take your recorded footage and modify it inside the game engine itself, but most of the time you'll be editing your work in an external package, such as Adobe Premiere, Avid Free DV, iMovie, or Sony Vegas. See Chapter 9 for more on editing your movie.

With the growth in powerful home-video editing software, there's a lot you can do during the editing process. You can add titles, special effects, and a huge variety of transitions between shots. You can composite shots on top of each other, or modify how they look through paint-like techniques. You can even take static shots and animate them in your video editor for shots that you just couldn't create any other way!

8. **Release.**

Personally, we think that you've only really made a film when you've released it to an audience and heard their reactions. Fortunately, with the boom in Internet video fostered by YouTube and similar sites (see Chapter 10), that's easier than ever.

You can either upload your finished movie to a movie-hosting site like YouTube, or you can host it yourself. Either way, there are dozens of forums and Web sites out there whose viewers will be eager to watch and comment on your film — perhaps you'll become famous, or perhaps you'll just learn more about being a filmmaker so that you can make an even better film next time!

# Controlling the Action: Live Versus Scripted

When making a Machinima movie, you can control the action you're filming in two ways: scripted or live. Each has its advocates and detractors. Which method you use is essentially up to you, but your choice will probably be dictated (at least in part) by the game engine in which you choose to make your movie.

✔ **Scripted sequences:** Scripting allows you to preprogram the sequence you want to film. When we use the word *scripting* here, we don't mean writing the lines and dialog of your film, but rather writing a series of computer code instructions (a *script*) that tells your actors, cameras, and other peripherals what to do (see Figure 1-4).

Although writing line upon line of computer code may seem pretty intimidating, many games provide an editor program or some other similar interface. By using the editor, the amount of actual code that you need to write is reduced dramatically. Often, an editor will eliminate the need for manual scripting altogether.

When you come to shoot the footage, you simply trigger the script, sit back, and record the on-screen action. If you run the script a second time, the resultant action will be (or at least should be) exactly the same.

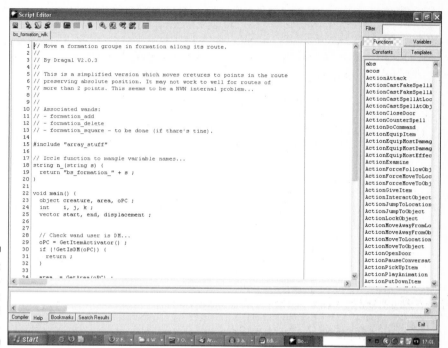

**Figure 1-4:**
An exam-
ple of a
Machinima
script.

Using a script gives you a great deal of control over the on-screen action. You can experiment and refine your pre-scripted sequence until it's exactly the way you want it. Preparing the script in the first place is often a lot of work and requires a good knowledge of the editor or scripting language that the game uses. Some of the more powerful game engines have a horrendously complicated scripting back-end, which require a considerable investment of time to learn even the basics.

While, in theory, scripting gives identical results every time, the combination of game physics and artificial intelligence means that sometimes things can go a little wrong. Don't expect animation-level accuracy; game events may interfere with the AI characters' attempts to play the script. If this happens, it's usually simple enough to restart the sequence, but sometimes this sort of behavior can cause problems.

Engines that offer scripting include Half-Life 2, Unreal Tournament 2007, Neverwinter Nights, and Second Life. Depending on how you look at it, The Sims 2 and Moviestorm arguably work in a similar way, but their scripts are generated live in the game, which we think makes them more like . . .

✔ **Live recording or virtual puppeteering:** The other way of filming is to control the on-screen action live, in real time. When you're playing the game you're using to film with, for example, you might use the mouse to change your in-game character's viewpoint. When you're using the game to make Machinima, you'd use the same mouse movement to pan your virtual camera about your set. The footage that you record will feature a camera pan at the same speed that you chose to move.

Likewise, you issue commands to your virtual actors by moving them around in the game and record the results as they happen. That's why we call this method *virtual puppeteering* — you're controlling the actors as you film, just like you would if you were making a puppet show.

If you use this technique to record a sequence that you don't like, you've no option but to go back and do it all again. The results won't be exactly the same the second time around, which can be a good or a bad thing. Using this technique on anything but the simplest shots requires practice, particularly if you're on your own.

Most movies made in this way are made by a team of people, all of whom control characters within the same multiplayer game. Controlling and instigating action live gives your movie more of an organic feel and can often inject life into your characters, but you sacrifice a degree of control over the precise on-screen action.

Engines that allow live filming include World of Warcraft, Unreal Tournament 2007, Battlefield 2, and Halo 2.

There's actually a third option for Machinima production. The third option is downright devious, but can produce some great results if used properly.

Many games provide a *model viewer* tool that allows you to examine each of the game's character models without loading the game itself. Often, you can also trigger any of the model's animations from within the model viewer program. If you capture this footage, you can then mix it onto a background at a later date. It's like a virtual green-screen studio!

If the game you're using doesn't come with a model viewer, it's quite possible that an enterprising fan of the game has written one. Search online. You may be surprised at what you can find.

You can use this same technique to generate a background, using a map viewer program. A *map viewer program* lets you view any of the games maps (the sets, from our point of view) and move around it. Composite footage from a model view and a map viewer, and you've got yourself a film. Engines with map and model viewers include World of Warcraft and Half-Life 2.

In practice, you might not use any one of these techniques exclusively. Many Machinima creators adopt a combination of these techniques, scripting the more complicated aspects of their movie, instigating the rest of the action live, and faking anything they have to.

*BloodSpell* was shot in this manner. Although we filmed the entire movie live in the game, many of the more complicated sequences were (at least partially) pre-scripted. As well as that, we wrote scripts to control much of the game's behavior, as well as scripts to control the camera and to return a character to a specific location.

Wondering which to use? Use live filming if

- ✔ You like working quickly and spontaneously.
- ✔ You've got friends who want to help.
- ✔ You're working in a Massively Multiplayer game.
- ✔ You're shooting shorter shots without complex camerawork.
- ✔ Your engine doesn't support scripting!
- ✔ You've got film experience or want to work in a way similar to conventional filmmaking.
- ✔ You want split-second control.

Use scripting if

- ✔ You're working alone.
- ✔ You're a computer programmer or enjoy programming.
- ✔ You're shooting very complex shots, particularly ones with complex camerawork.
- ✔ You want as much control as possible over your Machinima.
- ✔ You're working in an engine where multiplayer control is impractical, or where you can't easily pause the game action.
- ✔ You want to control some aspects of a live filmed shoot, such as camerawork or background characters.

Remember, you don't have to stick to just using scripting or just using live filming. Many engines, like Neverwinter Nights, Unreal Tournament 2007, and Half-Life 2, support both. We list which engines can use which method of filming in Chapter 5.

# Chapter 2

# Your First Machinima Movie

## In This Chapter

▶ Creating your first Machinima movie

▶ Using Moviestorm to make a simple scene

*T*o quote Morpheus in *The Matrix,* "No one can be told what Machinima is. You have to see it for yourself." (Actually, we think he was talking about, you know, the other thing. But we wear black leather coats sometimes, so it's nearly the same.)

In this chapter, we make a simple movie. We choreograph characters, record dialogue (if you've got a microphone), add cameras, and edit the end result. You create your first Machinima movie in about 15 minutes.

Because we're just giving you an introduction to the power of Machinima here, this is the only chapter where we're going to stick to a fixed script. If you want to change anything you see, Chapter 17 covers Moviestorm, the engine we use, and you can find out how to change our movie there!

## Installing Moviestorm

The installation of Moviestorm on the DVD that comes with this book contains the set and characters we're using for this film. Installing Moviestorm on your computer is an easy task. Just navigate to the Moviestorm folder on the DVD and double-click the file `moviestorm.exe`. The Moviestorm installation process starts.

After Moviestorm is installed, you can start the program by double-clicking the icon on your desktop or through the Start menu. The first time you run the software, Moviestorm will probably prompt you to download a new and updated version of itself. If you do so, you'll have access to all the latest features and improvements in Moviestorm, but you'll also probably find that parts of the program have changed since we wrote these tutorials. If you want to follow along with this tutorial, don't update. If you have access to the

Internet right now, you can download an updated version of the tutorial (which will probably be compatible with the latest version of Moviestorm up to at least the start of 2008) from www.machinimafordummies.com.

# Walk before Running

Before you can do anything else, you have to tell your characters where to stand and where to walk. In Moviestorm, choose Your First Machinima Movie from the opening menu. A "Please Wait" sign appears, and then you find yourself in a 3D set, with pictures of two characters up at the top-left, a lot like Figure 2-1.

The set in Figure 2-1 is our rendition of a back corridor in the UK's Houses of Parliament. Currently, the walls aren't visible, but don't worry. They're there.

We're dramatizing a moment from history — to be precise, a moment from the life of Winston Churchill. In our characters selection, we have Mr. Churchill himself, somewhat sleeker and more svelte than in real life, and an elderly, disapproving lady, who will be playing the formidable Lady Astor, with whom the famous politician had more than a few disagreements.

You may suspect that we're playing a trick on you here, and that we've spent hours creating this set and characters to give you a slick, fast demo. We're too lazy for that. The set and characters took Hugh less than an hour to create from scratch in Moviestorm.

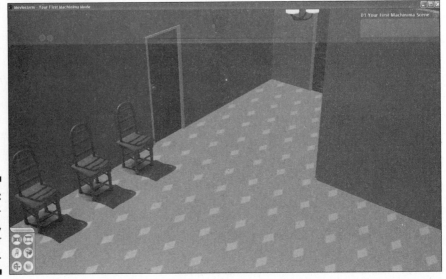

**Figure 2-1:**
A Machinima set, ready for shooting.

To get your characters into position:

1. **Right-click the ground near one of the hard wooden chairs next to the door and choose Place Here.**

   The Disapproving Lady Astor appears on that spot, as she's the character who is selected by default.

2. **Right-click the chair next to her and choose Sit Down.**

   Lady Astor sits down. A line moves along the blue rectangle at the bottom, and some things appear on it. That's the *timeline;* it's a record of everything that happens in the scene. Don't worry about the timeline for now — if you do want to know more, Chapter 17 is your friend.

   If you need to move your viewpoint to see what you're doing, you can use the following controls:

   - Right-click, hold, and drag the mouse to look around.
   - Click the middle mouse button, hold, and drag to move around the set.
   - Use the mousewheel to zoom in and out.

   Now you're ready to add Churchill into the scene.

3. **Click Winston's portrait at the left side of the screen.**

   Notice that a blue box appears whenever you move your mouse to the left of the screen. That's the Character pane, and it contains a list of all the characters that you can use in your current scene.

4. **Right-click behind the door with the bookcase next to it and choose Place Here.**

   Winston duly appears.

5. **Right-click about six feet in front of your Disapproving Lady and choose Move Here.**

   Winston walks to the door, opens it, walks through, and stops in front of Disapprove-O-Woman.

# *Making Winston Drunk*

Winston's striding confidently. He looks like a man who's in charge, a man who gives V-signs, and most importantly not at all like a man who has just consumed his own body weight in 25-year-old single-malt Talisker. Fortunately, we can fix that.

1. **Drag the time marker back until just after Winston comes through the door.**

   You'll probably have noticed a vertical bar or rule moving along the timeline as Winston walks. That's the *time marker,* and it controls the time you're currently seeing the scene from. To watch Winston walk again, drag it left along the timeline — you'll see him rewind. Now, press the Play button over at the bottom right, and you see him walk once more.

2. **Rewind to the start, and then right-click the light blue line on the timeline, just to the right of the time marker.**

   This light blue line represents Winston's walk, and the menu that appears gives you the option of deleting it or customizing it.

3. **Choose Customize.**

   The Customize window, shown in Figure 2-2, appears.

**Figure 2-2:**
Customizing
a walk.

4. **From the Gait drop-down list, select the Tired walk.**

   Winston's walk alters appropriately, all the way across his walk action.

5. **Drag the Stride slider to about the middle of the slider.**

   Winston's strides become shorter, making him look drrrrr . . . rrrr . . . unk.

6. **Close the Customize window by clicking the cross.**

# Time for a Witty Retort

Historiophiles (if that's a word) will already have guessed what you're about to reenact. There's a famous retort from Winston Churchill to Lady Astor, when the latter came upon the great politician, uhh, tired and emotional.

> *Lady Astor: Mr. Churchill, you are exceedingly drunk.*
>
> *Churchill: And you, madam, are ugly. But in the morning, I shall be sober.*

In common with filmmakers everywhere, we've not allowed anything as mundane as the facts to stand in our way whilst re-imagining this scene, so if this isn't how the event occurred, or indeed how either Churchill or Lady Astor appeared, we apologize in advance.

Lady Astor will presumably want to start her insult a little while before 250 pounds of drunken Prime Minister staggers past her:

1. **Select Lady Astor by clicking her portrait at the left side of the screen.**

2. **Right-click Lady Astor and choose Say.**

   The Record Line dialog box, shown in Figure 2-3, appears.

3. **Record Lady Astor's line.**

   Here's how:

   • If you've got a microphone and you fancy that you've got a pretty decent disapproving-old-woman voice, you can record the line yourself. Get your microphone ready to record by clicking the red button. Say your line, "Mr. Churchill, you are exceedingly drunk," and then click the red button again to stop recording. Click the white space and type the line you just said, so that you remember which line you just recorded and to help the program figure out its lipsynching. Then click the check to accept the line.

   • If you don't have a microphone or want to hear your humble authors' thespian ability, click the teeny, tiny button on the right of the red Record button. Open `Lady Astor.wav` from the DVD that accompanies this book. Now click the white space and type the line into it. Then click the check to accept the line.

**Figure 2-3:** The Record Line dialog box.

4. **When you come back to the main Moviestorm window, click the Play button to hear your line.**

   If you move your viewpoint so that you can see the Disapproving Lady as you do so, you see that she's lipsynching to the line.

5. **Add Churchill's devastating response.**

   To do so, drag the time marker as far as it will go to the right, select Churchill's portrait, right-click Churchill, and choose Say. Either record Churchill's line — "And you, madam, are ugly. But in the morning, I shall be sober." — or select Churchill.wav (see Step 3 for the details).

6. **Play Churchill's line.**

   Like Lady Astor, Winston lipsynchs automatically.

# A Quick Exit

This scene looks a bit static. You can do a lot to animate the scene using Moviestorm (see Chapter 17 if you want to know more), but for now, just have Churchill walk off, delivering his cutting final remark over his shoulder.

1. **Rewind the scene a bit with the time marker and then play through until just after Churchill says, "And you, madam, are ugly . . ."**

   You want to have the time marker just before he says, ". . . but in the morning . . ."

2. **Right-click the floor next to the door in front of Churchill and choose Move here.**

   Churchill walks off while delivering his final quip. Even more, because he is talking, Lady Astor automatically looks at him.

If you want to, you can also adjust Winston's walk so that he walks drunkenly. See the section "Making Winston Drunk," earlier in this chapter.

# Cinematography!

Something's missing — a camera! This movie is not ready yet! You need to add a simple wide shot to cover the scene as a whole.

1. **Drag the time marker right back to the start of the film.**

2. **Right-click the ground near the potted plant and choose Place Camera Here.**

   Your view changes. You're now looking through a widescreen camera, and you've almost certainly got an exciting view of a floor, wall, or basically anything but what you want to look at.

3. **Click the Set Up A New Shot icon.**

   Everything but your viewpoint goes dark, and you see a black grid appear. (Johnnie's had evenings like that after too many vodka tonics.)

4. **Use the same controls you use in the Director's view to change your shot to a shot of the room as a whole.**

   You want a shot that shows Lady Astor, the corridor, and (when he walks in to shot) Churchill.

5. **When you're happy, click the check sign to accept the shot.**

You can click Play, and you see your entire movie through that camera! It suddenly looks like a film, doesn't it?

Finally, you cut to the camera after Lady Astor has sat down, and then render your film out as a movie that you can view in Windows Media Player (or the player of your choice).

1. **Move the time marker to just before Winston walks through the door and click Insert A Cut To This Camera.**

2. **Click the window in the bottom right.**

   It has the Moviestorm logo in it. Now you're viewing the Master Monitor, which shows you what the film will look like when it's rendered.

3. **Click Play to see that you're now viewing the entire film through your camera.**

   Notice that the section before you cut to the first camera is white. Normally, you'd edit the movie in a standard video-editing package — see Chapter 9.

4. **Finally, render your movie to an `.avi` that anyone can view.**

   Move your mouse to the top of the screen.

5. **Click the Film Reel icon.**

   The Render Settings window appears. Choose the directory you'd like to render to by using the Browse button and then choose a filename to save your movie as.

6. **Click the green check to start the rendering process.**

Don't do anything! Your movie will now render out. If you use your computer for anything else while this is happening, the render won't work properly.

# And That's All, Folks!

You may be worried that your first Machinima movie looks a little simple. Well, currently it is. But the techniques used in this chapter are the same basic techniques you use to refine your film, fine-tune it, or make anything a feature-length movie. Congratulations — you're now a Machinima filmmaker.

# Part II
# Getting Serious

The 5th Wave                    By Rich Tennant

"I finally mastered all the game levels and thought
I'd set up a blacksmith shop and sell swords.
Two days later, a Wal-Mart goes up just
outside the village square."

# In this part . . .

In this part, we cover the basics of filmmaking in depth, including cinematography, storytelling, and scriptwriting. We also take a look at each of the major Machinima engines at the time of writing and weigh the pros and cons of each. We help you to choose the right engine for your new project.

Then we cover the rest of the filmmaking process, including how to create a virtual set, design your characters, and get your hands dirty with your first real piece of directing, using The Sims 2 to shoot a short, simple movie. Not only do you edit the resulting footage, you also explore the numerous distribution options available for your finished movie.

# Chapter 3

# Filmmaking 101

*J*ust to warn you: This is the chapter in the book where we confidently expect, unless you're already an experienced filmmaker, you'll come out feeling like you know less than when you went in. Sorry about that. But filmmaking is a huge, huge topic.

Both Hugh and Johnnie learned their filmmaking via the School of Hard Knocks, or in this case the School of Poor Shots. Hugh discovered early in 1997 that hyperactive Quake players on three liters of filter coffee make better cameramen when they're not trying to dodge the invisible rockets. It took another two or three films for Strange Company to start making movies that looked like, you know, actual cinema.

The reason isn't that Hugh's an idiot, although it's always worth considering that as a potential cause. It's because he didn't realize, until about two months after he made his first movie, that in order to make a movie, you have to speak a new language.

## Film Is a Language

We're used to thinking of language as verbal. However, cinematography is a language, with a vocabulary of shots and techniques, and a grammar of editing and spatial awareness. If you can't speak the language at least a little bit, you can't make a film. Hugh and Johnnie speak it well enough to order a coffee and find the nearest toilet. Meanwhile, Ridley Scott and David Lynch are the equivalent of Graham Greene and Ernest Hemingway.

To shoot a film that will make sense, much less have an emotional impact, you need to unlearn a lot of obvious potential mistakes with a camera. You need to know how the eye interprets the camera's vision, and how the brain will assume that one shot should flow from another, or how it will interpret a single frame.

This stuff isn't Machinima-specific. It's applicable to all forms of filmmaking, and some people have forgotten more than either Hugh or Johnnie knows on the subject. We give you some pointers to further sources of filmmaking expertise at the end of the chapter.

## Faking the eye

To watch a film is not a natural act. The brain isn't designed for it. We're fooling our audience's brains and eyes into thinking they're watching actual events, when they're seeing nothing of the kind.

If you're making cinema, you need to know how the brain will attempt to make sense of the sequence of disjointed images you're creating. Some movements and some shots will smoothly slot into each other, while others will jar and confuse their audience.

Here's a quick thought experiment. A brown sedan races across the screen from left to right, followed by a police car. Then, in the next shot, the brown sedan shoots across in the opposite direction, again followed by the cop car. That means that the chase has turned around, right?

Not necessarily. It could just mean that the director has failed to take account of the *line of action* (see the section "Mastering Shot Flow," later in this chapter) and as a result you've misinterpreted his intentions. You'll get more confused later on in the movie, as you're now working under an interpretation that the director hadn't taken into account.

A shot doesn't stand alone, any more than the word "artichoke" stands alone in a story. "Hugh hit Johnnie with the artichoke" is a totally different sentence from "steam the artichoke lightly with butter." In just the same way, a shot of a guy looking up, followed by a shot of a girl at a window, suggests one thing. A shot of a falling piano, followed by a shot of a guy looking up, suggests something else; it's a different sentence in the language.

Not only action, but intent, and even mood, carry across shots. A sequence of shots carries meaning that a single shot never can.

## Painting with light

Just to make things even more challenging, you're not just about to learn a new language. You're also about to become a painter.

filmmaking is an audio-visual medium. And that means that your movie will first be judged on its visual appeal. Does it look attractive? Do the visuals you've created stir emotion in your viewers?

Some of this appeal is down to the quality of your engine, obviously, but far more of it is down to the skill of the director or cinematographer. Which means you need to learn to paint, too. You'll discover how to draw the eye, balance a portrait, strike a balance between empty space and a cluttered screen, and use light and shadow as your paintbrushes on a scene.

The best advice Hugh ever received as a filmmaker was to make sure that every shot stands on its own as a piece of art. Now, to be fair, he hasn't managed that. Indeed, he'd say a fair number of his shots are a piece of something else entirely. But as soon as he started trying to achieve that, the quality of his filmmaking dramatically improved.

Film is audio-visual, not just visual. Sound plays a vital role in a movie, and without it, your movie won't — or shouldn't — make sense. You can use sound to tell the story, or to provide elements that aren't otherwise present. Never, ever forget about it. See Chapter 13 for more on sound.

# Interpreting Animation

You're not using conventional film and conventional actors here, you're using Machinima. That means three things:

- ✔ **You don't have brilliant acting to rely on.** Whereas *The West Wing* can just sit on a shot of Martin Sheen for 35 seconds while he does all the work of the scene, you'll need to draw emotion from your frankly wooden actors, using intelligent cinematography and framing.

- ✔ **Your film looks like animation, not real life.** Humans have millions of years of evolution to fall back on when trying to interpret pictures of real life — we can do so fast and effectively. By contrast, humans aren't nearly so fast or effective at interpreting drawn images, meaning we need more time for the brain to figure out what they mean.

✔ **You have to convince your viewers that what they're seeing is real.**
Computer-Generated Imagery (CGI) filmmakers try very hard to mimic
the look of real film, paying attention to how real cameras look, move,
and act.

# Making the Film: Anatomy of a Scene

Cinematography and shooting descend in complexity just like a story. In
order, here are the levels to consider, consciously or subconsciously.

1. **Style**

2. **Blocking**

3. **Camera positioning and shot flow**

4. **Micro-flow**

5. **Framing**

6. **Action**

The preceding steps describe how we shoot a film, not The One True Way. It
works for us, but different ways work for other people, many of them much
more famous than us. We heartily, enthusiastically, and without even a hint
of profit-sharing recommend you pick up as many books on filmmaking as
you can!

## Style

Style is the most obvious and arguably least vital element of a film. People
like this level — it's broad, sweeping, and sexy, and it makes good coffee
conversation.

Style is also probably the last thing you should be thinking about. Sure, it's
good to make some stylistic decisions (like *BloodSpell's* punk theme), and it's
worth thinking about the symbolism you're using in your film (David Lynch is
a master of this sort of filmmaking), but a lot of the style of your movie will
come from your subconscious preferences and your view of the world.

Your personal preferences and view will affect you as you plan individual
shots, but they'll be consistent through the movie, and before you know it
you'll have a style. Later, when you're a more experienced filmmaker, you can
start to tweak that.

Confused? Here's a (mostly) hypothetical example:

> Hugh: *"Okay, so I'm thinking that this is a very fantastic film, so we need to shoot in a very realistic way. I'm thinking* Firefly *and* Battlestar Galactica *here — handheld shots, shakey cam, not a lot of crane shots, keep it all very grounded."*
>
> Johnnie: *"Shaky cameras? In Machinima? Kill me now."*
>
> Hugh: *"No, seriously, it'll be cool. We can totally do that. Dragal can write us a tool."*
>
> Dragal: *\*Splutter\* "I can?"*
>
> Hugh: *"Relax. It'll be fine."*

# Blocking

Now we descend to a scene level. The first thing you need to do when you're planning a scene — and we do mean planning, well before you point a camera at anything — is to decide how your characters move and react in each scene. In theater, these decisions are referred to as *blocking*.

We're talking about the broad stuff. Where are your characters standing? Where do they walk to? Where do they fight? How does the flow of the fight work?

You need to think about the characters' motivations. Where does your character *want* to end up standing, and why? You need to think about the way the scene will look; will the character be framed against a dramatic backdrop?

You need to think about keeping the scene interesting. How do you avoid two characters standing in the same place talking for five minutes? Can they move around? Step closer to each other? Turn away from each other?

Blocking is hard, because you're acting for your characters at the same time as you are starting to design your shot flow. At the same time, remember that what you're doing is about effect, not about physical realism: The characters' locations should be chosen to interest the viewer and give them clues about the characters' relationships. Think dramatic and symbolic.

Here's an example:

> Hugh: *"And now they're getting pretty intense, but I'm looking at this, and we'll have been swapping back and forward in a couple of two-shots for about a minute here. So, Jered's looking scared, the Master's getting really angry, what's happening?"*

*Johnnie: "Er. . . . They move closer?"*

*Hugh: "Naah, dull, dull. Barely changes the shot. Okay, here we go. You're Jered, right? And . . . \*Rustling\* This coat on a stick is the Master. Now, see, he's getting angry, he's intimidating."*

*Johnnie: "Hugh, it's a coat on a stick. I'm worried that you're going to hit me with the blunt end."*

*Hugh: "Work with me here."*

*Johnnie: "Okay. So Jered's feeling like he can't show he's scared, right? So perhaps he deliberately turns his back."*

*Hugh: ". . . And that moves us into a new two-shot!"*

## Camera positioning

After you know where your characters are, you need to think about where you position your cameras. Note that you're not actually looking through a camera at any point here, except maybe to scout the location. Plan your cameras on paper, for the entire scene. Then, and only then, move onto the next stage.

Of course, this is Machinima. You can put a camera anywhere you darn well want. You can use a different camera for each shot in a 200-shot sequence. You can shoot the entire thing from a spinning crane shot. And you really don't want to do that.

Humans thrive on consistency. We're also really good at spotting when something isn't real, even when we're trying to pretend it is. Real-life camerawork tends to be as simple as possible for cost reasons, so if you want to mimic real life, you should start there.

In addition, overly complex camerawork gets in the way of the story. As director, your job is to shoot the scene in the simplest way that gets the story and its emotional content across — but, under no circumstances, to get any simpler than that.

Imagine an invisible producer shouting about the cost of crane shots in your ear. Can you shoot that conversation more simply? Do you really need a crane shot there? Can you trim five close-ups elsewhere into a single long dolly sequence? Simple and elegant.

Of course, sometimes you've just got to crank the special effects up to 11 and get with the Peter Jackson mad flying camera action. But the less you use awesome-mad shots, the cooler they'll look — and the more time you'll have to make sure that your uber-camera shot looks incredibly awesome.

Here's what we mean:

> Hugh: "So I'm thinking that we shoot this conversation a bit like this."
>
> *Slaps Figure 3-1 down on the table*

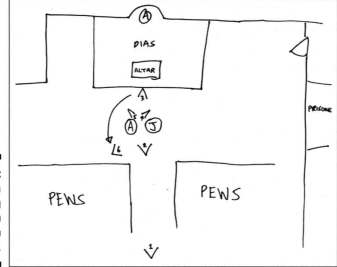

**Figure 3-1:**
Camera
positioning
diagram
from
*BloodSpell.*

> Johnnie: "Good. Because I can totally understand all of those random squiggles."
>
> Hugh: "No, look, it's simple. We've got a wide shot, a two-shot, and a reverse covering this conversation, and then when Jered turns, we'll just dolly around to face him."
>
> Johnnie: "Into the coffee stain?"
>
> Hugh: "Yup."

## Micro-flow

After you decide your camera positioning, you can start thinking about two or three shots at a time — maybe up to 12. This is the point where Hugh will generally start storyboarding — by which we mean drawing out rough images of his intended camera shots (see Figure 3-2).

Figure 3-2:
Rough
storyboard
from
*BloodSpell.*
You really
don't have
to be a fine
artist!

In conventional films, storyboarding is a way of saving money — it's cheaper to draw your shots than to crank up a film camera and get Sir Ian McKellen on set just to figure out what you want.

However, this is Machinima. We don't have to pay for film by the foot, and even if by some miracle you've got the man we call Gandalf in your film, he'll be looking confused in a closet lined with duvets (see Chapter 13), rather than on an actual stage. There's very little point drawing detailed storyboards.

But rough drawings of the shots you're trying to achieve are still useful, so that you can remember what you're trying to shoot, and so that you can check that your proposed shot sequence will work visually.

Your storyboards don't have to look good! Provided you as director can understand them and visualize the end shot, that's all that matters.

Hugh will usually draw out a dozen or so shots at a time, in his inimitable — not to say unintelligible — artistic style, and then close his eyes and fly his hand around like he's pretending it's an airplane:

> Hugh: *"Okay, here's a quick storyboard of the next dozen shots. Questions?"*
>
> Steve: *"A squiggle attacks another squiggle, and then there's . . . an incontinent elephant?"*
>
> Hugh: *"Oh, shut up."*

# Framing

Now we're cooking with gas. Unless we're using Neverwinter Nights. Then we're cooking with ghast. My, that's geeky even for us.

Finally, after all that nonsense, we get to actually shoot some darn shots. You're in the map, you've got any assistants you need, er, assisting you. It's time to figure out how each individual shot will look.

You'll need to sort out *framing* — exactly where are your characters in your shot, and how does that relate to your background? If you've got moving characters or a moving shot, you'll need to check your framing and composition at each key point within the movement and sort out the intended timing.

Now's also the time to cue up speech and animations, either in the game or by discussing with your filming assistants. And lastly, you need to move and arrange your lighting, in whatever form you have it, to make your shot look both pretty and clear.

This is the "painting with light" part.

> Hugh: *Tap* "Okay, Johnnie, left a bit." *Tap* "Right a bit." *Tap* "Okay, now back." *TAP* "He's nearly there — just move him back a bit more." *TAP!* "Oops. I meant forward."
>
> Johnnie: "I kill you. With my mind."
>
> Hugh: "And we're done with the framing. Now, lighting. Someone get me an invisible glowing badger and put it next to Jered's bottom."

# Filming

The next step is to shoot. Or rather, to try to shoot. Filming is where it all goes horribly wrong. In real film, and ten times more so in Machinima, this is where Mr. Reality stomps in the door, bleary-eyed and hung over, and proceeds to do something unmentionable to your lovely theoretical planning — which is why you planned in the first place.

Characters who just won't go to the right place, timings that require your assistants to have the dexterity of a concert pianist, poor understanding of exactly what's meant to happen — all these things will force you to re-do, re-try, think laterally, re-think the shot, or, in extreme cases, write entire new tools just to make this shot possible.

Given all these factors, you absolutely don't want to be trying to figure out the creative details of the film at the same time! The actual process of filming will stretch your creativity to the limits, not to mention your patience. On

*BloodSpell*, it wasn't uncommon for complex shots to take upward of an hour and ten takes to get right.

> *Hugh: "And, rolling. Take 14. And, action. Cue Jered!"*
>
> *\*CLICK\**
>
> *Hugh: "Cue the Master."*
>
> *\*CLICK\**
>
> *Hugh: "And animation 3 at the same time as he looks . . ."*
>
> *\*CLICK\* \*CLICKCLICKCLICKCLICK\**
>
> *Various crew members: "OH, S\*\*\*\*\* (\*&(£!!! O\*&(\*!! @@@!"*
>
> *Hugh: "And the Master turns into a giraffe rather than, as we'd hoped, playing his bow animation. Again. More coffee, anyone?"*

# Thinking about Aspect Ratios

You should make one very important decision when you start making your film: the *aspect ratio* you'll be shooting in. By *aspect ratio,* we mean the shape of the screen. Figure 3-3 shows three popular aspect ratios you should consider.

Aspect 4:3

Aspect 16:9

Aspect Cinemascope (2.39:1)

**Figure 3-3:**
Common
aspect
ratios for
film.

- ✔ **16:9:** We generally recommend 16:9. It's the most commonly used ratio in film and TV and provides a nice filmic feel without the intimidating size of Cinemascope. Plus, if you've got a widescreen monitor, you can shoot in this resolution without cropping your footage later. If you can, you should aim to shoot at a high-definition resolution like 1,280x720.

- ✔ **4:3:** The old TV format, 4:3 is also the format used by a lot of online video sites, notably YouTube. If you're aiming primarily for YouTube, a 4:3 aspect ratio (800x600, 640x480, 320x240) ensures that you get the most use out of your available screen space.

- ✔ **Cinemascope** is the high-end format used by blockbuster films. If you're shooting something seriously epic, it can look great in Cinemascope. However, its size means that it's difficult to display on non-widescreen monitors, and it'll suck horribly on YouTube. The sheer available screen size can also feel quite empty if you don't have epic vistas to deploy on it. And by vistas, we don't, nor will we ever, mean Windows.

# Framing Your Movie

Every time you set up a shot, you're essentially painting. You're constructing a 2D image that should convey both information and emotion. And you can ensure that both come across by improving your shot composition.

## Painterly composition

You can learn a lot from painters and photographers. Here are some tips on creating an artistic scene:

- ✔ **Keep it simple!** Don't crowd your shot. A shot should have at most three important elements — more often one or two. Your audience won't be able to follow more than three separate elements in a shot at the same time.

  Keeping it simple doesn't mean that you can't have a flight of 50 dragons in shot — that's a single element! But if you try to shoot a battle between dragons and eagles as your hero cleaves his way through an army toward the heroine, all in one static shot, your audience may get confused.

- ✔ **But don't make it too simple.** Most shots will work better with more than one element contrasting. That's not a hard-and-fast rule; close-ups of characters, for example, are definitely the exception. But if you can, try to capture two elements in shot at once — a contrasting or important element of the background, part of a crowd or passers-by, or two of your characters.

✔ **Remember the Rule of Thirds.** Divide your frame into thirds horizontally and vertically. You'll have four points where the dividing lines cross. If you center key elements of your shot — a character's face, for example — on one of those four points, you will tend to create a strong image. You can also sometimes center an element on one of the points where the lines meet the edge of the screen — for example, if you're framing one character with another.

✔ **Break the frame.** If you're shooting a crowd sequence, it's tempting to shoot in such a way that all the background characters are neatly enclosed by the frame, rather than having arms or legs cut off by the frame. But that's exactly the wrong way to shoot! If you arrange your frame so that key characters are in frame but background characters overlap the frame, it suggests a bigger, more continuous crowd.

✔ **Be dark or light — don't be brown.** Don't be afraid to use total darkness as part of your frame. Shooting through a doorway, for example, where only half the frame is light, is fine. If only the key character's face is light and the rest of the frame is dark, great.

However, don't shoot if the key element of your shot is poorly lit. If there is even a chance the audience won't be able to see the action, add more light. It's always better to be over-lit than to be a gray mush.

✔ **Use quick and dirty lighting.** You can write an entire book about lighting (and many people have). If you want a quick-and-dirty way to make your lighting look good, make sure that one side of your character's face is darker than the other or lit in a slightly different color. Contrast between the sides of the face nearly always looks dramatic.

✔ **Include lines.** Diagonal lines look dynamic on-screen. If you can, shoot walls, doors, and pylons so they aren't straight in frame. You can use suggested lines to point to key elements of your frame: a horizon pointing to your key character or shadows on the floor lining up to point toward your villain.

✔ **Shoot curvy lines!** Curves look great on-screen. In particular, paths that form an S-shape heading away from the camera look very nice indeed. See *Lord of the Rings* for about a million examples. Human shapes and silhouettes, particularly, ah, the kind of female silhouette you'll get from many computer games, also look great.

✔ **Hang it on your wall.** Before you take any shot, ask yourself this question: Would you be happy to take a still from it, have it printed, and display it on your wall? If so, you've got a good shot.

✔ **Change your Field Of View (FOV).** The default field-of-view for most games is 90 degrees. To make your work look less like a game and more like a film, if you have an engine that can change FOV, try changing to an angle closer to 40 degrees. Changes in FOV also alter how close objects appear to each other laterally. If you want to fit two objects into your shot but can't quite manage it, try changing your FOV.

## Framing characters

Knowing how and where to place your characters in frame governs the kind of story you can tell with them:

✔ **Don't center your characters on-screen.** Most of the time, your character should be on the left or right of the screen, talking either to the center screen or past the center screen. Only put them center-screen or directly facing the camera if you're sure you know what you're doing.

✔ **Handle sympathy.** As a rough general rule, the closer a character appears to the center of the screen, and the more head-on he is shot, the more sympathetic he will appear to the audience. This effect is subtle but powerful. Set up two shots, one where your hero is talking from a bit right of center, almost head-on to the camera, and another where your villain is right on the left of screen, talking across to the hero. Suddenly, your hero and villain will feel heroic and villainous, respectively.

✔ **Frame!** If you can frame a character with natural features, such as an arch, in the background it will make the image stronger. Likewise, on a wide shot, finding something — a rock, a candle, a doorhandle — to place in the foreground to give depth to the shot often improves your shot, too.

✔ **Shoot from up and down.** You can dramatically change the impact and overtone of a shot by changing the vertical angle you're shooting from. In general, shooting down on a character will often make him look vulnerable, while shooting up at him will make him look impressive.

Even in a field full of unreliable advice, this piece is particularly unreliable. For example, if you have a character look down (so that you're shooting him effectively from above) and then have him look up at the camera, he'll look menacing, in a Hannibal Lecter–style.

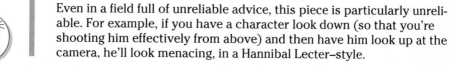

## Mastering Shot Flow

On the other side of the filmmaking coin are shot flow and storytelling. If your shots don't tell your story, you're in trouble, no matter how beautiful they are.

Fortunately, you can follow a few simple rules to help ensure that your shots make sense:

- ✔ **How will your audience know what's going on?** Make sure that you've got shots that establish everything important in the scene. You don't have to use them immediately — it's an old trick to start on a series of close-ups and then go to an establishing shot that explains their relationship — but make sure that you know how and when your audience will find out what's going on.

- ✔ **Be consistent with direction of action.** If your character runs out of the shot from left to right, and the next shot is of him running in the same direction, he should run from left to right on-screen again. Direction of action is super-important in making a sequence viewable: Anything that moves out of shot moving one way across the screen should nearly always move the same way in the next shot.

  (There are a few exceptions to this rule — notably if you're pulling out from a close-up to a new wide shot, or if you're going from a character running into screen to the same character running out of screen.)

- ✔ **Follow eyelines.** Viewers follow the direction a character is looking. If you're going to go from one character to a new character entering the scene, it'll make a lot more sense if the first character looks around in the direction of the second character's entrance before you cut. Likewise, if you're setting up two characters who are talking to each other, make sure that they look like they're talking to each other. Watch out for eye heights in frame in particular.

  That doesn't mean they actually have to be looking at each other. Perception is king. If your character is in reality looking right at his co-conversationalist, but it looks a bit funny when you shoot it, by all means move him around until it looks right on film, even if he's now staring at your lighting badger's left nipple.

- ✔ **Left, then right!** If you're shooting two characters, an easy way to make the scene make sense is to put one on the right and one on the left. This positioning holds if you're shooting a close-up, a wide shot, or a two-shot. At some point, if it's a long scene, you'll want to swap them around somehow (see the sidebar "The line"). But until then, shoot them left, right, left.

- ✔ **Remember the details.** Forgetting to shoot close-ups of items, characters holding items, characters opening doors, and other such things is easy to do. But these little elements really add a lot to the intelligibility of the scene. If you can, shoot close-up inserts of action that may be even slightly unclear — or even just action that looks cool. It'll help the flow of your sequence.

# The line

It seems that every area of technical knowledge has one deeply arcane and highly specific piece. With the programming language C, it's pointers. With Machinima, it's Half-Life 2. And with filmmaking in general, it's the *line*.

The basic rule is this. Any time two characters are interacting, an invisible line of action extends through both of them (see figure). If you ever cut over that line, you'll confuse your audience.

Now, nothing stops a camera from moving over the line, using a dollying shot, or the line from moving over your camera, if one of the characters moves. Both methods are reliable ways to change the line — if you want to reverse the positions of characters on-screen, for example. But you must never, ever (well, almost never) cut over the line, or everything will reverse places, and you'll confuse your viewers.

Sounds simple, right? Well, it is — provided that you're dealing with only two characters. If five or six characters are all talking to each other, determining where the line is at any time is difficult. As a general rule, the line is between the two most active characters at any time. But really, once you're past fairly simple scenes, you've just got to take your best guess, go for it, and fix the results in pickups!

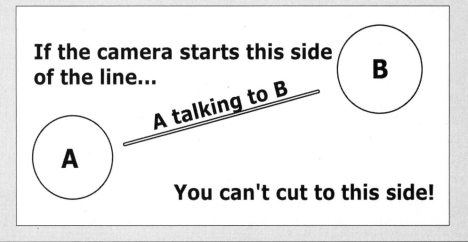

# The Components of a Film

Before you construct your novel, you need to know what words you have to work with. Here's a whistle-stop tour through the varieties of shots available to you.

You'll notice that we very rarely give specific details as to how to shoot a particular shot. Most shot types are more general categories than specific framings. The way you frame each shot layers on top of its general intention to give the meaning and purpose of that shot and that sequence.

Sounds complicated? Don't worry. Just come up with a rough idea, try it, and then junk it if it doesn't work. You'll get the hang of filming soon enough.

## Shot types: Wide

Arguably the simplest type of camera shot, a *wide shot,* shown in Figure 3-4, captures an entire scene or large part of a scene. A wide shot shows spatial relationships, gives the viewer an emotional break in intense scenes, shows action happening over a wide area (or full-body action, as in a martial-arts fight), and establishes a scene.

Whatever else you do during filming, make sure that you take a wide shot of your action. You'll never know when you need it.

## Shot functions: Establishing

Above all else, your film must establish in the viewer's mind what's going on, and where it is happening. Your establishing shot, or shots, set the scene. It may be a single wide shot that shows the area and the characters, or It may consist of a close-up shot of a sign or other salient detail, followed by a wide shot. Your establishing shots may even be a series of close shots followed by a wide shot (à la the bar scene in *Star Wars*), or a mixture of general visual shots around an area.

**Figure 3-4:**
A wide
shot from
*BloodSpell.*

A new establishing shot is often required after a period of action. Cut to a wide shot to update the viewers on what's happening now, who's still up, and who's lying down bleeding.

## Shot types: Two-shot

A two-shot (see Figure 3-5) is, unsurprisingly, any shot with two characters who are significant to the shot in frame. This type of shot is typically used for interactions between those characters.

A particularly strong type of two-shot is one arranged so that both characters' faces are visible. While this type of shot is sometimes a nightmare to shoot, being able to see both characters' interaction makes for a very strong image.

The infamous *over-the-shoulder shot* is arguably a type of two-shot. In this shot, part of one character's body (usually shoulder and head, hence the name) is used to frame another character in shot. This shot is usually used during dialoged sequences. Many directors hate it, but it's still worth having in your toolbox.

## Shot types: Reverse

A *reverse shot* is — er, well — how do we put this? It's like the shot before it, but backward. So, for example, if you're shooting two characters head-on, looking out over some battlements, and then you go to a shot from behind them looking out over their shoulders, you're shooting a reverse.

**Figure 3-5:**
A two-shot from the end of *BloodSpell.*

Reverses can be useful for revealing plot elements — a shadow appears at your heroine's shoulder as you're looking at her from behind, and you then reverse to a shot in front of her. Reverses are also a rare example of a shot that is acceptable to use even though they (often) cross the line. (For more about the line, see the earlier sidebar in this chapter.)

A reverse has to have some obvious clue that you've reversed. So, if both characters are looking forward and you're cutting from looking at their faces to looking at their backs, that's okay. But if they're facing each other, and you cut from one side of them to the other, that shot will jar as you cross the line, because the visual clues aren't obvious enough.

That's not the only meaning of the term *reverse* in filmmaking. As distinct from a *reverse shot,* filmmakers or editors will sometimes refer to *a reverse,* which is an opposing shot in a conversation sequence. Which might sometimes also be a reverse shot. Or not. Aargh!

## Shot types: Point of View (POV)

A Point of View (POV) shot is taken as if from the point of view of a character, usually just after or just before a close-up on that character, which cues the viewer as to which character's POV you're using. You can break all sorts of rules in a POV shot. Most notably, you can shoot other characters head-on, as you're saying to the viewer, "Okay, so this is what it looks like for this character."

Use a POV shot when you want to put the viewer in the character's place — when the character's creeping through a shadowy house, when an authority figure is shouting at him, or when he's watching his love interest anxiously after she's been shot.

## Shot types: Close-up

You know what a close-up is — a shot with only a character's face in shot (see Figure 3-6). These shots are great — they're emotionally intense, and they're simple to shoot because there's rarely more than one or two elements in frame.

There's another use for a close-up, too: When you're short on time and need to get a scene wrapped. A close-up is almost always the easiest type of shot to take — there's not a lot else in the scene.

**Figure 3-6:**
A close-up from, yes, you guessed it, *BloodSpell.*

Don't over-use close-ups. In general, you should save close-ups in conversations for emotionally intense moments. The closer you are to a character, the more strongly you feel his emotion.

You can have a *two-shot close-up,* where two characters are close enough or appropriately positioned that you can fit close-ups of both of them in frame. You can also go in closer on a character, to mouth and eyes, for an Extreme Close-Up (XCU). Don't be afraid to use them; they can be very powerful.

## Shot types: Medium shot

The absolute workhorse of character shots, a medium shot, shown in Figure 3-7, shows a character's torso and perhaps a little bit of her legs. It's the shot used for news reporters, interviews, and any shot where you're not in a wide shot, but you don't want the intimacy of a close-up. Get used to medium shots — you'll be using them a lot.

Be careful with the framing on a medium shot. In general, never cut a character off at the waist — either frame above it, at chest level, or below it, around the hips to mid-thigh.

**Figure 3-7:**
A medium
shot from
*BloodSpell*.

## Shot types: General Visual (GV)

Go watch any James Bond movie. Wait for him to travel to a new country. See that you've got a couple of quick shots of flavor of the country — Big Ben and a big red bus for London, a guy in a kilt for Scotland, the Kremlin for Moscow? That's a GV (see Figure 3-8). It's used to immediately establish the look and feel of the area, which carries over to the main scene (which was probably shot in Burbank, but now feels like it's in Scotland!).

**Figure 3-8:**
A GV of the
cathedral in
*BloodSpell*.

# Shot types: Reveal

Any shot that reveals a plot element is a (what else?) *reveal shot.* The absolutely classic reveal is the two-shot over a heroine's shoulder, shot from in front of her, which then changes focus to reveal the villain standing behind her.

Give some thought to your reveals. As a general guideline, if it's genuinely a dramatic reveal, you either want to ramp up the tension as high as you can in earlier shots or (as more modern films like *The Descent* have started to do) simulate the randomness of real life with a sudden reveal with no warning at all. The latter technique's hard to get right and relies a lot on genuinely shocking material, but if it's used well, it hits really hard.

# Shot types: Insert

Bond's sitting in the villain's office, pointing a silenced gun at the unfortunate Blofeld. But secretly, the man with the white cat is going for the button that will dump Bond into a tank full of sharks. How do you show that? With an insert, of course.

An *insert* is a close-up that isn't centered on a character's face (see Figure 3-9). It can be of something that is hidden or just something that wouldn't otherwise be obvious. Martial arts movies live, eat, and breathe inserts to show off the neato blocks, punches, and brutal violence that's going on.

**Figure 3-9:**
An insert from Strange Company's *Matrix: 4x1.*

You nearly always need more inserts than you've got. Sprinkle them in liberally. If a scene doesn't quite flow and you don't know why, chances are that you either need another wide shot or another insert.

## Moving camera: Pan

When you're turning the camera without moving it, you're *panning*. Pans are among the cheapest of camera moves in real life — all they need is a tripod. They're also quite hard to use well.

In general, a character's movement should suggest a pan — panning to track a character through a crowd, for example, or panning to follow a character's eyeline as she looks off-screen. They can also serve to introduce a scene. Otherwise, pans with no obvious cause and no other movement tend to look forced.

## Moving camera: Dolly/crane

Any time you're moving the camera in two dimensions, without changing height, you're *dollying* — so called because the platform on which a real camera is moved is called a dolly. Add height to that mix and you're probably looking at a crane shot, so called because — oh, right, you got it.

Both dolly and crane shots are comparatively cheap and common in real film, meaning that you can afford to use them relatively freely in your Machinima, too. It's worth thinking about how a crane, in particular, actually moves — it's a platform on the end of a long lever. Try to fake this movement for more realistic-looking shots.

Cameras moving in real 3D space are great for adding life and movement to a scene; many Machinima filmmakers have made a style out of continual subtle movement within a scene. They're also great ways to change your position in relation to the line, move between a wide shot or medium shot and a close-up, or shift from one character shot to another.

## Moving camera: Zoom

A *zoom* isn't actually a camera movement at all, but a change in the FOV of the camera, which appears to make some things closer and other things further away. Zooms went out of fashion through the '90s, but the handheld style of series like *24* and *Firefly* have ensured their return to popularity, at least in hand-held-shot series.

---

# Where to find more on filmmaking

You can find dozens of good books on film-making. Here are a few that we've found particularly valuable over the years:

✔ *The Guerilla Film Maker's Handbook* — **Chris Jones and Genevive Joliffe, published by Continuum International.** More focused on filmmaking as a whole package than shooting in particular, and quite UK-focused, this book is our bible for all aspects of real filmmaking. Use it to learn about everything from funding to filming to publicity.

✔ *Shot by Shot* — **Steven Katz, published by Michael Wiese Productions.** One of the classic tomes covering the basics of camerawork, the book is a bit dry, but very informative. The techniques it shows aren't particularly flashy, but they work well and are a good basis for springboarding your own work while being confident that you've got the bases covered.

✔ *Hollywood Camerawork* — **Per Holmes (www.hollywoodcamerawork.us).** This isn't a book — it's a set of DVDs, and a pricey set at that. But you get a fantastic introduction to some very sophisticated camerawork techniques, from the very basics to Hollywood-level shooting.

✔ *The Grammar of the Shot* by **Roy Thompson, published by Focal Press.** Comes to us highly recommended as a story- and edit-focused guide to shooting.

Other than these books, watch movies and TV. In particular, turn the sound off and then watch them. You'll pick up a lot more of the technique that way because you won't be distracted by the story.

And don't be afraid to try to copy sequences shot-by-shot for your own education — you'll learn fast by doing what your heroes do, and learning what works and why.

---

Zooms tend to look rather clunky, which you can sometimes use as a deliberate feature. You can effectively use a subtle zoom to heighten tension in a scene, à la classic Sergio Leone Westerns. Otherwise, you won't have a lot of uses for them unless you're going for a hand-held style.

It's worth noting that by zooming in one direction while tracking in the opposite direction, you can achieve a very weird effect, as the entire scene appears to foreshorten or lengthen. Peter Jackson is a particular fan of this trick, called a *dolly zoom,* which was pioneered in the film *Vertigo.*

## *Moving camera: Handheld*

Jerky, blurred hand-held camerawork has become increasingly prevalent in modern filmmaking and TV. Handheld camerawork is almost more of a style unto itself than a technique, and it's very hard to replicate in Machinima. While you can achieve something similar using mouse control, the typical handheld shake really has to be added in post-production or camera control. Medieval II: Total War does particularly fantastic handheld simulation (see Chapter 12).

Nonetheless, a handheld feel — characterized by rapid swish pans between subjects, fast crash zooms, and jerkiness — is a great way to achieve a feeling of realism, particularly in Machinima. If your film would benefit from such a style, it's worth considering, particularly for fast action and fight scenes, where the blurriness and jerkiness of the style can conceal a thousand dodgy Machinima animations. See the trailer for *The Return 2* by Rufus Cubed for a very good example of handheld simulation in Machinima.

# Chapter 4

# Storytelling and Scriptwriting

*W*e can't tell you how to make a Machinima film — or film period — that will definitely succeed. But we can tell you how to make sure that your film sucks. And what's more, it's simple: Don't have a good script.

Making a good film from a bad script is quite literally impossible. Can't be done. If your script sucks, so will your film. It's the nearest thing you'll be seeing in these pages to a hard-and-fast rule.

A few people are irritatingly talented gits who can just knock out brilliant stories without thinking about it. We hate them. But chances are that you're not one of them. If it's any consolation, neither are we.

The good news is that it's possible to learn to write good stories. It's not easy, and it takes time, but this chapter gets you started.

## Debunking Storytelling Myths

Storytelling is a misunderstood art form. Because storytelling (as opposed to writing — they're not the same thing) is so rarely taught or studied, there's a lot of nonsense talked about how to tell a story. The following sections outline common, and totally incorrect, factoids about storytelling.

### You can't learn to tell a story

A lot of people — including some very smart storytellers — will say that you can't learn to tell stories. You've just got to write a lot, they say, and one day the magic will flow.

Well, like any skill, you have to practice storytelling to learn it. You can read about storytelling until you're blue in the face, but unless you actually write stories you'll never become a good storyteller.

And you really do need life experience to tell great stories. When you write a story, you're recreating the world as you see it. The more penetrating your insights into the world, the more likely your story is to touch people.

But to say you can't learn storytelling is baloney. You can learn how a good story is constructed, just as you can learn any other skill. Sure, you can become a great football player by playing a lot of football. But if you've got a football coach who teaches you tactics and technique, you'll become more skilled, much faster. It's the same with storytelling.

## You'll ruin your storytelling by learning story structure

Hugh was infected with this particular meme for years. He worried that if he read how-to guides on storytelling, his writing would become stale and formulaic. He worried he'd end up struggling to fit his writing into rigid, predefined structures.

That's a potent fear. It's not helped by the number of guides that claim there's one true way to write a story. If you try to write every story the same way, you certainly will feel constricted.

Story techniques are tools, nothing more. You can use them if they help your work, you can ignore them if you feel you need to. By ignoring that information, you're trying to reinvent an art form that a lot of other people have already gotten very good at. Reading about storytelling gives you access to faster, neater, more involving, and more powerful ways to tell your stories.

## There's one true way to write a story

You'll encounter a lot of books promising to show you The Hidden Story-Form Behind All The Blockbusters! Some of these guys will be abusing poor Joseph Campbell's *Hero's Journey*. Others will be peddling some stinking, half-rotted monstrosity of their own creation. We're not very fond of these guys. Can you tell?

There. Is. No. One. Way. To. Write. A. Story.

Find us any book that claims all great films fit into one specific story structure, and we'll find you a counter-example. There are tips, and tricks, and generalities, and useful general rules; but there ain't no magic bullet. Thank goodness. Otherwise writing stories would be darn boring.

## Writing a story is easy

Imagine that you've decided to go and compete in a tennis match. You've played a bit of tennis; your friends say you're pretty good. So you've signed up for a tournament. You're standing at the side of the court, and you look down the list of your competitors. And said list goes a bit like this: Agassi, Becker, Sampras, Henman, McEnroe . . .

Welcome to storytelling. Any time you throw your hat into this particular ring, it's time to look at the competition you're facing for your audience. There's Stephen Spielberg leaning against the wall over there. J.R.R. Tolkien's on the green smoking a pipe. Ernest Hemingway's having an argument with the ball-boy, and in the distance there's a guy with silly hair called Will Shakespeare.

The standard of storytelling to which your audience is accustomed has been set by legions of stories from artists at the very top of their game. Handily, you can just learn the techniques they had to invent, but still — you're gonna be needin' some phat skillz.

## You don't need to write like the pros do

We've heard this one from professional filmmakers, believe it or not. "You don't need to write in conventional script format if you're directing the film yourself." "There's no point doing a focus test unless you've got thousands to spend on it".

If you hear about a technique that your storytelling heroes use to make better films, chances are it'll work for you, too. Sure, there are fewer reasons to use a standard script format if you're not submitting it to a $10-million production team. Sure, your focus group may not be so focused. But these techniques are in use because they work. The magic ingredient that makes them work is rarely money.

## Fire hot . . . fan films bad

A lot of people choose to set their first stories, or indeed later work, in a favorite fictional world. Some people — we won't name names here because they've embarrassed themselves quite enough already — claim these stories are somehow inferior to original work, or that it's impossible to learn story-telling by writing *fan-fiction*. That is patent nonsense.

Apprenticing by copying the work of the masters has been an accepted way to learn to create art since before the Renaissance. Shakespeare wrote what would today be considered fan-fiction, if not outright plagiarism. Hunter S Thompson learned to write by copying the works of his heroes word for word. And anyone who has worked in the television or comics industry has almost certainly worked on universes and characters created by others.

Fan-fiction is as valid a form of storytelling as any other. If you want to write it, do.

# Outlining the Form of a Story

So, what is a story, and what is a script? A *story* is the collected events, emotional changes, and action that form the skeleton of the script. A story can be expressed in any storytelling form.

The story of *Casablanca,* for example, could be told in a comic, a novel, a poem, or a film. The actions behind *Casablanca* are the story. The scaffold on top, the stuff that makes this version of *Casablanca* a film or a book — that's the *script.*

A story, in its most basic form, is just a sequence of events. In the movie *When Harry Met Sally,* for example, Harry meets Sally when they're both young. They don't get on. They meet again over the years. They come to care about each other. They try to find each other partners. Then one day they sleep together, and for some reason, the friendship's ruined — until they realize they're in love with each other.

If the story of a film is worth re-telling like *When Harry Met Sally,* you know it's good. Anyone can make up a series of events, but to know how to create a compelling series of events is the craft of storytelling.

But there's more to *When Harry Met Sally* than just the main story. The characters each have a story of their own, a story within a story. The themes and action of these sub-stories, or "spines", make the story resonate with the audience. We're interested in people and how their lives relate to ours.

Harry spends the film trying to convince himself that men and women can't be friends, when it turns out that the only woman he wants to be with is the one who is his friend. Meanwhile, Sally claims to be horrified by the idea that men and women can't be friends without sex getting in the way, when she believes just that, and she has to overcome the belief that sex and friendship can't coexist in order to be happy. (At least, that's our interpretation. We may be, and in fact almost certainly are, wrong.)

Then there's the setting of the story. Contrast the world of *When Harry Met Sally* with the background of another so-called real-world drama — the television series *24*. Just think about the backgrounds — which are both ostensibly the real world — being transposed.

*"I'll have what she's hav- — aargh, terrorists!"*

The background itself has a story — which many people would call a theme. In *When Harry Met Sally,* the story is that people will stress a lot about being single. They'll get together with some people, and it won't work out. Then finally they'll meet someone special. It'll be up and down, and at times, it'll look like it won't work out, but then it will. And before you know it, they'll have been married for 45 years.

In *24,* the story is that most of life isn't very important. But every so often, something Very Bad happens, and a number of people will conspire to harm others. Then the complexities of life will intervene to ensure that no one's plans, good or bad, go as expected, and everyone involved will go through horrible trauma that they have no choice but to endure.

All of these stories depend upon things not happening as expected. That's the most fundamental aspect of a story — the *reversal.*

# Getting the Scoop on Reversals

Stories are made up of a series of reversals on varying levels. Robert McKee, the author of *Story,* says that a story happens when a gap occurs between the expectations of a protagonist and reality.

*24's* Jack Bauer gets up expecting to spend another pleasant day hiding from the Chinese — but someone's trying to kill him. Okay, okay, this is *24*. They're trying to kill him more than usual.

Sally expects to spend a pleasant, but unmemorable, day driving to New York with her friend's boyfriend. Instead, he's a charming jerk who tries to sleep with her, but who she can't forget.

Zornhau, who writes about storytelling at http://zornhau.livejournal. com, describes this fundamental element of storytelling as a QABN: Question, Answer, But Now.

Can Jack Bauer continue to ever-so-politely try to get into the underwear of the cute single mother? No, because someone knows where he is and is trying to kill him. Now he needs to go after them before they come for him.

We used the word "pleasant" to describe both our heroes' expectations. Some part of a reversal — the question, the answer, or the But Now — always sucks. That's what drives the story — the avoidance of suckitude.

But the reversal doesn't work unless the characters are constantly trying to improve their lot. They're not just sitting waiting for the story to happen to them; they're actively searching for whatever they think will improve their lives. Your characters are made understandable and sympathetic by what they want. And when searching for wants meets incoming suckiness, the ensuing crash scatters story all over the sidewalk. So — the protagonist tries to improve his lot. Something happens that either sucks or has the potential to suck. But now. And we move on.

Conflict is drama — one of the oldest storytelling rules, dating back to Aristotle.

## Sizing your reversals

Reversals come in a variety of sizes, like particularly dramatic washing powder. There's the cute li'l-laundrette–sized reversal: Can Jack get to the elevator before the guards come around the corner? Yes — but now the elevator's under control of the terrorists and is in a free-fall!

Then there's the average-size single-guy-who-actually–remembered-to-buy-washing-powder-shocker! reversal: Can Harry and Sally manage to pair each other off with their respective best friends? No — the friends end up hooking up, leaving Harry and Sally together again.

And then there's the super-economy you'll-still-have-most-of-the-box-left-when-the-kids-go-to-college–size reversal: Can the Fellowship take the Ring to Mordor? No, the Ring's power corrupts the Fellowship. Now Frodo and Sam must travel on without protection.

These three levels of reversal — called *beat*, *scene,* and *act* respectively — are the keys to most stories.

If you're working on a gigantic project — the length of a full TV season or more — there's a higher level still, called *arc.* At that point, you're way past our experience, and frankly, you're out there on your own.

## Beats

The *beat* is the smallest practical unit of story, just like a beat in music. It consists of a single reversal — someone does something, it doesn't turn out as expected.

## "They have a Cave Troll"

Drums, drums in the deep! Orcs are coming, and our heroes are trapped in a room inside the dwarven halls of Moria. Boromir rushes to the door, looks right, and nearly gets an arrow in the eye. Aragorn's bellowing instructions and rushing for the door, too. Aragorn and Boromir struggle to close the doors — they make it!

"They have a Cave Troll", says Boromir — we don't know what a Cave Troll is, but we can guess from Boromir's expression that it's unlikely to lead to hugs and puppies. Everyone pulls out pointy things.

Gimli's getting with the aggro — "Let them come! There's one dwarf in Moria who still draws breath!" The Orcs are bashing on the door — one manages to break a hole in it and gets an arrow in the face for his trouble. Then they bash through it: But being the first Orc into that room was never going to be a career-enhancing move, as Aragorn and Legolas open up with bows. Orcs drop by the bucket-load, but they're closing on the Fellowship.

Everyone's fighting now, and Orcs are falling over left, right, and center — but then Sam looks up, and there's something big and ugly in the room. So that's a Cave Troll, then. My, that's large. Legolas tries to shoot it — but that does nothing but annoy it. It raises its hammer, ready to clobber Sam — but then he dives through its legs. And on we go.

Quite what happens in a beat is varied. It may be a single line, or several lines, or a small amount of action. In action movies, the fights often seem to be split up into moves.

In *Pirates of the Carribean: Curse of the Black Pearl,* Jack Sparrow and Will Turner fence until Jack's got his back to the door. Jack runs for the door. Will throws a sword at the door to block it. Jack turns and comes at Will with a sword. Will picks up a poker to defend himself. That's a series of beats.

The best way to understand how beats work is to deconstruct a sequence from a particularly brilliant story.

First up, the fantastic Cave Troll fight from *The Lord of the Rings: The Fellowship of the Ring* — see the sidebar "They have a Cave Troll." We heartily recommend checking out all three *Lord Of The Rings* movies for their story structure.

You can probably spot some of the beats in there already:

- Boromir wants to know what's going on. Are the Orcs close? Ooh, yes they are — close enough to reenact a Strongbow ad with Boromir's face. Now what is the Fellowship going to do?

- Aragorn and Boromir rush to close the doors. Can they close the ancient doors in time? Yes, they can — but now Boromir's seen what's out there, and it looks like they're in more trouble than they thought. Now the Fellowship has to get ready to fight.

- ✔ The Orcs want to get to tasty human meat, so they're getting rid of the door. Can the Orcs break down the door? Yes — and even though they'll get facefuls of arrows for their troubles, they're in the room.

- ✔ Can the Fellowship beat the Orcs up? Yes, because the Fellowship collectively kicks ass. But now they've got more than Orcs to deal with.

- ✔ Legolas would like that Cave Troll to stop its annoying living. Can Legolas drop the Cave Troll in one shot? No — this thing is a lot tougher than any Orc around here. Now Sam has to face its wrath.

- ✔ Can Sam avoid becoming Hobbit pâté courtesy of an irritated Cave Troll? Yes — he can dive through its legs. But now he's on the ground, and the Cave Troll's still on him.

If you can re-watch this sequence while reading this book, you'll notice that these beats vary enormously in length. Some of what you're seeing wasn't in the script, but was added later in filming (see Chapter 3). All the shots of people waiting for the Orcs to break down the door, for example, were added in the storyboard. But some of the apparently nonbeat action was in the script — Gimli's line, for example, or Aragorn's instructions.

It's important to allow the characters time around each beat to react to the events of that beat. A story structure is a framework — characters should both react to events and plan ahead for their next action.

When Gimli's shouting about how he wants the Orcs to come so that he can kill them, he's thinking, "Well, that's arguably a bad reversal, but these guys killed my friends, so I can look on this as a revenge-crazed, combat-junkie upside."

And when Aragorn starts shouting orders, he's thinking, "Oops, this is about to get a bit eventful. Better take charge and start giving everyone plans and instructions so that we can, you know, not die."

It's not just the events of the story that make people enjoy it. It's the characters' reactions to those events. Around every beat, you should be weaving the characters' personal stories and reactions. Beats also vary in length to boost suspense. There's jeopardy in each one, but in the first three beats, you're really hanging suspense off the beat question in each case. These beats work best if you've got time to wonder and worry: What *is* out there? Let's see some worrying shadows.

Character reactions heighten the suspense as you see your heroes getting scared. Face it: If Gandalf's looking worried, anyone else should probably advance straight to panic.

But the last two beats in the sequence work precisely because of their speed. Aargh, Troll! Oh, no, he's — phew. He's out of — oh, no, tha — phew. Here, you don't want any extraneous reaction or action, because it's all in the thinking time. If that hammer is coming down right now, you panic. If it's coming down some time next Tuesday, no worries.

All the preceding advice applies to scenes that aren't big fights, too. Drama is built on conflict, so virtually every scene is a fight in some way or another, whether physical, verbal, or even internal.

## Scenes

At the next level up from the beat, we've got the *scene*. A scene is a larger reversal within the story — it's about as low in the structure as you'd go if you were telling your story in a few minutes. Often, your scene will be limited to one location (the theatrical definition of scene), but sometimes it'll be spread over several locations, as in a chase — er — scene.

A scene is a single unit of story. So, any scene should have one important change — one major expectation gap, which breaks down into beats.

Let's take a look at the third act of *The Lord of the Rings: The Fellowship of the Ring:*

1. Frodo has brought the Ring safely to Rivendell. Can he now go home? No — the Ring is causing chaos in Rivendell, and the only way Frodo can see to avoid disaster is to volunteer to take the Ring himself. Now he and a few others must attempt to carry it all the way to Mordor.

2. Can the Fellowship reach Mordor via the Gap of Rohan? No — Saruman's birds are watching the Gap. Now they must cross the mountain Caradhras.

3. When Frodo falls in the snow, and the Ring slips from his grasp, will Boromir take it for himself? No — but it is clear he wants to. Now the Fellowship must guard against one of their own.

4. Will the Fellowship make it over Caradhras? No — Saruman's hold over the weather is too strong. Now, they must face whatever it is that Gandalf fears in the dark of the Mines of Moria.

5. The doors are shut. Can Gandalf even open the door to Moria? Yes — but something that lives outside Moria is awoken at the same time, and the ensuing fight brings down a landslide on the doors. Now, the Fellowship must go forward, because it can't go back.

6. In amidst the wonders of Moria, Frodo notices Gollum following them. Will they turn to deal with this threat? No — Gandalf advises against killing Gollum, believing he has a further part to play. Now Frodo must go on, both aware of Gollum and considering Gandalf's words.

7. The Fellowship comes across the tomb of Balin. Will they face the same threat that killed him? Yes — Pippin makes a mistake, alerts the Orcs, and now the party must fight.

8. The Fellowship is fleeing Orcs — can they escape? No — they are surrounded. But then the Orcs flee in turn, as a greater threat emerges from the Mines — the Balrog.

9. Can the Fellowship flee down the steps of Kazad-dum before they collapse? Yes, but only through Aragorn's athleticism.

10. Can the Fellowship escape Moria and the Balrog? No, not before the Balrog arrives. Now Gandalf must face the creature he fears.

11. Can Gandalf defeat the Balrog? Yes, by shattering the stone under it and casting it into the pit. But at the last minute, the Balrog drags Gandalf down to his doom, too — and now the Fellowship must continue without him.

The first thing to notice about this structure is how many scenes aren't there. There are whole heaps of the Fellowship's journey that are barely touched on, or skipped over altogether. The Fellowship walk for nearly a hundred miles without a single scene. Entire movies have been made about climbing a mountain, but it's only two short scenes in the film.

Those scenes that made it into the movie are there because they have important roles to play in the story. Each of the scenes starts as late as possible — straight into the terrible weather and Saruman from Boromir returning the Ring — and ends as soon as it can. It's always better to start in the middle of the action than to include pointless buildup.

The first draft of *BloodSpell* included an entire four-minute introduction scene that was cut from the feature version. We simply didn't need those four minutes, but cut straight to the action.

You'll run into the problem of how to rescue your characters from some plight again and again. In Scene 8, the Fellowship is "rescued" from the Orcs by the appearance of the Balrog.

Normally, it's a bad idea to have your characters rescued by an outside force, as it gives the audience the sense that the writer has just arbitrarily decided to save them! However, in Scene 8, we move from "In Danger" to "In Even More Danger," as a result of temporarily saving them, which means the rescue doesn't feel cheap. You might call this a Frying Pan to Fire reversal.

Scene 11 is the classic end-of-act setup. In general, each act ending will escalate from the last. So after a series of comparatively small scenes, we now have an absolute humdinger, drawn directly from the act structure, with which to go on to the first scene of the next act.

There's no fixed number of scenes that appear per act. When you're writing, you can aim for as many or as few scenes as will fit your act questions.

You may not agree with our scene breakdown here — and that's exactly as it should be. What we're doing here is reverse-engineering a structure that normally disappears as a script is written. Were you to write *The Fellowship of the Ring* yourself, you might start by writing a structure like this, but as you add detail and flavor to the script, the exact scene lines will blur.

Nonetheless, this sort of analysis is very useful because it allows you to look at the mechanics of a great story and get at least some idea of why it works so well. You're losing a lot of the story's greatness, but you can still see some of what makes it such a powerful and viewable sequence.

It works the other way around, too. If you find a film that really sucks, you can learn a lot about why and how stories suck, and how to avoid those problems in your own stories, by analyzing it as we're doing here.

# *Act*

Acts are the big questions. They encode the point of your film. If your act structure isn't totally kick-ass, everything below it will be weak.

There is no hard and fast rule as to how many acts you need in a film. Three is the norm for a standard-length feature film, while U.S.-format TV drama tends to work on a four-act structure.

*Lord of the Rings: The Fellowship of the Ring* is arguably a four-act structure:

1. The Baggins family of hobbits own a Ring of Power, which is arguably the most dangerous item in Middle-Earth. Will they manage to understand its danger before it is too late? Yes, just. Now Frodo Baggins must flee with the servants of Mordor on his heels.

2. Will Frodo meet up with Gandalf and travel to Rivendell safely? Barely — he delivers the Ring to Rivendell on the edge of death from an encounter with the Ringwraiths. Now he must decide whether he will carry it further still, all the way to Mordor.

3. Frodo can't give up the ring to the Wise. Will he succeed in carrying it to Mordor? Not yet — the Fellowship's enemies force the Fellowship to travel through the dangerous Mines of Moria, where Gandalf falls. Now the Fellowship must go on without its guide.

4. With Gandalf gone, can the Fellowship fulfill its mission? No — the Ring is working its evil again, and the party turns upon each other as Orcs attack. Now some of the broken Fellowship must search for their captured companions, while Frodo must travel on, with only Sam's companionship, toward Mordor.

With these big reversals, you've got to be especially careful that they're strong, and that the audience can't predict them in advance.

In particular, any reversal or climax that depends on a decision by the protagonist must be one that can be decided either way.

Frodo deciding whether to give the Ring to Sauron isn't a strong decision to hang an act on. The audience knows perfectly well he's not going to do it.

On the other hand, Frodo's decision of whether to stay with the Fellowship is a really strong climax — there are huge dangers on both sides, and it's a decision that the audience simply can't guess ahead of time.

With any reversal, but particularly on the Act level, you must also be careful not to go back on yourself. If, for example, Act 3 ended with Gandalf dying, and Act 4 ended with him returning to lead the Fellowship onward, that would be a very weak structure. The third and fourth acts would essentially cancel themselves out, leaving the Fellowship exactly as they were at the start.

Finally, if your Act structure doesn't grip people if you tell it in your local coffee shop, it's not yet strong enough.

# Developing Your Characters

Your audience comes for the action. That's a given. But they stay for the heroes and the villains — the characters of the piece.

There's an argument (one thing you may have noticed about storytelling by now is that there's always an argument) that the function of a story is to allow viewers to understand a character — an imaginary person — in a way that they generally can't understand someone else in real life. All the trials and tribulations (or, as the case may be, tribbleations, if you're writing *Star Trek* fanfic) your characters go through are purely there to expose the choices your characters make in steadily more extreme circumstances.

You'll already have ideas for your characters as part of the base-line plot you've constructed. But how do you fill them out?

- **Character = opposition.** If you want to make your hero cooler, make your villain scarier. Heroes, in particular, are reflections of their antagonists: the bigger and scarier their opposition, the cooler and more impressive your hero will look, by simply overcoming the odds.

  Hans Gruber, the villain from *Die Hard,* is a super-impressive villain. He's smart, he has overwhelming force, and he keeps out-thinking his opposition. Bruce Willis's hero gains points just from being the only man who can face him off.

Be aware: A villain who makes stupid decisions, overlooks obvious pitfalls in his plans, and fails to do anyone any harm is never going to appear impressive, no matter how theoretically overwhelming his resources.

- ✔ **Character versus characterization.** Don't get these two things confused. You need both of them to make a strong character, but they serve fundamentally different roles. *Characterization* is the trappings of a character — Jack Bauer is a devoted father, husband, and highly trained ex-special forces counterterrorist officer. Kinda cool — certainly good material for a hero.

  But what made him the driving force for the juggernaut of *24* was his *character* — the choices he makes when he's put under pressure. Will he let his daughter die at the hands of terrorists? No, he'll do anything up to, and including, shooting at a U.S. senator — despite the fact that he's also clearly a man of duty. Conflict is drama. How a character reacts to conflict is dramatic.

- ✔ **Passive isn't interesting.** Take your favorite hero or villain. Buffy, Aragorn, James Bond, Rambo. Now, stick them inside a locked room and leave them there. What do they do? Well, they'll all react differently, but you can darn well expect to meet them outside about 15 minutes later. They're all men and women of action. Make sure that your heroes are action-driven. They can make good choices, they can make bad choices, they can hurt people or make them better. Just have them do *something!*

If you're very clever, you can produce a character who appears to be passive, but actually is anything but — it's just that all his conflict is happening internally. See Stephen Donaldson's *Chronicles of Thomas Covenant* for a fantastic example of the apparently passive character. But watch out — this one is very hard to do well.

- ✔ **Injustice is a winner.** This almost falls under the dirty-tricks-to-make-your-audience-like-you playbook. The modern Western audience hates to see anyone unjustly oppressed. If you want your audience on your character's side, make them the victim of injustice. Have the school principal think your star is a delinquent when she's actually a superhero (*Buffy the Vampire Slayer*). Have him hunted not only by the bad guys, but also by his own team who believes he's a traitor (*24*).

- ✔ **No one is a villain.** No one gets up in the morning and thinks, "Aha, now I shall do hideous evil!" No one. And no good fictional villain does, either. Your villain should be doing what he's doing for very good reasons. Perhaps he believes that he can't stand against the powers of Darkness and must join them to survive (Saruman in *Lord of the Rings*). Or perhaps he believes he can earn incredible riches with minimal, acceptable levels of violence (Hans Gruber in *Die Hard*).

How does your villain live with himself? Does he blame others for what he has become? Operate under a compulsion he can't control? See himself as a reasonable man doing what he must?

✔ **Don't write chicks.** Or dudes. Or black people. Or Native Americans. It's hard to write people who aren't quite like you — say, if they're the opposite gender, or from a different ethic background. So don't.

Ignore the bits that are different (at least for now) and write the bits that you understand. Don't write a spunky female sidekick, for example; write a geek who's good with a gun and ignore gender. Then, later on, change the name in the script to one that's appropriate and ask someone who is familiar with the character's unique identifier to check that there's nothing in there she feels a girl/black guy/Native American from that situation wouldn't do. This is a cheat, but it's one that works a lot better than struggling to write the unknown and ending up with a cliché. Fundamentally, people are people.

✔ **Make your hero understandable, not likable.** This is a mistake Hugh makes all the time — he tries to write a hero people will like and ends up with a guy who's a bit bland and for some reason, whiny.

Think about the great heroes of film and books. Think Gandalf — grumpy, mysterious, secretive old git that he is. Think Han Solo. Would you buy a used TIE Fighter from this man? Think Jack Bauer. "Hi. I'm Jack. We're in grave danger from terrorists, so I'm going to attach you to mains electricity on the off-chance you know something about it."

Heroes tend to be understandable — we can see why they're how they are, and we forgive them. Jack's doing what he has to. Gandalf's not telling all because it would put people in danger. Han knows he can only rely on himself. Heroes do the right thing in the crunch. But you'd rarely want to go out for a drink with them.

A corollary to this last point is that when heroes meet, they rarely get on. Don't forget to have Hero A distrust/flee from/hit with a poker Hero B.

✔ **It's all about layers.** You discover more about any interesting character as you go on throughout the film. This doesn't necessarily mean back story — we don't know anything about James Bond that we didn't know four films ago. But it does mean that we reveal new layers to the character's personality — what they care about (Oh, so Jack Sparrow really is quite bitter about that whole mutiny thing!), what they will or won't do (My gosh, there's someone Jack Bauer won't shoot!), or what they hold dear (Who'd have thought Buffy would care so much about a school prom?).

✔ **Do the smart thing.** Try not to have your characters be stupid. This one's hard, we know — there's an ongoing joke about Jered, the hero of *BloodSpell,* being the stupidest man in the entire film — but do try. Talk over their plans and try to remove any obvious flaws. Brainstorm solutions to their problems.

Making characters super-smart is hard, but if you can manage it, you've got a chance to create a filmic moment that will live forever. Remember the end of *Die Hard?* We do.

# Actually Writing a Script — Or Not!

So you're brim-full of acts, themes, beats and all that good stuff. How do you actually write a script?

Well, the one thing you don't do, under any circumstances, is start writing a script. That's putting the cart before the horse in a big way. Rather than trying to write everything about your story all at the same time, you should work on one thing at once.

## 1. The pitch

First, you need to figure out the grand structure of your story. Just how high-level you start depends on the scale of your movie. If you're aiming to write a feature-length movie, start working on act-level plot. If you're aiming for a five-or-ten-minute short, you'll only have about three to five scenes, so you can start out at the scene level; in a film that short, acts and scenes are essentially the same thing.

Start with your overall idea and decide what you already know. How long a story are you writing? (Shorter is a lot easier.) Do you know what the ending is? If so, does it kick ass? Who are your characters?

Now, get yourself a whole pile of paper or, ideally, index cards. Come up with ideas for each of your scenes or acts. What are the biggest reversals that you can find? What are the most exciting events? Don't worry about fitting this stuff together — instead, just concentrate on getting the ideas down on paper.

Now start winnowing your ideas until you've got a series of events that combine to give you the fastest, deepest, most moving and yet exciting story you can work out of your raw materials. Write it up as a short story (and we mean one page or less), practice until you can remember it, and then go tell your friends this story and listen to their reactions. Watch their expressions. When are they rapt? When are they bored? If you stop halfway through, do they prompt you as to what happens next or go to the bar?

Then go back and improve it based on what worked and what didn't. And repeat. You know you're ready to move on to the next section when you're getting complaints if you don't finish the story.

## 2. The skeleton

Now you lay the entire movie out in structure form, down to the individual beats of each scene. If it's a big movie, lay it out at scene level first. Again, brainstorm all you're worth, then winnow down, brainstorm again, then winnow, then seek criticism, then brainstorm, and winnow some more. You should end up with a series of scenes for each Act.

And now go down to the level of the individual beats, and carry out the brainstorming and winnowing process again as you lay out beats for each scene. Think about your characters. Think about how they would react, but also about how they could react. What would happen if they did something wildly out of character? What if the heroine suddenly turned on the hero? What if the villain revealed a sensitive side? If you come up with a particularly cool twist, work it in there if you possibly can. You may have to do some re-engineering at higher levels to make it work, but it'll be worth it.

You'll notice we say engineering. That's what you're doing at this point. Storytelling is a craft just like carpentry, and currently you're sawing wood for the legs and planing the top smooth. It should be fun, but also exhausting, as you explore every possibility you can, to make the best story possible.

## 3. The narrative

Okay, you've got your scenes. Now, you write each of those scenes up as mini-stories, paying particular attention to what the characters are thinking and feeling — but absolutely do not write any dialog at all! Explain what the characters mean, how they say it, and what they're thinking, but don't under any circumstances write a word of dialog. You'll probably find that the stories end up being quite long — a few pages for each scene. That's a lot of writing, but it'll pay off.

What you're doing here is deciding exactly what's happening in the scene, from the point of view of all your characters. When you've finished writing, you know what they're thinking and feeling. It'll be a real struggle not to write their speech here — and that's good. You should be bursting to make them talk by the time you've finished, now you know who they are and what they'd say.

You may find that the story wants to change at this point. Perhaps a character's choice feels wrong, or you want something else to happen than what you've planned. Listen, and listen carefully, to these instincts. Go back and alter your structure to accommodate them.

Hugh didn't do this bit the first time he worked on the *BloodSpell* script — he only started doing it for the rewrites. And he's here to tell you that this step is an absolute must. It may seem like going through all these steps is very time-consuming, but you'll actually save time working this way, rather than writing and then trying to edit a flawed script.

## 4. The script

And now, and only now, do you write the script. By this time, actually writing the script will seem like a breeze — and it should, because you've done all the hard work already. Because you already know what's happening behind the scenes, and you know you've got a strong story, the writing will be a pleasure.

## 5. The s****ing editing

Your script's sitting there, fresh, pristine, and beautiful. And your job, from now until the end of the film, is to keep going through it, cutting, changing, and adding, until you've gotten rid of all the hidden shoddy bits.

This process takes up all the rest of the production, starting right now. Ruthlessly cut anything that doesn't add to your movie. In particular, look out for points where characters go through a beat sequence and come back to the same point they started. Remove them without question or doubt.

Keep cutting and changing as you cast your actors. Cut and trim as you record your dialog. Chop like a mad axeman on a caffeine high when you're editing.

You stop editing about five minutes before you release your film. And even then, three months later, you'll want to release a Director's Cut.

# Writing Natural Dialogue

But how do you write natural dialog? How do you make the characters sound cool? Well, the process described in the preceding sections will help. You'll be gagging to get at the page by the time you've finished, and the chances are you'll know exactly what you want your characters to say.

But there are still a lot of tricks to writing convincing dialogue — more than we have time to write about here. Here are a few quick pointers:

- ✔ **Interrupt me, please!** Real people don't wait patiently for each other to finish speeches, particularly if they're trying to kill or seduce each other at the time. Have your characters interrupt each other. Have them cut off each other's speeches. Have them start to say something and then realize that they didn't want to because it revealed too much. Have them sound convincingly impatient and flawed.

- ✔ **They don't all sound the same.** Make very sure that you can tell which character is speaking at any one time. Your characters should have different mannerisms, different favored phrases, and different levels of vocabulary. Would the posh Englishman really say that our hero fancies the villain, or would he say he has "a certain regard" for her? Or would he just go all Hugh Grant and say something like, "Well, of course, I don't really know for sure, but, well, he might well have, oh, you know, some kind of — oh, never mind."

  Hugh finds it sometimes helps to thing of a specific Hollywood actor and write as if you're writing the part for them to play — you'll write differently for Alan Rickman than The Rock.

- ✔ **Subtext, subtext, subtext.** People don't say what they mean. You'll know that if you've ever asked or been asked on a date. If a character's talking about something that's important to him, he should talk around the subject, talk through it, talk in metaphors, be unclear, and talk about something else entirely. Anything but actually say what he's thinking.

- ✔ **Listen to your actors.** Your actors are the best tool you've got for polishing characters if they're already pretty strong. Listen to their suggestions and listen in particular for lines they have trouble saying. Why is that? Can you say something else? Does the actor have a favored phrase or turn of speech that would work for the character, too?

# Adhering to Script Format

There's a standard format for Hollywood scripts. People who are aiming to break into Hollywood writing obsess over it and follow it slavishly, to the extent that you can find arguments on writers' forums about the type of manuscript binding that will best help your chances of getting picked up by an agent or a studio. That level of obsession is silly. But the standard script format, shown in Figure 4-1, is there for a reason, and it's worth following.

# More information

There's a wealth of information out there on storytelling and scriptwriting. Despite the length of this chapter, we've barely scratched the surface.

*Story,* by Robert McKee. This is It. This is The Tome. It's The Daddy. It's huge, and it's kinda dry, and it has a ton of graphs, but it's the best resource for understanding and writing story on this or any other planet.

*Adventures in the Screen Trade* and *Which Lie Did I Tell?* by William Goldman. *The Princess Bride. Butch Cassidy and the Sundance Kid. All The Presidents Men.* He wrote them all, and now he's written about writing them. Fantastic insights on every page.

*The Complete Book of Scriptwriting* by J. Michael Straczynski. The writer of *Babylon 5* gives us the low-down on, in particular, television writing. Fantastic for, amongst other things, a very clear and pretension-free guide to the standard episodic TV format.

www.janeespenson.com by Jane Espenson. One of the most experienced and talented writers working in TV today, Jane Espenson has worked on *Buffy the Vampire Slayer, Battlestar Galactica, The O.C.,* and a whole bunch more. And now she's writing a blog on how to write. Particularly brilliant info on humor and characterization here.

www.wordplayer.com. One of the top scriptwriting forums on the Internet, with a whole pile of helpful articles and some great discussion boards.

Your scripts should:

- ✔ Be written in 12-point Courier or Courier New font.
- ✔ Have dialog indented and character names (when speaking) bold, centered and capitalized
- ✔ Have action directions left-margin aligned.
- ✔ Capitalize major character action verbs and camera directions.
- ✔ Scenes should be marked as such and should include directions as to the location they take place, and the lighting there.

**Figure 4-1:** A standard script format.

```
                      JERED
         What's the stupidest thing I could possibly do here?
     He turns around and PUNCHES the metal golem.
     CUT TO
     Act 2, Scene 3
     INT, HOSPITAL - SOME HOURS LATER
```

Everything else is more or less optional, but if your script looks like the one shown in Figure 4-1, you'll find it's easier to read and understand. You'll also be able to use the old script-reader's trick of estimating duration — one page of properly formatted script, all else being equal, is about one minute of film.

Finally, you can compare your scripts with those of your heroes. You can learn a lot even from looking at how your script is laid out on the page, compared to, say, Peter Jackson's work, or a script by Quentin Tarantino.

Are your blocks of dialogue shorter or longer? Why? How do they lay out action? Why? Are your action scenes too short, or your dialogue not full enough of changes of speaker? Look at their work, look at yours, and compare. You'll learn more that way than we can teach you in a few thousand words, that's for sure!

# Chapter 5

# Engines, Engines Everywhere

**In This Chapter**

▶ Choosing the right engine for your project

▶ Reviewing the available Machinima engines

"*M*achinima sounds great, but I can't find a link to it anywhere. Where do I download this software?"

Of course, Machinima isn't a piece of software, but a technique that can be employed using a variety of computer game engines. In this chapter, we take a look at some of the most popular and most promising engines and tools and discuss their suitability for Machinima.

We list the pros and cons for a Machinima maker, suggest the most common genres of movie to which the engine lends itself, and rate each engine for Machinima usage.

We've tried to make the information in this chapter as up-to-date as possible, but clever modders and generous games designers reveal new game tools and features on an almost weekly basis. We keep a list of updates to this chapter on the *Machimima For Dummies* Web site at www.machinimafordummies.com.

# *Exploring Key Features*

A number of features are key for Machinima creation:

- ✔ **Import new animations?** Can the engine import animations designed in a separate 3D package and make them available for use in the game? **Engines:** The Sims 2, The Movies (with serious effort), Half-Life 2, Unreal Tournament, Neverwinter Nights, DooM 3, Moviestorm, IClone, Second Life, Battlefield 2.

- ✔ **Import new models?** Can you import entirely new character or prop models? **Engines:** Half-Life 2, the Sims 2, Unreal Tournament, The Movies (tricky), Neverwinter Nights, Neverwinter Nights 2, Medieval II: Total War, DooM 3, Grand Theft Auto, Moviestorm, IClone, Second Life (created within game), Battlefield 2, Company of Heroes.

- ✔ **Make custom sets?** It's hard, but not impossible, to make Machinima in an engine where you can't customize a set. **Engines:** See Chapter 6 for a full list.

- ✔ **In-game camera mode?** If the game offers a way to create and operate a virtual camera, that's a real plus point for a Machinima maker. **Engines:** The Sims 2, The Movies, Half-Life 2, Unreal Tournament, Neverwinter Nights (very limited), Neverwinter Nights 2 (very limited), Medieval II: Total War, Grand Theft Auto (with mods), Moviestorm, IClone, Second Life, World of Warcraft (kinda), Battlefield 2, Company of Heroes.

- ✔ **Add-on potential/scripting language?** Certain engines make creating third-party tools and add-ons easy. Other games don't, but that won't necessarily stop enterprising hackers from writing a plug-in. **Engines:** See Chapter 18.

- ✔ **Animated eyes?** The ability to animate a character's eyes (and therefore his eyeline) is tremendously useful as a narrative device. **Engines:** The Sims 2, The Movies, Half-Life 2, Unreal Tournament, DooM 3, Moviestorm, Second Life.

- ✔ **Manual head movement?** Being able to control characters' head movement is nearly vital. **Engines:** The Sims 2, Half-Life 2, Halo 2, Unreal Tournament, Neverwinter Nights (limited), DooM 3, Moviestorm, Second Life.

✔ **Create new characters on the fly?** If you can just click Create New Castle Guard rather than having to shut down the game, open the editor, drag a guard to the castle steps, save, and reload, your filming will be a much smoother and speedier process. **Engines:** Half-Life 2 (with scripting or add-ons), Neverwinter Nights, Neverwinter Nights 2, Grand Theft Auto (with mods), Moviestorm, IClone.

✔ **Pause mode?** If you're trying to control eight characters at once, cue up a magical explosion, and start your camera track all at the same time, you'll appreciate a Pause button. **Engines:** The Sims 2, Neverwinter Nights, Neverwinter Nights 2, Medieval II: Total War, Grand Theft Auto (with mods), Company of Heroes.

✔ **Control more than one character?** A game that provides the facility to control only one character at a time is quite limiting for Machinima purposes. A much better scenario is one in which the game allows you to swap between several characters, or even control a squad of characters at the same time. **Engines:** The Sims 2, The Movies, Half-Life 2 (with mods), Neverwinter Nights, Neverwinter Nights 2, Medieval II: Total War, Unreal Tournament, Grand Theft Auto (with mods), Moviestorm, IClone, Company of Heroes.

✔ **Multiplayer?** Does the game have a facility for more than one person to control aspects of the game at once? In other words, can you have your friends control the actors in your film while you control the camera? **Engines:** Half-Life 2, Halo 2, Unreal Tournament, Neverwinter Nights, Neverwinter Nights 2, Medieval II: Total War, DooM 3, Grand Theft Auto (with mods), Second Life, World of Warcraft, Battlefield 2, Company of Heroes.

✔ **Commercial license?** Most Machinima engines have legal hurdles (see Chapter 15) preventing you from selling or otherwise commercially exploiting your film. However, some engines allow you to sell your work. **Engines:** Unreal Tournament (expensive — $5,000), Moviestorm, IClone, Second Life.

Beyond these features, you're likely to care about a few general features of an engine. Table 5-1 lays out our opinions. Remember, 10 is the highest rating an engine can receive.

| Table 5-1 | Engine Ratings | | | | | | |
|---|---|---|---|---|---|---|---|
| Area | The Sims 2 | The Movies | Half-Life 2 | Halo 2 | Unreal Tournament | Neverwinter Nights | Neverwinter Nights 2 | Medieval II: Total War |
| Prettiness | 7 | 4 | 10 | 6 | 8 | 3 | 8 | 9 |
| Diversity of content | 7 | 6 | 3 | 1 | 5 | 8 | 6 | 4 |
| Community | 9 | 6 | 7 | 8 | 7 | 9 | 6 | 6 |
| Popularity | 8 | 6 | 8 | 9 | 8 | 5 | 6 | 7 |
| Ease of use | 6 | 9 | 2 | 7 | 6 | 4 | 3 | 9 |
| Control | 5 | 2 | 9 | 3 | 10 | 7 | 5 | 8 |

| Table 5-1 (continued) | | | | | | | |
|---|---|---|---|---|---|---|---|
| Area | DooM 3 | Grand Theft Auto | Movie-storm | IClone | Second Life | World of Warcraft | Battle-field 2 | Company of Heroes |
| Prettiness | 9 | 8 | 8 | 8 | 2-7 | 9 | 9 | 9 |
| Diversity of content | 3 | 7 | 6 | 5 | 9 | 7 | 4 | 4 |
| Community | 5 | 7 | 5 | 3 | 8 | 10 | 6 | 5 |
| Popularity | 4 | 8 | 5 | 3 | 7 | 10 | 6 | 6 |
| Ease of use | 1 | 5 | 8 | 9 | 5 | 8 | 8 | 3 |
| Control | 8 | 4 | 9 | 2 | 9 | 3 | 5 | 6 |

# The Sims 2

You'd think that a game that comes with its own built-in story mode and a bunch of filming tools would be a Machinima maker's dream come true.

We cover The Sims 2 as a Machinima engine, including pros, cons, and three chapters of tutorial, in Chapters 6, 7, and 8. Table 5-1, though, gives you our ratings of the engine.

Use this engine if you want to make a low-violence, modern-day movie, preferably without too much dialog.

# The Movies

A game in which you play a movie executive and get to create your own movies using a dedicated movie creation tool? Is The Movies the greatest Machinima tool ever? Well, sadly, no, although it does have its pros:

- ✔ **Ridiculously simple:** The Movies is probably the easiest engine in which you can make Machinima. You can churn out your first movie in less than an hour. It will, mark our words, be utterly dire, but it's still an impressively quick turn-around.

- ✔ **Widely adaptable:** The Movies is one of only a few game engines that are as suited to corny science-fiction as it is to a modern-day rom-com or a slapstick comedy. You can tackle an astonishingly wide range of projects with The Movies.

Ah, but the cons:

- ✔ **Filming by numbers:** The very simplicity of this game makes it hard to create something stunning. You need to buy the expansion pack to even choose your own camera angles freely, and even then, you're quite heavily restricted. It's very hard to avoid creating a movie that just screams "I've been made using The Movies!"

- ✔ **Basic edits only:** Although The Movies does ship with a simple video editor, it's very basic. There's no way it can compete with a "real" video editor.

- ✔ **One-stop-shop:** The game is reluctant to allow you to use any external tools, including video and audio editors, to edit your movie. It's possible with effort, but you'll be swimming against the current.

- ✔ **Oh, look, it's that living room again:** Imagine if every show on TV used the same 20 or so sets. Thus it is with The Movies. The sets, costumes, camera shots, and props soon become all-too-familiar.

It's also worth knowing:

✔ You can import new models into The Movies, although to do so requires a lot of complicated hacking and a knowledge of 3D model formats.

✔ Even with the additional camera controls provided by the Stunts And Effects add-on pack, the precision control that you'll have over your camera is severely limited.

✔ Manual head movement is only partially achievable. It's possible to ask the characters very nicely to look in a certain direction, but there's no guarantee that they'll listen.

✔ The Movies community has been hard at work creating tools to overcome its limitations. They're pretty technical, but you can find out more at http://dcmodding.com/main.

✔ The lack of a pause mode shouldn't be considered a negative point for this game. The nature of The Movies is such that is has no need of one.

You can use The Movies for virtually any genre. Use The Movies if you've got a specific idea you know you can pull off, or you just want a very basic introduction to Machinima.

# Half-Life 2

Half-Life 2 may have been the most anticipated game of all time, and it's still one of the most technologically advanced. It's also a modder's dream: The game is supplied with a lot of tremendously powerful, and mind-bogglingly complicated, modding tools, including Machinima utilities.

In many ways, Half-Life 2 is the polar opposite of The Movies (see preceding section). It's possible to do just about anything you can imagine in this engine to an incredibly high degree of quality, but even the simplest things may be a huge struggle.

The pros include

✔ **Ooh, it's pretty!** Half-Life 2 looks visually incredible. Produce a movie in this engine, and it will look good, no two ways about it.

✔ **It's phenomenal.** Half-Life 2 includes an incredibly advanced lip-synching tool, called Faceposer. It can create lipsynch automatically for speech in any language, and if that's not enough for you, you can then tweak that speech down to the finest details.

✔ **Yes, there is a tool for it.** Half-Life 2 features tools for *everything*. There's a full camerawork tool, just for Machinima. The Garrysmod add-on, available on the Internet, adds tons of new functionality equal to other games' Dungeon Master modes. And so on.

✔ **See whether you can balance the Jeep on top of the wall!** The Half-Life 2 in-game physics were justifiably lauded by all and sundry upon the game's release. Clever use of the game's physics can add a level of realism to even the most uncomplicated movie.

But, unfortunately, there are some cons:

✔ **Error: Brain is out of swap space. Please restart.** Half-Life 2 is very, very, very complex. Strange Company's regular video editor, Dr Ross Bambrey (who once interviewed for a job as Stephen Hawking's assistant), has been struggling with Half-Life 2 for a couple of years and still ranks himself as a beginner. Yikes.

✔ **Not him again!** It's not impossible to add new characters to Half-Life 2. Technically. True, to do so requires so much 3D modeling and texturing expertise that you should probably quit this Machinima thing and go and work for Pixar. But it's not impossible.

✔ **Engine coding from the future. Editor from the Stone Age.** There's one area where Half-Life 2 isn't super-advanced, and that's in its map/script editor, Hammer, the original Half-Life editor from 1999. It's utterly horrible for anyone who has used another gaming editor this decade.

Half-Life 2 works best for near-future dystopian science-fiction only. However, the game assets can be cleverly employed for other genres. Randall Glass' *A Few Good G-Men* is a modern-day courtroom drama, for example, that works well.

Most Machinima that has been produced in Half-Life 2 to date has used the Garrysmod add-on (`www.garrysmod.org`). If you want to make Machinima in Half-Life 2, Garrysmod is probably the easiest way.

Use Half-Life 2 if you want the best possible quality, you can use the existing characters, and you're prepared to work hard on very technical software.

# Halo 2

*Red vs Blue* is responsible for introducing more people to the Machinima community (both as producers and consumers) than anything else. It's astonishing how many people watch *RvB* and think "I want to make something like that".

But be warned: Rooster Teeth, the makers of *Red vs Blue,* are very good at what they do. You can create a movie using Halo 2 with comparative ease, but creating something as accomplished as *RvB* is trickier than you may think.

Here are the pros of Halo 2:

- **Faceplates:** Most computer game characters, let's be honest, are not really capable of competing with Johnny Depp for the full gamut of human emotions. But if all your characters are wearing helmets, as in Halo 2, that's a whole lot of emoting you don't have to worry about.

- **Big audience:** There's a big audience for Halo Machinima, thanks mainly to *Red vs Blue*. Chances are, if your movie is any good, it'll attract viewers almost immediately.

- **Simple enough:** It's easy to control and manipulate Halo 2 to achieve most of the shots you'll need. The tricky shots really tax your ingenuity, but you'll quickly get the hang of the basics.

And here are the cons:

- **Hard to hack:** As a primarily console-based game, Halo 2 is hard to hack or modify. Running the game on a PC rather than an X-Box can help, but it won't entirely alleviate the problem.

- **Very, very, very limited scope:** You're going to be making a film with Marines and aliens. They'll either be in futuristic corridors or outdoorsy countryside bits.

- **No facial animation:** Well, no faces, period. It's great if you can justify within your plot the fact that your characters never remove their helmets. If you want Bob to wink at Susie, though, forget it.

- **You're not as funny as Rooster Teeth:** Deal with it.

Halo 2 works well for self-referential comedy set within the game world. Again. Or a range of science fiction.

Use Halo 2 if you want to make a quick sci-fi movie, or you want to tell a story specifically set in the Halo universe.

# Unreal Tournament

A great multiplayer game, and also a potentially great Machinima engine, Unreal Tournament (UT) is heavily customizable and highly robust. It's also continually updated. We're looking at the 2004 version here, but the 2007 version, due to come out soon, looks super-slick.

Unreal Tournament's pros:

- **UnrealEd just rocks:** It really does. The UnrealEd editor (free with the game) can be used to create very detailed and impressive maps. A talented modder can modify the game in amazing ways.

- **Mountains and corridors:** UT is traditionally associated with low-lit metal corridors, but now includes the ability to create great-looking outdoor sets as well. Trees, lakes, and mountains are all achievable.

- **Built-in Machinima package:** UT includes a specially designed and highly regarded cinematics creation package, called Matinée, which was partially designed in consultation with Machinima creators.

And UT's cons:

- **Guns, big guns:** UT's biggest disadvantage is its available set of character models. Because it's a first-person battling game, they're a wide variety of heavily muscled space Marine and alien types.

- **No lipsync on player models:** UT ships with a high-quality lipsync tool called Impersonator and a couple of high-detail models. However, the player models aren't lipsynched by default, and these features are generally hard to use.

UT works best with sci-fi. However, lots of people have created mods, models, sets and art for UT. Lots and lots of people. If you want new content, go check the Internet first — someone may have already created it.

If you want to create new art, meanwhile, pretty much anything is possible.

You'll need to investigate the headache-inducing world of scripting if you want to animate characters' eyes or create new characters in-game. You don't need to do any scripting to control as many characters as you like, though — you can do that through the Matinée Machinima tool.

You can commercially license a version of the Unreal engine that doesn't include any of the art assets usually bundled with the game, for a few thousand dollars.

Use UT if you want to do something you can't do in any other Machinima package, and you're pretty technically adept.

# Neverwinter Nights

Your humble authors are quite familiar with Neverwinter Nights, having spent the last three years using it to make a feature film. It's quite an old engine now, and it's quirkier than a British sitcom character. But it does do some things better than just about anything else:

- **Dungeon Master Client:** NWN's *Dungeon Master* tool is one of the best Machinima production environments we've ever seen. It allows multiple users to spawn and destroy characters as needed, control every character in the set, place special effects, and so on.

- ✔ **Lots of characters:** NWN is one of the best available engines in which to shoot complex scenes with many active characters. We frequently shot fight scenes with upward of 30 combatants.

- ✔ **Huuuuuge range of (fantasy) content:** There are literally tens of thousands of custom models, sets, and props available for Neverwinter Nights. Most of them are targeted at the fantasy genre that NWN inhabits, but given that, you can find almost anything you want.

- ✔ **Fantastic set editor:** NWN's Aurora editor is incredibly fast and easy to use. Based on a tile and prop system, it can be fiddly to achieve precision, but for sheer speed and user-friendliness, it's hard to beat.

Now the cons:

- ✔ **No lipsynch without TOGLFaceS:** NWN doesn't have any sort of lip-synching available, at all. We wrote a tool to get around that, which we're happy to share (e-mail us at info@bloodspell.com), but it's fiddly and very technical. See Chapter 18 for the story.

- ✔ **Old:** NWN isn't the prettiest engine on all the Earth. It's possible to achieve some astonishing results with it, but straight out of the box, these days, it looks kinda ugly.

- ✔ **Horrible camera.** The camera controls for Neverwinter Nights are just plain horrible. Because the camera is attached to the character it's following, you can't move it around freely, but have to jiggle it around the invisible character you're following. This engine works well for fantasy, in all its varied forms. It's also possible to do modern-day or sci-fi using some content on the 'Net.

Use Neverwinter Nights if you want to make a fantasy movie, you're not too concerned about graphical quality, and you want more control and documentation than either NWN2 or World of Warcraft.

# Neverwinter Nights 2

The sequel to Neverwinter Nights came out in 2006, five years after the original. It's early days for the NWN2 modding community yet, but there doesn't seem to be the same frenzy of custom content creation as there was for the original Neverwinter Nights.

The pros:

- ✔ **Pretty:** The graphics for NWN2 are considerably upgraded from the original. In particular, NWN2's townscapes are lush, realistic, and convincingly dirty.

✔ **Dungeon Master Client, Nice toolset, et al:** NWN2 has many of the same advantages for Machinima as NWN1. It has retained the flexible Aurora editor, has a very similar scripting language, and has a nascent Dungeon Master's Client for Machinima directors to use and abuse.

The cons:

✔ **In theory:** The NWN2 toolset is, at time of writing (2007) a little incomplete. Many engine features are not yet available to modders, as they're based on expensive ($10,000+) tools used by the developers.

✔ **Buggy:** At time of writing, more than a hundred bugs were listed on the official toolset bug list on the Neverwinter Nights 2 forums. Patches are dramatically improving the situation, but right now, creating content using NWN2 is hard.

✔ **Unattractive heads:** While some aspects of NWN2 look astonishingly cool, we've seen very few NWN2 character heads that didn't look distinctly odd. Thick brows and strong jawlines — on the women — may be ironed out with better toolset usage, but currently the characters we've seen don't look great.

✔ **Limited characters:** Adding new character models is hard due to the animation problems, but it's not impossible.

✔ **Fiddly camera mode:** The in-game camera mode is still very fiddly.

Use Neverwinter Nights 2 if you want to make a fantasy movie, want more control than World of Warcraft will give you, want better graphics than NWN1, and you're prepared to put up with or hack around bugs and arbitrary limitations.

# Medieval II: Total War

The Total War series of games has reached a pinnacle with Medieval II: Total War. In this game, you control armies of thousands of knights, peasants, cannoneers, and even elephants. We cover Medieval II: Total War, and its sophisticated Machinima creation tools, in Chapter 12.

If you want to re-create the massive battles of *Lord of the Rings,* this is the engine for you — and it's really the only engine that can do that.

# DooM 3

DooM 3, the second sequel to the genre-defining DooM, was released in 2004. Its graphics were stunning, featuring real-time lighting and shadows, and monsters more realistic than anything we'd seen. But since then, virtually no Machinima work has been seen coming from DooM.

DooM 3's pros include:

- ✓ **Incredible graphics:** DooM 3's graphics are still state-of-the-art today. They're dark, they're involving, and they look fantastic. Full lipsynching and sophisticated animation complete the package.

- ✓ **Machinima production tool:** Fountainhead Entertainment produced a Machinima tool called Machinimation for DooM 3. Only a beta version was ever made available, but it's still out there and still usable.

- ✓ **Very flexible:** A lot of the DooM 3 engine is exposed for editing. It's another the-sky-is-the-limit engine.

- ✓ **Fantastic custom characters:** Imported custom characters can potentially look fantastic, but they'll need to be of an equivalent detail level to Hollywood 3D models.

For the cons:

- ✓ **Really, really, really, really complicated:** DooM 3 may be the most arcane engine ever created. Even simple editing work requires huge amounts of scripting, programming, and 3D art ability.

- ✓ **Very limited game art:** Unless you're aiming to produce a movie about space marines fighting demons, you'll not get a lot of use out of the heavily muscled heroes and Geigeresque villains of DooM 3.

- ✓ **Small community:** There's basically no one making DooM 3 Machinima. Some people are making mods for it, but again, information on the engine is quite limited.

DooM 3 works best for sci-fi featuring space marines or weird demonic aliens in a space station or Hell. If you want to do anything else, you'll need to start creating models, which is hard.

Use DooM 3 if you really want to use the graphics engine and are prepared to do a lot of work.

# Grand Theft Auto

Hip, violent, and controversial, the Grand Theft Auto (GTA) series has been one of the more visible game franchises of the last few years. If you've somehow missed hearing about GTA, the series is a collection of crime sims — sand-box cities where you can commit mayhem to your heart's content.

It's extremely difficult to create Machinima using the tools built into Grand Theft Auto. Fortunately, one Machinima maker (Ceedj from pioneering GTA filmmakers Pawfect Films) has designed an entire toolset to allow more sophisticated Machinima creation. You can download it from www.pawfectfilms.com.

The pros:

- **Real-time puppetry:** Using the Pawfect Films San Andreas Studios, you can control an entire group of characters in real-time, giving you a fast and flexible Machinima production studio.

- **Huge and cool:** There's a lot of content in San Andreas, and it's all well-rendered in a slightly satirical style.

- **Modern-day action:** Car chases! Gunfights! Fisticuffs in buildings! GTA opens up a whole vista of potential action and adventure for your Machinima.

- **NC-17:** With the exception of Second Life, most Machinima-capable engines tend to be a bit tame. Not so GTA — if you want guns, violence, and scantily clad women, this is the engine for you.

The cons:

- **Very hacked:** All the Machinima tools available are hacks, and their reliability and ease of use isn't up there with professional packages.

- **Limited setting:** There's no map editing or character creation in GTA. You'll have to make films with what you can find.

- **Still limited:** Because you don't have perfect (or even Pawfect) control, what you can do with GTA is still limited. You can create some pretty cool stuff, but the control mechanisms you've got available will break down if you want to, say, re-create the famous "thousands of cop cars" chase at the end of Blues Brothers.

GTA is modern day, but within that limitation, it offers a pretty wide palette. You can shoot sitcoms, à la the series *PEDS,* or post-apocalyptic drama like *The Days After.* In many ways, Grand Theft Auto is one of the more flexible games available for Machinima.

However, keep the following points in mind:

- It's very difficult to import custom animations or new models into the game, although it can be done.

- You'll need to SA Studios mod to create new characters on the fly, or control more than one character.

- You make GTA into a multiplayer game with the SA Multiplayer mod, available from www.sa-mp.com.

# Moviestorm

Moviestorm is the new kid on the block — so new, in fact, that we only had a beta preview copy to play with while we were writing most of this book. Moviestorm isn't a game: It's a dedicated Machinima filmmaking package. It allows for character creation, modelling of sets, camera scripting, and on-the-fly filming, as well as sound editing and post-production.

Chapter 17 covers Moviestorm in full detail, including sets, characters, and editing. Oh, and you can find a copy of Moviestorm on the DVD that accompanies this book.

Use Moviestorm if you want to make a commercial Machinima production, you want to use a dedicated Machinima production kit without the hacking hassles of other engines, or just because it came on the DVD!

# IClone

One of the first professionally licensed Machinima toolkits on the market, IClone is now in version 2.0, with version 3.0 due some time in the months after publication of this book. Billed as "accessible 3D animation", IClone has so far failed to attract a major following in the Machinima world.

Here are the pros:

✔ **Very simple:** It's no exaggeration to say that you can create a movie within five minutes using IClone.

✔ **Nice character customization:** Sophisticated morphs and a great new garment creation system mean you can quickly create attractive 3D characters.

✔ **Automatic lipsynching:** It's trivially simple to have a character in IClone lipsynch a line. Simply record the line live in IClone or attach a `.wav` file, and the program automatically animates the character's face as they speak their lines.

✔ **Built-in Motion Editor:** While it's very primitive, Iclone does ship with a built-in animation editor.

And the cons:

✔ **Too simple:** It's very easy to create a simple scene in IClone, but it's very hard to go beyond the basics. You can't adjust the lipsynch, there's not a lot of adjustment you can make to the animation, and you can't control a character's face beyond very basic expressions.

- ✔ **No AI:** There's no intelligence in IClone allowing you to simply tell a character to walk.

- ✔ **No new sets:** IClone doesn't have a set editor beyond basic templates. You'll need 3D Studio Max ($3,500) to create new sets.

IClone comes with a couple of basic characters, a dozen basic sets ranging from a fantasy temple to a newsroom, and about 20 props. It's possible to make a modern-day or fantasy film with these props, if you're careful. Use IClone if you want very simple talking head characters, and you don't need them to walk or interact.

# Second Life

There's a Chinese company called Anshe Chung Studios, Ltd, which currently employs about 30 people. Its business is entirely conducted in the virtual world of Second Life. This fact alone should give you some idea of how vast Second Life is, and how much potential the game world provides for the most diverse of ventures. Machinima creators are migrating there in droves.

The pros:

- ✔ **Great potential:** You can create almost anything you can imagine using Second Life. The sheer scope and variety of locations, props, and characters within Second Life is staggering.

- ✔ **Free to join:** A basic Second Life account is free. You're required to enter your credit-card details, but you aren't charged a dime unless you choose to upgrade your account.

- ✔ **Machinima-friendly:** Linden Labs, the makers of the game, are big Machinima fans and actively encourage its users to produce movies within the Second Life world.

- ✔ **Commercial license:** The default game license for Second Life allows you to record footage from the game and use it for commercial purposes.

- ✔ **Active community:** Machinima makers are very active in Second Life and may be able to help you with land fees, casting, and technical support.

Linden Labs recently announced that it would make the server code for Second Life open-source. That will change or make irrelevant a lot of the following con points — notably the first, the second, and eventually the fourth and fifth — and make SL a much more attractive Machinima platform.

- ✔ **Aargh! Our eyes, our beautiful eyes!** A lot of the content in-world is very adult. Your humble authors were shocked by some of the sexual imagery we found in the game — and we don't shock easily. In our experience, the in-game mature content filter isn't very effective either.

- ✔ **It'll cost you:** Although a basic Second Life subscription is free, you'll need to pay real-world money to buy in-game items and rent in-game land. It would have cost Strange Company more than $7,000 to make *BloodSpell* in Second Life. Most movies would cost less, but free it ain't.

- ✔ **Not all that pretty:** Unfortunately, the graphics engine behind Second Life is distinctly last-generation. It is being continually developed, but currently Half-Life 2, DooM 3, and later engines leave Second Life eating their dust. In particular, there's no lipsynching without Neverwinter Nights-style hacks (see "Neverwinter Nights", above).

- ✔ **One player, one character:** If you want a character in your movie, even as an extra, even just propping up a bar, you'll need an actual live person there to control them. That can quickly become a major logistical problem.

- ✔ **Lag:** Second Life is very prone to slowdown or lag, and you can't do to control it unless you own your own server (Island), which is expensive. Half the art of SL Machinima is avoiding said lag.

Your imagination is your only limit with Second Life. Almost any genre can be catered for.

Here are a few more points to consider:

- ✔ The quality of created content within Second Life varies enormously, as does its visual quality.

- ✔ You need the separate software Poser ($250) to import new animations.

- ✔ Camera movements are scriptable, and your viewpoint character can go virtually anywhere.

- ✔ Second Life is a moving target even more than the rest of the engines in this chapter. As we were finalizing this chapter, a major graphical improvement for SL's lighting arrived in our inbox. You can keep on top of the latest improvements in SL at www.machinimafordummies.com.

Use Second Life if you need a commercial Machinima environment, you've already got a budget and plenty of contacts in Second Life, or you don't want to use third-party modeling tools.

# World of Warcraft

World of Warcraft is the biggest media property of all time, offering you the opportunity to become an Orc, a Troll, or a Night Elf in a sprawling fantasy world inhabited by literally millions of other players (0.1 percent of the entire world, according to some reports). World of Warcraft has also spawned a massive Machinima following. We cover Machinima creation in World of Warcraft, including using third-party tools and organizing shoots in a virtual world, in Chapter 11.

Use World of Warcraft if you want to make a fantasy movie, you want to make a World of Warcraft fan movie, or you just want to make a movie with a potential audience of 10 million plus.

# Battlefield 2

Battlefield 2, the modern-day first-person shooter/strategy game, seems at first glance to have limited scope as a Machinima engine — but looks are deceiving. It provides an excellent setting for modern-day war or military-conflict-based movies and comes with a powerful and flexible editor.

Battlefield 2's pros include:

- **Superb editor:** By far the most appealing thing about Battlefield 2 as a Machinima engine is the excellent editor that ships with the game, which allows you to create Battlefield 2 sets very quickly.

- **"Poop-poop!" murmured Mr Toad:** The game includes myriad vehicles, from jeeps to helicopters, all of which can be driven or piloted as appropriate. Most of the vehicles can accommodate more than one character at a time, and they all look superb.

- **Movie-making add-ons:** Several third-party add-ons provide excellent tools for a budding Machinima maker. Particularly worthy of note is the Battle Director, which enables easy modification of recorded game files.

And the cons:

- **Hidden costs:** You can import new models and animations into Battlefield 2, but the only 3D packages it supports are 3D Studio Max and Maya, neither of which retail for much under $2,000.

- **Don't get too close:** Very close up, character models are ugly and alpha-channel transparency mapping is unpleasantly obvious.

- **You said that without moving your lips:** None of the game's character models have any ability to open their mouths or change their expression.

As far as genres, a modern-day war story is your only real choice. Use Battlefield 2 if you want to make *Black Hawk Down 2* (or a new *24*), and you don't need your characters to emote too much.

# Company Of Heroes

Released in fall 2006, Company of Heroes has the distinction of being the only game engine to win two Machinima Film Festival awards for cinematics created for the game itself. It's a spectacular World War II real-time strategy game, with detailed graphics and a great, realistic feel.

Its pros:

- ✔ **Sophisticated Machinima tool:** Company of Heroes comes with the Non-Interactive Sequence Editor (NIS Editor), which was used to create the Machinima Film Festival–winning movie.

- ✔ **Demo recording:** You can record in-game action as you're playing and then come back and re-film it from cinematic angles later. This is a rare and valuable feature.

- ✔ **Extremely graphically sophisticated:** The animations are highly detailed, all the in-game models are extremely high-resolution for a real-time strategy game, and the art direction is exquisite.

- ✔ **World War II:** If you want to make a movie set in the ground battles of World War II, Company of Heroes is your best option.

The cons:

- ✔ **Not designed for close-ups:** While Company of Heroes does much better than many RTS games in close-up, its focus is still very much on the big picture. There's no lipsynching capability accessible, and no manual head or eye control.

- ✔ **Very small Machinima community:** If you're intending to create Company of Heroes Machinima, you're almost on your own.

- ✔ **Hard or expensive:** You'll need 3D Studio Max ($3,500) to create character models. Meanwhile, CoH's scripting language is infamously hard to use.

Use Company of Heroes if you want to make a World War II Machinima movie focused primarily on the infantry, without too much dialogue.

# Chapter 6

# Making Your World: Set Design and Texturing

. . . . . . . . . . . . . . . . . . . . . . . . . . . . . . . . . . . . . . . . . . . . . . . .

*In This Chapter*

▶ Discovering how you can use game level editors to make your set

▶ Making your first set in The Sims 2

▶ Polishing your set design skills

. . . . . . . . . . . . . . . . . . . . . . . . . . . . . . . . . . . . . . . . . . . . . . . .

S o you've written your story. You know how to shoot it. And you've chosen your engine, set it up, and wasted a few days in playing — er, researching — the game with which you'll be getting scarily intimate. No, not that intimate. Put away the credit card and step away from the dodgy Web site.

Sets are really the hidden characters of a film. Think of any great film, from *Lost In Translation* to *Aliens,* and you think of the locations that made that film. Would *Lost In Translation* have worked if Bill Murray and Scarlett Johannson hadn't been flirting in such an empty, faux-hip hotel bar, or hadn't been looking quite as confused in all the Japanese minimalism? Would *Aliens* have been as scary with Doctor Who–level cardboard walls?

Since the days of DooM, back in the early 1990s, the majority of PC games have shipped with a built-in set design tool. They don't call it that, of course — they'll call it a *Map Editor, Mission Editor,* or *Level Editor* — but that's how we use the design tool.

# Knowing What Game Engines You Can Use

The following engines have sophisticated set design tools of the type we discuss in this chapter. As you can see, that's the vast majority of modern games suitable for Machinima.

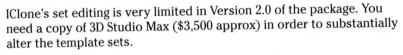

- The Sims 2
- The Movies
- Half-Life 2
- Unreal Tournament (various iterations)
- Neverwinter Nights
- Neverwinter Nights 2
- Medieval Total War 2
- DooM 3
- Moviestorm
- IClone

    IClone's set editing is very limited in Version 2.0 of the package. You
    need a copy of 3D Studio Max ($3,500 approx) in order to substantially
    alter the template sets.

- Second Life
- Battlefield 2
- Company Of Heroes

World of Warcraft, Halo 2, and Grand Theft Auto have a very limited set
editor or no editor at all. You have to *location scout* in these engines for suitable places to film rather than creating sets.

# The Design Phase

Before you touch your computer, you need to have a good idea what you're
designing. Game set designers are fast and sophisticated, but they're still not
as fast or easy to use as a pen and paper. Grab your script, grab a piece of
paper, and sketch a couple of quick designs for the set.

Your design doesn't have to look sophisticated or artistic — Hugh's set designs
certainly don't (see Figure 6-1) — they just need to get the key features of the
room across, to make sure that your design is practical before you spend
time on realizing it.

After you pick a favorite from your potential designs, grab your script and go
through it line-by-line, checking that nothing in the script makes your design
impractical. Have you forgotten a significant static prop? Does the action
move in such a way that your design can't work? Will you end up unable to
get a shot you've been visualizing since your story treatment?

Once you're certain that your design will actually work in your movie, *then*
it's time to open your set editor.

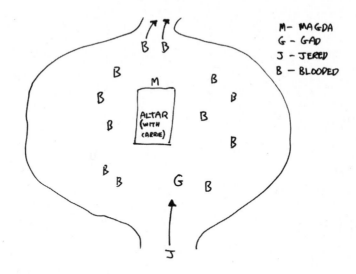

M— MAGDA
G — GAD
J — JERED
B — BLOODED

**Figure 6-1:**
Hugh's set
designs
wouldn't
pass muster
with an
architect.

Don't skip this phase. It's very tempting to just say "Oh, I know what I need for this scene", but there's a huge chance you've forgotten something, or just not thought about it. Pen-and-paper is a great tool to force you to think through your design before you spend days constructing it.

# Creating a Set

So how are we going to create our set? You can visualize a 3D world in a variety of ways, but every game engine we can think of has settled on a single standard: polygon modeling.

*Polygons* are two-dimensional shapes — triangles, squares, pentagons, hexagons, and so on. In the case of game engines, everything is eventually broken down into triangles.

Those triangles are then placed into the game world and make up all the objects you see — big triangles stacked up against each other to create walls, smaller triangles bent in funny patterns to make objects, furniture, and even characters. Sounds weird and implausible, right? But it's the truth — that's the reason that, if you get up close to an item in the game, it will have lots of hard edges and points. The pointy bits are where the triangles end.

Of course, a modern game world uses lots of polygons. Figure 6-2 gives you a quick look at the set from Strange Company's Ozymandias, which is 7 years old now, in both its original and trianglized forms.

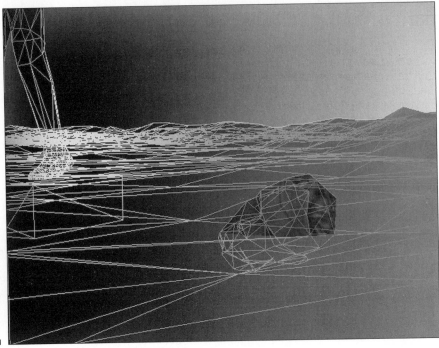

**Figure 6-2:**
A set from Ozymandias, showing underlying polygons.

So we've got our polygons. Early virtual reality engines from the 1980s used to just color those polygons a flat color, and that was your world. In theory, we could still do that and just model all the fine detail of the world from triangles — but that's a horribly complex and processor-intensive way of working. Instead, nowadays, we fake all the fine detail by wallpapering our set with a 2D image, called a *texture*. That image then provides the fine detail, which can be anything from the wood grain on a door to the keys on a telephone. Of course, those keys wouldn't work, but they look great.

Some advanced engines, such as DooM 3, layer more complex textures on top of the basic texture layer. These extra textures provide additional information for the game engine:

- **Bump maps:** Information about the depth of the surface
- **Specularity maps:** Information about the shininess of the object
- **Normal maps:** Information about sub-geometry in the engine
- **Environment maps:** Information about objects reflected in the object

In the old days of 3D games, we designed our sets right out of the bare polygons. Editors had the ability to form simple 3D shapes — pyramids and cubes — from triangles, and we built our sets from them and then textured them manually, designing and assigning images to make our world.

## Other 3D ways?

Other ways of visualizing 3D worlds include *Voxels,* which are essentially 3D pixels that make up a world (mostly used in medical imaging) and NURBS, which are horrendously complex mathematical objects describing 3D curves.

It's entirely possible that game engines may swap to one of these methods in the future, but for now, polygons are the way forward.

Strange Company's *Eschaton* series was entirely produced using those techniques. But these days, we've become a lot more sophisticated, and the tools that you use to create your sets probably won't go near a polygon editor.

So why do you need to know this stuff? Every object has a polygon count and a texture that it uses. Your graphics card can render a certain number of polygons, and it has space for a certain amount of textures. If you go over those limits, things start to run slowly and jerkily. The closer to your hardware limits you get, the more pronounced this degradation can be. Of course, computers these days can render terrifying numbers of polygons, and fit ridiculous numbers of textures onto their cards.

But still, if you're trying to model Helm's Deep from *The Lord of the Rings* or re-create the flight across the Death Star — or even just shoot a vista like the hills of *Brokeback Mountain* — you need to think carefully about how you spend your polygon budget.

# Entering the Modern Age

It didn't take long for game designers to figure out that making endless game levels using polygon-modeling tools sucked (see preceding section).

Most game engines now treat creating world objects and placing them as separate tasks. Modern set editors usually work from a mixture of precreated world items and simple design tools:

- **Heightmaps:** If you've played any of the Populous games, or The Sim City games, you'll be right at home here — you start with a flat landscape and then click it with your mouse to raise or lower sections of it, create harsh cliffs, gentle rolling hills, deep valleys, or whatever.

    Sometimes the set editor automatically decides that a particularly harsh slope must be a cliff and gives it a cliff texture, or that you've lowered your land below water level so it fills a valley up with water; sometimes, you have to assign those things manually.

You can also paint features onto your landscape using your mouse like an airbrush — those things may be simple textures, like a road running through your landscape, or they may be grass, trees, or even crowds of people.

✔ **Tiles:** Alternatively, you can build parts of your world using pre-set *tiles,* equal-sized parts of a map that could be the floor of an inn or the streets of a city.

Some map editors, mostly older ones, don't use heightmaps, and your world is solely constructed of tiles. Other game engines, such as Unreal Tournament, don't use tiles at all. Yet others, such as The Sims 2, use both.

✔ **Placeables:** You'll do the majority of your world creation by simply selecting items from a library in your set editor and dragging them into the world. If you're making a bedroom, you create a south-facing slope with your heightmap and lay out the floor plan of the room with your tiles. Now, you navigate through your menus, select a bed, and drag it around in the world.

Some game engines use placeables for everything other than landscape. In other engines, placeables are mostly smaller objects, such as chairs, tables, telephones, or swords. You're often able to set attributes on these placeables, too — for example, you may be able to choose the texture of a stained-glass window.

✔ **Weird stuff:** Most set editors will allow you to control other elements of your world. They can include the time of day in the game, the sky that you see above your world, or the ambient sounds in that set.

✔ **In-game:** Finally, a really good engine lets you change or add aspects of your set on the fly while you're shooting. That's an incredibly handy feature. You may want a super-long shot on one character, but you need to remove a wall to get far enough out. In real life, a huge problem. In Machinima? No worries.

We're generalizing. Specific game editors have specific features — Unreal Tournament, for example, still includes old-style polygon-editing tools.

# Creating a Set in The Sims 2

The Sims 2 has one of the most feature-packed set editors of any game. The following steps demonstrate all the features of the engine's set construction by creating a classic *Spooky House On The Hill.* Legally, we're not allowed to say we're basing this set on any film in particular, so let's say this set is for an imaginary movie called, ooh, *The Schining.* Or perhaps *Pschycho.* Or *The Texas Schainsaw Schmasacre.*

1. **Start up *The Sims 2* or the relevant expansion if you've got that installed.**

   You see a series of amusing loading screen messages, which relieves us of the need to come up with a joke for this section. Then the Choose A Neighborhood To Play screen appears.

2. **Click the arrow marked Next, and click Create Custom Neighborhood.**

   You see a confirmation message.

3. **Click OK, and you're on your way to the Choose Landscape screen.**

   You're now given a choice of landscapes on which you can build your neighborhood.

4. **Select the landscape you want and click the Load Template button.**

   For this example, we chose Aridia as our landscape.

   Now you can name your neighborhood whatever you want and change the terrain type.

5. **Select your terrain type and then click the check mark (shown to the left in the margin) to Load Neighborhood.**

   We're thinking Maine more than New Mexico, so we chose Lush.

   If you've got Sims 2 Nightlife installed at this point, the game asks you whether you want to associate a Downtown with this neighborhood.

6. **(If you have any Sims 2 Expansion Packs) Click No when the game asks if you want to create any other areas (Downtown and so on) to associate with this neighborhood.**

   Now the game asks you whether you'd like to write a story for your neighborhood. This answer has no effect on the game.

7. **Click OK.**

   At this point, you're looking at your brand-new landscape. You'll only be building on a small section of this landscape, so you need to find a suitable "Lot" for your set here.

8. **Right-click and drag on the set to move around.**

   You can only place your set near to a road, but other than this, your placement doesn't actually affect the look of your set. Find somewhere suitable near a road.

9. **Press F2 to go to the Lots And Houses menu.**

10. **Click the empty square below the House icon (it has the ToolTip Empty Lots), select Huge Lot, and click your chosen section of ground to place that lot.**

    You see an overlay of the lot, which turns green when you position it in a space the game likes.

    Plan before you choose a lot. Larger lots are more demanding on your computer. Strike a balance that works best for you. If you have a powerful modern PC, you may not notice any degradation at all.

11. **Click to set your lot down.**

    You see another dialog box, giving you a chance to name your lot.

12. **Name your lot.**

    For this example, we named our lot the Shmates Motel.

13. **Ignore the rest of this scene and click the check mark.**

14. **Left-click your lot and click Enter Lot.**

15. **Click No to disable game tips.**

    They're very annoying. And, hey, presto! You can actually start building!

# Landscaping for the Win

After you create your lot (see preceding section), you can look around it by pressing Ctrl+right-click and dragging, or by holding down the middle mouse button and moving the mouse. You can move around by right-clicking and dragging. You can zoom with the mousewheel if you want to get a closer look.

We start with a spot of landscaping; we create a mini-hill that leads to the back of the lot where you'll build your house.

1. **Press F3 to go to Build Mode.**

    The menu at the bottom changes.

2. **Click the Terrain icon, which looks like a spade.**

    Now you can use the tools at the right of the menu to raise and lower your terrain.

3. **Use the Elevation tools to raise up a big, evil-looking hill on your lot and then use Level Terrain on the middle of that hill to flatten an area of about 10 to 15 squares across.**

    This spot is where we build our house.

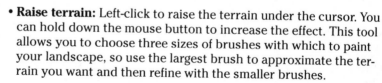

You have four landscaping tools available to you under the Elevation category.

- **Raise terrain:** Left-click to raise the terrain under the cursor. You can hold down the mouse button to increase the effect. This tool allows you to choose three sizes of brushes with which to paint your landscape, so use the largest brush to approximate the terrain you want and then refine with the smaller brushes.

- **Lower terrain:** Second verse, same as the first, except you're lowering the terrain.

- **Level terrain:** Left-click and drag to define a rectangular section of terrain to be totally flattened. This tool is useful for ensuring that you have sufficient level ground on which to create buildings.

- **Smooth terrain:** Use this brush to smooth out areas in which the height contrast is perhaps too harsh. Apply this brush in increments and, using the small or medium brush size, create a much more realistic-looking landscape.

4. **Add an idyllic-looking stream to your set by choosing the Terrain menu and then clicking the Water tool. Click some of the terrain at the bottom of the hill, and hold down and drag to draw out a stream.**

   Of course, in traditional horror movie juxtaposition, the idyllic beauty of this babbling brook only serves to hide the horror that lies in wait.

5. **Take a look at your creation from the ground.**

   To do so, press Tab to switch to Camera View and use Q to lower your view and S to move backward to get a good view.

6. **Press Tab again to escape from Camera View.**

7. **Use the Ground Cover tool to add a quaint little pathway leading up to the house.**

   Click, drag — you know the drill by now.

8. **Click Back and then press the Flooring tool to take a look at flooring choices.**

   You probably won't find any grimy cracked tiles that can almost make the shape of a human face if you squint, so try Smitty's Distressed Floorboards instead.

9. **Select a floor texture.**

10. **Drag a generous covering onto the flat area at the top of the hill.**

    This step creates the main floor.

11. **Make a small tiled entryway as well.**

    Slate For Days should do, under the Stone tab. Hey, we didn't name these textures.

Switch to the top-down view to place ground floor textures. It's much easier to see what's going on. When you come to place textures and items on the upper floors of your building, the top-down view is less useful.

# *Build Me Up, Buttercup*

If you created a house, you need some walls, obviously, so the following steps show you how to make them.

1. **Use the Walls tool to click and drag single walls into place, or use the Box tool to define entire rooms at once.**

    Ctrl+left-click removes a section if you make a mistake.

    We need a second story for this crumbling edifice.

2. **Click the Go Up A Floor button.**

    It's just above your cash total in the bottom left-hand corner — the Page Up key also does the trick.

3. **Place a floor and walls on the new floor — er, story.**

    Just click and drag to place floor tiles or walls. Any floor textures you place now are placed on the next floor up. You can only build on areas that have rooms underneath them on the ground floor. You also need to add walls for this story, too.

4. **To add a roof, click the Roofing tool, choose Roof Types, and pick an appropriate type; drag that out to cover the entire roof area and then choose a suitable roof pattern.**

    We went for the Mansard roof type with Stormy Slate tiles.

    If you can't see the roof, make sure that you're viewing the very top story of your building — keep pressing the Home key until you've moved up as far as you can.

5. **Click Back and choose the Wall Coverings tool (the paint brush).**

    Now you're ready to do some interior — well, exterior — design.

6. **Choose whichever wall covering takes your fancy, and click and drag that over all of your external walls.**

    We decided on Industrio Brick Wall for our spooky motel.

7. **Add an imposing door and windows by choosing the door and windows type from the Doors menu.**

For this example, we chose Colonial Tract Door.

The motel is a bit too exposed and welcoming still. Conceal it with some sinister trees.

8. **To add trees, choose the Garden Center tab and browse the selection of trees until you find the one you want.**

We couldn't resist the Creaky Branches Designer Tree — throw a few of those along the pathway, and the atmosphere is starting to look like a film that you can't legally watch without being of voting age.

# Adding the Finishing Touches

Chances are, you'll want a few appropriate furnishings and decorations on your set. No problem. Here's what you do:

1. **Press F2 to enter Buy Mode.**

2. **Add a few appropriate furnishings.**

3. **Add a few decorations by choosing Sort By Room⇨Outside, grab the decor you want, and place it where you want.**

We chose Bust Of Tylopoda (it's not what you think; she's a very respectable girl) and placed it at the entranceway.

4. **To add lighting, choose Sort By Function⇨Lighting⇨Spike Light and place it to one side of the door; place another inside the building so that it illuminates one or two windows.**

Now, doesn't that look spooky? If it's a little too spooky for the set you have in mind, choose another type of light from the Lighting menu.

You can play around with your set and customize it to your heart's content. There are props and building tools for almost everything you can think of just in the default Sims 2 installation. You can add a telescope on the roof of the building or make your set a little more up-market with a customized private swimming pool.

# Grabbing Props from the "Intarweb"

Even with the vast quantity of props and textures available to you in The Sims 2 (or another engine), a time will invariably come when you want to use something that's not on the disc. Perhaps you need a set of wings for your fairy godmother, or you just can't create the hero's distinctive hairstyle to your satisfaction. It's time to harness the awesome power of the Great Gestalt. To the tubes! It's Internet time!

Since the '90s, games developers have learned (via things like DooM, which started out as a game but became a phenomenon) that a good game will spawn its own following of passionate content creators. As a result, there's been an increasing trend for games companies to actively support and encourage development and expansion of a product by its fans. Creating new content for your favorite game is known as *modding*.

Modding prolongs the game's life — there's still an active and prolific content creation community for *Neverwinter Nights* five years after its release — and effectively provides the developers with a huge, talented staff that will create constant new content and never claim a paycheck.

In order to encourage modding, most games are released with a complex and powerful set of editing tools not just for maps, but also for item models, textures, and more. Often, the developers used this suite of tools themselves to write the game in the first place. This is great news for us.

## Finding mods

At the time of writing, typing "sims 2 custom content" into a search engine returns about 1,300,000 results. There's a lot of content out there, even for more obscure game engines than Sims 2, and a lot of it is really not of the highest quality. So how do you separate the wheat from the chaffing "Lara Croft Nude!!!!!" mods?

The first place to try are the most reputable and popular sites. You can often find links to favorite community sites on the game's official Web site. It's also worth checking the entry for the game in Wikipedia (`http://en.wikipedia.org/`) or other online encyclopedia. Useful sites are listed at the end of the entry and often include links to popular fan sites.

If you can't find a definitive list of popular sites for your game engine, then try searching for the name of the game plus "custom content" or perhaps "mods" (short for modifications, and often a slang term for custom content).

If you know exactly what you need, try a search specifically for it — "empire-line black evening dress sims 2", for example. You may just get lucky, especially with some of the more popular game engines.

This stuff was created by individuals on the Internet. And we know what that means — porn. You may well find, particularly with some of the more, ahem, intimacy-friendly engines like The Sims 2, that you run into some "naughty" material. Don't worry — there's probably nothing too bad on any vaguely reputable site. But if you're offended by nudity, or your parents/boss/SO are likely to look over your shoulder at an inconvenient moment, surf with caution.

When you've found your perfect item, check it in the game to make sure that it can do everything that you need it to. Some items may look great until you try to use them. That perfect black evening dress is pretty useless if it warps into an explosive mess of bad polygons every time your character kneels down. Unless you're sure that your character will never need to kneel down, of course, in which case you may just be able to get away with it.

## Installing a mod

The custom content installation process (and the complexity of it) varies between games. Often, you're just required to uncompress a .zip file, and place the compressed files into a specific folder within the game installation. If the game manual doesn't tell you the process to follow, any decent custom content Web site certainly will. Some even provide their own custom tools to make the installation of additional content even easier (such as the Sims 2 Q-Xpress Installer, from www.q-xpressinstaller.com).

A piece of custom content may have specific requirements — in that case, look for a Readme file within the package that the mod comes in, usually a .zip or .rar file. It'll tell you what to do.

We're probably not the first people to tell you this, and we're sure we won't be the last, but it bears repeating: Always run a virus-checking program before opening any files that you've downloaded from the Internet.

## Making a Quality Set

But how do you make a good set, one that will get across what you intend it to? Originally, when drafting this book, we wrote a big, slightly pompous section here on color theory, and use of space, and other things we heard about while watching *Changing Rooms* reruns. But about half-way through writing it, we realized there was a big problem. We don't really understand use of space. Or color theory. Or interior design. Sure, we've picked up some stuff, and we integrate what we know into our films — if we remember. Or we think of it. Or we're not hung over. But if we tried to write an "expert" guide to any of these things, we'd be bluffing.

So, here's a grab-bag list of things that helped us when we've been making sets for films, all in the slightly disorganized, stream-of-consciousness way that we tend to work. Welcome to Machinima.

## Research

If you want a "feel" for an area that you're not able to achieve, go find similar scenes in movies. Now watch for the things that are common over several different examples of the scene.

When we were researching for *BloodSpell,* we noticed that several filmmakers used white rim lighting around dark rocks to give the impression of a spooky, underlit cave. We copied that trick, and it worked like a charm.

Here are a few other techniques to try:

- ✔ **Take a test drive.** Build several different simple versions of your set, not spending more than half an hour on each one, and then look at how they come out in the game engine before you choose which one to develop further.

- ✔ **Use photo references.** If you're recreating something you'd see in the real world, look at as many pictures of that thing as you can before you design. You'll spot a lot of small details that you wouldn't have otherwise thought of.

- ✔ **But don't get hung up on the details.** You don't need to exactly re-create the Oval Office if you're only going to see it for a few moments.

Consider what elements are vital to convey the feel of the set. Think about how you can make your life easier and your set design quicker by eliminating things that aren't vital. It's the shots that are important, not the set itself.

Often what you will need isn't a mass of detail, but one or two pivotal points of detail. These will focus the eye and give a sense of realism.

## Color and light

Although it may not seem so at first, light and color are two of the most important tools in your arsenal. You can change the entire feel of a set simply by lowering the overall lighting value slightly or changing your dark brown walls to a light pastel blue.

Here are a few tips for working with light and color:

✔ **Painting with light is easier than painting with paint.** Lighting is the easiest way to customize a set using standard game objects. Intelligent and attractive lighting can do more for the mood of your set than just about any other technique, in terms of bang for time spent.

✔ **Try to avoid lighting that can't be moved.** As you shoot, you'll want to move your lighting around for best effect. You need to re-light for actor movement or changes in mood. Try to avoid relying on lighting in the set that you can't change in-game.

On *BloodSpell,* we used dynamic lights spawned on invisible characters for most of our lighting and used very minimal lighting in the set itself. That way, if we needed to move the source of a light, we didn't have to go back to our editor. We'd just tell our glowing invisible badger to move out of the way.

✔ **Avoid lighting soup.** As any amateur painter knows, the more you mix colors together, the more you head toward a nondescript brown. Keep your lighting simple and elegant — a single color, or at most two colors strongly contrasting.

✔ **Too dark is usually better than too bright.** If in doubt, underlight your set. It's far better to have interesting shadows and suggestions of shapes than horrible flat over-lighting.

This applies to sets only, not characters! It's fine to have your hero's face half in shadow. But as soon as the audience can't figure out what's going on, they'll tune out, and you're lost.

✔ **Painting with light and painting with dark.** Imagine that black is one of the colors you're lighting with. Manufacture interesting shadows and suggestive dark spots as much as you manufacture points of light and interesting shades. You can change the appearance of a set very rapidly with clever usage of dark and shadow.

# *Space*

Even though your movie is going to be shot on an entirely virtual set, you still need to consider a few basic points about the use of space:

✔ **Don't supersize me.** It's very easy to create a huge set in Machinima, but the bigger the set, the more work you'll have to do to fill it. Your sets should be as small as you can reasonably make them and still tell your story. If you're making a living room, don't make it the size of a whole house, unless you've got a very good reason.

✔ **Peter Jackson had hobbits.** If you're creating a set at an immense scale, your audience needs to be able to tell what size it is. Make sure that you've got items that contrast with the size of the set and show just how large it is.

✔ **Overclutter and then spring-clean.** It's very easy to underdetail your sets. To avoid doing that, deliberately overdetail. Stick all the details you can think of into the set.

After you do that, work with a couple of other people to figure out what's not needed in there and slowly strip the set back until you've got a good balance. Everything that's in there should be there for a reason.

✔ **Scale is important.** Make sure that everything you create is in scale to your characters. That applies to chairs, tables, telephones, doors, and especially rooms. It's very easy to create a room in which your hero appears to be about the size of a large house cat.

✔ **Vertical space is key.** The hidden key to creating a set that "feels" right is the vertical space. Make sure that your ceilings are appropriately sized and well-modeled.

High ceilings will give a feeling of scale and awe. Very low ceilings make a space claustrophobic. Think vertical.

## Practicalities

Like it or not, you're not working in the real world here — you're working with a game engine.

✔ **Always check in the engine.** Don't rely on your editor's preview window for anything, be it lighting, draw distance, or field of view. Always check your set in the game itself. Otherwise, you may be setting yourself up for nasty surprises later.

✔ **Minimize fiddly detail.** Even with today's processors and graphics cards, it's depressingly easy to end up watching a slide-show because you've tried to fit too much small detail into a scene.

✔ **Dress rehearse.** Start studying your set from the perspective of the shots you're going to use as early as possible, with character models in place. Until you get in there in the engine and try to set up shots as you would with a camera, with characters in place, you'll have no idea how usable your set will be. And that means you don't know what you can do to improve it.

✔ **Think about whether you could live there.** How practical is the set for its alleged function? If it's an evil cult's meeting place, where do they hang up the robes? Do they scrub the floor? Is there enough space to stand around the mystic circle? Where's the toilet? You don't need to model the lavatory, but even a doorway off the meeting room increases the sense of realism.

✔ **Think about whether the set fits its occupants and environment's descriptions.** If you're riffing off *24,* where are the empty cigarette packets and piles of briefing paper? If you've got a cave inhabited by wild animals, are bones scattered around? Is the owner very neat (line up the pens, then) or obsessive and too busy (pizza boxes on the floor, ahoy)?

# Chapter 7

# The Casting Couch: In-Engine Character Design in The Sims 2

· · · · · · · · · · · · · · · · · · · · · · · · · · · · · · · · · · · · · · · · · · · · · · · · · · · · · · · · ·

## In This Chapter

▶ Understanding the theory of in-game character creation

▶ Creating a character in The Sims 2

▶ Improving your character design and creation

· · · · · · · · · · · · · · · · · · · · · · · · · · · · · · · · · · · · · · · · · · · · · · · · · · · · · · · · ·

$W$hile sets are important for a film, the characters are really the most vital element. (This message brought to you by Hugh's secret super-hero identity, Captain Obvious.)

In normal computer animation, characters are hard to create — brutally hard. They're the most expensive element of any production, and so they tend to be used sparingly and avoided whenever possible. You wondered why Pixar's first film featured a bouncing desk lamp? That's why.

In Machinima, by contrast, you're working with technology specifically designed to allow you to throw characters around willy-nilly. In the last few years, that character technology has developed so that you can quickly and simply design whole hosts of characters, each of them individual and hand-crafted. No armies of identical robots for you (unless you want them) — if you want background actors, you can design them in minutes, drop them into the scene, and have your new guys drinking coffee in the background as easy as saying, "Call the MPAA. We've got a threat to our business model!"

And *then* you can have a giant robot break through the window and blow everyone to bits.

## How Do They Do That?

A few years ago, game designers started to realize that their players enjoyed customizing their characters, and so they started incorporating techniques for simple modification of a character's look. From a few simple initial options — different colored hair, perhaps a few different faces — these options rapidly extended into full-fledged human design studios.

You can model your character in-game in four simple steps:

1. **Choose a base character model — male or female.**

   These days, every character starts with a simple, generic human shape, usually one for male and one for female.

2. **Morph that model or choose different body parts until you're happy with your actor's appearance.**

   Morphs may include (but aren't limited to):

   - Longer or shorter nose

   - Stronger or weaker jaw

   - Heavier or lighter physique

   Some games take a different approach, most commonly offering a variety of body part meshes without morphs, but with very different physical characteristics. For example, you may have a head with long, slightly '70s hair and a Dominic Monaghan jaw, and another one with a spiky hairstyle and a jaw that appears to have gone for an early lunch. Swap between the two, and do the same for torso, legs, and so on, and you can change your character from looking like Johnnie to looking like Hugh.

3. **Choose a texture and change its characteristics in the engine.**

   Next, a texture is overlaid onto the basic model. This simple 2D image, much like a digital photograph, is designed so that when it's overlaid onto the mesh, just like wrapping paper onto a parcel, the image gives the character details that aren't in the basic 3D mesh — eyes, mouth and skin color, and so on. Some games use multiple textures for different parts of the body — head, arms, hands, and so on. Usually, options are built into the texture to change its characteristics — hair color, skin color, eye color, and so on.

4. **Add clothing parts to form a character outfit.**

   From there, you can then equip the character with a variety of clothing items — some of these will simply be changes to the texture (for example, a unique T-shirt can be modeled just by changing the color of part of the texture), while others are 3D models overlaid onto the base model — a wristwatch, for example, or boots.

All these options are built into the game, or associated tools. You may be wondering what you can do with your particular engine. Table 7-1 lists the capabilities of each engine.

## Using advanced character creation techniques

You can get more advanced in character creation and use two other approaches to edit your characters:

- You can modify the texture for your character in an image editor — adding a tattoo, for example.

- If you want to get really advanced, you can often bring your character's mesh or meshes into a 3D modeling package and modify them on the level of the triangles themselves. This approach is definitely for advanced users only, but it gives your character a really unique look. We're not going to cover 3D modeling in more detail in this chapter, but if you really have a jones for polygons, head on over to Chapter 18.

| Table 7-1 | Features Available in Engines |
|---|---|
| *Game* | *Features* |
| The Sims 2 | Full morphing character creation |
| The Movies | Full morphing character creation |
| Neverwinter Nights 1 | Multiple body part choices (no morphing) |
| Neverwinter Nights 2 | Full morphing character creation |
| Moviestorm | Full morphing character creation |
| IClone | Full morphing character creation |
| SecondLife | Full morphing character creation |
| World of Warcraft | Multiple body part choices (no morphing) |
| Half-Life 2 | Limited character customization |
| Halo 2 | Limited character customization |
| Unreal Tournament | Limited character customization |
| Medieval Total War 2 | Limited character customization |
| Doom 3 | Limited character customization |
| Grand Theft Auto | Limited character customization |
| Battlefield 2 | Limited character customization |
| Company of Heroes | Limited character customization |

If you're working with an engine that offers only limited character customization, you'll have to get out the 3D packages or texture editors to alter your characters. A number of the engines that don't offer much character customization are also on our less recommended list. That's no coincidence. Character customization is really important for Machinima creation.

# Creating Characters in The Sims 2

The Sims 2 is one of the poster children for high-quality character creation. It ships with a fantastically powerful editor called Body Shop (see Figure 7-1), which offers a tremendous amount of control and creativity over your actors, their costumes, and their personal props. Body Shop runs as a separate program to the main Sims 2 game. You can find it in your Start menu in the same folder as your main Sims 2 game.

Body Shop was released ahead of the main Sims 2 game as a free download. Even if you don't own a copy of The Sims 2, you can easily find Body Shop available for free on the Internet.

**Figure 7-1:**
The Sims 2
Body Shop.

Once Body Shop has loaded, you see a big, friendly Sims 2 logo on the right side of the application, and an empty 3D room on the left side. When you're creating or editing a Sim, you can see your changes in the left pane, modeled for you by the Sim himself.

If you've installed any of The Sims 2 expansion packs, such as Nightlife, Open For Business, University, or Pets, each expansion pack has created a separate folder for itself in your Start menu. Each folder contains a link to The Sims 2 Body Shop. Be sure to run the copy of Body Shop associated with the most recent expansion pack you own. If, for example, you've installed The Sims 2 and Nightlife, clicking the link to The Sims 2 Body Shop in Start⇨Programs⇨ EA GAMES⇨The Sims 2 results in a nasty error message and little else. You should instead choose Start⇨Programs⇨EA GAMES⇨The Sims 2 Nightlife⇨ The Sims 2 Body Shop.

To make a new actor, follow these steps:

**1. Click the Build Sims button at the top of the screen, on the right side.**

Body Shop asks you whether you'd like to Build Or Clone Sims, or Package Sims. Don't worry about the Package Sims option for now.

**2. Choose Build Or Clone Sims.**

Well, look at that. You see a list that looks suspiciously like a big casting call full of hopeful virtual actors. These are all the sample Sims included with the game. You may well be able to find a model suitable for your lead character right here, without doing any editing at all. If so, just select the character, and click the green check. You don't have to do any further editing.

But we know you better than that. You're a perfectionist, and picking a model from a pre-made selection just won't do. It's time to roll your own.

The first Sim in the list is nothing but a blue cross on a green background. Don't worry, he hasn't got some sort of horrible disfiguring disease. That's the button to create a new Sim, and you're going to click it.

**3. Click the blue cross on the green background.**

Even though you've edited nothing so far, you already have a Sim. What gives? Body Shop has automatically created a Sim for you to use as the basis of your new creation. Everything about your new Sim, from skin tone to choice of outfit to the length of his nose, has been randomly determined by Body Shop.

You can click the Randomize button (the dice icon) to generate another random set of values, and another randomly generated Sim appears. Be warned, though: some of the characters that the Random tool comes up with are strange and freaky-lookin' indeed. These images may not be suitable for small children.

Although the Randomize button changes most things, the sex and age of your Sim remain the same unless you choose to change it using the buttons just above Randomize.

It's important to have an idea in your head of the character you want to create. You may even like to have a couple of reference shots on hand of somebody who resembles them. We often find it easiest to hit the Randomize button a few times until the random Sim bears a passing resemblance to the final character that we're after and then fine-edit from there.

# Customizing Your Character

At the top of the panel on the right are five icons: Genetics; Faces; Modifiers; Facial Hair, Makeup, And Glasses; and Clothing. The following sections tackle each icon in order.

## Genetics: A new pair of genes

Clicking the Genetics buttons brings up a menu with three options: Skin Tone, Eye Color, and Hair. No bonus points will be awarded to those who can guess what each of these does. Go ahead and choose options from the menus below. You'll see your changes updated automatically in the model on the right.

You can reverse your changes at any time with the Undo function in Body Shop. The Undo and Redo buttons appear at the bottom left of the window.

You may assume that any hats your character can wear will be available under the Clothing category somewhere, but actually hats are stored under the Hair tab in the Genetics category. In fact, The Sims 2 game engine doesn't know the difference between a new hairstyle and a new hat; hence, both appear under the same tab.

## Faces: Tragedy, comedy, or chimp

When you're happy with your new actor's skin tone, hair, and eye color, take a look at the next tab, Faces. You have six menus to choose from here: Face,

Brow, Eyes, Nose, Mouth, and Jaw. Pretty self-explanatory. Clicking any of these menus brings up a whole series of potential face shapes.

Each potential shape has a slider beneath it. By default, these sliders are all set to minimum, so they'll have no effect on your model. Turn one of the sliders up by moving it to the right, and you see that your character's face starts to morph toward that shape (see Figure 7-2). The further right you move the slider, the more pronounced the effect will be. Body Shop displays eight potential shapes for you to choose from, but there are plenty more. Just hit the arrows to the left and right to scroll through all the available choices.

You can achieve a lot of control over the look of your Sim right here, just by combining the two face shapes: your randomly generated Sim and the face shape attached to the slider. You can't use more than one of the sliders at the same time, but you can achieve even more flexibility using the Modifiers tab (see the upcoming section, "Modifiers: The real power awaits you"). You're only aiming for an approximation of your character here. Don't be hesitant to play around — you won't be able to tell whether an adjustment will work until you've tried it.

**Figure 7-2:**
Affecting face shapes using the sliders.

## Modifiers: The real power awaits you

The Modifiers category is where the real power of Body Shop lies. At first glance, you may not see the difference between Modifiers and Faces — after all, they both have the same six categories. Explore a little more, though, and you see that modifiers allow you control over one single aspect of your character's face at a time. Unlike Faces, you can combine these effects to your heart's content.

Theoretically, there's nothing to stop you from modeling absolutely any face with remarkable accuracy. Accurate modeling takes time and skill, and the more you invest the better the result.

You may be tempted to keep fiddling with your character model until it's exactly, perfectly correct. Think before you spend a lot of time on this step. Resist the urge to spend hours on every character. The time soon adds up, and it's time taken from other (perhaps more productive) aspects of your movie.

The trick to achieving good results with Modifiers is subtlety. Make a small change, take a look at the effects, and make another small change.

## Facial hair, makeup, and glasses

The Facial Hair, Makeup, And Glasses category allows you to accessorize your new Sim to within an inch of his street-cred. You can choose the shape of your character's eyebrows here, as well as give him a fine Lincolnian beard (and all-over stubble at differing designer lengths, too, if you so wish). Before you ask, no, you can't easily give beards to your female Sims, so that great idea for *Badger Bristles: Confessions Of A Bearded Lady* will have to wait.

You can give your Sim glasses in this section, as well as apply makeup and face paints in a variety of frightening shades. In a blatant display of sexism, your male Sims can wear whatever fabulous color of lipstick you choose, thereby proving once and for all that men have it easier in life.

Although the Eyebrows tab allows you to choose the shape of your character's eyebrows, it doesn't determine their thickness (or lack thereof). There are seven different Modifiers for that, under the Modifiers➪Brow tab. Thoughtlessly excessive use of these modifiers can create a *Buffy The Vampire Slayer* bumpy forehead effect, so be careful — unless you're trying to film a *Buffy* fan-film, that is, in which case your humble authors can always be thanked through the medium of alcohol.

If you can't find that perfect item, you can always make your own. Once again, Body Shop makes this task easy. Load up the application and choose Create Parts rather than Build Sim.

The three options you see — Create Genetics, Create Facial Hair, Makeup & Glasses, and Create Clothing — correspond to the three categories of the same name in the Sim-building part of Body Shop. You can create new eye colors, makeup, clothing, glasses, and so on.

Say, for example, that you want to give your character a distinctive tattoo:

1. **Click Start a New Project and give your project a name.**

2. **Click Create Genetics.**

3. **Click the Skin Tone button, which is the first one on the lower row.**

   The description Skin Tone is something of a misnomer. What you're actually going to be editing is the texture that gets applied to the model's skin, underneath any clothing and makeup he's wearing.

4. **Select the lightest of the four default skin tones and click Export Selected Textures at the bottom of the screen.**

   Body Shop prompts you for a project name.

5. **Name your project.**

   You can choose anything you like.

   Body Shop exports all the textures used by the light skin tone to My Documents⇨EA Games⇨The Sims 2⇨Projects, in a folder named the same as your project. You already knew that, though, because a helpful message at the top of the Body Shop window tells you so.

6. **Click Cancel in Body Shop.**

   You can reload this project after you've edited the image.

   Take a look at what's been exported. Yikes, that's a lot of stuff. What you have here are image files for every potential age, sex, and body shape, with separate images for faces. You're only going to change one file, and that's the image for a standard adult female body. It has the catchy name of `afbodynormal~top~stdMatBaseTextureName.bmp`.

7. **Open the file in your favorite editor.**

   This file is just a standard bitmap image. Notice that the texture file makes it seem that your character has been involved in some sort of horrific steam roller accident. That's just because the texture has to be flattened to convert it from a 3D wrapped shape to a flat 2D texture. (You can find out more about this topic in Chapter 16.) You can see the approximate position of your character's shoulder.

8. **Edit the image to add a tattoo at that spot.**

9. **Save the altered image and reload the project in Body Shop.**

   Your changes appear on the model. If not, check that you edited the right image file, and that you're displaying the new skin tone using a model of the correct sex, age, and body type. If your edits aren't quite right, just cancel the project in Body Shop, re-edit your image(s), and open the project again

10. **After you're happy with your edits, click Import To Game.**

    After a few moments, your new skin tone is imported into the game for you to use in just the same way as the standard skin tones.

    You need to edit your existing model in order to use this texture.

11. **Choose Build Sims⇨Build Or Clone Sims and select your character.**

    You can't edit this model directly, so you need to create a clone and edit it.

12. **Press the Clone Selected Sim button at the bottom right.**

13. **Change the Sim's skin tone to your new skin tone, which you can now find under Genetics⇨Skin Tone and save.**

    You've now got two, seemingly identical, Sims in your collection. The one on the left is your new, fully tattooed, Lead Character Version 2.0, and she's ready to start filming.

# Clothing

After you have a character model that you're pretty happy with, it's time to send him off for a costume fitting. Click the Clothing button.

Clothing in The Sims is divided into six categories. Body Shop randomly picked an outfit in each category for your Sim when you first generated him (see the section "Creating Characters in The Sims 2," but you can choose something more appropriate here. The selection of clothes available is limited by the sex of the Sim that you're dressing, as well as his age. Most items of clothing can only be worn by Sims at a certain life stage.

You can edit as many of your characters outfits as you want, but only one of them will be saved along with your character when you exit Body Shop. Don't waste time assigning six separate outfits to each character at this stage. You can assign more clothes later, when you come to actually import the character to the game.

### Going shopping on the Web

If you need a specific piece of clothing and can't find it in Body Shop, your first resource should be the wide-open seas of the Great Internet. There are a lot (and we do mean a lot) of Web sites dedicated to custom content for the Sims 2, and most of them are free to access.

Custom content is usually distributed as a `.package` file. To install a `.package` file and make it accessible in The Sims 2, simply place that file in your `My Documents/EA Games/The Sims 2/Downloads folder`.

Custom content can also come as a `.Sims2pack` file. This is, essentially, a self-extracting archive of multiple `.package` files. If you have The Sims 2 (with or without any of its expansion packs), double-clicking a `.Sims2pack` file automatically installs the custom content where it needs to go (after first giving you a list of items to confirm). When downloading custom content for The Sims 2, make sure that you've downloaded the correct pieces. Sims 2 Custom content can be composed of two parts: the mesh and the texture. If the dress or hairstyle you download is simply a new color scheme for an existing Sims 2 mesh, it's called a *recolor* and typically will just be one Sims 2 `.package` file.

If it's an entirely new shape, then sometimes the mesh comes as one `.package`, and the recolor(s) will come as another. Sometimes these are available at the same location, other times they are not.

Always read carefully when downloading, looking for any references to other files required to get your content to work. If you install a hair color for a custom mesh and neglect to download the mesh, the new hair color doesn't show up as a choice until its mesh is present.

Many pieces of custom content are distributed as compressed archive files, usually in the ZIP or RAR format. You have to uncompress these files before you can access the content. If you're using Microsoft Windows XP, you can read ZIP files already, but plenty of simple programs specifically designed to read archived files are available. We recommend 7-Zip, on the DVD.

# Designing a Character's Look

There's a difference between knowing how to design *a* character and knowing how to design *your* character. So, once you've written your script, breakdown, and story treatment, how do you translate the words on the page into a finished character? Just follow these steps:

## Perfect designs considered harmful

If you know exactly how you want your character to look, you're probably sunk. As soon as you get into character design, you're into a process of compromise with the game engine and its available assets.

If you come into the design process with a vision of exactly how your character should look, you'll invariably be disappointed by the results of your work. You won't achieve the vision in your head, and if you keep aiming for that, you'll probably rule out other possibilities that could have produced an even better result.

1. **Have a flexible idea for the character's look, based on his role and personality.**

   Come to your character design with a vague idea of the character's look but a firm grasp of his role and appearance in the story and experiment from there. By being willing to experiment with the strangest ideas and play with the editor, you'll come up with a much fresher look that plays to your engine's strengths. (To find out why you shouldn't know exactly how your character will look, see the nearby sidebar.)

2. **Do your research, and scour the 'Net for the look you want.**

   Start your design process with unimportant extras and create your most important characters last, to ensure that you've got a good grasp of the strengths and weaknesses of your tool. You need to learn your tool before you do your important work, and there's no better way than to use it for less vital production design.

   At the same time, scour every add-on site you can find for game mods that can make your characters look better. If it looks even vaguely relevant to your character design process, download it and try it.

   And keep a written journal of any add-ons or particular setups inside the character editor that may be useful for your main characters. If you don't write it down, you'll forget it. Hugh has a piece of paper hanging down from his monitor stand that he scrawls notes on whenever he spots something he likes.

3. **Don't create a look — create a range of looks.**

   When you're ready to start designing your main character or characters, the first thing you should do is go through the editor and assemble a potential look for the character. Done that? Good. Now do it again. And again. Get as wild and crazy as you want — experiment with different visual styles. What would the character look like if the film used a '40s noir style? What about if she could only wear orange?

Once you're running out of ideas — and it's a good idea to work with some-one else on this stage to ensure that you don't wear out your brains too quickly — and you've got a bunch of outfits, it's time to start winnowing.

4. **Go over your designs with the whole team.**

   Get everyone working on your film, or a bunch of people you trust who've read the script, together with a computer running your charac-ter editor. Now show them each of the designs for each of your charac-ters in turn. Discuss them. Edit as you're talking. Perhaps you like the shoulders from one but the jacket from another? Try it. How would the hair look spiked? Try it. From this process, you should be able to narrow down to a single design that you like, and you've got your character.

You're the director during this process — and make sure that your helpers know that although you appreciate their input, you're the vision keeper for the film, and you have the final word. If everyone else hates a look, but you're absolutely certain it's the right one, then go for it.

5. **Don't be afraid to change later.**

   After you've been filming for a bit, or shooting a storyboard, it often becomes obvious that a character's look just doesn't work in the story. At that point, the absolute worst thing you can do is to keep going with the style you've chosen.

   If there's any way that you can go back and re-shoot the sections that don't work, do it. Go back to Step 1 on this list and start developing the character again, based on what worked from his/her last outfit.

   Technology and mods have probably moved on since you started work, so check the latest character modifications. Then settle on a new look, and get on with the filming.

On *BloodSpell,* we changed our lead character's appearance at the start of filming, after a year of filming our animatic. The process of re-designing Jered was a nightmare — it took a month and many iterations of his models, and nearly resulted in Hugh bouncing his head off his monitor a couple of times. But we look back on the animatic now and cringe. Jered looked like a total idiot before we fixed him. And that's how you'll feel about your old character designs after you've redesigned for a better look.

# Mastering Visual Character Design

As you experiment with Body Shop, or with any other character-editing tool, you'll slowly gain an intuitive sense for what works and what doesn't. We guarantee that you'll look back on your early attempts a little further on down the line and wince. That's okay, though — the best way to learn is by doing.

Here are few tips for creating competent, striking, and well-designed characters. You can apply most of these tips to character design using any engine, not just The Sims 2.

- ✔ **Practice makes perfect.** Your characters on your first film won't look as good as the characters on your fifth. That's fine — just get on, do the best you can, and don't obsess on any one character. If she looks a bit ropey now, you'll probably figure out how to make her look better soon enough.

- ✔ **Try to give your character a style.** Notice how characters in your favorite television show have a particular dress sense that is peculiar to them; that's the costume designer doing a good job. Perhaps your character tends to wear long, flowing skirts or always dresses in smart business clothes.

- ✔ **He's like Blade, but he has *two* katanas.** You don't have to avoid cliché, but be aware that you're using them and make sure that you've explored other options. Does your brooding vampire hunter *have* to wear a black trench-coat? What about jeans and T-shirt? Or a business suit?

- ✔ **Spend time on your textures.** A few hours immersed in a image-editing program can often prove beneficial. As well as customizing your textures to better suit the character, you may be able to improve on, and add detail to, the texture that you're using. If you're using one of the default game textures, chances are that the texture will already be of a very high standard, but if the texture is from a third-party or fan-made add-on, the quality isn't guaranteed.

- ✔ **Place your character across a crowded room.** Put your lead character in a room with a dozen game extras. If she's not so striking that you can't find her straight away, you need to do more work.

- ✔ **The eyes have it.** Your character's eyes are extremely important. We subconsciously associate a lot of information from a person's eyes. Make sure that the eyes are clean and detailed. You may think that your character's eyes are so small as to not be worth worrying about, but you never know when you're going to need an extreme close-up.

  You can suggest innocence or trustfulness by subtly enlarging your character's eyes. (In the same way, contract or narrow the eyes slightly to give a villainous or untrustworthy look.)

- ✔ **Do Deformed Rabbit; it's my favorite.** Your character will be more interesting and memorable if they make a good physical silhouette, which also helps to define them easily within a frame. The shape of your character's outline is of particular importance in Machinima, where a low-polygon game engine or character model can appear to consist of nothing but harsh straight lines when viewed up close.

✔ **Think about yin and yang.** Be aware that your character is going to be seen against other characters and against the backdrop and set that you've created. Make sure that the colors you've chosen are well-defined. Your character should contrast with the background of a typical scene unless you've got a very definite reason for not doing so.

On *BloodSpell,* we had to drop an entire scene from the feature-length version, because both the background and the outfits of the characters were brown. Oops. Our bad.

✔ **Define features.** You're working on what is basically a cartoon, so your characters need to be immediately distinctive and possibly even slightly caricatured. To make them memorable, ensure that your characters have a single very distinctive feature — think Batman's incredibly strong jaw, or Lex Luthor's bald head.

✔ **Be bold.** Use bold colors for your character and try to avoid murky browns, grays, and dark purples. There are other ways to make your character look moody and angst-ridden, and these sort of colors rarely come across well in Machinima. You can create a much stronger effect with stronger and brighter colors like reds and blues. You can always darken these colors with lighting in your game engine. This tip is of primary importance. Get it? Primary. Oh, never mind.

✔ **Make it clear which *Charmed* sister is which.** It's equally important to make your characters distinct from one another. If all four of your lead characters are blond-haired Caucasians wearing dark tops and jeans, you're going to end up with a very confusing movie about a schizophrenic who keeps changing his tie. Think Buffy versus Willow versus Faith, and you've got an idea of how to distinguish your characters visually.

Hair is a great way to make a character distinctive. Have it blond, have it red, have it not be there.

✔ **Feel blue.** Psychologists and interior decorators know that, in the western world at least, we associate specific colors with certain emotions or character traits. Black is death, the unknown, power, and corruption; blue is a sad color (but also calm and regal); and so on. This idea is called *Emotive Color Theory,* and it's worth researching and following for your characters. You can find out the basics at Color Wheel Pro (www.color-wheel-pro.com/color-meaning.html) or Wikipedia (http://en.wikipedia.org/wiki/Color_Symbolism).

✔ **Use the color wheel.** The *color wheel* is a tool that has long been used by artists and graphic designers in order to select complementary colors. A circle is divided into three parts, one for each of the primary colors (red, green, and blue for visual media). Each segment is then divided into two, which are then filled with the so-called secondary colors, created by combining two of the primary colors.

The great thing about the color wheel is that, if you pick two colors that sit opposite each other on the color wheel, you can be almost guaranteed that they will complement each other and go together well. If, on the other hand, you pick two colors that are adjacent on the color wheel, your eyes will bleed at the ugliness.

# Chapter 8

## Cut! Directing Machinima with The Sims 2

*In This Chapter*

▶ Hacking the game to make it a movie studio

▶ Controlling the camera and setting up great shots

▶ Getting tips from Michelle of Brittanica Dreams

*T*he Sims 2 — possibly the most popular computer game of all time. In The Sims, you control a family of little computer people, who have just moved into a new house. Just like real people, they have aspirations in life, fears, and the need to use the toilet (believe us, that's a big part of the game). You get to control them, direct them to fulfill themselves and their goals, buy goods and services to improve their home, and hopefully avoid them dying of hunger or thirst, setting themselves or their house alight, or otherwise failing in their life's aims.

As a Machinima maker, you can create almost anyone you can imagine, place them in virtually any situation you can think of (from modern day to mermaids), and film the results.

## Making Movies in The Sims: The Advantages

The makers of The Sims were taken by surprise when players started using their game to tell stories. Hence, when they were developing the second game, in full 3D, they decided to take these possibilities a step further, and incorporate tools to allow its users to make movies.

The Sims 2 is one of the most advanced Machinima toolsets available today:

- ✔ The Sims 2 boasts full camera control, including simple tracks and pans, as well as a pause mode to set up your perfect shot.

- ✔ Characters have a huge range of potential animations and reactions. In particular, for romantic or emotional films, The Sims 2 is way out in front of any other engine for the average filmmaker.

- ✔ The game includes both set construction and a fantastic character creation tool.

- ✔ The range of additional content for The Sims 2 on the Internet is huge. There are thousands of new sets, new characters, new props, and almost anything else you can imagine. (And, in some cases, things you really didn't want to imagine, and now can't scrub clean from your brain.)

- ✔ Many Machinima makers have also created add-ons for the game, and so you can find lots of utilities and add-ons that make creating movies easier.

- ✔ Sites like `www.sims99.com` provide a community of people eager to help new Machinima makers.

# Checking Out The Sims Disadvantages

We have to tell you now that The Sims 2 has one honking, massive problem as a Machinima tool: The characters can't talk. Or rather, they can't lip synch to movie dialogue. They do talk, but in a weird, Sim-lish dialect.

Just before we went to press, a Sims 2 filmmaker named Decorgal released two game hacks for The Sims 2, which give an amazing degree of control over speech in the game. With a bit of work, you can use these tools to achieve pretty accurate lipsynching. You can find these tools on the included DVD or online at `http://decorgalinc.com/blog/?p=157` and `http://decorgalinc.com/blog/?p=179`.

The Sims 2 has a few other problems:

- ✔ Many animations are quite overblown, which can be a problem for less melodramatic films.

- ✔ The Sims 2 is best for nonviolent, or at least not action-packed, films. The game doesn't really have a lot of facility for violence — romance, yes, violence no.

- ✔ The Sims is best for films set in the modern day. You can find content for nonmodern sets, particularly historical romances, but most available content is for modern-day settings.

✔ The game has a number of weird little flaws. For example, it's nearly impossible to have a character interact with a door. You can't have them open it or close it on demand. Many of these problems have been worked around by the community, but some — like the door thing — haven't been, which can crop up to bite you unexpectedly.

✔ For very serious moviemakers, it's worth noting that it's very difficult to add new animations to the game. So, if you want your characters to do anything normal Sims can't, you're out of luck.

If you really have to import a custom animation, take a look at Miche's Sim's body animation converter (`www.jd-movies.com/ animtutorial.php`).

# Preparing to Film with The Sims

Several useful additions to The Sims's movie-making capabilities were added in the expansion pack, Sims 2: Nightlife. You'll need that to make most Machinima movies and to fully follow along with this chapter.

Getting started filming with The Sims 2 is relatively easy. Although the game has a few quirks as a Machinima platform, you'll be able to set up your first shot pretty quickly. In brief, the Sims 2 process of filming consists of the following stages:

1. **Create your cast in the Body Shop application and create your set in the game itself.**

   For more information on the mechanics of Sims set design, see Chapter 6. To find out how to create your cast, see Chapter 7.

2. **Import your main cast into your main set, ready for filming, and your supporting cast into the neighborhood ready to be called in whenever you require them.**

   See the upcoming section "Getting Your Sims onto Your Lot."

3. **Configure The Sims 2 for Machinima creation.**

   See the upcoming section "Configuring The Sims 2 for Machinima."

4. **Shoot your film more or less live, telling your characters what to do and then freezing the game, setting up a shot, and watching as they do what you've told them.**

   The game exports this footage live as you shoot as AVI files.

5. **Take these AVI files and edit them as a normal movie.**

Want to get a laugh out of a group of filmmakers? Say, "We'll fix it in post-production." It's a truism in filmmaking that the earlier you get something right, the less time it will take you — or, to put it another way; screw it up now, pay for it later. Hence, you should set up as much as possible before you actually start filming. It's much more efficient to line everything up from the start instead of fixing them during filming.

## Getting Your Sims onto Your Lot

After you've designed your set, you need to set up your actors, ready for filming. Assuming that you've already created your actors in the Sims Bodyshop (see Chapter 7), here's a simple procedure to get everyone ready for shooting:

1. **Load The Sims 2 and then load your custom Machinima neighborhood from the Choose A Neighborhood To Play screen.**

   If you haven't created a custom neighborhood yet, see Chapter 6.

2. **From your Neighborhood screen, press F1 to go to your Families tab and then press the big Create New Family button at the bottom of the screen.**

   Yes, in The Sims 2, your actors really are one big happy family (see Figure 8-1).

3. **Give your family a name — the Machinimators, say — and then click the Create a Sim button.**

4. **Click the new button that appears (not the baby comforter). Confusingly, that button is also called Create a Sim.**

5. **Choose the appropriate age and sex for your sim (as you set them up in the Body Shop) and then click Choose Existing Sim.**

   The oh-so-hilarious Sim Bin appears. (Oy, Wright, we do the jokes around here, not you!)

6. **Select your pre-created sim for your first supporting character (see Chapter 7).**

   Don't select your lead character/characters yet. The next step is the time to choose additional costumes and outfits for your character. Each character will have been imported from Body Shop with only one set of clothes, but you can add more here.

7. **Click Step 5: Clothing (the number 5) and select additional clothing from the six tabs that appear.**

   If you only need one set of clothes for your actor (the one that he appears in by default), you can skip this stage. You can also only select one of each type of clothing for your Sim (Everyday, Formal, Undies, PJs, Swimwear, and Athletic).

**TIP**

If you want a character to change T-shirts, for example, during your film, you can either create two identical characters with different T-shirts, or you can send your character to a Shop in the game to buy herself additional clothing.

8. **Name your first supporting character whatever you want and click the number 6.**

9. **Give your character an Aspiration (ooh, we think Romance), and two Turn-ons and one Turn-off.**

   We leave those personal details up to you. They have no effect on filming, so choose anything you fancy.

10. **Click the check box and add your first supporting character to your family.**

    He appears next to a backdrop, facing a camera, ready for that lovely family photo.

11. **Repeat the preceding steps for each of your supporting characters and click the check mark in the bottom-left corner to accept that family.**

    Now you need to set up a new family for your lead character(s). Yes, even in Machinima the stars get their own trailer.

12. **Repeat the preceding steps, this time calling the family The Talent, and importing your lead characters.**

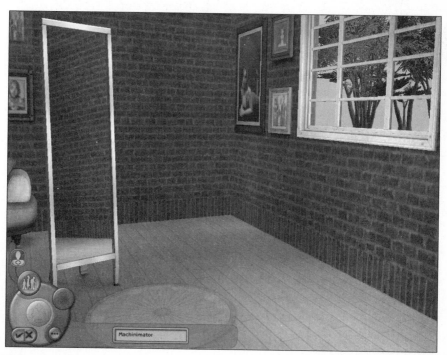

**Figure 8-1:**
The Add
Family
screen.

Sometimes it's useful to create two versions of the same lead character in one family. Suppose, for example, that your movie calls for your character to have two different hairstyles. Rather than constantly switching out to Body Shop, editing your lead character and re-importing, just create two copies of the character in Body Shop. Because the second character is a clone of the first, they'll be identical. All you have to do now is to give one version a different hairstyle. Now, when you come to create you Lead Character family, you can add both versions of this character. You can also have a character change outfits using this method.

After you have your two families set up — one with your lead character, the other with your extras — you need to move them into the neighborhood ready for filming.

1. **On the Neighborhood screen, press Ctrl+Shift+C to bring up the Cheat Console.**

   It's a lot easier to make money in The Sims 2 than it is in real life, so make all your actors millionaires. It'll only take a second.

2. **Enter the following line, substituting your family name for The Machinimators if you chose a different name:** familyfunds TheMachinimators 1000000.

   Now your family has access to all the virtual money you could possibly need.

3. **Do the same for your lead character family, The Talent.**

Now you need to move your characters into their houses. Move the Talent, your leads, into the main set and put The Machinimators in a cheap lot nearby, ready for you to call them later.

Be sure to back up your set so that if something goes wrong, you can reload it later. If you've not created a set yet, now is a good time to go to Chapter 6 and create one.

1. **Press F2 or select Lots And Houses and click your set.**

   The For Sale dialog box appears.

2. **Select the Package Lot icon from the left side of the pop-up dialog box.**

   The Package Lot dialog box appears.

3. **Select the Package Lot To A File radio button and click the check button to accept.**

   The Sims 2 pops up another helpful little dialog box to inform you where it has saved your lot. Now, if you accidentally delete, burn down, or whatever else your set, it's trivial to re-create it. Take that, Real World filmmakers!

Now you can create a cheap house for our Machinimators. Or a very expensive one. Darn these inflating Hollywood budgets.

4. **Select a house from the pictures at the bottom of the screen.**

   The cursor changes to a picture of the house in question. It doesn't matter what house you pick; you're not going to visit there.

5. **Find a spot on the screen where you can place the house and click to place it.**

   You can place the house next to a road on flat land. The picture of the house on your cursor turns green when it's placeable.

   The Rename This House dialog box appears.

6. **Accept the default name and press F1 to move to the Families tab; click the picture of the Machinimators family.**

   If you've forgotten what they look like (extras, who can tell them apart?), you can hover over the pictures to see a pop-up of their name.

   After you click them, your cursor changes to a picture of the family.

7. **Click the house you just placed.**

   The Sims 2 asks you whether you want to move the family into that house.

8. **Click Yes.**

   The Sims 2 loads up the lot. We don't want to be here yet, so exit.

9. **Press F5 to open the Options menu and then select the Neighborhood icon.**

   Now, you need to move your lead actors into the set where you'll be filming.

10. **Move your second family into your set rather than the Machinimator's house.**

    And you're done! Now you can set your engine up for filming.

Whatever you do, don't now move your leads out of the set again. If you do that, all their belongings — in other words, all the set-dressing you've done — will be deleted!

# Configuring The Sims 2 for Machinima

After your characters are on the set, you still have some setup work to do. You need to modify a couple files that the game uses, which gives you more flexibility in filming.

The following steps may look intimidating, but they're actually no harder than opening a letter in a word processor.

1. **Go to** `Program Files\EA GAMES\The Sims 2\TSData\Res\Config` **folder.**

   If you've got Nightlife installed, which is a really good idea for filming purposes, go to `Program Files\EA GAMES\The Sims 2 Nightlife\TSData\Res\Config` instead.

2. **Make a copy of** `GlobalProps.xml`.

   This is one of the main Sims 2 configuration files.

3. **Open the original file in Notepad and add the following line after**

   ```
   <AnyBoolean key=allowCustomContent
   type=0xcba908e1>true</AnyBoolean> :
   ```

   ```
   <AnyBoolean key=testingCheatsEnabled
   type=0xcba908e1>true</AnyBoolean>
   ```

4. **Start The Sims 2/The Sims 2 Nightlife.**

   You're done with the config editing.

## Adding a community add-on

Next, you need to add a community add-on: The Sims 2 Studio, from Pawfect Films, which is pretty much a necessity for Sims 2 Machinima creation. This particular add-on gives you access to a whole bunch of animations that are a total nightmare to access by any other means. Here's what you need to do:

1. **Download from the add-on from** `www.modthesims2.com/showthread.php?t=100738`.

2. **Unzip the file into the following directory:** `My Documents\EA Games\The Sims 2\Downloads`.

   When you start the game, you're asked whether you want to enable the add-on.

3. **Click the radio button for Enable Custom Content and click OK.**

## Adding game cheats

You also need to add a few cheats to your game of The Sims 2 to make your life easier. *Game cheats* are hidden ways to change the way that the game runs. A cheat can give your game character unlimited lives or show you the location of all the important in-game items. We use cheats a lot in Machinima to get around in-game limitations.

You can enter a lot of cheats here. Most cheats skew the balance of your game so much that they'll probably ruin your playing experience. We're not here to play, though, so you can unashamedly take advantage of all the cheats that can help you film. Here's what you need to do:

1. **Start The Sims 2 and choose your custom Machinima neighborhood.**

2. **Press Ctrl+Shift+C and then enter the following command into the cheat box exactly as it appears:** `boolProp enablePostProcessing true`.

3. **Press Enter.**

   Don't worry if nothing seems to happen. All that this cheat does is allow you to run other commands that are normally unavailable to you.

4. **Press Ctrl+Shift+C and then enter the following command into the cheat box exactly as it appears:** `boolProp testingCheatsEnabled true`.

5. **Press Enter.**

Now, you've got a few cheats you need to enable to stop The Sims from being a game and turn it into more of a movie-making tool. You can enable them in any order:

- ✔ To enable all interactions, meaning that your Sims will do what you want when you want, press Shift+Ctrl+C and then type `AllMenus On`.

- ✔ To stop your beautiful Sims from losing their looks, press Shift+Ctrl+C and then type `Aging Off`.

- ✔ To remove speech and thought bubbles (kinda vital), press Shift+Ctrl+C and then type `boolprop useEffects false`.

  You can also use `boolprop showHeadlines off` to accomplish the same thing.

- ✔ To get rid of the green spinny thing (technically known as the plumb-bob, but we like green spinny thing), press Shift+Ctrl+C and then type `plumbbobtoggle`.

- ✔ To make your Sims dumber (oh so very vital), go to the Options screen by pressing F5, then Game Options (the cogs), and then select Free Will Off.

- ✔ To allow you to move any and all objects around, using the Build screen press Shift+Ctrl+C and then type `moveobjects on`.

Only turn this cheat on when it is needed. Don't leave it on during filming; bad things can happen. Turn it on when you need to move something in a particular way and then turn it off afterward by moveobjects off.

✔ To allow you to move any and all objects around, using the Build screen, press Shift+Ctrl+C and then type MaxMotives on.

✔ To allow you to move any and all objects around, using the Build screen, press Shift+Ctrl+C and then type motiveDecay off.

You've now totally ruined any chance that you could enjoy a nice game of The Sims with your character. On the upside, you can now make a movie with them! Oh, choices, choices.

# Starting to Film

Try a gentle start to your new life as a filmmaker. Fire up The Sims 2 and load the Lot that contains your main character's house. (See the earlier section "Getting Your Sims Onto Your Lot.") Once you're in, you need to do a little bit of preparation to ensure that you're filming in an optimal environment:

1. **Click the Camera Settings button and make sure that you've disabled the option that records sound along with video footage.**

   The game records much slower if you leave the sound-recording option on. It's always best to compose, layer, and add sound later, when you're compositing your video footage together.

2. **Set other Camera Options (see Figure 8-2), if necessary.**

   You can choose the size and quality of the footage you film here. Depending on the speed and power of your computer, you may need to lower these setting a little, but in most cases, you can film with Video Capture Size set to large and Video Capture Quality set to high. Go ahead and make those changes now if you need to.

3. **Within Options⇨Graphics/Performance Options, set Object Hiding to Off.**

4. **Press Ctrl+Shift+C to get the cheats box up and then type letterbox 0.2.**

   If you didn't enable the cheats in the section "Adding game cheats," earlier in this chapter, you need to now. You're going to be using them.

   Now, *that* made a difference. You should see a black bar at the top and bottom of your screen, as if you're watching a wide-screen movie on a standard TV screen. If you don't, check that you've entered the two cheats exactly as they appear.

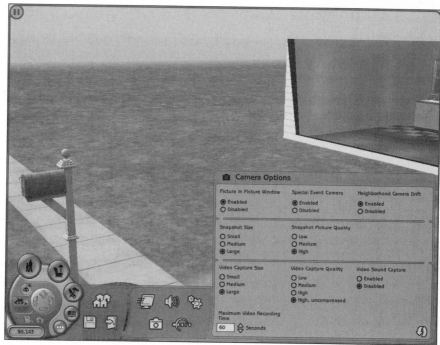

**Figure 8-2:**
Camera
Options in
The Sims 2.

This letterbox command allows you to adjust the *aspect ratio* of the footage that you're going to be recording. The number that follows is how extreme this effect is. We've chosen 0.2 here in order to replicate the wide-screen aspect ratio called Cinemascope, in which most Hollywood movies are filmed.

5. **You can turn the letterbox on again later, but turn it off for now with the command** letterbox 0.0.

Great, you're back to normal, and you can see what you're doing a little better.

## Static shots

So, this is The Sims 2. Have a look around. Try making your character interact with some of the objects in his house. When you're ready to start filming, press Tab and get ready for your first shot.

We're going through exactly the same procedure here that we would if we were filming live footage on a conventional film set. You have to position your camera within your film space and then check the view through it. If it's not quite right, you'll adjust until you're satisfied. The only difference is that our actors, set, filming space, and even the camera itself all exist within a virtual space that you can view on your computer monitor.

Notice that the view on your screen changes to Camera View when you press Tab. You're now viewing the action through the lens of your virtual camera. You'll be switching between this view and the standard game view a lot while you're filming. What you see on-screen now is exactly what will be recorded if you start filming.

Before you start filming, you need to position your camera properly.

You can move the camera in Camera View using the keyboard, as described in Table 8-1.

| Table 8-1 | Moving the Camera in The Sims 2 |
|---|---|
| *Key* | *Movement* |
| W | Forward |
| S | Backward |
| A | Slide Left |
| D | Slide Right |
| < | Turn left |
| > | Turn Right |
| Z | Zoom in |
| X | Zoom out |
| Q | Move up |
| E | Move down |
| PgUp | Raise walls |
| PgDn | Lower walls |

For your first shot, find something static you want to film — a plant, a piano, or even your house. Now zoom in until it fills your entire screen. This will be your first camera position, so press Ctrl+4 to save it.

The Sims 2 allows you to save six different camera positions and return to them later. By pressing Ctrl+4, you've just assigned this camera position to the 4 key. You can assign other camera positions to keys 5 through 9. (Keys 1, 2, and 3 are out of bounds, as they're already used by The Sims 2 to control the game speed.)

The Sims 2 remembers any camera positions that you save, even between sessions of the game, which is a great timesaver. They're saved with your lot.

Make sure that the walls of your house are displaying in full before you save a camera position. If you save a camera position with the walls down, The Sims 2 switches back to that mode of display when you load that camera position, even if you've changed it.

After you save that first camera position, use the X key to zoom out a little until you can clearly see some of the surrounding space. Now is a good time to turn the letterbox effect on so that you can check that the shot still works. Shift+Ctrl+C and then type **letterbox 0.2**.

Assign this new camera position by pressing Ctrl+5. Now you can switch between the two camera positions by pressing 4 and 5. (Don't hold down Ctrl this time.)

## Lights, camera, action!

After you set up your camera (see preceding section), you're ready to film your first shot:

1. **Press the P key to pause the game and then press 4 to move the camera to your first recorded position.**

2. **Press the V key.**

   The Sims 2's built-in camera recorder begins, and the red border around the screen turns yellow to indicate that the view on-screen is currently being recorded.

   You'll probably find that everything starts moving really slowly. The game hasn't gone wrong — The Sims 2 just slows the game down while its recording to ensure that the quality of the recorded footage is as good as possible. When you review the footage that you're capturing at the moment, it plays back at the correct speed.

3. **Press V again to stop recording.**

   The Sims 2 provides you with a helpful message about the location of the footage you just recorded.

Congratulations! You've just shot your first piece of Machinima footage in The Sims 2. It's sitting on your hard drive right now, just waiting for you to view it. Don't do that just yet, though — after all, it's a pretty boring shot on its own.

Even the highest-quality setting in The Sims 2 produces only 640x480 video. You'll almost certainly want higher quality than that. To accomplish this, edit `Videocapture.ini` in the `My Documents/EA GAMES/The Sims 2/Config` folder and change the Large Settings and High Quality Settings fields to change resolution and framerate, respectively. Ideally, you should be capturing at the same resolution you're running The Sims 2 at, to minimize the impact of resizing. Watch out: Changing these settings will make your video files much larger.

## *I like to move it — moving shots*

If you set up your camera in the section "Static shots," earlier in this chapter, you can easily set up a transition for a nice pan or tracking shot. Just press 4 to get to the first position and then press 5 — and you move!

Does that look a bit faster and jerkier than you'd hoped for? Us, too. We'd better fix that. Press Alt+Tab to leave The Sims 2 temporarily and return to Windows; you need to engage in some old-skool hacking:

1. **Open up your My Documents folder and navigate to** `EA GAMES/The Sims 2/Cameras`.

2. **Open the file called** `FirstPersonCameras.txt` **in Notepad or your favorite text editor.**

   If you're not used to editing and hacking game configuration files, you may be feeling a little out of your depth here, but there's no need to panic. Machinima is all about finding ingenious ways to make a game do what you want it to do, and you can always re-install if things do somehow break. Get your hands dirty — this is what you signed up for, soldier!

   You now see that you've got a whole bunch of settings and code in front of you. You're not concerned with most of these settings, and you can, in fact, ignore most of them. You do need to change just a few, though.

# Camera parameters in The Sims 2

The movement of your in-game camera is governed by four separate types of parameter.

✔ The *translation* dictates the amount of movement between one location and the next.

✔ The *orientation* dictates the direction in which the camera faces (and the change thereof).

✔ The *velocity* is the speed at which the camera moves.

(Note to physics geeks and pedants: Yes, we know that technically 'velocity' describes a directional vector as well as a speed, but in this instance it's much simpler to think of velocity as applying purely to speed. Just trust us on this one. It is.)

✔ The Field Of View, or *FOV*, describes the cone which is visible to the camera at any one time — wider FOV means that you can see more in front of the camera, but it also tends to exaggerate distances between objects (see Chapter 3).

In The Sims 2, we have the option of specifying two values for each of these parameters.

✔ Firstly, we can specify the number of *steps,* which dictates the number of individual changes that the camera will implement during the course of a single movement. Think of this as the number of frames in an animation, or the number of pages in a flickbook comic.

✔ Secondly, we can specify the *minchange,* or minimum change. The minimum change tells The Sims 2 how large (or small) we want each step to be. The larger the *minchange,* the more significant a change will be performed with each step.

We think. No-one outside the developers of The Sims 2 is exactly sure what these features do — these explanations are our best guess based on observation.

A lot of Machinima tends to function in much the same way — Machinima creators hack the game and exploit features that the game developer wasn't really expecting to be exploited, and hence didn't document.

During the course of filming, you'll probably need to make changes to only nine of these lines. They are the lines that start with the following:

```
setparam orientationminchange
setparam orientationsteps
setparam fovminchange
setparam fovsteps
setparam velocityminchange
setparam velocitysteps
setparam translationminchange
setparam translationsteps
setparam ticklimit
```

For this first shot, make just two changes to `FirstPersonCameras.txt`.

3. **Change the line** `setparam fovsteps 3` **to read** `setparam fovsteps 300`.

    You're changing the number of steps from 3 (which made the camera movement quick and jerky earlier) to 300. This step makes the camera movement much smoother, but it also takes much longer to perform, so the camera will appear to move at a slower rate.

4. **Change** `setparam fovminchange 0.1` **to** `setparam fovminchange 0.001`.

    You reduced the minimum movement so that the camera can now move less distance with each step. Combined, Steps 3 and 4 make the camera move slower — exactly the effect you want.

5. **Save the file, but don't close it.**

    You'll need to edit it before too long.

Alt+Tab back into your game again and switch to Camera View with the Tab key. Try the camera again (press 4 and then 5). Much smoother. It looks like you're finally ready to film.

Repeat the recording steps in "Lights, camera, action!" — the file will be saved separately — and you're done with the moving camera.

---

# More camera changes

You can make similar changes to these to achieve a wide variety of effects. For example, if you want to make the camera physically move slower, substitute the appropriate lines in the text file with these:

```
setparam translationminchange
    0.00018
setparam translationsteps
    5500
setparam maxvelocity 0.1
setparam velocitysteps 50
```

Those changes will make the camera move slower and more smoothly.

Likewise, if you want to slow down the camera's turning, use

```
setparam orientationminchange
    0.001
setparam orientationsteps
    7500
```

There's really no hard-and-fast rules here. Set up your shot, plug in some numbers, see whether they work, and if they don't, wash, rinse, and repeat. You'll get there in the end.

There's one more thing you need to know. By default, The Sims 2 doesn't allow you to point the camera directly up or down. If you need to do so, make these edits in your text editor:

```
setparam upperpitchlimit 90
setparam lowerpitchlimit -90
```

# Diving in to Character Filming

Cameras are all very fun, but you're here to make films about people, right? Okay, then. Start your film with your lead character waking up from a nice nap. You'll need a couch in your set.

With your lead as the active character, click the couch and choose Nap from the menu. All being well, your character curls up on the couch for some much needed R&R. If he doesn't do so immediately, check that the path to the couch is unobstructed. You may also want to turn his/her *Energy* value right down.

If you've already enabled the `boolProp Testing` cheat (see the section "Adding game cheats," earlier in this chapter), you can simply click the Energy bar and drag it to the left.

If your character curls up on the couch, but faces the opposite direction than what you want, tell him to get up and stand him directly in front of the couch. Whichever end of the couch he's standing at is the end that his feet will occupy, so if you want him to sleep the other way around, simply move him to stand at the other end of the couch.

Now, switch to Camera Mode and maneuver your camera until you have his face centered on-screen. Doesn't he look sweet when he's sleeping? Save this position with Ctrl+6 and record it as in "Lights, camera, action!"

If your character is feeling particularly uncooperative, there's a possibility that your lead character may go for a wander halfway through this shot. If he does, you can't really do anything but shout a word that your mother doesn't know you know and retake the shot.

Although you can limit the amount of independent thought and behavior exhibited by your sims, you can't mute it entirely. Some days they just *will not do* what you tell them. (This situation can be a problem with real actors, too, but at least you can fire them.)

Next, have your lead wake up:

1. **Pull your camera back a bit so that you can see the character and the couch (paying attention to the Rule of Thirds — see Chapter 3).**

2. **Pause the game with P.**

   You'll be using this key a lot.

3. **Select your character from the left side of the screen and then give him another command — walk to the chair, say.**

4. **Click the Nap action in the top-left of the screen to cancel it.**

5. **Press V to record, P to unpause, and then V again when he's gotten up.**

This process is exactly how you'll film all of your characters' actions — pausing, selecting an action, and then filming it.

Have a play around in the set now, finding out how the character can interact with all the objects and people around them. You'll probably already have film ideas springing to mind!

# Using Advanced Animation Tools

The Sims 2 Studio is a lovable little black box that will make your Sims 2 movie-making life a whole lot easier.

Go to Buy mode, go into Hobbies, and then go into Creative. Grab the black box with paw print that's in there and put it somewhere easily visible outside the set, on the grass.

You're going to use this box to make our lead character talk. If you were shooting a full film, his talking animations wouldn't exactly mesh with his lines, but they'll be close enough to be usable with some editing.

You can use Decorgal's new Sims 2 hacks to improve his talking, too. (See the earlier section "Checking Out The Sims Disadvantages.")

1. **Set up a good close-up on your lead character and save it as Shot 4 in the same way you've saved the other shots.**

   See the earlier section on static shots.

2. **Select your lead character as the active sim, if he isn't already.**

3. **Click the couch, select Sit, and then click The Sims 2 Studio box.**

   You get a huge series of menus here — this box offers dozens of animation options. Pause the game with P, select TS2 Studios, select Talk, select Stand or Sit (most animations require the lead character to stand up, but these don't), and then select Talk You.

4. **Tab back into camera mode, press 4 to get your shot back, and press V to record, then 1 to start the game playing.**

5. **Watch the animation, give it another couple of seconds of the lead character sitting there, and stop recording.**

The Sims 2 Studio is an example of an add-on, downloaded from the Internet. A number of filming tools are available for The Sims 2, as well as hundreds of new sets, new characters, and new props. Check out a site like `http://modthesims2.com` to browse some of the vast selection available.

# Creating Character Interaction

Want your lead character to look over his shoulder, as though someone else is knocking on his door? This is one of the tricks you can use as a Machinima filmmaker to make your characters do your evil bidding.

For this interaction, you need another Sim for your character to look at. And, handily, for a film, you need to invite all your Sims over anyway.

1. **Go to Build mode and create a box on the lot, with four walls and no door.**

   You'll use this box to ensure that your extras can't get away once they've arrived! Think of it as . . . you know . . . an unusually restrictive trailer.

2. **Shift+Click the mailbox and choose Invite All Neighbors.**

   Wait a little bit. All the neighbors will show up en masse — in this case, all your extras.

3. **Go to Buy mode, enable the `MoveObjects` cheat (see "Adding game cheats") and drag all the extras apart from one into the Box Of No Escape you created in Step 1.**

   They'll be fine. Turn off the sound if their crying disturbs you. No, seriously.

4. **Drag one of your extras into the set, Shift+Click on him, and then choose Make Selectable from the menu.**

   Sometimes this command is under "More" on the menu, for no apparent reason, so if you don't see it on the first screen, don't panic.

5. **Click your extra's portrait.**

   Bang! You're controlling him, and his picture appears at the bottom of the screen.

6. **Click next to your lead character, sitting on the PC, and select Go To.**

   Your extra walks toward your lead character — but will remain out of your shot, with any luck — and your lead will look at him. However, there's a problem.

7. **Select Go To, skip into Camera mode with Tab, and press 4.**

   Your lead looks up — but he looks awfully happy about it. That's great if he's greeting someone he likes, but dammit, this is drama, and drama is about conflict! We want him to look irritated. So, we need to irritate him.

8. **Go back to Live Mode, click your lead while controlling your extra, select More, and then select — yes — Irritate.**

9. **Choose one of the options here and enjoy the fun.**

   Your extra will proceed to — well, irritate — your lead actor.

10. **Repeat Steps 9 and 10 a few more times, and your star won't be smiling any more when Mr. Extra comes a'visiting.**

Machinima is all about using the features of the game in a creative way, and the shot described in the preceding steps is a perfect example of that. If you run into a problem in Machinima filming, brainstorm as many ways as possible around it using the features of the game. Don't be afraid to try silly ideas — they're quite likely to work!

# Case Study: The Snow Witch

Michelle Pettit-Mee and Kheri Batal met face to face for the first time in 2006, in the online world of "The Sims Online." By that time, they'd already been working together for three years, entirely online, and had quickly established themselves as one of the most pioneering Sims 2 Machinima-making teams in the world.

When the two started telling stories using The Sims 2, neither of them had even heard of Machinima. They had no professional film training and lived thousands of miles apart — Michelle in the UK and Kheri in the United States.

Under the name Brittanica Dreams, Kheri and Michelle have produced success after success, from the moving *Highwayman* to the beautiful *Mermaid's Tale*. But their most ambitious and arguably most successful production has been the short film *The Snow Witch,* an interpretation of an old Japanese ghost story, which you can find on the DVD.

Following are Kheri and Michelle's top tips for The Sims 2:

- ✔ Don't expect it be easy. Making a movie in The Sims 2 is a heavy technical achievement.

- ✔ Use the game's animations in nonstandard ways. To make the Snow Witch bend over, Kheri and Michelle used a custom mod to trigger the browse store shelves animation from the Sims 2 Open For Business expansion pack.

- ✔ It may not be cheap. Expect to splash out on a decent video-editing suite like Vegas Video at the very minimum.

- ✔ Download high-quality skins to improve your film. Brittanica Dreams used custom, high-detail skin textures for The Snow Witch, downloaded from Sims 2 mod sites like www.modthesims2.com, to add a sense of realism to their otherwise mildly cartoon-like appearance.

- ✔ Know the game inside-out. Learn all the animations and interactions. Kheri and Michelle played the game for several hours a day for almost nine months before they started making movies with it. Every time a new expansion pack is released, they have to spend time learning that, too.

- ✔ Make use of the in-game cheats and hacks. In particular, don't be afraid to use the boolprop cheat. You just won't manage without it.

- ✔ Get really nit-picky about set building. You've got to spend some time on it — it's a big part of the finished product. There's nothing worse than a movie with a set the size of a football pitch, with nothing but a single sofa right in the center.

- ✔ Use the lighting hacks available online and the Radiance lighting that's available.

- ✔ Watch as many Sims 2 movies as you can to see what other people have been able to achieve.

# Chapter 9

# Get Out the Scissors: Editing Machinima

## In This Chapter

▶ Using Vegas Video to edit your Machinima

▶ Importing clips

▶ Adding transitions and sound

▶ Exploring editing techniques

▶ Editing specific styles of scene

*Y*our hard drive is straining at the screws with all the footage you've recorded for your groundbreaking new Machinima movie. You've got at least five different takes for each shot, and you also filmed a few seconds of the sun shining through the trees because the lens flare was so darn pretty. You've just *got* to put that in somewhere.

So, how do you take all this disparate footage and turn it into a slick, narratively coherent movie? It's time to start editing.

In this chapter's examples, we use Sony Vegas Movie Studio 6.0. You can find a trial version of this program on the book's DVD, but the techniques we cover here are equally applicable to most similar video-editing packages.

## Understanding What You're Achieving with Your Edits

In its simplest form, *editing* is merely the process of stringing together all the bits of footage that you've recorded, thereby creating one long piece of footage that you can then call a movie. In practice, though, there's far more to video editing than that.

You'll need to shorten some clips and outright discard others. You'll be making pass after iterative pass over your video edit, tightening all the time. Eventually, you'll use advanced editing techniques to tell part of your story purely by composing and contrasting different clips in a specific order.

Most scenes have a similar structure. In general, you need to achieve the following things in your edit.

- **Tell the audience what's going on and where.** Obviously, this goal is vital. It's easy to believe, as the filmmaker, that your audience will know the layout of your scene, just like you do. But that Just Ain't True. You need to show details both large (epic, sweeping landscape) and small (gun in a desk drawer) at the appropriate time for the audience to follow your story.

- **Show the audience cool stuff.** Don't underestimate this step. If you've got a fantastic visual, a great vista, a neat animation, or a tense moment, make sure that the audience sees it! Baz Luhrmann and Peter Jackson are both masters of this sort of editing. But don't let your visuals get in the way of the story.

- **Tell the audience what your characters are thinking.** You need to direct your audience's eye and suggest where your characters are looking, what they're thinking, and what they're aware of.

- **Tell your audience what to expect.** If something important is about to happen, you must make sure that your audience is in the appropriate mindset for it — either expecting it, or really not expecting it!

- **Control the movie's pace.** A movie is like a piece of music. No two pieces will have an identical tempo. Some will be fast and furious, some slow and melodic. But consciously controlling and crafting that tempo is one of the editor's most vital functions. An audience will get bored with a random or monotonous pace to a movie.

- **Tell the audience what the director thinks is important.** To a considerable extent, the edit and camerawork combine to form the editorial of a film. It's here that you can craft a theme or a mood, from David Lynch's sparking electrics and deep woods to John Woo's slow-motion doves. Think about what the style of the action in *Aliens* says compared to what *Rambo's* style says about the director's vision for what's important in his world.

- **Don't bore anyone!** And this is the first and greatest commandment of the editor: Bore not the crap out of your audience. If you ever wonder what you're doing here, just remember this: You're here to put the shots in the right order and cut out the boring bits.

If anything is boring, not vital, not adding anything to the movie, be it a half-second pause or a five-minute scene, chop it!

# *Figuring Out How to Edit*

Editing is a very intuitive process. If you've watched many films or much television, you'll quickly pick up the process. Add some basic knowledge of film language, and you'll have very few problems editing your movie together.

In general, the editing process for a Machinima film comprises five phases:

1. **Assemble your footage.**

   When you start editing, you're faced with an intimidating pile of footage. Your first task is, quite simply, to trim out all the obvious rubbish and put your shots in the right order.

   Start at Shot 1, cut it down to size, drop it into the timeline, and on to Shot 2. Try to cut as tight as possible, but don't obsess over the right sequence just yet.

2. **Fine edit your movie.**

   Now you start from the beginning of the movie and preview it in your editing package. Every time you see something that's not perfect, stop previewing, go into the edit, tighten it or alter it to make it better, and then watch it again.

   When it's perfect, or as close as possible, move on to the next part of the film. It's at this point that you should be adding fades, dissolves, and necessary effects.

   It's possible to simply stop after this stage — and many Machinima productions do. This is a huge mistake. The next few steps will make the difference between an okay, slow film, and a great production.

3. **Preview.**

   Find some friends who haven't been involved in your film, preferably people who aren't particularly familiar with Machinima and hence won't excuse its limitations. Sit them down in front of a complete copy of your fine edit. Now give them all paper and pencils and ask them to watch it and make notes about anything they don't like, don't understand, or think can be improved.

   Do the same yourself at the same time. We warn you now, you'll suddenly realize that your allegedly perfect edit is nothing of the kind. Collect their comments, then figure out how to fix the problems you find.

4. **Pickup shots.**

   Some problems you've found in Step 3 will probably require new shots to fix. Shoot these now.

**5. Conduct a final edit.**

Take your notes and your new shots and edit the film again. Depending on how many problems you discovered in your fine edit, you may need to do another preview now and repeat Steps 3 through 5 again. Otherwise, congratulations. You've got a finished film!

# Getting Started with Vegas Video

The Vegas Video editing package (see Figure 9-1) is an excellent all-rounder.

To start a new project, follow these steps:

**1. Run Vegas Video.**

**2. Close the dialog box and choose File⇨New.**

**3. In the dialog box that appears, click the "Match Media Settings" button.**

If you want your final movie to have the same settings as a file already on your computer, you can just check this box and select this file in the next dialog box; Vegas automatically sets up your project to match it.

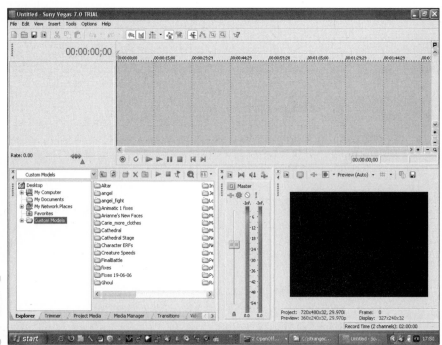

**Figure 9-1:**
Vegas
Video.

4. **Give your project a name and choose a location on your hard drive to store all the files that Vegas creates; then click Next.**

5. **Click OK.**

# Importing a Clip

Before you start editing, you need to have something to edit! Fortunately, you can easily add a Machinima clip to your Vegas project. Simply choose File⇨ Import⇨Media and, in the Import dialog box import the clips you want to edit. Once a clip has been added to the project, it appears in the Project Media tab on the bottom half of the screen. You can use the clip multiple times in different places, if you want.

# Adding a Clip to the Video Track

To start editing, you need to move a clip onto the main editing track. This track is sequence of video clips, all timed to a single timeline above, which eventually becomes your film.

Import a clip and drag it from Project Media to the main window. (If you're not sure how to import a clip, see the preceding section.) Notice that the audio from the imported clip is automatically added as a second track.

# Trimming a Clip

One of the things that you'll be doing most often during the editing process is *trimming* a clip: removing excess material from the start and the end of a piece of footage to leave just the essential parts.

There's a very simple rule for all but the most expert editor: Once you've chopped your scene down as tight as you think it can possibly go, it'll be even better if you cut another 10 percent.

There's always junk in there.

Here are some prime candidates for the chopping block:

✔ **Shoe-leather shots:** Audiences are smart. If they see someone getting into a car, they can figure out how he got to the front door in the next scene. In fact, they can figure it out if they just see him heading toward a car. Anytime all you're showing is how someone or something got from A to B, you can cut it.

- ✔ **Awkward pauses:** Just because it sounded great in the recording studio doesn't mean it'll sound good with visuals. Anytime the pace of a conversation drags or a pause feels unnaturally long, cut it down.

- ✔ **Nasty Machinima clunks:** Your engine will have its own quirks. Some engines can't have a character turn around without a second of foot-skating first. Perhaps your engine's facial animation works like treacle for the first second, or there's a short delay before scripts run. Cut it out. Trim it, chop it, cut away from it. There's no better way to make a film feel like a game than to include all the clunky game animation.

- ✔ **Dodgy script moments:** If the script doesn't feel right in the edit, trust the edit, not the script. Lines, actions, even entire scenes can cheerfully come out if they don't work. A classic example is the zero-advance beat: If a script beat ends up with the situation not changing at all, you can drop it with no problems.

Fortunately, Vegas has a separate editing window for trimming clips, called (usefully) the Trimmer:

1. **Right-click a clip on the Project Media tab and choose Open In Trimmer.**

2. **Click and drag the small yellow arrow at the top left of the trimmer window to define a selection.**

   You can click and drag the start or end of this section to the exact frame you want — the preview window at the right updates to show the currently selected frame.

3. **Once you've highlighted the part of the clip that you want, just drag it to the timeline.**

   Notice that the original clip remains unchanged. You can reuse it (in whole or in part) by performing exactly the same process.

Don't be afraid to be ruthless when you're trimming clips. The snappier your footage, the better your movie will flow.

# Adding Transitions

One of the things that will set your movie above the pack is good transition editing. A *transition* is a change between one screen and another, or even just the change from one shot to the next. Fades, dissolves, and more obvious (some would say cheesier) effects are all transitions.

Inexperienced editors almost always overuse transitions. Only when you're absolutely certain you need a different transition should you use anything other than a simple cut. Here are the most common forms of transition and their uses:

- ✔ **Cut:** Used in 99 percent of all transitions. A cut from one camera angle to another implies continued action, with no passing time between the last shot and the current one, even if the cut is between two different sets.

  Sometimes a cut will appear jarring, usually because there's too small a difference between the shots, or because you've made a filmic mistake (see Chapter 4). This is referred to as a *Jump cut* and is sometimes useful as a deliberate choice, but usually needs to be fixed with pickup shots or an alternate edit.

- ✔ **Fade:** The next most common transition, usually a fade to and from a black screen. A fade implies the passing of time; a fade-out followed by a fade-in is usually used to signal the start of a new scene. In TV, a fade-out is also used before an ad break, and hence shows that were originally TV format will sometimes fade out on a cliffhanger and then fade in again at the same location.

- ✔ **Dissolve:** One shot dissolves straight into another. A dissolve forms a bridge between two disparate shots; it can be used where it's not obvious that two shots are in the same location, to bridge time in the same way as a fade, or to fix a jump cut.

- ✔ **Wipe:** One shot is very obviously wiped over another, either from a single direction or in a geometric shape. George Lucas's *Star Wars* uses wipes extensively to mimic the style of the '30s pulps. A wipe is a very obvious, almost crass, transition and is usually used only to make a stylistic point.

- ✔ **Invisible wipe:** An object moving across the screen can signal an invisible wipe, where what follows the object appears to be a continuation of the shot but is actually a different shot altogether. *The West Wing* and *Buffy the Vampire Slayer* both use the invisible wipe all the time. This technique is handy for Machinima, but obviously requires two shots specifically set up with this goal in mind.

- ✔ **Other transitions — 3D boxes, shaped dissolves, and all that nonsense:** Editing packages generally come with a package of a hundred or so cute transitions: expanding hearts, peeling pages, nifty 3D effects, and so on. You should only use them if you're being ironic (à la *Wayne's World*), if you have a very specific idea that you're absolutely certain about, if you're a far more experienced editor than your humble authors, or if you want your film to look like a badly edited wedding video.

Vegas automates much of the transitioning process. If you add two clips to a single track, for example, and move the right clip so that it overlaps the left clip, Vegas automatically creates a dissolve transition for you.

You can also create a fade in or out for a single clip on the Vegas tracks:

1. **Move your cursor to the top-left corner of the clip until the cursor changes to an arc shape.**

2. **Click and drag to the right.**

   The further you drag, the longer your fade-in will last. You can see a curve appear to indicate the range of the transition.

3. **Repeat this process at the end of the clip to create a fade-out.**

With Vegas (and most similar editing packages), you can apply a fade to either the video or the audio channel of a clip, which lets you treat each aspect of the clip separately.

Try starting the audio of a clip a few frames before the visuals fade in. This teasing technique is good for grabbing the viewer's attention for the first few seconds of a new scene.

If your audience will notice a transition, then the transition is probably too extreme. Tone it down or cut it altogether. Not all section changes need a transition to frame them.

---

# Creating other transitions

We warned you, but you just couldn't stay away, could you? Very well. It's your movie. Before we go any further, though, we must insist that you sign this waver, solemnly swearing to only use your powers of transition for good, and never to exploit an innocent piece of footage just for your own selfish pleasures. Sign here. And here. And initial here. Thank you.

Without further ado, then, we present: Hugh And Johnnie's Crazy Transition Show!

1. **Position two clips that will feature the transition on the track before applying the transition.**

   Move the right clip so that it overlaps the other clip. Vegas automatically applies a dissolve transition.

2. **Click the Transitions tab at the bottom of the window and choose a fun-looking transition.**

   We particularly like *Spin Away* under *3d Fly In/Out*, but it's up to you.

3. **Drag the transition from the transition window and position it over the dissolve that Vegas created for you.**

   Your chosen transition replaces the cross-fade.

4. **Close the Transition Editing window that appears unless you want to make any changes to the default transition.**

There. See the damage you've done? Are you happy now?

# *Working with Sound*

You can add an audio track to your Vegas project in exactly the same way that you added your movie clips. (See the section "Adding a Clip to the Video Track," earlier in this chapter, for more information.) Simply choose File⇨Import⇨Media and choose an audio file. You can now add and adjust this clip independently in the Vegas editing window.

If you import a video clip, chances are that it will provide its own audio track. When you drag the clip to the track, the audio will be imported onto one of Vegas' audio tracks as well. You can't just delete this audio — it's grouped with the video clip, so deleting one deletes both.

If you want to delete it, right-click either the audio or video clip and then choose Group⇨Remove From (or press *U*). This action separates the audio and video, which you can then move or delete independently.

# *Speeding Up or Slowing Down a Clip*

Time-stretching, or *slow motion,* is a handy tactic that can add emphasis or emotive overtones to a sequence when used correctly.

A slo-mo effect (and we promise never to use that phrase again) can be achieved by artificially stretching a clip during the editing process. Vegas makes stretching a clip a one-click process.

Hover your mouse cursor over the end of a clip and hold down the Ctrl key. The cursor changes to include a wave symbol. Click and drag the end of the clip to the right (while still holding down Ctrl). Voilá: A time-stretched clip.

## Emo slo-mo

Try altering the speed of short but significant shots to increase the emotive impact: for example, slow a shot of the main characters walking toward the camera on their way to the final confrontation; or the hero spotting a child crossing the road but reacting too late to stop the car. Likewise, speed up some shots, like a character turning their head toward the sound of a noise, to increase urgency.

# *Adding Title Sequence or Credits*

If you want any credit for your project, want to thank other people, or even want your audience to know what your movie's called, you need titles.

You can use the Media Generators tab at the bottom of the screen (see Figure 9-2) to add text to your project.

Here are a couple of points to consider when adding text:

✔ Choose Text to add a single line of text as an overlay to the video footage. You can use this to add *X-Files*–like location information or to add subtitles to a piece of dialog that is spoken in a different language. Make sure that the track containing your text is on top of all your other tracks.

✔ You can add credits at the end of your movie by using Vegas' *Credit Roll* plug-in. Select Credit Roll from the Media Generators tab. Drag one of the preconfigured credit rolls to the end of your project. You can add text and credits one line at a time in the properties box that appears.

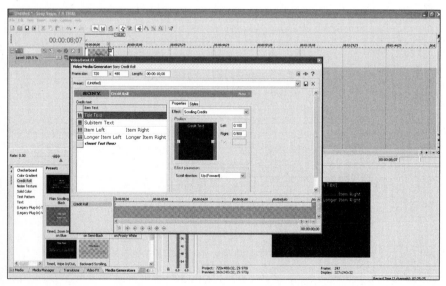

**Figure 9-2:**
Using the
Media
Generator
in Vegas.

# Rendering Video

Once your movie is ready, you'll want to render it into a viewable format. Nobody can watch it right now unless they also have a copy of Vegas (or whichever video editor you've used). Here's what you need to do:

1. **Choose File⇨ Render As.**

2. **Make sure that Save As Type is set to Video For Windows (\*.avi), and click Custom.**

   The Project tab of the Custom Template Window appears.

3. **From the template drop-down menu, select Default Template (uncompressed).**

4. **Turn off "Render loop region only" and click OK.**

5. **Give your movie file a name and click Save.**

   Vegas renders out your completed movie file. Be aware that this is an uncompressed video file, and as such, is very, very large (approximately 1GB per minute for NTSC format). You're done.

Obviously you can't upload a multi-gigabyte video to YouTube! See Chapter 10 to learn how to compress and distribute your movie.

# Identifying New Shots

After editing, most directors find that they're missing some shots that would enable them to polish their movie. If you're shooting in real life, refilming is a pain, as you've often lost your actors or have blown up the key props.

In Machinima, though, it's not a problem. Whenever you're editing, you should be looking for new shots that would improve your edit. Trust your gut: Any time you're looking at a shot sequence and it's disappointing, try to consider what shots would make it better, smoother, or easier to follow.

Pick-up shots are particularly useful for clearing up confusing points in a film. An extra wide shot or a close-up of a character interacting with a prop can make the meaning of a shot obvious.

# Editing an Action Sequence

*Action sequences* — anything from a fight to a chase sequence, where the key elements are violent action and speed — are among the most challenging sequences to edit, particularly in Machinima, where you'll often be covering for weaknesses in the engine or in the actors' reactive abilities.

Remember these key points when you're editing an action sequence:

- ✔ **Keep the action coming.** Action sequences are really, really fast. Make sure that you've cut your shots down to the bone, and there's no waiting around, no moments where the characters are bobbing up and down waiting to do something, and generally no pauses. Shots will often be a second long or even less.

- ✔ **Tell a story within a story.** A successful action sequence is a story within a story. Can Bond tackle the bad guy before he leaps off the crane? Yes, but now he is hanging from his fingertips while the bad guy stomps on him!

  If there's no story, there's no interest. See Chapter 4 for more on story.

- ✔ **Remember — action, then reaction.** The edit for an action sequence often follows the pattern Action (wide), Action (close), Reaction from a character. Reaction shots humanize the sequence (so that we care about what's happening to the characters) and allow you to slow the action for a moment as characters react to the latest development.

- ✔ **Shoot wide, close, very close.** Don't sit in one distance of shot, either wide, which can make the action feel distant and static, or close, which can be confusing. A well-framed action sequence has an even mixture of intense close-ups and jaw-dropping wide shots, so that the audience can both feel a part of the action and see it clearly.

- ✔ **Speed is your friend.** Changes of speed are your friend in an action sequence. Slow motion is almost vital, particularly during impacts, and sped-up footage can be helpful to tighten slow game engine animations.

- ✔ **Reshoots happen.** You'll probably not get your action sequence right the first time you film it. Pickup shots are your friend — use them liberally.

# Editing a Conversation

Conversational editing is a comparatively simple and pleasurable job as an editor. If the script works and the actors are on-form, it should take vastly less time to edit a conversation than a more visual sequence.

- ✔ **Trim mercilessly.** Particularly in Machinima, pauses are your enemy. Once you've gone through your initial edit, watch it again with a critical eye. Any time the sequence seems to drag even for a moment, cut something. There will be lots of pauses that sounded great in the voice recording session that now drag the film down. (For more on trimming, see the section "Trimming a Clip," earlier in this chapter.)

- ✔ **Don't be afraid to edit the script.** Video editing is, in many ways, the final phase of script editing. Kill any bits of your script that aren't fitting or that are slowing the story down. If a line isn't necessary, cut it. If the sequence would work better in a different order, try that order instead.

- ✔ **Don't use too many angles.** In a conversational scene, the camerawork should be unobtrusive. You'll probably use only three to four shots (one wide and either one medium or close for each actor, or perhaps a two-shot) for each stage of the conversation. If the camera jumps around, it'll distract from the content.

- ✔ **Your Machinima characters can't act.** Unlike a live film director, you can't really just let an actor's performance carry the moment. Your audience will get bored watching your characters, even in the tensest of verbal confrontations. Cut to a wide shot or a reaction shot as needed.

- ✔ **Don't always watch the speaker.** Just because a character is speaking doesn't mean that the camera has to be on them. Particularly if your engine has good facial animation, cut to reaction shots and don't cut away for every quick interjection.

Play around with the times you cut in. Cut in on a significant phrase or cut away to a reaction shot. Your editing will feel more organic and natural.

# Editing a Romantic Sequence

Hoo, boy. You're not going easy on yourself, are you? Romance is . . . how can we put this? . . . nontrivial in Machinima. Our actors' lack of expression make romantic scenes hard, hard, hard. And not in a euphemistic way. Having said that, here are some tips that can make your scenes more slushy:

- ✔ **Kuleshov is your friend.** The *Kuleshov effect* is a vital part of Machinima, and no more so than in romantic scenes. Lev Kuleshov was one of the pioneers of filmmaking, before World War I. He proved that an audience would attribute thoughts to a static character if shots of him were interleaved with shots of other objects. Man followed by baby, tender thoughts; man followed by gun, violent thoughts. We can use this technique to get around our limitations in Machinima. Shots of roses, hands intertwining, and then back to a shot of your protagonist's face — all help imply emotion.

✔ **Soft transitions.** It's a bit '80s Meatloaf video, but cross-dissolves soften the sequence. If a cut feels a bit brutal, try a dissolve instead.

✔ **Take it slow.** Most romantic scenes contain a good chunk of suspense. Take your time here. Cut back to a wide, cut to a shot of downcast eyes, but give yourself plenty of time. At the same time, be ruthless in cutting out anything that reduces rather than contributes to the mood you're trying to set.

# Editing a Suspense Sequence

There are a lot more scenes that rely on suspense in most films, particularly even vaguely action films, than is immediately apparent. Look over your favorite action movie — *Aliens, Lord of the Rings, Star Wars, The Matrix,* whatever — and notice how much time is spent on people creeping around, people waiting for something to happen, slow zooms with violins playing.

Editing a suspense sequence is very visual, and quite difficult. These pointers should help you out:

✔ **No, you can give it longer.** If you've become used to tightening your visuals on almost every other strand of editing, you'll almost certainly not leave enough time in your suspense sequences. Just keep cutting to more build-up of suspense: hands on weapons, gritted teeth, reaction shots, shadows slowly creeping along the floor, whatever.

✔ **Come in.** Generally, you can build suspense by starting from a wide shot and getting gradually closer and more personal with each shot from there on. Look at the classic Western shootout sequence to see how this technique works.

✔ **Focus group it.** It's very hard to tell whether you've gone far enough, not far enough, or too far, particularly on a suspense sequence. Show it to some people who aren't involved with your project. They'll give you much better feedback than you can give yourself.

# Chapter 10

# Fifteen Minutes of Fame: Distributing Your Movie

*In This Chapter*

▶ Encoding video for the Internet

▶ Distributing your movie online

▶ Making your movie available as streaming and downloadable video

*A*fter you make your movie, you'll probably want to distribute it, probably either via Internet downloads or DVDs. In this chapter, we tell you everything you need to successfully distribute your masterpiece.

# Codecs, Codecs Every . . . What?

Isn't a *codec* the thing the Pope carries around with him? No, no, wait, it's a big book with laws in. No, it's Superman!

Okay, for real now. *Codec* is a portmanteau word, compressed (appropriately enough) from Encoder/Decoder. It refers to a piece of software that compresses or uncompresses audio or video content. A good codec compresses an audio or video file, making the file size noticeably smaller, without a perceptible loss of quality. It accomplishes this goal primarily by discarding excess audio information in ranges that are almost undetectable to the human eye or ear. Probably the best-known codec of all is the MP3 audio codec from Fraunhofer, beloved of music lovers everywhere (and when we say music lovers, we mean, of course, "Yaarr! Run up the mainsail, you scurvy dogs! Avast!").

So, essentially, a codec is just a glorified Zip program. But because these codecs deal with specific types of data, and data that'll be fed to a human rather than a machine, they can achieve compressions vastly better than any normal compression program — which is good, because video data, in particular, is absolutely huge.

An uncompressed episode of Strange Company's *BloodSpell* is about 13,000MB. After we compress it with DivX, it's down to 70MB with very little perceptible loss in quality.

Why do you need to know all this stuff? Because you're eventually going to want to distribute your movie, and to do that, you need to get it down to a reasonable size, most likely for other people to download it, but perhaps to put it on a DVD.

# Video Formats

Videos don't just come in a variety of compression technologies; they also come in different *video formats*. Where a codec is a way of compressing video, a *format* is a way of saying how that video data is then stored and what programs can read it. Just like word processor files, different video formats are readable in different programs — Word can't read OpenOffice.org files (something our editor is no doubt cursing quite literally as we write), and Windows Media Player can't read QuickTime files.

You need to be aware of three popular video formats: QuickTime, AVI, and Windows Media.

## QuickTime

QuickTime is the oldest of the current video formats, initially released in May 1991 by Apple. Since then, it has been the main Mac video codec, with some support on Windows via the Windows QuickTime player and most editing packages. It's the primary editing format for the Avid video editors in particular. QuickTime files are also sometimes called MOV files, because the file extension for QuickTime is .mov.

You can download the latest version of the QuickTime software , which you need to play QuickTime files, from www.quicktime.com. If you're on a Mac, you've probably got it already.

So, if you're on a PC, why would you care about QuickTime? Well, there are three reasons:

- ✔ Mac users have a real time of it trying to play any other video format. A savvy Mac user can do it but it's hard and requires them to use slightly unreliable software. You'll lose a lot of your Mac audience if you don't have a downloadable QuickTime version available.

- ✔ At time of writing, QuickTime is winning the compression wars. The H.264 codec offered in QuickTime 7 takes about half the age of the earth to encode, but offers the best quality for downloadable video currently out there.

✔ QuickTime is the de facto standard for professional video. AVID and Final Cut Pro, the two most used professional-editing packages, both use QuickTime. So if you end up working with TV, you'll have to get used to it, just like you'll need to get used to spiky gelled hair, ironic thick black rims on glasses, and perky assistant producers called Debbie.

If you want to output QuickTime video, you probably need to invest in QuickTime Pro from Apple, for $30 — anyone who was wondering why QuickTime isn't as omnipresent as AVI or WMV, you now know why. A free, open-source alternative called FFMPEG (`http://ffmpeg.mplayerhq.hu`) can encode QuickTime, but it's command-line based, quite limited, and definitely not for beginners.

In QuickTime 7, by far the best choice for video compression is called H.264. It comes with two options — either fast encode, which is approximately comparable in compression speed to DivX, or best quality, which is, uh, slower. A lot slower. We're not talking put the kettle on here so much as prepare a three-course meal to Michelin standards. A five-minute *BloodSpell* episode takes approximately three hours to encode at Best Quality on our MacBook Pro.

If you're super-worried about compatibility, you can also encode with Sorensen 3, another, older codec, but the quality will be noticeably worse and the size noticeably larger.

# AVI

Originally introduced by Microsoft in 1992 as a response to QuickTime, Audio Video Interleave (AVI) is the main Windows video format, much as Microsoft would like to change that. These days, Microsoft has moved on to WMV, and AVI is mostly supported and extended by third-party developers. It's probably the most widely used, hacked, and developed-for format in the world.

On a PC, Windows Media Player can play AVI by default. However, you will still need to install the appropriate codec for the video you're viewing. On a Mac, you need to download VLC (`www.videolan.org/vlc`) to be able to play AVI files.

To be honest, you may as well download it if you're on a PC, too — VLC is a cross-platform piece of software that plays most common AVI codecs without needing them to be installed separately, and many people prefer the user interface to that of Windows Media Player.

AVI is by far the simplest video format to play on Linux. VLC comes in Linux flavor, too, although plenty of other excellent media players are out there for the Linux platform.

The chances are that any video you capture on a PC will be captured in AVI format. Because all PCs can play AVI format, it's really a no-brainer to have an AVI version available.

The absolute best tool for any kind of AVI encoding — and arguably the best video-encoding tool available short of $500, anywhere — is VirtualDub, which you can download from www.virtualdub.org. This free, open-source, powerhouse of video-encoding potential allows you to resize, reformat, and generally mess around with your video to your heart's content.

All modern AVI codecs are developed by third parties and downloaded from the Internet. Windows comes with some older AVI codecs, but with the exception of Uncompressed Video, which isn't really a codec at all, none of the standard Windows codecs are of any use these days.

The codec of choice for the modern downloader is DivX, available from DivX.com. There's a good chance that you've already heard of the DivX codec and perhaps installed it, as it's the No. 1 codec for, ahem, redistributing video via peer-to-peer programs like EMule and BitTorrent. (Hey, we're not judging. Just remember that Piracy With Violence is still punishable by hanging in the UK, so whatever you do, don't punch anyone while you're BitTorrenting the latest episode of Heroes.)

From our oh-so-legal point of view, many or most of your viewers will already have the DivX codec installed and can watch your video without having to install DivX first. Some won't, though, which means that they'll either have to download DivX before they can watch your movie or watch an alternative version like WMV.

DivX is very definitely a commercial product these days, and the free version is slightly limited. For most people, it will be fine, but if you need more power without price, you can use an open-source equivalent called XVid, which you can download ready-to-run for Windows from www.koepi.org/xvid.shtml.

## *WMV*

Windows Media Video (WMV) is the new(ish), more or less closed and proprietary Windows Media format for video. Technically, WMV video is actually video in Microsoft's Advanced Systems Format (ASF) using WMV codecs, but frankly, no one cares.

There are basically only two reasons for using WMV.

- ✔ It gives comparable compression to video formats like DivX, meaning it's a decent video format for downloaded videos.
- ✔ Everyone with a PC running Windows XP or Vista can play it by default.

The second reason's the biggie. Unlike DivX or QuickTime, all modern Windows PCs can play WMV with no additional software needed. Macs can play WMV, too, using the MS WMV Player, although it's a headache to get it to work. (It took Hugh about an hour to get his MacBook Pro to play WMV, as opposed to about five minutes for AVI.) Needless to say, because WMV is controlled by Microsoft, it can be an absolute pain in the proverbial to play it under Linux.

You can create WMV files using the free Windows Media Encoder, download-able from `www.microsoft.com/windows/windowsmedia/forpros/encoder/default.mspx`. There's no question of choosing codecs here — the WMV codec is the only one available — so it's a fairly simple process to encode.

# Thinking about Bitrates

All the codecs mentioned in the preceding sections are based loosely on the MPEG-4 standard, developed by the Moving Picture Experts Group.

MPEG-4 controls the size of files produced by means of a single variable: the bitrate of the file. This single number represents the maximum number of bits allowed per second of the video. It's usually expressed in terms of kilobits or megabits per second (Kbps or Mbps, like Internet connection speeds).

Now, as we're sure you can dimly recall from years-old computer science classes, 8 bits are in a byte, and 1,024 bytes are in a kilobyte, and so on. So, by remembering these numbers, you have a relatively simple way to control the size of your video: Choose the size you'd like your end file to be in bytes, multiply that number by 8, divide it by the length of your movie in seconds, and you've got your target bitrate.

Whether the movie is viewable or indeed identifiable at your chosen bitrate is another question, and this is where the black magic of bitrate estimation comes in. You need to choose the smallest possible bitrate, based on your codec, format, and the size and content of your video, that will give an acceptable level of quality while keeping files as small as possible.

How do you do that? Well, here at Strange Company, we use a highly techni-cal process called 'guessing'. No hard-and-fast rules allow you to determine your optimal bitrate. You can start from a rough guess (for example, we knew that around 1000 Kbps normal PAL video looks pretty good), but after that, the best way to find an optimal bitrate is as follows:

1. **Find the ten-second clip of your movie that contains the most action, color contrast, and precise detail and export it as an uncompressed video.**

2. **Run this video off as one of your target formats (DivX AVI is usually fastest) at a variety of bitrates — say, 500 Kbps, 600 Kbps, and so on up to 1500 Kbps, as an example.**

3. **Watch the videos, from the lowest bitrate to the highest, and choose the bitrate that gives the best balance of size and quality.**

For the rest of the chapter, we use the standard BloodSpell bitrate, which is 800 Kbps at 800x450 using 2006 video technology. But it's really up to you to determine the bitrate that will suit your movie, particularly if you're releasing in high definition or something similar.

The good news is that bitrates don't differ much across the various video formats. We used 800 Kbps for QuickTime, AVI, and WMV.

## Encoding Your Video

Assuming that you've got your final movie available in uncompressed video AVI format, and you've installed programs to encode either QuickTime, AVI, or WMV, the following sections walk you through encoding your video down to a final downloadable movie in each of the three main formats.

We recommend always making your movie available in each format. However, if you don't want to pay $30 for QuickTime Pro, you can just do AVI and WMV. You may also want to consider making different sizes of movie available, but, in our testing of *BloodSpell,* we found that very few people would download anything but the highest-quality format!

## QuickTime

You need your version of QuickTime Pro installed. To encode your uncompressed video into a final downloadable movie:

1. **In QuickTime, choose File⇨Open File and open your AVI file.**

2. **Choose File⇨Export and select a name and location for your finished file.**

   The Save Exported File As dialog box appears.

3. **Select Movie To QuickTime Movie from the Export drop-down list**

4. **Click Options.**

   You see the Movie Settings dialog box, shown in Figure 10-1.

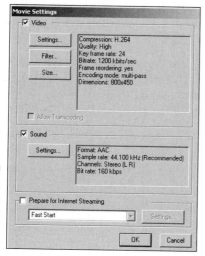

**Figure 10-1:**
The Movie
Settings
dialog box.

5. **Select both Video and Sound.**

6. **Click Settings.**

   The Standard Video Compression Settings dialog box appears, as shown in Figure 10-2.

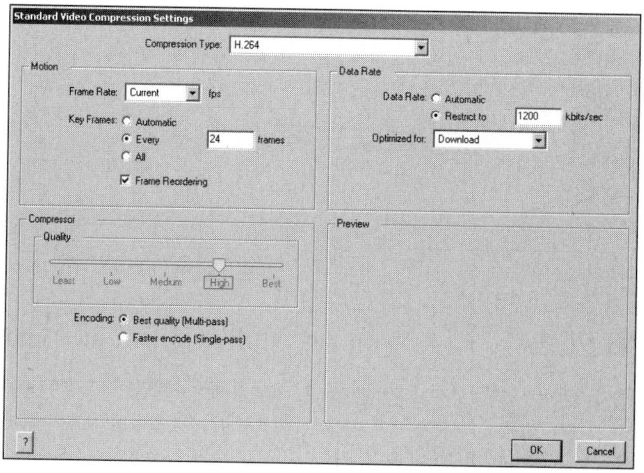

**Figure 10-2:**
The Standard Video Compression Settings dialog box.

7. **From the Compression Type drop-down list, select H.264.**

8. **From the Frame Rate drop-down list, select Current.**

9. **Select the Restrict To radio button under Data Rate and set the number to 800.**

   This number is the bitrate of the finished movie.

10. **Under Encoding, select Fast Encode and click OK.**

    Or, select Best Quality if you're not doing anything for the next few hours, or you really want the best possible quality (say, if you're about to release your movie to the big wide world).

    The Movie Settings dialog box reappears.

11. **Click the Size button.**

    The Export Size Settings dialog box appears.

12. **From the Dimensions drop-down list, select Current and then click OK.**

    The Movie Settings dialog box reappears. You're nearly there!

13. **In the Sounds area, click the Settings button.**

    The Sound Settings dialog box, shown in Figure 10-3, appears.

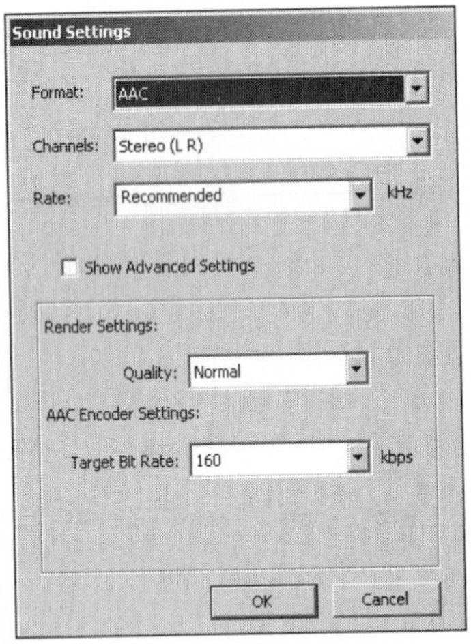

**Figure 10-3:**
The Sound
Settings
dialog box.

14. **In the Format drop-down list, select AAC.**

15. **From the Channels drop-down list, select Stereo if you have stereo sound on your video**

16. **From the rate drop-down list, select the maximum allowed and click OK.**

    The Movie Settings dialog box reappears for the last time.

**17. If it's checked, uncheck Optimize For Internet Streaming and then click OK.**

The File dialog box appears.

**18. Click Save.**

A progress bar appears after a moment. When it's done, you're done, too!

# *AVI*

To encode your video in AVI format, you need to have VirtualDub installed, which is just a question of unzipping it into a folder. You can launch the program using Vdub.exe. You also need the latest version of DivX installed.

To encode your uncompressed video into a final downloadable movie:

**1. In VirtualDub, choose File➪Open Video File and open your uncompressed AVI.**

**2. Choose Video➪Compression.**

The Select Video Compression dialog box appears.

**3. Select the DivX codec from the list on the left side of the dialog box.**

It's called something like DivX 6.4.0 Codec (1 logical CPU) depending on your PC and the latest version of DivX when you read this book. If it's gotten past DivX 10 by now, e-mail us and tell us to hurry up and write *Machinima For Dummies,* 2nd Edition!

**4. Click Configure.**

The DivX Codec Properties dialog box, shown in Figure 10-4, appears.

It looks a bit frightening, but the good news is you can ignore most of it.

**5. Set Bitrate to 800 and click OK to close the window.**

**6. Click OK again.**

**7. Choose Audio➪Full Processing Mode.**

Many options under the Audio menu are now selectable.

**8. Choose Audio➪Compression.**

The Select Audio Compression dialog box appears.

9. **Select MPEG Layer 3 from the left-hand window and then select 56 kbit/s, 24000 Hz, Stereo from the right-hand side menu.**

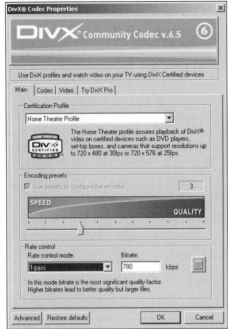

**Figure 10-4:**
The DivX
Codec
Properties
dialog box
appears.

10. **Click OK.**

11. **Choose File⇨Save As AVI, choose a name and location, and click OK.**

Your AVI starts to save.

If you want better audio compression, you can install the LAME MP3 codec, available from `www.free-codecs.com/download/Lame_Encoder.htm`. You can then select that from the Audio Compression dialog box in VirtualDub, and it allows you to select a huge variety of compression modes for your audio. *BloodSpell* used LAME MP3 audio at 44 kHz and 128 Kbps.

# *WMV*

To encode your video in WMV format, you need to have — you can guess what's coming here — the Windows Media Encoder installed. To encode your uncompressed video into a final downloadable movie:

1. **Start Windows Media Encoder and choose Custom Session.**

   The Session Properties dialog box, shown in Figure 10-5, appears.

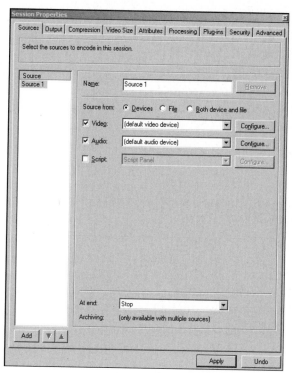

**Figure 10-5:**
The Session
Properties
dialog box.

2. **In the Source From area, select the File radio button.**

3. **Select Browse and find your uncompressed video file.**

4. **Click the Output tab.**

5. **Deselect Pull From Encoder (as professional video producers, we're here to tell you we have no idea what that does) and select Archive To File.**

6. **Click Browse next to File Name on this tab and select where you'd like your video to end up.**

7. **Click the Compression tab and then click Edit on that tab.**

   The Custom Encoding Settings dialog box, shown in Figure 10-6, appears.

Tab name varies. Click to alter settings.

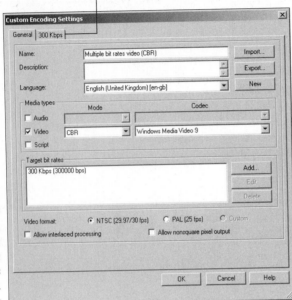

**Figure 10-6:**
The Custom
Encoding
Settings
dialog box.

8. **Click the tab marked something like 282 Kbps.**

   It'll be a number followed by Kbps.

   The Custom Encoding Settings dialog box now shows the 282 Kbps tab (see Figure 10-7).

9. **Check Same As Video Input and then set the Frame Rate to the correct rate for your source footage.**

   That frame rate is 29.997 for NTSC and 25 for PAL.

10. **Set the Video bitrate to 800K.**

    It's very important you put the K at the end here, or the Encoder, in its near-infinite wisdom, will attempt to encode your movie at 800 bits per second, which is, shall we say, a little low — a thousand times too low.

11. **In the Audio Format drop-down list, select 128 Kbps, 44 kHz, CBR from the list and click OK.**

    You return to the Session Properties dialog box.

12. **(Optional) Select the Attributes tab of the Session Properties dialog box and fill out the attributes there: your name, the name of your movie, and so on.**

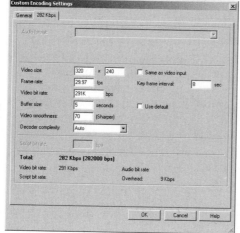

**Figure 10-7:**
The 282 Kbps tab of the Custom Encoding Settings dialog box.

13. **Click Apply.**

    The Session Properties dialog box disappears, and you just see the main Windows Media Encoder screen.

14. **Click Start Encoding.**

    You're encoding a Windows Media file!

# Streaming Video

By now, if you're an experienced Internet user, you're probably asking, "What about streaming video? Why should my viewers download my movie? Can't they just watch it instantly, like on YouTube?"

Well, actually, yes, they can. Video that is streaming, as opposed to downloading, plays across the Internet immediately, with no waiting for the file to arrive. High-quality streaming video has been the Holy Grail of Internet video for the last ten years, and, like the Holy Grail, is probably a reinterpretation of earlier pagan myths of renewal and endless plenty.

No, wait, that second bit is actually a lie.

Flash, formerly known for rock band Web sites and incredibly annoying Web site intro screens, has emerged from the shadows in the last three years to become the de facto leader in streaming video. Popularized by sites like YouTube, Flash video is simple to create (with the appropriate tools), plays on 95 percent of browsers, doesn't require a separate download for 99.95 percent of the Web browsing population (an absolute killer for past streaming media standards), and looks reasonably good at encoding rates that most Internet connections support.

You can make your movie instantly viewable on the Web in two ways: external hosting and personal hosting.

## External hosting

The simplest way to get your video into streaming Flash Video is to upload it to one of the many, many video hosting sites currently available. The grand-daddy of them all is YouTube, `www.youtube.com`, which is viewed by millions of people daily. But many other options, including Google Video (`http://video.google.com`) and Lulu.tv (`www.lulu.tv`), are available.

The advantage with an external site is that uploading your movie is simplicity itself. Click on a Web link, wait a bit, and you're live on the Interweb. In addition, these sites, particularly YouTube, offer you a potential audience of millions.

The price you pay for that convenience is control. Many filmmakers don't like the reduction in quality that almost always accompanies the automated encoding process these sites use, which can vary from some grain to virtually unwatchable. And by uploading to an external site, you're relying on them to support your movie — if they go bust or decide that your movie isn't suitable and remove it, you can't do anything about it. You should also check the legal terms on any site to which you're uploading — some sites, which we can't really name-and-shame here for legal reasons, demand a whole host of rights over your video once it's uploaded, essentially meaning that they can exploit your video however they choose, without sharing any potential profits. But if you're willing to live with the quality loss, these sites are the fastest way to get your video immediately viewable live on the Net.

To achieve maximum quality on a video-streaming site, upload your video in as close as possible to its existing standard. For example, for YouTube, it is highly recommended to use VirtualDub to create a 320 x 240 MPEG4 (DivX, Xvid) AVI and upload that. VirtualDub is much better at resizing your film than YouTube's automatic process will be.

If you can, encode your own Flash video and upload that. See the upcoming section "Personal hosting."

Among the best-regarded video sharing sites are

- **YouTube:** `http://youtube.com/my_videos_upload`
- **Lulu.tv:** `https://www.lulu.tv/?submission=1`
- **Google Video:** `http://video.google.com/videouploadform?utm_campaign=gv-ww-hdr&utm_source=EM&utm_medium=link`
- **Revver:** `http://one.revver.com/video/new`
- **Stage 6:** `http://stage6.divx.com/users/login/register`

# Personal hosting

Alternatively, you can encode, upload, and publish your streaming video yourself, all with free tools. First, you need an encoder for your video to convert it into the FLV format that Flash plays. The free Riva Encoder, made by a company specializing in Flash Video, is the best free solution for FLV encoding, although it's also possible to use the Open-Source tool FFMPEG if you're fairly technically competent.

You can also use a combination of the two: the Riva Encoder simply authors a batch file that you can then use to run FFMPEG, which means you can add additional functions that Riva doesn't support. That's particularly useful if you're encoding in widescreen, and it's the approach we used for *BloodSpell's* streaming video (`www.bloodspell.com/film/list/`).

Then, you need a player for that video, which you embed into your Web page. The Open-Source Flow Player is the best option here, providing a lot of features for a attractive cost of zero. You embed this Flash file, in SWF form, into your Web page using a little bit of HTML, and you're ready to go.

Obviously, this process is a bit more complex than uploading to YouTube (see preceding section). You also need to make sure that you're with a host that can take the bandwidth usage of a popular video file — as we write, Dreamhosts offer some of the best low-cost plans for this sort of usage, but given the high speed of change in the Web-hosting industry, there's no guarantee that will be true when you read this, so shop around.

On the plus side, however, using your own encoder and player gives you a lot more control over the viewing experience. You can fit your video into your Web pages more neatly, which gives you a more professional look, and you'll almost certainly achieve higher visual quality for your videos.

Here are some URLs you need:

- ✔ **Riva Encoder:** `www.rivavx.com/index.php?encoder&L=3`
- ✔ **Flow Player:** `http://flowplayer.sourceforge.net`
- ✔ **Tutorial on Riva and Flow:** `www.boutell.com/newfaq/creating/video.html`
- ✔ **Dreamhosts:** `www.dreamhost.com`

# Getting Your Video Out There

There's little point in spending whole days of your life filming and editing your magnum opus if nobody can see it. Assuming that you've managed to vault the myriad legal hurdles, you'll probably want to distribute your finished movie to the great unwashed on the Internet. There are quite a few ways to go about this. Some are free, and some will cost you Real Life Cash (TM). You can follow any or all these routes, which are described in the following sections. The more exposure your movie has, after all, the better.

## Standard (paid) Web hosting

Standard Web hosting is the one that will cost you money, unless you're very fortunate. It's the most obvious and direct solution to the distribution problem: Upload your file to your own Web server and then point people at it.

It's quite likely that you already have some Web server space, although you may not know about it. Most ISPs provide users with a small amount of very basic Web server space as part of the customer's ISP account. Unfortunately, free Web space such is rarely up to the task of distributing even a moderately successful movie.

Aside from the fact that you may well find that your movie is too large in file size to fit on the Web server that your ISP has provided for you, it's often the case that the ISP will have pretty strict limits on the type of files that can be uploaded to your public space. In hosting a movie file, legal or not, you may well be breaking the terms and conditions of your ISP account. Check first — it'll be a far bigger problem further down the line.

So, your ISP's free Web space is out. What's left? Plenty, thankfully, although you're probably going to have to put your hand in your pocket.

Look at buying a basic starter package from a reputable hosting company. You can pick up these sort of packages for about $50 a year, or even less. It's important to check what happens if you exceed the monthly bandwidth that the package provides. Some hosting companies have a retroactive charge per GB for additional monthly bandwidth — although watch out, because a really popular movie can rack up enormous bills. Other companies simply block any Web traffic to your site until the next monthly period starts, effectively shutting down your site.

If your movie becomes staggeringly popular . . . sorry, sorry, we have total confidence in you . . . *when* your movie becomes staggeringly popular, check that you can upgrade your hosting package to one with a larger monthly bandwidth allowance.

Buy a domain name. Dedicated domain names are nowhere near as expensive as you may expect. It's worth looking into purchasing a domain name for your movie's publicity Web site, even if you're not planning to host the file yourself. The URL `www.afistfulofmolars.com` is much better and catchier than `www.myisp.com/userspaces/johndoe123/machinimamovies/badwesterns/afistfulofmolars`. A `.com` address is the most expensive, but you can purchase domain names ending in `.org`, `.org.uk`, `.co.uk`, and so on for the equivalent of a handful of loose change if you shop around.

# *Internet Archive*

The Internet Archive (`www.archive.org`) is a nonprofit organization run by a group of modern day heroes who are trying to preserve, archive, and document the ever-changing maelstrom that is the World Wide Web. Its flagship application is the Wayback Machine, which grabs snapshots of Web sites are regular intervals, preserving them for all eternity, but the Archive also offers free hosting for certain files.

Machinima movies are one of the things that the Internet Archive is interested in preserving, so much so that it has a distinct Machinima section at `www.archive.org/details/machinima`.

Uploading your movie to the Internet Archive is pretty easy, and you can take advantage of its blisteringly fast HTTP and FTP servers, which can take any traffic you can throw at them without even blinking. Visit `www.archive.org/create`. You're asked to register with the site if you haven't done so already and then follow the simple steps to upload your movie. You're given a URL to your file(s) at the end of the process.

Stop the press! If you upload your movie to the Archive, it'll now also automatically encode and provide a streaming version, too!

## Why *Male Restroom Etiquette* worked

Phil Rice was more astonished than anyone at *Male Restroom Etiquette*'s extraordinary success. His blog entry Why It Worked (http://z-studios.com/blog/2006/10/03/why-it-worked) is great reading and full of tips on how to market, publicize, and capitalize on a movie's release.

YouTube, Google Video, Daily Motion, and all the other video-sharing sites are free and easy ways to get your movie out there. Users of these sites tend to pass on great video finds to each other. Effectively, these sites provide free, word-of-mouse publicity if your movie grabs the site admin's attention.

Sounds great, right? Well, it is — so great that we use the Archive for *BloodSpell*'s hosting. But there's one wrinkle to be aware of: In order to qualify for Archive hosting, your movie must be distributed under a Creative Commons license (see Chapter 15), which, at a minimum, allows your users to redistribute it freely for noncommercial purposes. We can't see why you'd have a problem with that, but if for some reason you do, the Archive isn't for you.

## Web video sites

In 2006, Google bought YouTube for a reputed $1.65 billion. Web video is big business, and if you can find the magic formula to tap into the constant demand for new content, you're on to a winner. When Phil Overman Rice released his short *Male Restroom Etiquette,* the snowball effect of video-sharing sites such as YouTube quickly brought him over 1.5 million views within days of release. At the time of writing, the total traffic on YouTube alone has hit 3 million and climbing. We're not at all envious, really we're not.

## Peer-to-peer distribution

As we all know, peer-to-peer services (the most famous of which is, or rather was, Napster) are only used by pirates and terrorists. Honest. Unbelievable as it may seem, though, we're about to propose a use for file sharing that is (a) legal, and (b) extremely useful.

A peer-to-peer file-sharing service, such as Kazaa, Limewire, or EMule, allows you to share files on your computer with other users of the same software. You can also download files from other people. In order to release your movie onto a file-sharing network, you just need to have the software installed (most of them are freely downloadable) and then place your movie file in a shared directory on your hard drive. Easy.

Of course, your movie file is likely to be downloaded only by people who are specifically searching for it already, or who stumble upon it by accident. There's not really any way to publicize your file to other users of the network. If you've got other means of publicity in play, releasing your file onto file-sharing networks is a useful alternative means of distribution. Just mention in your publicity that the file is available on Kazaa (or wherever), and let interested users search for it themselves.

There's another form of peer-to-peer distribution, using a program called BitTorrent (www.bittorrent.com), which mimics conventional downloading but uses peer-to-peer techniques to share the load of downloading popular files. Essentially, using BitTorrent, a popular file should be fast and easy to download because all the downloaders assist in distributing it.

Releasing a file over BitTorrent is somewhat more complex than a standard peer-to-peer solution. You need access to a tracker and a Web server for the torrent. In the bad old days of the BitTorrent community, you had little choice but to run and configure these items yourself. In our more enlightened times, many of the popular torrent sites provide a tracker for free public use; Downhill Battle's Broadcast Machine (www.getdemocracy.com/broadcast/) is one of the easier services to use.

Once you have your tracker details, you can create a torrent from the video file that you want to share. Most BitTorrent clients enable you to do this from within the program.

Once the torrent is created and running, you should announce it on some of the major BitTorrent search sites, such as bittorrent.com, torrentspy.com, and mininova.com, as well as provide a link to the torrent in any publicity you release. Remember, the more people accessing the torrent, the faster it goes.

A downside to peer-to-peer (and torrent) distribution is, assuming that you release the file yourself, you need to leave your computer on, with the peer-to-peer or torrent software constantly running, until the file has been downloaded by enough users to sustain it. In the initial phase of the release, you're the only provider of this content, so absolutely everybody will be downloading from you. If your bandwidth isn't up to the task, your potential audience will quickly grow frustrated and cancel the download. Speeds will increase exponentially with the popularity of the file, though, particularly on BitTorrent, so keep at it.

Unlike peer-to-peer services, where each file is shared individually, a torrent can contain several files. That means that, if your Machinima series has several episodes, you can release them all as part of the same torrent. It also means that you can include a small text file in the torrent with a link to your Web site or just give yourself credit for all your hard work. It's good etiquette to credit the site that's providing your tracker, too, assuming that you're not hosting it yourself.

Although the use of BitTorrent and peer-to-peer services is perfectly legal, many files available on these networks most certainly are not. Your ISP may well impose limits or outright bans on the use of these services, partially to protect themselves from legal liability and partially to prevent heavy download users from clogging up their networks for everyone else. We also can't be held responsible for any, erm, special-interest material that you may find on file-sharing networks. Apparently, some people use the Internet for accessing and distributing pornography. We're as shocked as you are. If you're easily offended, steer clear.

# Publicizing Your Movie

Who should you tell about your movie? Absolutely everybody. If your friends and family aren't thoroughly sick of hearing about *Zombie Cheerleaders From Mars*, then you're not doing your job. Johnnie had a laptop screening a constantly looping showing of *BloodSpell* during his wedding. That's the kind of commitment we're looking for, soldier.

Specifically, though, you should announce your new movie on a few important Machinima Web sites: `mprem.com` (Machinima Premiere), `machinima.com`, and `Sims99.com`.

It's also worth targeting fan sites for the game engine you used, especially if your movie is set within the game world. If you've used World of Warcraft, for example, then `www.warcraftmovies.com` is essential, but any game will have a fan site full of fanatical users. Join the forums well in advance of your movie's release and try to become a part of the community. After all, you're hacking away at their favorite game on a daily basis — you can probably offer helpful advice and information to regular users of the game. If the community already knows you (and knows that you're working on a Machinima movie), then it'll be far more receptive when you eventually hit release day. Its members may even start publicizing the movie before release, simply out of expectation.

We've got an entire chapter full of more publicity tips. If you want to go the whole hog, hie thee to Chapter 14.

# Part III

# Advanced Machinima Creation

## The 5th Wave
By Rich Tennant

"Why don't you try blurring the brimstone and then putting a nice glow effect around the hellfire."

# In this part . . .

We looked at *The Lord of the Rings,* and we said, "We want to do that." Now we can. In this part, we delve into advanced Machinima creation. We discuss how to organize a Hollywood-style film shoot in a world that doesn't exist and how to combine different characters, sets, and special effects inside your editing package.

We also cover sound recording and editing, and why you should aim to have Ian McKellan standing in a broom closet. You also discover why *marketing* isn't a dirty word and how to sell your film to your audience without selling out. And finally, we put on our rimless glasses and pretend we're wearing $5,000 suits as we look into the legal status of Machinima.

# Chapter 11

# Massively Multiplayer Machinima: World of Warcraft

● ● ● ● ● ● ● ● ● ● ● ● ● ● ● ● ● ● ● ● ● ● ● ● ● ● ● ● ● ● ● ● ● ● ● ● ● ● ● ● ●

## In This Chapter

▶ Filming in World of Warcraft

▶ Organizing a massively multiplayer film shoot

▶ Using the World of Warcraft Map and Model Viewers

▶ Video compositing and chroma-keying

● ● ● ● ● ● ● ● ● ● ● ● ● ● ● ● ● ● ● ● ● ● ● ● ● ● ● ● ● ● ● ● ● ● ● ● ● ● ● ● ●

*T*he rise in Massively Multiplayer games over the last five years has been one of the great changes in gaming, possibly the greatest since DooM. More than 10 million people play World of Warcraft at the time of writing, which means that about 75 percent of our readers are skipping this section because they know it already. So hello, the other quarter of you.

The rise in MMO games (as they're known) has been met by a corresponding renaissance in Machinima created in those game engines. Why? First, it's the first time ever that so many people have all been actively involved in playing the same game — World of Warcraft, the most popular MMO by a huge margin. But it's more than that. Massively Multiplayer games offer a unique opportunity for Machinima creators, a genuine alternate world, a place where you can do everything from recruiting your cast to shooting your film.

Groups (called *Guilds* in the game) naturally form in these cooperative games, which offer immediate ways to find people to help with your film. The in-game community means that film-making can be much more social than other, sometimes isolating, ways of making Machinima. And with thousands of people online at any time, it's actually possible to recruit a cast of hundreds to shoot truly epic scenes inside these non-existent worlds.

There's an entire *For Dummies* book all about Massively Multiplayer Games, by the way. It's called *Massively Multiplayer Games For Dummies,* written by Scott Jennings, a.k.a. Lum the Mad. It's a great intro to the genre if you fancy actually playing the games as well as making movies in them! (There you go, Scott. We'll take our payment in U.S. dollars, pounds sterling, or stacks of Netherweave.)

# World of Warcrack — er, Warcraft

World of Warcraft is a fantasy MMO, which owes a lot to the traditional fantasy staples of J. R. R. Tolkien et al, as well as current pulp fantasy writers.

In World of Warcraft (WoW), you play a hero (see Figure 11-1). In the battered land of Azeroth, constant war rages between the smug, goody-two-shoes Alliance and the tribal warrior societies of the "We're not Klingons, honest" Horde. You play a hero of one of these two factions. As well as choosing a side, you choose your race — elves, dwarves, orcs, and the undead are all available, along with several other choices — and your sex. Your hero also has a class — Warrior, Priest, Mage, Hunter — which is effectively a fighting style, be it with a sword, a bow, or a magic wand. Sometimes you get a pet dinosaur, too. With all these choices made, you set out on your great adventure as a lowly first-level character: a newbie, or *noob,* in Warcraft-speak.

**Figure 11-1:**
Some of the characters of Warcraft.

Although WoW, like all online games, has its fair share of idiots bouncing around the servers just begging for a slap, it is, on the whole, a very friendly and welcoming community. The game itself is pretty intuitive and leads you by the hand through the first few hours of game play.

Since its release in 2004, World of Warcraft has gained an unprecedented level of popularity and is now hailed as the golden boy of the MMORPG revolution. It has also spawned a host of Machinima movies, including several award-winners in the Machinima Film Festival.

# World of Warcraft and Machinima

World of Warcraft is a great tool for Machinima. Nonetheless, it may not be the ideal engine for your project. Here are a few good points to consider:

- **My, Zeke, she'm purty!** There's no getting away from it: World of Warcraft is just darned pretty. Even on the lowest graphical settings, the game isn't hard on the eyes. With graphical power turned up to maximum, the astonishingly high-quality art direction in the game really does become apparent. This abundance of visual quality lends itself to a very visual form of story-telling, and some seriously impressive movies.

- **Are we done already?** For all but the most complex and ambitious shots, filming in World of Warcraft is easy and fast. You'll probably take most of your shots in-game while connected to one of the many live servers provided by Blizzard Entertainment (the makers of the game).

  If you need a shot of a character standing on a hill and pointing to the horizon, go find a hill and get a friend to stand his in-game avatar on top of it. Then tell him to point. Done. For the more complicated shots, you can use an external Model Viewer program (see the upcoming section "Model Viewer FTW!") to generate static shots (or simple animations) of any character (or monster) in the game, in any available costume and with any available props. You can take this footage and insert it into your movie using a process called *video compositing* (see the upcoming section "Mastering Post-Production Effects," which you can easily achieve with most movie editors).

- **More than 7 million players worldwide.** Far from being a world inhabited solely by stereotypical 14-year-old computer geeks, WoW players come in all shapes, sizes, ages, and sexes . This diversity provides you with a huge swarm of people who already have a predisposition toward the movie you're making. People love to see movies that make clever use of locations that they're familiar with, just as they love to see footage of places within the game world that they haven't yet visited.

- **The only thing missing is a 20-sided die.** WoW is classic, unashamedly clichéd fantasy at its very best. It has elves, dwarves, and goblins. It has treasure and dungeons. In short, it's a world built for telling fantasy stories.

  If your movie leans toward traditional fantasy or even pseudo-history in any way, a lot of your work has been done for you in WoW.

- **You see that Massively bit?** World of Warcraft was designed to accommodate many players in the same area of the game world at the same time. There's technically no limit to the number of players who can occupy the same area (although eventually the servers stop working!).

That means that big battles with dozens of protagonists on either side are entirely feasible, if a little complicated to organize.

✔ **Any high-level enchanters who can make my greatsword glow in the dark?** Every player wants his character to look cool, or at least unique. World of Warcraft fulfills this need admirably — all sorts of different clothing choices are available, from spiky demon armor to designer tuxedos.

There's also a reasonable amount of customization available on your character himself. You can choose hair color and style, skin tone, and facial features from a predefined range. As if that weren't enough, with access to Darjk's Model Viewer, you can spice up your movie with all sorts of weird and wonderful monsters, from a cast of literally thousands.

Of course, World of Warcraft does have some bad points when it comes to making Machinima:

✔ **Can someone generate a new female Orc character with blue hair and run her up to Ironforge? Er . . . try not to die, okay?** Unless you're using the Model Viewer or just outright cheating, every character in your cast is controlled by a real-life person at the other end of a keyboard. One player, one character. The Rule of Committees states that the chances of something going annoyingly wrong increases with the number of people involved, just as the chances of having everybody in the right place at the right time decreases exponentially.

✔ **No character scripting.** Understandably enough, the creators of World of Warcraft tend to look fairly harshly on people who attempt to automate any of their character's actions. It's therefore virtually impossible to pre-script anything other than the simplest actions for the character you're controlling. That means that if a take doesn't go well, you've no option but to go through the whole scene again manually, just the way conventional filmmakers do. Sorry, but there are no shortcuts for this one.

✔ **No third-party content.** Blizzard releases new content for World of Warcraft all the time. The game has all sorts of bizarre items, and you'll be surprised at just what you can find. Nonetheless, if you absolutely positively got to have an oversized ice-cream cone with two blue scoops and one pink, you're out of luck. If it's not in the game, it's not going to be in your movie without a lot of clever post-production editing.

✔ **No, UberkillR, you cannot do your special Leroy Jenkins dance in the middle of this scene.** The unfortunate fact is that, although most of the people you'll meet and recruit within World of Warcraft are friendly, keen, and helpful, sooner or later you're going to pick up your very own village idiot. There's nothing you can do about it other than grit your teeth, smile, and try to politely dismiss them as soon as possible. Remember that everybody is helping you out for little or no reward, out of their own free time — don't throw your weight around too much, or you'll end up with no cast or crew at all.

- ✔ **I'll buy all the pink fishnet leggings you've got. Don't ask why.** When you log in to World of Warcraft, you're joining a world that's being shared by thousands of other players at the same time. It's easy to understand, therefore, why you can't just hack the game to make it do the things you need it to do or change your character to give it infinite financial resources to buy all your virtual props and costumes. If your actors have to be wearing a specific piece of armor, you've no option but to visit the auction house or the trade channel and give up some of your hard-earned gold.

- ✔ **I love the artistic way in which we only ever see the backs of your characters' heads in this movie.** World of Warcraft suffers from a similar problem to The Sims 2 — there's no practical way to lip synch your characters to their lines of dialogue. It doesn't have to be a show-stopping problem — clever editing and dialogue-light scripting can alleviate the glaring errors — but it's something to bear in mind.

- ✔ **The game doesn't feature a laser-powered anti-gravity gun.** We've already said that World of Warcraft is perfect for fantasy movies. The reverse is also true. If you're planning a movie that's not fantasy in approach, if not in actual genre, then you'll find yourself heavily limited by WoW's iconic look and feel.

- ✔ **Just let me hit my next level and then we'll go back to filming, I promise.** Here is your official warning: World of Warcraft is addictive. You may set out with the admirable intention of dedicating your time to filming and nothing else, no matter what temptations may come your way, but take our word for it: It takes a strong will indeed not to get sucked in.

## Tools of the MMO trade

Before you log in to WoW, you'll need a few more toys if you want to get the most out of your moviemaking. Most of these tools are either free or pretty darn cheap, and they'll come together to give you the Massively Multiplayer Movie-Making Experience of your dreams.

- ✔ **FRAPS:** FRAPS, shown in Figure 11-2, is the best tool around for recording video out of games that don't have an in-game recorder (like WoW). If you've got a fast dual-core CPU and a second hard drive, you can easily record High-Def video from WoW at nearly cinema resolution.

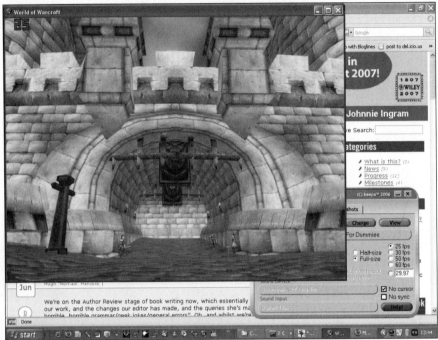

**Figure 11-2:**
FRAPS in
Record
mode.

If you're planning on doing serious Machinima production in WoW, you need to register FRAPS to unlock all its features. It costs $37 to register, which may seem like quite a bit, but for that price, you get fantastic, error-free performance. If you're not certain about shelling out, you can use the free version, but you're limited to 30-second shots, and a nasty www.fraps.com watermark appears along the top of the screen.

For best performance in FRAPS, you need a second hard drive in your machine. It doesn't react too well to recording onto the same hard drive you're running WoW and your operating system from. After you've installed FRAPS, set it to capture at either 25 FPS if you're in Europe or 29.97 FPS if you're in the United States, at full resolution, with no sound.

✔ **CameraPlus:** CameraPlus is a simple add-on that gives you easy access to some of WoW's hidden camera functions. You can find the latest version of CameraPlus at www.wowinterface.com/downloads/info6795-CameraPlus.html. To install it, just unzip it into the Interface directory in your World of Warcraft installation. Then, run World of Warcraft and make sure that CameraPlus is enabled. You may have to go into the Add-Ons screen on the WoW character selection menu and select Load Out Of Date Add-Ons if CameraPlus hasn't been updated lately.

Now you can configure CameraPlus's various tools through the normal Key Bindings menu in World of Warcraft. It gives you control over the horizontal and vertical speed of the in-game camera and allows you to define a key to switch to Shooting Mode, where all in-game interface elements are hidden.

✔ **World of Warcraft Model Viewer:** Need an Orc in a bikini and dungarees? Well, you could make a new Orc character, level them to 35 (taking about two weeks), and go do the quest that gets you the [Dungarees of Power] — or you can just install the WoW Model Viewer and select 'em from a list.

The Model Viewer is a brilliantly clever piece of coding from John "Darjk" Steele and Zoltan Szego that allows you to browse every creature, character, item, and special effect available in WoW, place them, animate them, and then save video footage that you can later composite into your film. Nearly every successful World of Warcraft Machinima film, including massive hits like *The Return* and *Edge of Remorse,* used the Model Viewer extensively. You can find the latest version at www.wowmodelviewer.org.

✔ **World of Warcraft Map Viewer:** From the team that brought you the World of Warcraft Model Viewer comes the Map Viewer. And yep, it lets you view all the maps and areas in World of Warcraft. You'll probably find you use this add-on less often than the Model Viewer; it's a bit less developed, it doesn't quite work in every situation, and frankly, it's easier to get to an area in WoW than it is to acquire items. You can find it at the same place as the Model Viewer: www.wowmodelviewer.org.

✔ **Voice communications:** If you're doing anything but the most trivial filming, you need to be in voice communication with your peons — er, valued crew members. Text is great, but it's hard to communicate exact timings or easily organize a milling group of 40-plus trained killers into a smoothly functioning unit. While the complexities of choosing voice communications software is a bit beyond the 100 words or so we've got here, top packages include TeamSpeak (www.goteamspeak.com) and Ventrillo (www.ventrilo.com).

Configuration for each package is different — some need a dedicated server, some don't, some require a Ph.D. to set up, some are brain-dead simple. Fortunately, many online guides show you how to set up these programs, and hey, it's just possible that *Massively Multiplayer Games For Dummies* may have something about this topic, too.

As this book was going to press, Blizzard Entertainment announced that the next big World of Warcraft patch would include voice communications built in. This should be in place by the time you read this and will make communicating with your cast and crew much easier.

✔ **Image editor:** You'll benefit from having access to a decent 2D image editor for WoW moviemaking, particularly if you're getting with the humor. It's handy to be able to add in details to backplates you've created with the Map Viewer or add titles or zany captions.

✔ **Some mates:** That's the sound of our poor editor bashing her head off the desk you hear. So let us quickly clarify. By mates, we, in our quaint British fashion, mean pals. Buddies. Companions. Comrades, Associates. Acquaintances. Gentlepeople of your social circle. Men and women of fine reputation and considerable influence. The very cream of society, and by that we don't mean the thick and the rich. In a word, friends.

If you want to shoot a cast of thousands in-game, you're going to need thousands of people behind their keyboards obeying your every command. Fortunately, the setup of the game makes finding people easy, and it's tons of fun to shoot this way.

# Writing for WoW

Writing for a World of Warcraft movie presents unique challenges. In some ways, it's much more like writing a conventional low-budget film than your usual Machinima film. With World of Warcraft, you've got a strictly limited palette of locations, characters, and props, and your challenge is to tell the best story you can within those constraints.

Before you start writing, you need to know exactly what you've got available. Investigate every location you can. Either go there physically with your in-game character or look at it using the Map Viewer (if you don't mind spoilering yourself for the game).

You need to know what you've got — from the medieval streets of Stormwind (which look a bit like Annecy in France, as it happens) to the sinister tunnels of the Undercity, to the pastoral fields of Westfall. Essentially, what you're doing here is location scouting, just as you would in a real-life film. As such, don't just think about the large-scale elements of what you're seeing. Note whether you see an interesting feature or a particular view across a zone that looks cinematic.

It's definitely worth doing this well before you've got a story in mind. One of the great things about working with such a well-designed and directed world as WoW is that the locations and characters themselves suggest stories to you. It's hard for Hugh to look across the rolling plains of Mulgore without wanting to set a Clint Eastwood-style spaghetti Western there, for example (and you could do it!), or to wander around Stormwind without wanting to start writing grimy political intrigue à la Game of Thrones.

Likewise, make sure that you know what the characters can look like — the Model Viewer's definitely your best choice for this — and what items and special effects are available.

## Why BloodSpell isn't made in WoW

Obviously, we didn't make *BloodSpell* using World of Warcraft, and one of the reasons was that we couldn't achieve some of the locations we wanted, like the huge steps that cross *BloodSpell's* City.

But if we had been shooting in WoW, we would have just had to think about the essential function of that scene — it's a dialogue sequence between our two characters, on their way to a religious ceremony. We could have easily re-set it walking through Stormwind's streets and used the tiny alleys and hundreds of little features of the city to our advantage to create a very claustrophobic, tense moment in the film.

## Decide what sort of story you want to tell

You can make three types of film in WoW, and all three options have advantages and disadvantages:

- ✔ **Satire or other humor (either jokes based in-game, or using the game to poke fun at something else).** Humor tends to be both more popular and easier to pull off in Machinima.

- ✔ **Drama set in the World of Warcraft (like the enormously popular *Return*).** In-game stories find a huge audience, and the background's rich enough to tell plenty of stories in, but many people find working in an existing canon limiting.

- ✔ **Drama not set in the World of Warcraft, but using the art assets available from the game to tell a different story.** Nongame stories are harder to promote and write, but may have a wider potential audience and greater apparent artistic value.

Watch other well-known Machinima movies to see what they've done, what stories they have told, and how much success they've had, as well as how they've done it.

## Write your story

Now you can work just as you would for any film. Write down all the ideas you've had, choose a story structure from them, and build a script just as you would for any Machinima film. Just remember to keep a close eye on what you can and can't do in the engine. Where in other Machinima engines, some of the things you may be suggesting would be difficult, it's entirely possible that in WoW they'll be totally impossible. Be flexible and be ready to re-set or re-cast shots if you have to.

# LFG 3,745 More 4 Helm's Deep PST!

WoW Machinima filming is very, very similar to real-life shooting, even more so than most Machinima. You've got to do everything you'd have to do in a real film: Break down the script, buy the props, hire the actors, clear the set, design costumes, the lot.

In other words, welcome to being a virtual Executive Producer. And Assistant Producer. And 1st Assistant Director. Yes, in order to organize a complex WoW shoot, you have to do all the jobs you'd have to do on a real set. If you forget that you need a posse of flowers for the next shot, you really will have to send someone to go buy them from the flower seller in Stormwind. If you're shooting in Feathermoon, approximately 15 minutes' gryphon flight away from said vendor, that'll really suck. And don't forget that you'll need the money to buy them.

Bearing all this in mind, it's worth reading a guide to real filmmaking if you're planning to shoot in WoW, because a lot of the tasks are very similar, and you can pick up good organizational tips.

The following sections offer a quick guide to some of the organizational roles you need to consider for your film.

## Executive producer

In RealFilm, the executive producer does a lot of things, but the primary and principle one is this: He ponies up the cash or acts as a representative for the people who did. Bob and Harvey Weinstein, for example, crop up as executive producers on a lot of films — because they run Miramax.

If you're filming in-game and you need specific props, you're going to have to buy them. A lot of the time, you can cheat by using the WoW Model Viewer, but if you have a specific shot that you can't use the Model Viewer for (a big pan or a complex crowd sequence), you need your props. So you need to consider how to get hold of the cash.

Most of the time, you can find low-level — cheap — items that will outfit your characters appropriately. If you need the Destiny sword model, though, you need to find a couple of hundred gold pieces. At that point, though it makes us feel dirty to say it, you may need to think about contacting a gold-selling organization.

For a more ethical alternative, consider asking one of the large raiding guilds on your server to donate, in exchange for a mention in the filming. If you've got a really serious raiding guild on the server, they'll be able to totally outfit your film out of small change — and may make excellent cast and crew for the film, too!

## Permissions agent

In RealFilm, you need to get in touch with the authorities in your town or country of choice to arrange permissions for shooting. You don't have to do that in WoW, thank goodness, but you do have to choose which country — which server — you'll be shooting on.

Servers have a variety of properties. For starters, they've got a dominant language — we recommend you choose one that you actually speak — and then they come in several flavors: PvE, PvP, RP, and RP-PvP.

*PvP* means that Horde can attack Alliance characters at any time, and vice versa. Unless you've got very strong reasons to go to one of these servers, steer clear.

*RP servers* are meant to be servers where players act and talk as their characters, role-playing them, rather than just talking as themselves. In practice, this doesn't always happen, but RP servers do seem to attract a more mature and story-aware group of players. It's worth inquiring on a realm's forums (via www.worldofwarcraft.com or www.wow-europe.com) whether you'll be welcome filming on that server. If you are, an RP server is likely to give you less grief and more interested players than normal PvE (Player versus Environment) servers.

Finally, you've got the population of the server to consider. Here you've got a balancing act to consider. The emptier the server, the less trouble you'll have with unwanted players walking into your shot, but the more problems you'll have recruiting assistance, as there are less players on the server to choose from.

## Casting agent

Want a gigantic battle occurring on the Elwynn Forest road? Or an army of Orcs streaming out of Blackrock Mountain? Then you're gonna need warm bodies, and lots of them.

Fortunately, you've got some great tools available for recruiting. Start by posting on your chosen server's forums, asking politely whether any individuals are interested in assisting you. Make your pitch well here — this is your equivalent of the elevator pitch to Spielberg, so make sure that you paint a positive but accurate picture of the movie you want to make, and deploy all the sales knowledge in your possession to persuade anyone reading to sign up. Ask a few times, if you like, but be careful not to spam; more than once a week is probably too much.

Ask politely in game, too. General chat in the cities is probably the best place to do that. Remember, if you want both Horde and Alliance characters in your movie, you need a character on both sides to talk to them.

Finally, find the leaders of larger (and better behaved) guilds in your game and privately ask them whether they'd be interested in helping, or if any of their guild members might be. People are usually flattered to be asked for advice and assistance. Just remember to be polite and reasonable and take no for an answer.

## Costume department

You also need to assemble your costumes. Be warned: The more precise you are about costumes, the more gold it'll cost you, and the more hassle it'll be. But it's far from impossible to persuade an entire guild to outfit themselves identically for a shoot — if you really need your line of identically dressed guards, you can do it. Do check that you can't achieve the shot in Model Viewer before you shell out, though!

Your costume research will be easier if you can find someone who really knows his WoW kit already. Likewise, you'll probably benefit from having *crafters* — in-game characters who can make items — on-side if you need a lot of a particular item or set. Ask around among your helpers or via the channels we mention earlier in the section "Casting agent".

A lot of high-end, expensive items look similar to cheaper, lower-level items. Make sure that you can't find something similar for a quarter of the price.

# Crowd control

Hollywood has to hire security to stop inappropriate people getting onto its film sets. So do we. Virtual crowd control in WoW takes two forms: control of monsters and control of players. Monsters are the more common and annoying, but also the most easy to deal with — just enlist the assistance of a high-level player (preferably a Mage or someone else with effective Area of Effect damage) to clear 'em out every time they reappear. Their corpses fade seconds after they're looted, and then you're able to shoot.

Player crowd control is harder, because just like in real life, you can't kill 'em. Here, you probably need someone whose responsibility it is to message players who are getting into your shot and ask them politely if they wouldn't mind moving, just until the shot is finished. The keywords here are polite, reasonable, and short term; don't ask them to stay away from the area for an hour!

Obviously, try to avoid shooting in high-traffic areas, such as cities. If you absolutely need to shoot a scene outside the bank in Stormwind, for example, you may have to wait for the Golden Hour — in other words, the time when the server is quietest — and shoot then. Bear in mind that's likely to be about 7 a.m.!

# Transport coordinator

Travel takes real time in WoW. Hence, you'll want to have your shoot set up to minimize any travel time. Break down the scenes you're shooting well before you start and make a list of absolutely everything you'll need for them — props, weapons, costumes, characters, the lot — on a scene-by-scene basis. Make sure that you know what shots you're aiming for and where you'll be shooting from. And make sure that everyone involved knows to be at the shooting location at least 10 minutes before shooting starts.

You may still need to have people run back to cities or other locations to retrieve items. It'll help if you can enlist a high-level mage and make sure that he's got appropriate supplies to provide portals to any of the major cities. If you're shooting near or in a friendly town, have all your crew and cast set their *hearthstones* — transporters they can use once an hour — to that location. And if you can, try to enlist a Warlock character, too, as he can summon your crew to you, minimizing travel time.

# Shooting in WoW

This, you'll be pleased to know, will be a very short section. Once you've installed all your tools, run WoW. You should see a frame-rate counter in the top left of the screen — that's FRAPS showing it's alive.

1. **Log your character in, zoom right in (or press the Home key on your keyboard repeatedly) so that you're in first-person mode and you can't see your own character any more.**

2. **Set your resolution as high as you can while still keeping action on the screen smooth.**

    It's always better to have as high a resolution capture as possible.

3. **Hit the FRAPS record key (default F9).**

    Watch the numbers at the top left. They'll turn red, showing that you're recording. If they dip below 25 (for Europe) or 29 to 30 (United States), then you need to reduce your resolution a bit. Otherwise, you're ready to go!

4. **Press F9 again to stop recording.**

5. **Select your shot, press F9 once again, and press it again when you want to stop shooting.**

# Record pans in WoW

WoW has a really nice set of panning tools, complete with acceleration and deceleration on the start and end. With CameraPlus, they're really simple to use, too. You need to set up CameraPlus's various key bindings first, which you can do through WoW's main Key Bindings menu, off the main menu. We recommend using the number pad on your keyboard for these keys.

1. **Press the button you selected for CameraPlus's setup menu.**

2. **Select a speed for vertical or horizontal movement.**

    This is a guesswork job: Select a number, save, try the next few steps, see whether they're the right speed, if not adjust, and repeat. Obviously, low numbers mean slow, high means fast.

3. **Close CameraPlus's setup menu.**

4. **Check your camera speed by holding down the key for the direction you want to pan**

    Up, down, left, right, and so on. If the speed's too slow or too fast for what you want, go back and try a different number.

5. **Start recording with F9, and when you're ready, hold the appropriate key down to pan; let go to stop when you're where you want to be!**

# Record tracks in WoW

It's a lot harder to zoom or track in WoW than it is to pan. The principle's simple enough, but it's difficult to get right. Essentially, you track by moving your character around while shooting. You can move faster by running or slower by walking, but there's not a lot of fine control! Often it's easier to fake a track in post-production (and it's nearly always easier to fake a zoom the same way) by moving footage around on-screen.

1. **Point your character in the direction you want to track.**

   This doesn't have to be the same direction you'll be shooting in. Use the right mouse button to turn your character rather than your view.

2. **Toggle walk/run to set your speed.**

   The default key to toggle these is Numpad /.

3. **Point your camera in the direction you want to shoot.**

   You need to do this step with the left mouse button and hold that button down to keep your shot.

4. **Start recording with F9**

5. **Press Forward to start moving.**

   That's W in the default key bindings.

6. **Press F9 again when you want to stop recording.**

# Shoot characters acting in WoW

All the other characters in your film are controlled by other players, just as they normally would when playing the game. Make sure that they're set to walk unless there's a good reason they should be running and discourage them from doing anything else odd, such as turning too fast, turning in the air, jumping around, or similar things. You'll probably need to practice a few times for each shot to make sure that they know where they're meant to be walking to, and what they're meant to do when they get there.

They can trigger animations on their character via the slash emote system — see www.wow-europe.com/en/info/basics/emotes.html for the full, current list of emote commands. Some emotes are very useful, while others are . . . very silly.

To have your character perform a talking animation, simply type something in the chat window — anything will do. WoW characters perform their talking animations while standing, sitting, walking, riding — wherever! Make sure that you, as cameraman, have checked the box on CameraPlus that reads Hide Chat Bubbles before you start shooting.

Here are a few more tips on how to shoot well in WoW.

- **Kneel, peon!** If you want to shoot from a lower angle, have your camera-man sit down. Simple as that! If you want lower still, you'll need to be an engineer using the Gnomish World Enlarger, or a druid in cat form, to make yourself tiny. You can also create a few different characters to use as camera people for a range of heights.

- **I want to be a tree.** Shooting from a higher angle is harder. Taurens and Drenai are the tallest characters in the game. You can also get on a mount to get higher. We believe that you can get taller still by either using a Potion of Giant Growth or having a high-level healing Druid do the shooting and turn themselves into their tree form. Yes, tree form. Just go with it.

- **Dum da da dum dum, dum da da....** Want to get higher still? Want that *Lord of the Rings* feeling? This one'll be painful and slow, but if you really need flying shots, you need a flying mount or a Druid with flight form — and that means that your cameraman needs to be level 68 minimum for a Druid, and level 70 for a regular guy. That's about six months of work, minimum, if you're starting from scratch, so you're better off finding an addicted friend who has already gotten there. Just be aware that you can only shoot in-flight shots in the Outlands (from the expansion Burning Crusade).

- **Mark your man.** If you want to mark exactly where people need to stand for your shot, you've got a few options. Ideally, you'll be a Hunter, in which case you can cast Flare on the place you want them to go. If you're a Mage, Flamestrike will do the same job. Engineers can place Target Dummies, but be aware that they're quite short-ranged.

# Model Viewer FTW!

FTW means For The Win, just so you know. Nothing looms larger over the field of WoW moviemaking than the Model Viewer tool (see Figure 11-3). It has enabled literally thousands of WoW movies — virtually no well-respected movie team doesn't use it. From *Edge of Remorse* to *Illegal Danish Super Snacks,* it's the bee's knees for the WoW filmmaker.

Handily, it's also simplicity itself to use:

- **File List:** Here you can choose any model in the game to be displayed and animated. This area doesn't choose clothes, weapons, or anything else — just the basic model.

- **The model view window itself:** If you've got FRAPS running, you'll see the numbers counting in the top left of the screen.

- **Appearance Selection Frame:** This window appears only if you choose one of the character models rather than a Creature. Click through these options to customize the character's appearance in exactly the same way as when you create a new WoW character.

✔ **Item Selection Frame:** Again, this option is available only if you're using a character. These tabs allow you to select any item in the game — swords, armor, clothing, and even flowers. The character then appears holding or wearing them.

✔ **Animation frame:** From here, you can browse through all the animations available for this character, play them, and even combine them. Uncheck Lock Animations on character models to allow you to combine two animations together — walking and talking, for example.

That's all you need! With this simple tool, you can create any character you like, video capture him doing anything you want, and then paste it into your video!

One of the great arts of WoW moviemaking is knowing when to use the Model Viewer to shoot a scene that you'll stitch together, and when to shoot it live.

File List        Uncheck to combine animations        Appearance Selection frame

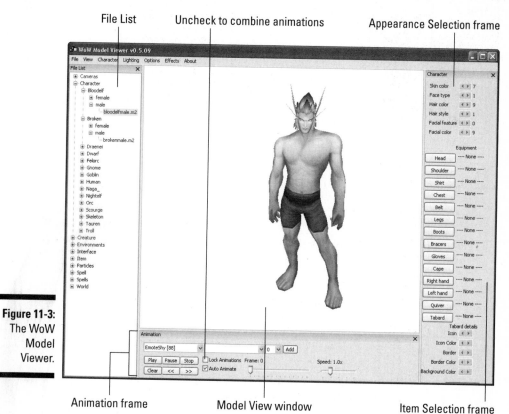

**Figure 11-3:**
The WoW
Model
Viewer.

Animation frame        Model View window        Item Selection frame

In general, you should use the game when:

✔ **It's easy.** If you need to shoot a character or couple of characters you have easy access to in an area that's not too overcrowded, do it in-game.

✔ **You're not planning on using post-processing effects.** The only way to put depth of field on a shot, in particular, is to composite, and that means Model Viewer.

✔ **You need to shoot complex motion.** If you're planning a shot where 40 characters run across an uneven field toward the camera while performing other actions, it's probably easier to shoot live.

✔ **You want to use in-game pans.** Compositing a character into a pan is a nightmare without very expensive tools. It's possible it will become easier with future releases of Model Viewer, but for now, it's live in the game for you.

You should use Model Viewer and Map Viewer when:

✔ **The shot is simple, but getting the kit isn't.** If you need a Night Elf Warrior in kit you can only acquire at Level 70, and your highest-level elf is Level 5, Model View it.

✔ **You want a lot of characters onscreen, but standing still or walking over simple surfaces.** Remember those *Helm's Deep* shots where there's a horde of Elves all standing behind a battlement, not moving? Perfect Model Viewer shot.

✔ **You want a shot that you just can't get with your character.** A classic example would be a very high-angle shot from somewhere where you can't put a flying mount. At that point, rush off to your Map Viewer for that high-angle goodness.

To capture video from the Model Viewer:

1. **Load up Model Viewer.**

2. **Select a model from the File List.**

   We chose `Character/Orc/Male/Orcmale.m2`. You can select any character model in the game. However, only models under `Character` are customizable player models. If you select one of these models, the Item Selection Frame appears.

3. **Click a body part in the Item Selection Frame.**

   You can go through the character parts in the Item Selection Frame and clothe your character. You can also customize your character's facial appearance in this pane. If you click Legs, for example, the Legs dialog box appears.

4. **Type the name of the item you want into the Filter text field.**

   Otherwise, feel free to browse! In this case, we chose the Black Tuxedo Pants. We could have navigated through every different piece of clothing (and it's an interesting exercise), but in this case we know what we want: We want dapper, and we want it now.

5. **Choose clothing and held items from the rest of this pane.**

6. **Go to the Animation Frame and scroll down through the list of animations; select an animation.**

   We chose one of the dance animations; they're well known for looking great. You can uncheck the Lock Animations check box and combine two animations here, too!

7. **Change the view in the Model View Window by dragging with left or right mouse button held down.**

   Once you've got a good angle, stop.

8. **Press F9.**

   FRAPS captures the model frame as a movie. It may also change your character's appearance a bit. We can re-map the movie key in FRAPS to avoid that happening in the future

9. **Press F9 again to stop capturing.**

If you're using the Model Viewer and one of your animations is a Walk, a Walk Backward, or a Run, hold down the forward or backward cursor key to have the model walk or run forward or backward — in the Model Viewer, at the correct speed! This is an incredibly handy feature for capturing movement.

# And Now, View That Map!

WoW Map Viewer is a little less documented and slick than the WoW Model Viewer (see preceding section), but it's still pretty darn Scooby, as we say in Scotland. To start it, use the `Windowed.cmd` item in the WoW Map Viewer folder. You can edit this `.cmd` file in a text editor to change the resolution it uses. Simply add the resolution after a dash at the end of the line `wowmapview -w` to make it, say, `wowmapview -w -1400x1050`. Sadly, it'll only accept more common resolutions: 1,280x1,024, 1,600x1,200, 1,024x768, and a couple of others.

Once you're in, you see a screen like the one in Figure 11-4. From here, you can either choose one of the Instanced dungeons listed or the continents of either Azeroth or Kalimdor (or the expansion continents — the first one, for Burning Crusade, contains the Drenai and Blood Elf starting areas plus the high-level Outlands). In the latter case, you can then select your starting point from the map that appears immediately afterward.

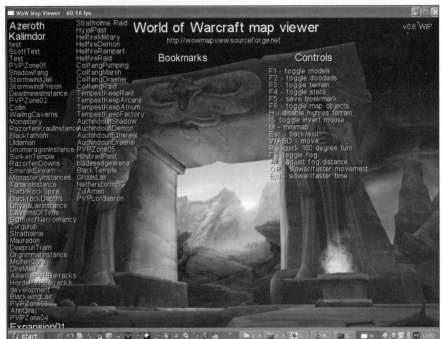

**Figure 11-4:**
The WoW
Map
Viewer.

Now you see a view of the map area you chose. You can move around in this using the W, A, S, and D keys as normal, plus Q and E to go up and down. O and P change how fast you move, F4 removes the stats, and you can control your forward direction by clicking and dragging with the mouse.

Using the Map Viewer is simple: Select the area you want to shoot, set up your movement speed (you can't pan at the moment, to the best of our knowledge), press F9 to start up FRAPS, and start moving! If you want to, that is. Otherwise, just capture yourself a nice bit o' landscape.

Do be aware that not everything will look identical in the game and the Map Viewer. The Map Viewer is actually the product of reverse-engineering the game's map files. While the guys who developed it did a great job, some things still don't look quite the same.

# *Mastering Post-Production Effects*

Thanks to World of Warcraft's rather brilliant art direction, your movie already looks pretty good. There's more that you can do, though. With a little effort and a copy of Sony Vegas (or your equivalently capable editor of choice), you can add clever effects to improve your film or just hide the ugly bits. And using the Model Viewer and Map Viewer, you can create hundreds of shots that you can't create any other way.

# Layering

*Layers* are a very simple but highly effective idea that first came to prominence in traditional hand-drawn animation. The basic idea is simple. Imagine you have to animate a scene in which Snow White walks through a forest. It's a couple of hundred frames long, and you have to draw each frame by hand. By about frame ten, you're going to be sick of drawing the same three trees, in exactly the same position, looking exactly the same as they did in all the previous frames. Why can't you just draw the trees once and use that same image for each of the 200 frames? They're not going to change, after all.

Good idea. Why not draw all the trees as one image and use that as background? That way, if you can draw Snow White onto some sort of transparent sheet, you can place her on top of the trees to produce a complete frame. For the next frame, all you need to do is draw another Snow White layer, still walking — you can reuse the same trees. You've just increased your productivity ten-fold and guaranteed yourself a nice pay raise at the next wage review. You've also invented a technique that is still used extensively in both digital and traditional animation, as well as in photo manipulation and montage.

Most World of Warcraft movies use layered video files in one way or another — most often, to layer video from the Model Viewer with backgrounds from the game or the Map Viewer. *Edge of Remorse,* winner of two Machinima Film Festival awards in 2006, was created entirely using these techniques.

In principle, layering Model Viewer footage and background footage is simple. You shoot your Model Viewer character against a solid color background, make that solid color transparent in your video editor, and place the image or video you want to use as your actual background behind it. It's the same technique that news stations use to show a weather map behind the forecaster.

## Compositing the Map and Model Viewer

You'll need some footage from the Model Viewer and some footage from the Map Viewer.

1. **Boot up Vegas and import your first clip: the background footage.**

2. **Drag your background footage clip into the Video Tracks Area.**

3. **Add the footage from the Model Viewer.**

4. **Drag your Model Viewer footage into the Video Tracks Area, above the background footage.**

   Vegas probably imported an empty audio track along with the video footage; if so, you can safely delete it.

   The preview window in the bottom right of the screen shows both clips combined — but not very well. You can use a technique called *Chroma-keying* to fix this problem. A *Chroma-key* is a specific color that you specify should be transparent. Whenever Vegas encounters this color, it shows the background through it instead.

5. **Right-click your Model Viewer footage and choose Media FX from the drop-down menu.**

   Vegas brings up the Media FX Plug-in Chooser. Unsurprisingly, you want the Sony Chroma Keyer plug-in.

6. **Select the Chroma Keyer plug-in and click OK.**

   The Chroma-key settings page, shown in Figure 11-5, appears for this clip. Fortunately, it's nowhere near as complicated as it looks. All you have to do is find the right color to set as the transparency color. To do so, first find the wrong color. Yes, you read that correctly.

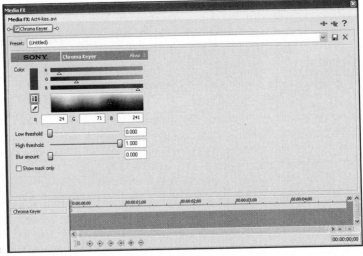

**Figure 11-5:** The Chroma-key window.

7. **Set the color to a garish pink or a lush green — anything other than the background color of your Model Viewer clip.**

   You can change the color by clicking anywhere in the rainbow-like color box in the center of the screen.

8. **Use the eye-dropper tool to select your background color.**

   It's the tiny icon that looks like a pipette, just to the left of the color palette (above the letter R). You'll know you've hit the right icon, because your cursor turns into a pipette.

9. **Left-click the ugly background square in the preview window at the bottom right.**

   Move the Chroma-key window out of the way first, if necessary. As if by magic, Vegas sets this color to be your new transparency color. Things should be looking a lot better in the preview window now, but they still aren't quite right: You see little bits and pieces of color here and there.

10. **Make small changes to the High threshold and Low threshold sliders until you're happy.**

    The lower you can get these values, the better. Leave Blur amount set to zero unless you really need it; this blurs the edge of the image to get rid of any ugly borders. It's a good cheat for when the basic Chroma-key filters can't get it right, but it does tend to lower the overall quality of the image and leads to that glaring this-scene-has-been-chroma-keyed look.

11. **You may have to tweak the color that the color picker pipette tool chose for you slightly.**

    The R, G, and B values below the color palette stand for Red, Green, and Blue and can be set to any value from 0 to 255.

12. **When you're happy with the effect, click the X at the top right to close the Chroma-key window.**

    You can always bring back the window by right-clicking the clip once again and choosing Media FX.

Any parts of the image that match the Chroma-key color will be made transparent. Make sure your character isn't wearing blue pants, or your final footage will look strange indeed. Change the background color in the Model Viewer options.

## Hiding Snow White behind the trees: Layer masking

If you want to achieve the opposite effect — you want to place a static or mostly static image over an animated background — you can use another technique called *masking*. You need to use a separate image-editing program for this. We recommend The GIMP (free and open-source, and on the DVD).

While working through these steps, keep an animated video file below your mask so that you can see when it's working!

1. **Open a copy of the static image that you want to overlay.**

   Don't use the original image. You'll use it again later, so you'll want to keep it intact.

2. **Use the tools in your image editor to fill the parts of the image that you want to be shown in solid white.**

3. **Fill the parts that you want to be transparent in solid black.**

4. **Open Vegas again if you've closed it; create a brand new track and add the original image to it.**

5. **Add another track and this time add the image mask to it; move this track so that it's above the original image's track.**

   Now it gets a little complex. You need to make the layer containing the original image a child of the layer with the black-and-white mask in it.

 6. **Click the Make Compositing Child button on the original image's track.**

   It's quite small and looks like a blue arrow pointing right and down. Notice that the track containing the original image appears slightly indented from the mask image layer, which indicates that the mask layer is the parent of the original image layer.

7. **Change the Compositing Mode on the mask layer from Source Alpha to Multiply (Mask).**

   The Compositing Mode button is next to the Make Compositing Parent button. That's masked out the original image, which is now only showing the areas that you painted white.

   Where's the animated footage that you placed underneath, though? Even if you've added it to a track below the other two images, you won't be able to see it. The solution lies in adding another type of mask to the mask layer.

 8. **Select Track FX from the buttons on the Mask track.**

9. **Select Mask Generator and close the Track FX windows.**

   The default settings should be fine; your animated background layer should now be visible behind the masked image.

Often, you use masking and chroma-keying in the same piece of footage. For example, in the Snow White example, the background image is a static shot of trees in the background. Snow White herself is shot against blue and chroma-keyed into the video. Finally, a masked layer of foreground trees is laid in using masking, behind which Snow White sometimes vanishes.

There aren't any really hard-and-fast rules as to when you use masking and when you use chroma-keying. You just discover which technique to use by trial, error, and practical examples.

# *Other compositing techniques*

You can do a lot more things with compositing in your video editor. Here are a few common tricks:

- **Depth of field:** You can layer several images and then apply blurs to them to simulate a camera moving in and out of focus on different parts of the image. This technique is powerful for achieving a filmic effect.

- **Special effects:** Using animated footage created elsewhere, or particle effects in powerful video editors, you can add special effects — smoke, lightning bolts, anything you like! — that aren't possible in World of Warcraft or any other engine.

- **Digital grading:** Most video editors allow you to adjust the image properties of your video — brightness, contrast, saturation, and more. You can use these changes to give more life to a dull image or evoke a specific feel in your footage.

# Chapter 12

# *Lord of the Rings* on $50 — Mass Battles with Medieval II: Total War

*H*ugh is smug right now. He's smug because he has, for about a decade, been predicting that Machinima will one day allow him to film battle scenes on the scale of *Zulu* or *Lord of the Rings.* Last year, a little game emerged into the market called Medieval II: Total War (MTW2, as we refer to it for the rest of the chapter). In April 2007, the makers of the Total War series, Creative Assembly, released a Machinima tool for it — with which, yes, you can create battles on the scale of Peter Jackson's *Lord of the Rings.*

The Total War engine was used for the historical recreations in the television series *Time Commanders* and *Decisive Battles.* With the release of the MTW2 Machinima tool, it's your turn. If you want to create a small, detailed love story à la *Brief Encounter,* this ain't the chapter for you. We recommend Chapters 6 through 8 or Chapter 17 for that sort of thing.

If, on the other hand, you want to create enormous, graphically detailed medieval battle scenes, with tens of thousands of characters fighting it out for king, cash, and country, read this chapter.

# The Ups and Downs of Medieval II: Total War

MTW2 is a fantastic engine, but it's highly focused on one purpose: really big fights.

Here are the pros:

- ✔ **Huge battles:** We really do mean huge. Its limits are somewhere upward of 30,000 troops. We guarantee a Wow! moment within your first hour of working with the engine.

- ✔ **Works well at close-up, too:** The Machinima potential of the previous Total War games was somewhat let down by the fact that, while they looked great from a distance, the individual character models were quite blocky and ugly. MTW2 has fixed that and fixed it good. Individual characters now move individually, play with their weapons, and shift their feet. Their individual fighting animations have to be seen to be believed. You can go in close, shoot an individual character being killed or the impact of a cannon shot, and then zoom right out to see thousands of characters fighting.

- ✔ **Wow. No, really. Wow.** The Total War games have always looked good, but MTW2, from a 2007 perspective, looks darned amazing. Your wide shots will feature sweeping vistas and rolling hills. Your medium and close shots will show beautifully textured armor glinting in the morning sun. MTW2 is among the most graphically accomplished games we've ever seen.

- ✔ **Great process and tools:** The process of filming in MTW2 is both intuitive and flexible. In Medieval, you make a set, you then control the action in that set using the standard game controls, and that action is then saved as a replay. You can then replay that footage as often and from as many angles as you want, and even add camerawork after the fact. This process used to be called *recamming*. It's tremendously flexible and is something offered by no other modern engine but Half-Life 2.

Of course, every game has its cons:

- ✔ **No facial animation:** It's only when you get in really close that the flaws in the MTW2 graphics engine become slightly apparent. The individual unit models are fairly low resolution. This is most noticeable on the character's faces, which can't emote at all. You're not going to be able to make your characters blink, let alone lip synch.

- ✔ **Some bugs:** The camera tools and map tools were designed to be used by the game development team itself. We're tremendously grateful they've released them. However, that does mean that they've not undergone the level of testing that a consumer piece of software would have done.

We're told by the designers that saving frequently is a good idea while using MTW2 as a Machinima tool. In addition, these tools aren't supported by the games publisher Sega — so please don't call Sega if they break!

✔ **No individual character control:** The recording facility records the actions that you, as the player, take in directing your units, not the movements of the individual characters within those units. If you've got an inconveniently positioned knight blocking your shot, you've got no choice but to take the shot from another angle. In this respect, filming in MTW2 is often a lot more like documentary filming than conventional Hollywood-style work: You may have Total War, but you don't have total control.

✔ **Designed for the Big Screen:** Once you start to work with the camera tools, you'll be grateful for a really big monitor. We found our 19 widescreen a little cramped when editing camerawork. Try to film on a small monitor at, say, 1024x768 resolution, and you'll soon be longing for a multiple-monitor setup.

✔ **Medieval:** That's it. We say you could re-create *Helm's Deep.* That's true, but you'd have to create all the models yourself. Medieval II: Total War does one thing and one thing well. It does war, which is often pretty total, in a medieval setting. If you want to make *Star Wars VIII: The Really Big Barney,* you've got a lot of work ahead of you. Having said that, the community for MTW2 was developing fast as we wrote this book, and some truly fantastic modifications may be available now. See `http://forums.totalwar.org/vb/forumdisplay.php?f=159` to get the state of play.

# The Filming Process in MTW2

The process of filming in MTW2 is a bit different than that of any other engine:

1. **Plan your film.**

   Because you don't have total control, you can't plan an MTW2 film down to a shot-by-shot level. Instead, you need a script and a general beat-level plan of the action (Cavalry charge. Pikemen get ready for impact. Cannon fires on cavalry).

2. **Make a map.**

   You can model virtually any terrain you can think of using MTW2's map builder. As well as choosing the height, layout, and surface terrain across your map, you can choose the weather and season. MTW2 also includes quite a number of small terrain features, such as monoliths or tilled fields, as well as several enormous (and superbly detailed) castles.

3. **Choose and place all the character units that you want to feature in your movie, from cannoneers to a Highland Rabble.**

4. **Record a battle.**

   This is the fun bit. You take your pre-set armies and map and play the game yourself. Either you and a friend or you and the computer take a side each and, using the normal game controls, order your troops into action. Cannon roar, knights charge. The game, meanwhile, records everything you do, ready to be played back and filmed.

5. **Add cameras.**

   You take the battle you just recorded into MTW2's Cinematics Editor. Here, you add key-framed cameras to any point of the battle, from giant sweeping helicopter shots to tight, close-in handheld-style shaky camera-work. Larger shots will probably come out as you've planned them, but you'll have to look carefully for individual action shots.

6. **Render the scene.**

   Medieval includes a fantastic feature similar to (but rather better than) The Sims 2: A full renderer, which creates a graphically perfect version of your film without the use of programs like FRAPS. It also, as an added bonus, turns all your graphics settings up to maximum while it does this — and MTW2 on maximum graphic quality is a very pretty thing indeed.

7. **Edit your movie.**

   Just like any other movie, once you've got your raw footage, you then edit it together using a conventional video editor — and lo and behold, you'll have a darn pretty movie.

# Getting Started

When you're ready to get on the MTW2 train to Carnage City, follow these steps:

1. **Install Medieval II: Total War.**

   If you haven't got this already, you can order a copy of the game through the link on the *Machinima For Dummies* Web site at www.machinimafor dummies.com.

2. **Download and install the latest patch.**

   You can find patches for the game at www.totalwar.com. You need at least *Update 2*.

3. **Navigate to the Medieval 2 folder on the book's DVD and copy all the batch files (files ending in** .bat**) to the root folder of your MTW2 installation (**C:/Program Files/MedievalTotalWar2 **for a default installation).**

4. **Double-click** `1editor.bat` **in your MTW2 folder to launch the game.**

5. **Click Options and then Battle Editor.**

   The Location Selection screen appears.

6. **Choose a location in which to set your battle.**

   If you click the map, the Battle Editor tells you what type of terrain you're going to be editing.

7. **Click Next.**

   You're now looking at the Battle Editor.

# Getting to Know the Battle Editor

You can navigate around the Battle Editor by using the number pad on your keyboard.

Table 12-1 clues you in on what each key does.

| Table 12-1 | Navigating in the Battle Editor |
|---|---|
| *Key* | *Action* |
| 8 | Move forward quickly |
| 5 | Move forward slowly |
| 2 | Move backward |
| 4 | Turn left |
| 6 | Turn right |
| 1 | Pan left |
| 3 | Pan right |
| * | Move up |
| / | Move down |
| - | Look down |
| + | Look up |

Each button along the bottom of the Battle Editor, shown in Figure 12-1, displays its name and function if you hover your mouse over it for a couple of seconds. You can also find a useful summary of their functions at the top of the screen once you click them. Table 12-2 describes each button.

**Figure 12-1:**
The Battle
Editor
controls.
The Battle
Editor also
contains a
big pile of
buttons at
the bottom.

| Table 12-2 | The Battle Editor Buttons |
|---|---|
| *Button* | *Description* |
| Edit Battle Details (1) | Edit the details of the battle. You can choose from a single-player or a multiplayer map. You can also edit the weather and the time of day, both of which have a huge effect on in-game graphics. The editor updates to reflect your changes when you click OK. |
| Create Army (2) | Probably the first thing you should do. Create an army and select the faction to which it belongs. You can choose anything from Scotland to the Holy Roman Empire. Choose a name for your commander and turn his Command slider up to maximum. You need to create at least two armies, or the battle will be quite dull! (Plus, the game will probably crash.) |
| Create/Edit Units (3) | See the upcoming steps on adding units, later in this section. |

| Button | Description |
|---|---|
| **Create Deployment Area (4)** | A deployment area must be set down for each army before you can place any troops. Select your commander and then click the map to define the corner points of your deployment area. You can deploy units only within this area. If you make a mistake, you can delete a point by right-clicking or move it by clicking and dragging. Don't make your deployment area too small, or you'll never be able to fit your unit of 200 elephants into it!<br><br>It can be a precision task selecting an individual point of a deployment zone in order to edit it. The selectable area is actually at the base of the point, where it connects to the map. |
| **Edit Landscape Heights (5)** | Click this button to display a new menu showing the different brushes available to modify the terrain. This tool works just like an airbrush tool in a paint program; the editor allows for various different sizes of brush, from tiny to enormous. Left-click and hold to raise the terrain. The longer you hold down the mouse button, the greater the effect will be. Shift+click and hold to lower the terrain.<br><br>There is no tool to apply rivers; you'll have to find a pre-existing map with a river if you want to use it in your film. |
| **Smooth tool (6)** | Applying the Smooth tool to a section of terrain averages out the height under the brush, effectively smoothing it down. |
| **Plateau tool (7)** | Flattens the landscape level with the point you first click. It is much like the Smudge tool, except that the Smudge tool will fall off as you get further from the point you first click. |
| **Smudge tool (8)** | Using this tool, you can move mountains. The editor takes the height of the terrain at the point you start clicking and drags that height across the areas you move your mouse, effectively smudging the terrain around the landscape. |

*(continued)*

**Table 12-2 (continued)**

| Button | Description |
|---|---|
| Texture tool (9) | Pops up a new window. With this tool, you not only get a list of the brushes available, but also the different textures that you can apply to the terrain. You can repaint using this tool to your heart's content, although you'll only have access to the type of terrain that's appropriate for your chosen terrain type. |
| Vegetation tool (10) | The vegetation tool works rather like the Terrain tool, except it adds plants, trees, and shrubbery. You can access all the different vegetation available in the game, but if a particular bit of brush isn't suitable for your terrain type, the editor simply won't allow you to place it. |
| Place/Edit World Package tool (11) | Also known as the Everything Else tool, this is the tool to use for placing wagons, rocks, and watch-towers, as well as castles, cities, and monasteries. Try adding the Aztec City from the Settlement package if you want to be instantly impressed. |
| Set Victory Conditions (14) | This tool is very important, and if you don't set it up properly, the game won't run your map. |
| Nonfunctional buttons | Buttons 12, 13, 15, and 16 don't do anything right now. But they're very pretty. |

The numbers at the bottom-right of the screen represent your current coordinates in the world. However, you can also view the current strength of the tool you're using there, if you change it. You can raise or lower this value using the < and > keys on your keyboard. These alter the overall strength of the tool, ranging from 1 (hardly any effect at all) to 100 (huge effect). This strength then applies to tools 5 through 10.

Press Esc to access the Game Options menu, from which you can save or quit.

To add units to your battlefield:

1. **Create a deployment area.**

2. **Click the button to the left of the faction.**

   A list of available commanders appears.

3. **Click the commander's name.**

   A new menu appears, with a list of all the available units that you can create under his command. The new menu will probably cover your main menu, so just click and drag to move it out of the way.

4. **Place units by clicking your chosen unit to select it and then clicking and dragging across the map to define the unit's facing and initial formation.**

   When you release the mouse button, the editor opens the Edit Unit Details dialog box where you can edit the size of the unit, as well as its equipment and general competence.

Once a unit has been placed, you're unable to edit it with a right-click, and clicking just places another identical unit on the map. The trick is to click the unit with both the right and left mouse buttons simultaneously. Then you can change its facing and deployment.

We can't say it often enough. The MTW2 editor is great, but it's not officially supported by the developers, and is still pretty buggy. Save regularly. You'll thank us.

# Making a Map

MTW2 is built primarily for outdoor scenes. Thus, it works entirely on a combination of height-mapped terrain and placeable objects, which range in size from individual rocks to enormous castles. (See Chapter 6 for more on map-making techniques.)

At the same time as making your map, you'll set up the initial positions of the armies you intend to have clash. Often, when you're making a more complex Medieval movie, you create several different maps, each of them with identical terrain but with units set up representing different stages of the battle.

Here's how to create your map and set up your armies' initial positions:

1. **Modify your terrain.**

   Using the various terrain and placeable tools in the Battle Editor, add hills, trees, cities, and farms to your heart's content.

2. **Click the Edit Battle Details and choose the weather and time of day.**

   Set the map as multiplayer if you'll be directing with a friend, or single-player if not.

3. **Move the camera around until you find a good spot to place your first army.**

   MTW2 maps are huge and can quickly get confusing. You'll probably find it convenient to deploy your troops somewhere near the center of the map. It'll be easier to find them when you eventually replay your recordings.

4. **Click the Create Army button and select your faction.**

   We're going for Scotland, obviously. Give your captain a good name. Scottish commanders can be called Hew, which is a fine name with a noble tradition of geekhood behind it.

5. **Create a second army.**

   An English army under the command of Captain John would seem a good choice to be trampled by elephants.

6. **Click the button next to Scotland and select Captain Hew (or whoever you chose).**

   Give him a nice deployment area using the Create Deployment Areas tool.

7. **Create another deployment area for Captain John.**

   Make sure that you give him plenty of space and that the armies aren't too far away from each other.

8. **Click Create/Edit Units and lay down a few troops for each side.**

   Remember that you need to select the appropriate captain to place troops under his command. The most important — nay, essential — unit to place is the General's Bodyguard, without which the game won't run. Other than that, go wild and place anything you fancy. We insist that you place a unit of Highland Rabble on the Scottish side, though. They remind Johnnie of the pub near his flat.

   Don't get too excited, but if you want to, you can choose some elephants.

9. **Click Victory Conditions and set your home faction to Scotland (or whatever you want your home faction to be).**

   You may want to paint half your face blue and recruit a famous Australian actor to do a very bad Scottish accent.

10. **Click the + button toward the top of the Victory Conditions window twice to add two Alliances.**

    Each row has two tick boxes available under the list of faction flags, as well as a further four tick boxes at the end of the row.

11. **Against Alliance No 0, place a tick beneath the Scottish flag (a white cross on a blue background) or the appropriate flag if you're not using Scotland the Brave as one of your factions.**

**12. For Alliance 1, place a tick beneath the other flag — English, in our case.**

Make sure that you get this bit right. If you make a mistake here, the game will crash spectacularly when you try to run this map.

**13. Set one of the factions as the attacker, by placing a tick in the A column at the end of the row.**

**14. Set the slider next to Select Alliance to 0 and click the + button next to Destroy or rout enemy.**

This step sets up the game in such a way that the first Alliance must completely conquer its enemies to win. Several other alternative win conditions are available to you, but this default choice provides the most flexibility and the least chance for the battle to end unexpectedly.

**15. Move the Select Alliance slider to 1 and again click the + button to add a Destroy or rout enemy condition for the Bad Guys.**

You should now have a screen that looks something like Figure 12-2.

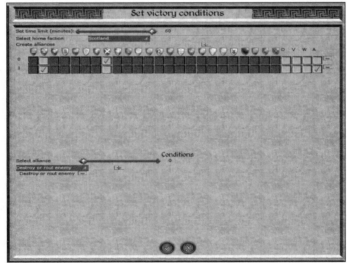

**Figure 12-2:**
The Victory Conditions screen.

**16. Click the tick to accept your modifications.**

**17. Hit Escape to access the Save menu and save your map.**

Hopefully, the editor doesn't report any errors during its Sanity Check. If it does, you need to rectify them before you carry on.

**18. Exit the program.**

You can do so through the Escape menu.

# Recording the Action

After you create your map, you can dive in and shoot some action! For the following steps, we're assuming that you're playing single player:

1. **Open** `2save_replay.preference.cfg` **from your main MTW2 directory and search for [replay].**

   It's just a text file, so you can open it in any text editor.

2. **Edit the line** `file = C:\mtw2_release_F52\replays\MfD1.rpy` **and change the name** `MfD1` **to whatever you want to call your first replay.**

   You can choose any name you like — just remember what you've chosen.

3. **Change the path to wherever you installed MTW2 — probably** `C:\Program Files\SEGA\Medieval II`.

4. **Double-click** `2save_replay.bat` **to start MTW2.**

   The game is ready to record whatever actions you take.

5. **Select Single Player, then Historical Battle from the menu that appears, and choose the map you created earlier from the following menu.**

6. **Click Next and then choose which army you want to control by clicking the appropriate flag.**

7. **Click Start.**

8. **Press P to pause the game as soon as it loads and take a look around.**

9. **It's up to you now: Play the game as normal.**

   If, like us, you've barely considered that this is, in fact, a game, you may want to quit and play a couple of the tutorials to get the hang of actually, er, playing.

If you do decide to go straight into playing, all the events of the battle are saved. Don't play for too long — a minute or so is fine. If you then exit, your replay is saved.

# Shooting the Carnage

After your glorious victory has been recorded for all eternity (see preceding section), you can reload the saved game and replay the action. This time, you add cameras and camera movements to create a cinematic story:

1. **Open the file** `3cined.preference.cfg` **in your MTW2 directory for editing.**

2. **Look for the line file** = `C:\mtw2_release_F52\replays\mfD3.rpy` **and change** `mfD3` **to the name of your saved game.**

3. **Check that the resolution specified in the file isn't too large for your monitor.**

4. **Double-click** `3cined.bat` **to once again load MTW2.**

   The CineEd window, shown in Figure 12-3, appears below the main MTW2 window. If you can't see it, you may not have enough room on your screen to display both windows at once.

Playback controls          Interpolation controls          Medieval II: Total War window

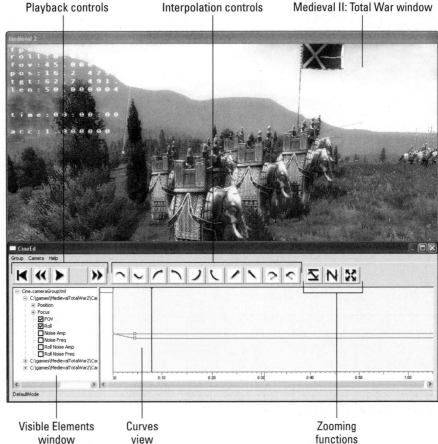

**Figure 12-3:** MTW2 running with the CineEd window also present.

Visible Elements window          Curves view          Zooming functions

The Cinematics Editor contains a few key tools and commands that you need to know to use it, as outlined in the following sections.

# 1: The Medieval II: Total War window

The main game view is rendered in the MTW2 window. You can press Tab to switch between a free view and a view through the current active camera. In this view, you can move around the map using the standard controls. If you're in free view, you can press P to get a picture-in-picture view from your currently active camera, and you can also see and move any cameras in the scene.

# 2: The Visible Elements window

This window selects the elements of the current camera displayed in the Curves View. You need to expand the tree view here to see the available cameras. Then you can expand the tree for those cameras to select:

- ✔ **Position (X, Y, and Z axis),** which defines the camera's position in 3D-space.
- ✔ **Focus (X, Y, and Z axis),** which defines the point at which the camera is looking. When you're looking up and down using the keyboard controls, what you're really doing is moving the focus point. Rarely will you need to manually edit the Position or Focus elements, because you'll do most of that through the MTW2 window.
- ✔ **Field Of View,** which you can modify only through the CineEd window.
- ✔ **Roll,** which governs the amount that the camera is tilted off-center.
- ✔ **The four Noise controls,** which you can use to add an element of random movement to the camera (to simulate a hand-held shot, or the ground shaking, for example).

# 3: The Curves View

In the Curves View, you see curves representing the value of all the camera elements that you've changed over time. A green line represents the current playback point for the recording, and a red line represents the current time on the active camera. Little white or red squares, known as *keyframes,* also appear at different points on the curves (see Figure 12-4). Keyframes represent specific values that you've told MTW2 to assign to a certain camera element at a specific time.

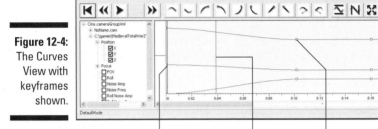

**Figure 12-4:**
The Curves
View with
keyframes
shown.

Active camera time    Playback point    Keyframe

If you were to place your camera at ground level and place a keyframe at 0 seconds, that would mean your camera would start at the ground level at 0 seconds. You'd see a keyframe on the camera position curve at 0 seconds, specifying ground level as the current camera height. Then, if you were to raise the camera up for 4 seconds (craning up to a nice high shot), you'd see another point for, say, 10 meters, appear on the position curve at 4 seconds.

Crucially, a curve or a line (which is just a flat curve) would be drawn between these two points, telling you that the camera moves from one position to the next. From that curve, you could tell, for example, that at 2 seconds into the movie, the camera will be about 5 meters off the ground — because that's where the curve lies at the 2-second mark.

You can navigate between keyframes by pressing the left and right square bracket keys ([ and ]) on your keyboard. You can only move the camera in the MTW2 window when the red line is on a keyframe. That's because CineEd needs a keyframe in which to record the camera's new position.

Here are a few more things to keep in mind:

✔ If you want to place a keyframe for the camera, you can do so by pressing the Insert key. This action adds a keyframe at the current camera time (the red line), on all tracks, whether visible or not.

✔ You can also double-click to place a keyframe at the point where you double-click. This only places a keyframe on visible curves.

✔ Left-click and drag in the Curves View to select multiple keyframes at once.

✔ You can click and drag a keyframe to move it up or down, changing its value. If you want to change its position in time, Shift+click and drag the keyframe backward or forward along the timeline.

- ✔ To delete a keyframe, select it and press Delete. Sometimes deleting keyframes won't work. If that happens, try de-selecting and re-selecting them and then deleting again.

- ✔ Shift+right-click anywhere in this timeline to set a rewind point. On long films, you may not always want to rewind right the way back to the start. Setting a rewind point ensures that the film restarts from that point only.

## 4: The Playback controls

You can use the Playback controls to move the action forward through time or fast-forward if you're impatient. You can also rewind the recorded footage to the very beginning. Unfortunately, there's no way to rewind just a few seconds. It's all or nothing, so if you miss the exact moment that you wanted to start your camera move, you've no option but to rewind the battle to the start and try again.

The replay can't rewind because it is a series of orders, not a recording of unit positions. So, in order to get back to the 2-minute mark on a recording, the game has to quickly run through all the orders that happened up to that time.

You can playback any camera movements that you've defined by pressing the Spacebar. The camera moves, but the action of the battle remains paused. This technique is great for checking your camera paths without having to rewind and re-edit every time.

Finally, if you're working on a long replay, don't forget you can create a rewind point by Shift+right-clicking in the Curves View so that you don't have to watch through the entire battle.

## 5: The Interpolation controls

Use the Interpolation controls to decide how the camera moves during the transition between two camera points (known as interpolation).

By default, camera changes use smooth interpolation, which usually generates a nice smooth movement, but may result in your camera doing something unexpected. If your camera decides to take a brief side trip between two similar keyframes, for example, change your interpolation settings. You can apply these controls to curves other than position, too.

The various interpolation controls are

- ✔ **Smooth in and smooth out,** which give you a generally smooth camera motion. Use these interpolation units by default unless they aren't working for you!

✔ **Easy-in and easy-out,** which tell the camera to accelerate and decelerate gradually at the beginning and end of its path. Ease-in gives you a very smooth start, which looks as though the camera is accelerating.

✔ **Hard-in and hard-out,** which causes the camera to accelerate to a very sudden stop (or vice versa). Useful for imitating a rough, warts-and-all hand-held style (think *NYPD Blue,* but with more elephants).

✔ **Linear In and Linear Out,** which you'll mainly use for a smooth continuation. You'll usually use only one of these on a keyframe, either in or out, depending on whether the shot follows another shot or leads into another shot. Linear In and Linear Out are useful particularly when two adjacent keyframes are meant to be in very similar positions — if you use other interpolation types, you may find the camera wanders.

✔ **Bezier-in and Bezier-out.** Theoretically, this should give you a very smooth, yet highly editable, curve on your camera path. We don't recommend you use these interpolations unless you're pretty familiar with Bezier curves; they're still quite bug-ridden.

## 6: Zooming functions

These three buttons magnify (or zoom out on) your timeline view, enabling you to concentrate on the specific part that you're currently editing. In order from left to right, the buttons are

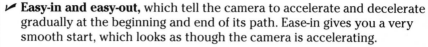

✔ **Vertical zoom,** which zooms the timeline so that all the currently selected keyframes fit into the screen view vertically (by value).

✔ **Horizontal zoom,** which does the same for the other axis — that is to say, it fits all the selected keyframes on-screen horizontally (by time).

✔ **Show all,** which zooms the Curves View as far out as it will go.

You can also use the < and > keys to zoom in and out on the timeline.

# Creating Camera Paths

Here's how you can create a simple camera:

1. **Select New from the Camera menu in the CineEd window.**

2. **Find a nice wide shot to use for your opening camera move.**

3. **Press the Enter key to start the replay playing.**

   The battle is played out on-screen just as it happened.

4. **When you've reached an appropriate point for the end of your opening camera move, press Enter again to stop the action.**

5. **Press Insert to add a new keyframe at this point in the action.**

Now you can move the camera to wherever you want it to end up — perhaps a slow pan in toward your assembled troops?

You can also insert a keyframe by double-clicking the timeline. This action adds keyframes only on visible tracks.

Drag the timeline back and press the spacebar to play, and your camera moves toward your troops.

## Adding a zoom

Here's how to use the FOV feature to add a zoom in:

1. **Expand the Visible Elements Window as far as it will go and tick the tick boxes for Position (all three controls), Focus (all three controls), and FOV.**

2. **Click Zoom Out.**

You've got two sets of keyframes now on the window, and some lines going between them.

3. **Deselect Position and Focus.**

4. **Double-click the remaining line (which represents Field of View, or FOV) at the point that the red playback line is currently placed.**

A keyframe is added on this line. Try dragging it up and down, and notice how the field of view changes. Drag it down a bit, to give you a zoom in.

5. **Double-click the FOV line about a second before the keyframe you just added and drag this keyframe up to where the line originally was.**

6. **Select this keyframe and click Linear In.**

This ensures the FOV stays constant before this keyframe. Now, if you right-click in the Curve View about 2 seconds before the first keyframe and then press space to play the camera, you see that you've got a fairly quick zoom in.

7. **On the CineEd menu, choose Camera⇨Save and choose a name for your camera.**

You should be saving your cameras fairly regularly.

Click the Save button in the Windows dialog box with the mouse. Don't press Enter, or the recording will start playing. Also note that when you save your camera, its name changes in the Visible Elements window to whatever you saved it as.

# Creating a close-up hand-held camera

Here's how to add a camera closer in to the action.

1. **Choose Camera⇨New, expand the Visible Elements window, and select NoName in the Visible Elements window.**

2. **Press Tab twice, press Insert to add a keyframe, and move your camera closer to the action.**

    Find a nice shot on some cavalry, elephants, cannons, or something else that will make the ground shake a bit. You're just going to use a static shot here, but you'll add some camera shake to it.

    Sometimes, when you change cameras, CineEd gets a bit confused. We pressed Tab twice here to remind CineEd which camera we're using.

3. **Go to the CineEd window and expand the Visible Elements on the NoName camera.**

    Just so we're clear, that's the Visible Elements window, not the Visible Elephants window. Depending on what you placed in your map, this may be an easy mistake to make.

4. **Save it as a new camera by choosing Camera⇨Save.**

    You may notice we have a bit of a saving twitch here. You can avoid problems by clicking OK on the Save dialog box instead of pressing Enter at any point.

5. **Select Noise Amp and Noise Freq and double-click the horizontal line that appears, about a second before where the red line is currently placed; then double-click exactly where the red line is placed.**

    You see only one line here, despite the fact that you've selected two values, because both values are currently the same.

    You've now created two keyframes for your noise. You can edit the levels of the second one now, and you'll get a nice ramp up from the levels that the first one is set to, meaning the camera will start shaking.

6. **Drag a box around the second keyframe (which is actually a set of two keyframes) and then click them and drag them up a bit.**

7. **Now right-click just before the first set of keyframes and play back by pressing the spacebar.**

    How does that look? Like the camera's being shaken, or like it's on a rolling sea? Try playing around with the settings on the second set of keyframes to see what happens.

    We've set some keyframes to cause camera shake at the appropriate point. It's unlikely that our camera would stay pointing perfectly forward while it's getting knocked around. We can add a bit of roll shake, too.

8. **Deselect Noise Amp and Noise Freq and select Roll Noise Amp and Roll Noise Freq.**

9. **Create two sets of keyframes about a second apart, like you did in Step 5, with the keyframes at the same time you created the Noise Amp and Noise Freq keyframes.**

10. **Drag a box around the second keyframes and try dragging them up and down, as you did in Step 6.**

   Play with this for a bit until you've got a camera that looks like it's being authentically shaken around as the elephants (or whatever) charge past. Now to hold onto that rumble while everything goes past.

11. **Select Noise Amp, Noise Freq, Roll Noise Amp, and Roll Noise Freq.**

12. **Move the play head to when you think the elephants (or whatever) will have gone past by right-clicking the Curve window; double-click at that point to add another keyframe.**

   The line between the two keyframes isn't flat. If you play the sequence back from the second keyframe, you see that the noise changes in intensity, rather than staying the same. That's no good.

13. **Drag-select the second keyframes and click Linear Out at the top of the screen.**

   The line changes as you do this step. Now the line should be flat. If you add more animation on the noise curves later on, you also need to give the third keyframe a Linear In, to avoid it curving again.

   Finally, go back to your original camera, change its duration, and get it ready to render.

14. **Choose Camera➪Save and save your second camera (over the file-name you already used).**

   You've now got some close-up shaky camerawork!

If you wanted to, you could add movement here, to simulate a cameraman moving closer, or add any other camerawork element you like.

## Rendering a camera

You render each camera in turn to an AVI file. You'll render the first camera here, but rendering subsequent cameras works exactly the same way.

1. **Deselect all the check boxes in the Visible Elements window and click your original camera.**

   The view changes to your first camera.

**2. Click the Zoom Out button.**

From now on, we're assuming that you started your camera at the start of your recording and want to continue using it until a few seconds after the end of the camera move.

**3. Press the Rewind button.**

The scene reloads.

**4. Press Tab to require your camera view and then press Enter to play back both camerawork and recording.**

When your camera move finishes and you think you've gotten to the end of the usable footage for the first shot, press Enter again to stop.

**5. Drag the black line from the end of the timeline window back to the position of the replay head (the green line, which may currently be covered by the red camera playhead).**

You've now told the game that you want to only use that section of the recording when you render this shot out.

**6. Save your camera again and exit CineEd.**

# Rendering a Shot

After you've set up a camera, you're ready to render out the footage from that camera as an AVI file. MTW2 renders using the highest graphical settings it can possibly manage, which makes your movie look really rather nice.

**1. Open up** `4render.preference.cfg` **in your main MTW2 directory for editing.**

**2. Edit the following lines in the replay section to point to your replay file and your camera file:**

```
file = C:\mtw2_release_F52\replays\mfD3.rpy
camera = C:\mtw2_release_F52\Cameras\MfD_Cam06_render.cam
```

**3. Edit the following lines in the cine section:**

```
width = 800
height = 600
```

**4. Set these values to whatever resolution you'd like your footage to be rendered as.**

You can only choose standard OpenGL resolutions here, unfortunately — 800x600, 1,024x768, 1,200x900, 1,600x1,200 and equivalent widescreen resolutions.

5. **Edit the following line in the** `capture_tga` **section if you want a different frames-per-second rate:** `fps = 60`.

We recommend leaving this setting at 60 unless you have good reason not to. It's double the rate you'll eventually need, which means that it'll be very easy to add fancy effects, such as slow-motion footage, in your video-editing package.

6. **Double-click** `4render.bat` **and then do nothing at all.**

This step is very important. MTW2 loads and starts to render your footage automatically. Unfortunately, it's a little precious, so just let it run; attempting any other task with your computer while the footage is rendering will probably cause your cavalry charge to be interrupted with footage of you checking your e-mail or browsing certain specialist Web sites.

Once the footage has finished rendering, an `avi` file appears in the `capture_tga` directory, under the MTW2 directory.

7. **Edit this footage in your video editor of choice, and you've got a pretty decent little movie.**

If you import your footage into Premiere or another high-end video package, you may find that they appear completely black. That's because MTW2's renderer has a bug in the way it exports Alpha Channels. Tell your video editor to ignore alpha for that footage, and you're away.

# Getting the Scoop on Tips and Tricks

Medieval II: Total War can create some fantastic movies with very little effort, but you can improve your efforts even more with a few simple guidelines. Here are a few tips and tricks, direct from Peter Brophy at Creative Assembly, to help you make your MTW2 Machinima absolutely stunning.

- ✔ **You can edit a lot of files in a text editor.** Many MTW2 data files — camera files and map files, in particular — are plain text. Don't be afraid to hack away at them. You can change camera duration, fix things you've broken, and more. Just remember to save a copy of the original in case your over-eager ministrations break the file beyond all repair.

- ✔ **Swish pans.** You can put together some great hand-held-style swish pans, à la *NYPD Blue,* using a hard in and a linear out. On a fast pan, this effect gives the handheld camera a jerking-around feel.

- ✔ **Wait for a good kill.** It's impossible to predict when you'll see a good fight or killing blow between two individual characters. Your best approach is to set up a lengthy fight in the recording and then play it back in CineEd, looking for a good moment. You can turn on show `fatality_markers = true` in the `3cined.preference.cfg` to have the game show a green marker above any unit about to perform a fatality.

✔ **Take close-ups from two different angles.** Remember that you can shoot the same piece of action several times, from several different cameras. Shoot any close-ups or action shots from at least two different angles. You'll be grateful for the choice of footage when you edit the movie together.

✔ **Watch your angles!** If you worry about nothing else while shooting MTW2 sequences, watch the line of action and the angles that characters exit and enter a frame. Getting confused in a fight is easy; keep a careful eye on your technical camerawork to make sure that the viewer knows what's going on and where he is.

✔ **Watch out for popping trees.** Occasionally, trees (or sometimes entire forests) spontaneously pop into existence during a camera movement. There's no way to avoid this mishap, unfortunately, other than to choose a different shot.

✔ **Avoid fights on slopes.** MTW2 has an amazing engine, but sometimes it still gets a bit confused. If two characters are fighting on a slope, they'll carry on using the same animations they would use if they were on flat land, no matter how high they are standing respective to each other. That can look funny, but it rarely looks good.

✔ **Vegetation, particularly long grass, looks great.** MTW2 produces great shots if the camera is low to the ground with some rocks or vegetation in the foreground. These shots also help maintain the illusion that the viewer is not simply watching a computer game.

✔ **Make sure that everything's a mini-story.** Take a shot of a cannon firing, for example. You can cover the entire thing in a slow, wide shot — or you can open with a wide shot, then cut to a shot of the cannoneer loading the cannon, cut to a close-up as he fires, cut back to the wide or to a reaction shot of the cannoneer, cut to a shot of the ball in flight, and then cut to a shot of it impacting and mud and stone flying everywhere. Which looks more dramatic?

✔ **Tell that cameraman to stay still!** Although it's tempting to plot a complicated sweeping camera path complete with noise and zoom for every shot, use these techniques sparingly. MTW2's camera plotting is all the more effective if you don't saturate your movie with it. A well-placed static camera is the best choice for almost every shot.

✔ **Fill your frame with distances.** MTW2 looks particularly great if you can emphasize the scale of your battlefield by contrasting foreground and background, near and distant. If you've got a close-up of a cannoneer, can you frame him with a castle looming in the background? If you're shooting a long shot of a cavalry charge, can you crane down to rocks in the foreground?

✔ **Re-attach split files with VirtualDub.** Footage rendered from MTW2 can get quite large — even a few seconds of uncompressed footage at 60FPS can take up hundreds of megabytes. MTW2 automatically splits the file into two or more parts if the size grows to greater than 1GB. VirtualDub (on the DVD for this book) can easily reattach these files and produce one single (huge) video file.

✔ **Get with the handheld camerawork.** Using noise, you can put together some fantastic handheld camera shots. As *Lord of the Rings* shows, that sort of camerawork is just fantastic for convincing an audience that what it sees is real.

✔ **Refine your camerawork in several passes.** You won't get your camera placement and pathing exactly right the first time you try, and it can be frustrating to rewind the replay file every time you make a change. The solution is not to worry about it. Establish your cameras in approximately the setup you want and then watch the sequence, noting the errors. Now make another pass through, tweaking the cameras as appropriate. Repeat this process until your cameras are perfect. You'll expend far less energy this way.

✔ **Get rid of the flags!** By default, all the MTW2 units have large flags floating above them. Up close, these look really dodgy. You can get rid of them by adding `show_banners = 0` under `[video]` in the `4render.preference.cfg`.

✔ **You can't really storyboard.** Peter describes attempting to predict exactly what will happen in an MTW2 battle as like trying to storyboard a riot. You can plan, but the joy of MTW2 Machinima is finding and using the spontaneous moments that occur.

To find out more and get the latest updates on Total War and the Total War modding scene, visit the Total War forums at `www.totalwarforums.com`.

# Chapter 13

# Noise! Sound Design and Recording for a Great Film

*Y*ou can always tell the movies with great sound design: They're the ones in which you don't notice the sound. That's the eternal irony of the sound engineer. If he does his work properly, nobody will notice. If he does a terrible job, you can be sure people will tell him so.

Sound design is one of the most important aspects of any Machinima production — it can give life to the story, help make your computer-generated world feel real, and even provide action and effects that you can't achieve in your engine. The classic Machinima productions, without exception, have great soundtracks.

A good soundscape is multilayered. It tells a story — audibly rather than visually, but a story nonetheless. A really good soundscape takes account of absolutely everything that's happening at that point in the movie, *on-screen and off*, and adds one or more audio layers for each of those events. That may seem like overkill. It certainly seems a bit too much like hard work, but if you want your movie to be really great instead of just good, multilayered sound-scaping is something that has to be done.

We can easily fill this book with tips, tricks, and techniques for sound design, and you can easily spend years learning the craft. Unfortunately, we've just got this chapter, and you probably want to get your movie finished before your grandchildren graduate, so we limit it to a crash course for now.

# *Figuring Out What Sound You Need*

A common mistake made by inexperienced filmmakers is to underestimate the importance of sound in their movie. It's all too easy to think of your movie's sound and audio production as the icing on the cake, rather than the flour. Far too often, a movie of potentially excellent quality is let down by shoddy sound design. Think about the different categories of sound that a movie requires:

- ✔ **Dialogue:** Assuming that your movie contains spoken (or sung) words — and there's no sacred law that says it should — you'll need to record this dialogue. It may not take up a large chunk of your movie — depending on the lip syncing capabilities of your chosen engine, it may occupy as little space as possible — but there's no denying its importance. It doesn't matter how cleverly you word your three minutes of heavy exposition if the audience can't hear it.

- ✔ **Foley sounds:** If a tree falls in a forest, it needs to make a sound. A loud, crashing, tearing, swishing thump of a sound. More subtly, if a character puts her purse down for a second, we need to hear it as it makes contact with the table. Almost every action in your movie, no matter how small or trivial, potentially requires an accompanying sound. These sounds are collectively known as the *foley,* after Hollywood sound designer Jack Foley, a pioneer of sound design during the early days of the new talkies.

- ✔ **Ambient noise:** The birds are chirping softly. In the distance, a stream gently trickles. The trees wave softly in the breeze. CUT TO: The mysterious old house. All is dusty and still, except for the constant ponderous ticking of the clock in the hall. It's raining heavily outside and droplets begin to spatter onto the hardwood floor . . . As well as winning the clichéd movie-of-the-month award, those few sentences contain enough ambient and background noise to give a sound designer sleepless nights. They won't record themselves, and if they're forgotten, their absence from the film will be painfully apparent.

- ✔ **Woosh! Zap! Boom!** If your film is a science-fiction tale, you'll definitely have to add special sound effects to your arsenal, but even a romantic period drama can have occasion to call on some Ka-zow! Buzz! sounds. Any sound that is out of the ordinary, or that is meant to represent the sound of something that has never actually been heard (the discharge from a Martian anti-proton laser rifle, say), is a special effect.

- ✔ **Musical soundtracks:** Music underscoring a scene is a long-accepted convention. Despite the music being, in theory, heavily incongruous, audiences have grown so used to musical soundtracks to movies that the lack of one can actually make them feel quite uncomfortable.

Subconsciously, the film sounds unfinished. It's always good advice to decide if your film will have a soundtrack or not early on in the process, and if so, what it will be. Of course, if you're making a music video, the decision is out of your hands.

Music also creates mood. It's much harder to achieve any emotional impact in your film without a stirring soundtrack.

# Winning a Losing Battle

In an ideal world, you'd record the sound for your movie on the same voice mike that you use for TeamSpeak, or by leaning over the built-in mike on your laptop and moving the FireWire cable out of the way. In an ideal world, it would be that simple to record brilliant quality audio, and you'd never have to worry about it. In an ideal world, your humble authors would be writing this book from the beach house on their exclusive private island. Life just isn't that kind.

However cleverly you go about it, and however many clever tools and techniques you employ, there's one key fact that you just can't get around: Any sound recording you make will be a digital approximation of a real-world analog sound. That's bad news before you even start — you have to resign yourself to an inevitable loss of sound quality. One of your key tasks as a sound designer is to keep this loss to a minimum.

# Understanding the Basics of Sound

When you record the sound for your movie, and later on, when you edit it, you'll constantly have your eye on a few key aspects of the sound:

- **Levels:** The simplest way of think about *levels* is to think of them as the volume (or lack of it), but sound levels are actually far more complex than that. Sound exists at a number of different frequencies, some more naturally audible to the human ear than others. (Audio compression formats such as OGG and MP3 work by discarding sounds from frequency levels that are all but inaudible anyway.)

  It's trivial to artificially boost a sound to increase its overall volume, or decrease it. By manipulating the volume of specific frequency brackets, you can gain far greater control of the final sound product. You can increase the volume of the low bass rumble from that big explosion (or decrease it if it's so bass-heavy that your speakers shake).

✔ **Clipping:** What happens if you amplify a sound further than your speakers can accommodate or your chosen sound storage format can represent? The sound *clips,* artificially cutting off the highest and lowest frequency noises (the top and the bottom of the audio wave). Clipping can have a significant effect on the generated sound and is rarely desirable. The very flat, dirty sound produced when an electric guitar is forced through an overdriven amp is typical of a clipped sound. You should always watch for clipping and try to avoid it as much as possible. Luckily, that's comparatively easy to do.

Extreme clipping is always detectable to even the most casual listener, but minor or moderate clipping — which is the really dangerous kind — can sometimes be difficult to notice when you first listen to a track. Most good audio-editing software packages include a graphical representation of the sound waveform. Often, you can easily identify regions of clipping by examining this image. Look for moments when the peaks of the sound curve flatten out, as if somebody's sliced the top off a mountain (and vice versa for the troughs).

If you do find areas of clipping, the easiest (and best) way to deal with them is to undo the last alteration that you made. If you just boosted the overall gain (or volume) on the track, it may well have caused the clipping. A bit of trial and error will soon produce the optimum compromise. If the clipping isn't the result of your manipulations, but is unavoidably present in the raw sound data, there's less you can do, but small iterative alterations to the sound can often limit the damage caused by the clipped areas.

✔ **Noise:** Hold on. Isn't noise exactly what you're trying to record here? Well, yes it is, but in this case, the phrase *noise* is used to refer specifically to unwanted audio artifacts within an otherwise pure sound. The hiss of a low-quality microphone; your lead actor's breath that makes every *f* or *w* sound like a wind tunnel test; a car driving by outside — all these things are classified as noise and need to be eliminated.

The easiest way to do so, of course, is to ensure that the unwanted noise never makes it onto the audio track in the first place. Buy a good-quality microphone; tell Dave that his voice will be picked up just fine even if his lips are further than 3mm from the mike; and find a recording environment that's further from the main road (or at least set up your make-shift sound studio properly — see our tips later in this chapter).

Of course, exceptions can prove the rule. Sometimes the low quality and distortion caused by noise or clipping is exactly what you need. A line of dialogue supposedly heard over a walkie-talkie, or the inhuman roar of the homicidal robot, both benefit from deliberate clipping. Don't go overboard, though. Remember that every change you make is discarding sound data; and once it's gone, it's impossible to add it back in.

# Getting the Kit — Recommendations for Cheap Equipment and Free Software

Okay, no lies. You're going to have to spend a bit of money to get good-quality sound. Not that much — certainly not as much as you need to spend to get a good video-editing setup — but you do need to part with a bit of cash.

## Microphone

You need a good microphone. It's as simple as that. There is just no way that your $10 mike from Fry's will do the job here.

Our recommendation is the Shure SM58 mike, which you can buy new for about $99, or on eBay for about $60. The SM58 is an industry classic whose design has stayed the same for about ten years — and there's a reason for that. It's virtually indestructable, very cheap (for a pro-grade microphone), and gives you sensational results — all of *BloodSpell* was recorded on these little beauties.

You should also pick up a mike stand when you buy the SM58, plus the appropriate leads — which are XLR to Minijack leads if you're going straight to your PC. Stands aren't optional — these mikes are, fairly obviously, very good at picking up sounds, and you make a lot of sound when you're holding one.

You also need a *pop shield,* which is a sheet of gauze or nylon that's placed between the microphone and the actor. It doesn't muzzle the audio quality at all, but it reduces the unpleasant artifacts from plosive sounds. (Peter Piper picked a peck of pickled pepper, and the like.) You can buy pop shields for a few dollars from any decent audio equipment store.

Overall, smart buying should ensure that you don't have to go above $120 or so for your kit. You can spend less — we don't recommend shelling all this money out for your first-ever film — but if you're doing anything serious, you really need audio of this quality.

## Mixing desk

A *mixing desk* (or mixing console) is a clever device that allows you to combine several audio signals into one glorious whole. You can change the levels, tonality, and dynamics of each track before it's added to the mix. You don't really need a mixing desk unless you're going to be recording more than one person at once — however, if you're making a film with a lot of dialogue, you'll want to do just that. Bear in mind that you'll need to buy another mike, stand, and pop shield for this approach, too! (For more on these items, see the preceding section.)

However, if you're recording multiple voices, you've got two choices available to you — either buy a multitrack recorder, which usually hooks up to your PC or Mac via FireWire, or buy a mixing desk, which can go via FireWire or via conventional audio cable.

The latter costs a lot less than the former — a 2-input multitrack from Presonus sets you back about $250, whereas a Peavey 4-input mixer costs just $100 or so. Unless you've got a truly professional recording space, you can't record separate tracks cleanly anyway, so a mixer is the best solution for you.

On *BloodSpell,* we went mad and bought an 8-input FirePod from Presonus. It was total overkill — if we were doing it again, we'd buy a simple mixing desk. Mixing desks also have the advantage that they output only a single track of audio, which makes the audio easier to edit and also widens the range of programs you can use to record.

Mixing desk technology changes fast. Find your local sound/music supply shop and ask the employees what they recommend. In the UK, we recommend calling Dolphin Music (+44 870 840 9060 or www.dolphinmusic.co.uk) and asking its staff for a recommendation. In the United States, ZZounds (800-ZZOUNDS or 800-996-8637 and www.zzounds.com) is an excellent retailer for audio equipment.

Don't forget leads. If you're using a mixing desk, you need XLR to XLR leads to connect the mike to the desk and then an XLR or phono jack to minijack to go to the PC.

## Headphones

Sorry, but your iPod headphones won't quite cut it here. The good news is that a decent pair of headphones really isn't expensive. While you can easily spend $300 on a pair, a $30 pair from a reputable manufacturer (Seinhausser, Shure, AKG, and Behringer) do just as well. Ask your friendly local audio shop for recommendations.

## Software

If you don't want to spend money on software, you're in luck. Audacity (http://audacity.sourceforge.net/) is one of the poster children for top-quality open-source software, offering audio editing that's on a par with low-end professional systems.

If you do want to spend money, on the other hand, you have a wealth of choice. As comparative sound-editing neophytes, we recommend Adobe Audition, formerly Cool Edit Pro. It's a great multitrack audio-editing package. Phil Rice, the sound design genius who produced the sound on *BloodSpell* in between authoring million-view films such as *Male Restroom Etiquette,* uses Steinberg's Cubase SX, a package that's primarily used for music, and does great work.

## Sound damping

You need to damp out sound in your recording studio. Hard surfaces cause reverberation (reverb, for short), which alters the sound of your recording, and noise can leak through from other locations.

Our recommended supplier for sound damping hardware is IKEA. Yes, IKEA, the Swedish home-decorating company that produces some excellent, and exceedingly cheap, duvets. Buy 4 or 5 (or 10 or 12, depending on the size of your room — more is better than less) of their cheapest, and you'll be sorted for things to thumbtack to walls to reduce sound bounce.

# Setting Up a Recording Studio in Your Bedroom

You need somewhere to record your audio. Sure, you can just use the microphone that came bundled with your budget PC. Why not just record everything onto a $30 Dictaphone and be done with it? If you want your movie to have an audio track that's actually audible, you need to spend a little time on your setup. Surprisingly, a minimum amount of effort can transform your own bedroom into a very passable recording studio.

You need to follow these steps as far as you can, whether you're planning to record spoken dialogue, foley, or anything else. Your aim is to record as much of the sound you actually want as possible, while recording the minimum of any other interfering sound.

1. **Find a space.**

   The first thing to do is to choose a room. Unless you're recording an entire chamber orchestra plus 300 voice choir, a small room is better than a large one. A large space can often absorb and reflect low to mid-end sound frequencies, leaving your recorded audio sounding flat and dampened, while echoing horribly. It's important that the space you use isn't too echo-ey or acoustically bizarre.

Don't be afraid to do some test recordings first or to fall back on the old favorite of snapping your fingers, clapping your hands, and moaning, all the while listening to the way the space treats the sound.

While you're at it, contravene all fire-safety regulations; the ideal recording room is one with only a single door and no windows. Every door and every window let in some extraneous sound from outside and change the way the room's acoustics act, probably for the worse. You can minimize the damage, though. You need your mom's (SO's/wife's/children's) best duvet.

2. **Pin the duvet up over any windows or doors.**

   Wait, don't put the book down. We're serious. This technique works — we've done it ourselves many times. What you're trying to do is reduce the amount of echo and delayed sound reflection in the room through the medium of quality winter bed coverage.

   Come to think of it, maybe Mom's best duvet wasn't the best idea. Better grab the grubby old one from the storage cupboard instead. We need to find a way to fix it securely over the window.

   We say "we" — you're the one who's going to have to do the work. In the past, we've used all sorts of techniques, from draping the quilt over the curtain rail, to three full rolls of liberally applied gaffer tape, to simply nailing the darned thing to the wall with huge tacks. The solution you choose probably depends on how much you value your wall, or (more importantly) if it actually is your wall.

   If you can't stick pins in your walls, you can always drape the duvet over your actor's head while recording. Doing so completely eliminates the room from your recording.

3. **Put something soft in the corners of your room, which are the primary danger points for reverberation, and to break up any flat surface.**

   You don't need to utterly cover flat walls and so on — just make sure that the middle of the wall is covered. Provided the wall's at least half duvet by the time you've finished, you'll be fine.

4. **Block up the edges of the doorframe.**

   Use bubble wrap, woolen scarves or even old T-shirts. If you can get hold of any spare duvets, all the better — pin them up to the other walls. It will isolate the sound even further. Call all your relatives and make up a story about a troupe of itinerant Bohemian finger puppeteers to whom you've offered sleeping accommodation in return for the secret of the mystical Pinky Finger Ballet.

5. **Once you've padded out The Special Room so that you can't hurt yourself, set up your mikes and your recording equipment and listen to the output on a good-quality pair of headphones.**

# Makin' Yer Aktual Recording!

Fortunately, recording your actor or actors is fairly simple. For the following steps, we assume that you're recording 2 actors, but the same process applies for 1, 2, or 75.

1. **Set up mikes and pop shields to appropriate heights.**

   Make sure that your actors can talk comfortably into their mikes by adjusting the height and angle of your mike stands. Also, make sure that their pop shields are about 3 inches away from the mike, and in between the mike and the actor!

2. **Check that you can record!**

   Have each of your actors talk randomly into their mikes. A classic question to get them talking is, "So, what did you have for breakfast?" while Hugh likes to ask people to talk about what random words like koala and indigestion mean to them. Now, turn up levels on your mixer to reasonable numbers and press record on your audio equipment.

   Are you hearing sound through your headphones? If not, it's time to use a technical expression and mess around until they miraculously work. Check connections. Make sure that you've got the leads plugged into the right sockets (Hugh tends to plug microphones into headphone sockets, and hilarity then ensues).

3. **Set levels.**

   Your actors will be getting sick of talking into their mikes by now. Hard luck. Have them continue to talk and adjust the levels on the mixing desk until the levels meter on your sound software is showing that their volume is peaking at about 50 percent of maximum. Setting levels now ensures that you don't get horrible clipping all through their otherwise brilliant performance.

   Make sure that you ask them to speak as loudly as they will in the scene you're about to record. Hugh nearly blew out his sound designer's ears during the filming of *Eschaton: Nightfall,* as he moved from conversation to shouting at a huge demonic entity voice pitch.

4. **Relax your actors.**

   Now that everything's set up, take a little while to relax your actors. Chat to them about the scene. Do some kind of thespian warmup exercise. Feed them vodka — whatever works to get them relaxed for the shoot to come.

5. **Aaaand . . . action!**

   Start recording. Make sure that you wait a couple of seconds before your actors start speaking, to give yourself some pre-roll time and ensure that you don't clip off anything important. And don't be afraid to do multiple takes, until you think you've got what you need.

# Recording from Different Locations

In an ideal situation, all your actors would be located in the same part of the world as you, enabling you to record their voices live in an environment you've created. The fast-moving world of Machinima being what it is, though, you may have a few cast members on the other side of the globe, communicating through this new-fangled Internet thingy. All is not lost.

You'll have to trust them to record their own audio, though. That's one of the many reasons that we don't recommend this approach if you can possibly avoid it. Most of the basic steps for setting up a recording environment can be replicated in your actor's bedroom four time zones away. (See the section "Setting Up a Recording Studio in Your Bedroom," earlier in this chapter.) And why not buy them a copy of this book? (Hey, we've got to eat, you know!)

At Strange Company, we've experimented with conducting a virtual audio recording session using a Voice Over IP (VOIP) connection via Skype (www.skype.com). That let the director and sound designer (seated around a bunch of computers in Edinburgh) listen to each take live and pass comments immediately to the actor (probably recording onto his laptop on a Los Angeles beach — you know what actors are like).

If you're going to do this, you need to have two microphones at each end, unless you're very, very clever. One (the good one) should be going to a decent audio recording package, while the other (the cruddy one, in all likelihood) should be going to your VOIP software.

We don't recommend recording from different locations unless it's absolutely essential. It's hard to direct an actor when she's hundreds of miles away, and the sound quality that you'll achieve won't be up to the standards of the rest of your dialogue. The more elements you add into the equation, the more likelihood there is of something going wrong.

# Cleaning Up Voices and Balance Levels

Although you may have recorded your audio, the process is by no means finished. Any audio file will benefit from optimization in an audio editor. In many cases, the improvement is dramatic. Here are some simple tips for processing audio:

- **Importing an audio file:** You need to bring your audio file into your editor of choice. In Audacity (see Figure 13-1), it couldn't be simpler. Choosing File⇨Open allows you to locate the source audio file. You should then immediately save the file as an Audacity project — that way, your original audio source file remains intact, in case your editing goes horribly wrong.

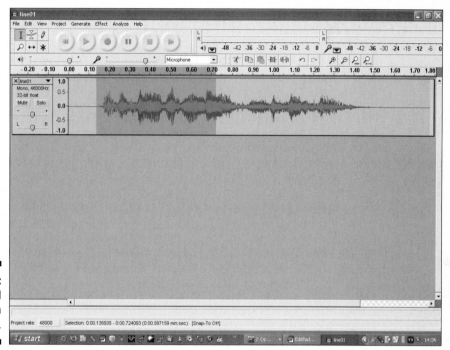

**Figure 13-1:**
Normalized
waveform in
Audacity.

✔ **Checking current levels:** The audio file is represented on screen as a graphical waveform. Although the waveform looks complicated, you can see the basic rises and falls of volume as increases in the size of the waveform (the blue colored block in Audacity). You can also see how wide a variation is in the track as a whole. If the overall track is too quiet, you can boost it by choosing Effect⇨Normalize and choosing a filter.

Be aware that normalization raises all levels in the track, including even the slightest background noise. Don't rely on normalization for anything other than fixing slight variances; try from the start to get good levels during recording.

✔ **Isolating specific sections:** To work on just a part of the track at a time, click and drag along from your chosen start point to the end point. The highlighted area is now being worked on. Any effects you apply are made only on this section until you deselect it.

✔ **Modifying overall levels:** You can further adjust the amplitude levels of the track by choosing Effect⇨Amplify filter. Contrary to the implication in its name, this filter can lower the sound levels as well as raising them.

Overzealous use of amplification filters is a classic way to clip your track. View the results of a transformation carefully and use a less intensive filter setting, if necessary

Don't attempt to perfect your audio using global changes such as this. They're a good shortcut and allow you to assemble the track into roughly the form that you want, but you should do further editing using equalization tools and frequency isolators.

✔ **Modifying specific frequencies:** Making everything generically louder won't help you if you need to emphasize a specific sound within the track. If you can find the frequency at which it occurs, though, and boost only those frequencies, you can effectively work on just that one sound without affecting the rest of the track. Audacity's Analyze➪Plot Spectrum tool is a great way to get a quick overall picture of the levels at different frequencies of the track. Note the frequency at which noticeable peaks and troughs occur and then choose Effect➪Equalization. This filter allows you to modify the relative intensity of different levels using a point graph (see Figure 13-2). Add a new point at each of the important frequency locations by clicking. If the track was too quiet at that frequency, move the point upward. If the sounds at that frequency were too loud and drowned out other audio, move the point downward. Click OK to exit the dialog box and view the Plot Spectrum once more. You should see that the overall spread is now much smoother.

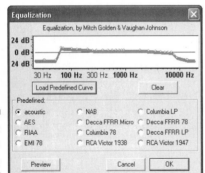

**Figure 13-2:**
Equalizing in
Audacity.

# Finding Foley Sounds and Effects

There are two basic approaches to acquiring appropriate sounds for all the actions of your movie. You can take the purist approach or the pragmatic approach. Imagine you need the sound of the hero's fist connecting soundly with the villain's jaw. The purist approach is to ask a gullible friend to stand still while you hit him repeatedly. The pragmatic approach is to smash a melon onto a concrete slab.

That's a silly example, but the idea of using completely unrelated objects to replicate a specific sound is a good one, and it's not new. The eponymous Jack Foley did that sort of thing all the time, which is probably why they named the process after him.

The melon technique, by the way, works well enough to have been used in several major Hollywood action movies.

Acquiring foley sounds can be great fun. Undoubtedly, you'll find yourself stomping on peas, throwing eggs at a wall, or snapping pencils at two-second intervals. The best tip we can give you is to experiment. Try as many bizarre things as you can think of.

The sound you're aiming for is one that automatically suggests the event taking place, even if the sound isn't truly authentic. When somebody gets punched, for example, even by a professional pugilist, it doesn't make that distinctive crunching smack sound at all, but that's the sound we expect to hear. The real sound of a thrown punch is rather disappointing and just sounds wrong when used on film.

You can often capture other ambient sounds from their real-world equivalents. What better way to create the sound of a bustling market street than to visit the market just down the road and hit Record? Be sure to record plenty of audio and make the recording from several different positions. You have very little control over the sounds you record, so you have to spend a long time editing, combining, and tweaking them to get the right result. At that point, you'll be grateful that you've got so much recorded audio to choose from. You should use this method only for ambient sound. Even after you've edited it, the track will contain a lot of noise and intrusion. Let it play as a general backdrop to a scene, but be sure it doesn't overwhelm it.

You've already got one great source of foley audio, of course — the game you're using to make your film. All the game sound effects are available for you to use, if you're using game art anyway, and they'll usually be of a very high quality. You need to extract them from whatever format the game saves them in, which can be a problem — ask around on the appropriate game modding forums and someone will soon point you to the appropriate tool:

  ✔ **The Sims 2:** SimPE, available from `http://sims.ambertation.de`

  ✔ **World of Warcraft:** MyWarcraftStudio, available from `http://wow-en.curse-gaming.com/files/details/446/mywarcraftstudio`

Finally, many sites, some free, offer foley effects for download. You can also buy a selection of sound effect libraries, with prices ranging from $100 to $5,000 or more. If you find a library that's ideally suited to a major project, and it's not too pricey, it may be a worthwhile investment.

# Locating Music

If you're remarkably talented, you can write the soundtrack to your movie yourself, perform it (including both guitar and vocals), and record the whole thing in your basement. A few irritatingly talented people like that are even around — did you know that Ezra Ferguson wrote and sang the song at the start of *The Return?* If your musical talents extend only as far as the average Joe, though, you'll need to look for an alternative soundtrack.

If you're just looking for a single song or musical piece to accompany one scene, you have plenty of options. The best idea is to explore the world of creative-commons licensed music at The Creative Commons Audio site (`http://creativecommons.org/audio`), and most of it is of a pretty high standard.

You can find music that is licensed for you to include in your film, modify, and even make commercial use out of. You can find more creative commons licensed audio at the Creative Commons Catalog (`http://commoncontent.org`), Magnatune (`www.magnatune.com`), and the Creative Commons Audio Remixes site (`ccmixter.org`).

It's also worth approaching unsigned or local bands and asking whether they'd be okay for you to use one of their tracks if they received full credit. Almost all music that we featured in *BloodSpell* was by unsigned bands, and all the artists were happy to license their work under a creative-commons license. We found most of this music either through hip indie friends or the unbelievably massive garageband.com.

Larger and more commercially successful musicians are less likely to grant you permission to use their work, and certainly not for free. There's no reason not to try, but if you've got your heart set on one specific track, you may well be disappointed. Many Machinima movies are music videos, a lot of the time set to the exact length of a full track from a commercial artist. Very few films obtain the appropriate permissions before using the track. You can avoid this step, and it may even be legal — but note the *may even* bit there. If you want to be 100 percent sure that your film won't get pulled from the Internet or, indeed, if you ever plan to show it anywhere other than the Great Wide Web, don't skip getting permission. See Chapter 15 for more details.

You may be very lucky indeed and find somebody who's willing to compose music especially for your movie. Finding these saintly individuals is hard, but they're out there. Don't just post on Machinima-related forums. Visit audio-lovers sites, as well as community sites for musicians and composers. You can also try your local music college, or find a contact within the local music scene. Many artists are striving to make themselves known anyway, and the chance for their music to be heard by anyone in the world as part of a global-released Machinima movie means that they'll see it as a good deal for both parties.

# Phil Rice's mixing tips

Once you've assembled all your audio, you have to take your music, dialogue, and audio and mix it together into a single soundtrack in your sound editor of choice. Phil Rice, audio editor on *BloodSpell* and the technical reviewer on this book, offers the following tips on mixing your finished audio:

✔ Special effects added to sounds are a distortion of the sound. All effects, be they EQ (equalization), reverb, even normalization, are distorting and corrupting the original sound to achieve their effect. As such, only use an effect if absolutely needed and then only in extreme moderation (unless the particular situation calls for that distortion).

✔ If your film has dialogue, make sure — above all else — that the dialogue comes through clearly in your mix. It should be the top priority in those scenes; everything else is secondary.

✔ Minimize use of ambient and minor foley (for example, footsteps, clothing rustles) when musical score is present. Music obscures the richest frequencies of these background sounds anyway, and their effect will likely be perceived as undesirable noise. In most cases, you can drop background sounds entirely when music is playing.

✔ Ideally, your audience should be able to set its volume at the beginning of watching your film, and never have to touch that knob again until it's finished. It's okay to have some quiet and some loud parts, but make sure neither make it so that the average user would have to adjust his volume to hear what is being said or to keep from suddenly blowing his speakers.

✔ Make it a regular part of your mixing technique to listen to your mix at a very low volume. At that low volume, do any sounds stick out? Can you still hear the dialogue or the main sound effects? Does everything seem balanced? Over the course of a mix, the natural tendency is to keep increasing the volume as your ears get tired. Make a deliberate point to crank back the volume from time to time; it's better on your ears, and you'll catch things you'd otherwise miss.

✔ Never rely on your headphones as your only mixing monitor. Effects sound dryer than normal in headphones, bass levels are deceptive, and perhaps most importantly, your ears grow tired from long sessions of headphones use, and tired ears mean flawed mix — every time. If your ears become fatigued enough, they'll start to ache a bit. If this happens, take a breather, go outside, and give them time to recuperate. Your ears are an important Machinima asset.

✔ Test your sound mix on every conceivable piece of audio equipment you have access to. Listen to it in your car, on your iPod, on your sister's old boom box and make notes with each listen. Sometimes a mix that sounds good in your studio can sound really bad elsewhere; ideally, you want to end up with a mix that sounds decent wherever you play it. Testing on various equipment is important, because your viewers will be listening to the sound on a variety of speaker configurations on their computers.

# Chapter 14

## Get It Out There! Publicizing Your Movie

*I*magine that we've imparted enough knowledge in your general direction that you've managed to create a tolerable movie using this Machinima thing. What now? Surely, you're not going to rest on your (admittedly fine-looking) laurels? When you're so close? Don't give up now! You're movie's great, so tell a few people about it — everyone, for instance.

## There's No Such Thing as Bad Publicity

It's an old and oft-touted adage, but the saying, "There's no such thing as bad publicity" is true. There are exceptions to the rule, of course, but the principle is sound. The nail that this cliché hits soundly on the head is that publicity is all about making people talk.

The next time you see an ad break on TV, don't grab a snack or answer the call of nature: Sit and watch. Television advertisements seem designed to irritate and annoy. They also get stuck in your brain. If they raise your awareness of the brand that the man in the chicken suit is singing about, they've done their job.

We're not suggesting that you dress up in a chicken suit (although what you do on your own time is your affair), but what we can't overemphasis is this point: You need to make some noise!

All right, you don't *need* to. You may be happy just showing your movie to a few friends, or just keeping it on your hard drive and never letting anyone else see it. If that's as far as you want to take it, fair enough.

It seems a shame, though, after all that hard work. Why not tell other people about it? You never know; they might like it.

There's nothing like a random e-mail from a complete stranger extolling your virtues to give you an instant ego-boost.

# Why You Should Always Lie

The late, great stand-up comedian Bill Hicks once said, "If there's anybody here who's in marketing or advertising, could you do me a favor? Kill yourselves."

It's true that a lot of publicity feels like coming as close to lying as possible without actually getting sued. That isn't really a bad thing.

Wait, hear us out.

You see, if you're publicizing something that you created yourself, you'll often find yourself being a little bit too honest. Of course, you can see the joins and the ugly bits. You've been staring at that horrible two-shot that you never had a chance to fix for the last two weeks. To you, it's so obvious that you assume that everybody else will immediately spot it as well.

In fact, they may not. They may be too busy watching the amazing action sequence with the three dozen exploding alien helicopters. You know the one — that sequence that you finished editing a little while ago and that you've watched so much that any novelty value has long since been drained out of it. What you don't realize (or perhaps you've forgotten) is that the helicopter sequence is some genuinely impressive work, the sort of thing that will make a first-time viewer mutter, "Whoa! That was cool!" under his breath.

The natural tendency when promoting your own work is to overemphasize the bad parts and play down the really great parts. So, do the opposite — even if it feels like you're lying a little bit. Plaster on a great big e-smile and talk about how pleased you are with your huge exploding alien helicopter battle. If you give the impression that you've achieved what you wanted to and you're proud of your work, people will be curious to see what you've created.

Feeling self-conscious now? Maybe you're thinking, "Well, I don't know. Perhaps this film really isn't that good!" But you've spent the time making it — that means that it has value to you. Just tell people why you liked the idea enough to make it and why you're happy enough with it that you've finished it, and you've got a publicity drive.

Don't *actually* lie. That's a pretty obvious point. Saying "Yes, I'm very happy with the movie" isn't really lying, because at some point your brain will resume normal function and you will be. However, do not make stuff up, claim people have liked your movie when they haven't, or say anything obviously untrue. It's just a bad idea. Spin good, lying bad — and learning to tell the difference is half the trick of the marketer's trade.

# Spin

Ah, spin. A word beloved of politicians everywhere, and liberally splashed over tabloid front pages as if there were a prize for the number of times it was mentioned. The word has some pretty depressing connotations for most people, but it's not a negative concept in and of itself.

Putting the *spin* on a news story simply refers to the technique of altering the emphasis of the story to improve the way in which it is perceived. "I've just made a marvelous Machinima movie!" is not a particularly interesting news story for the general public (although you'd get bonus points from certain publications for alliteration). "Local filmmaker takes on Hollywood in his spare room" is far more likely to attract attention.

It doesn't really matter that the primary purpose of your movie isn't actually to take on Hollywood from your spare room — just that you can argue that that's what you're doing. The purpose of adding an angle to the story is to catch the attention of the journalist or editor assigned to vet the story for publication, and eventually the public as a whole.

Though, the spin that you're putting on your story must be both true and interesting to readers or viewers; otherwise, it'll just be ignored. Your goal is to talk about your movie; their goal is to read something interesting on their lunch break. You have to satisfy both goals at once.

"Local Filmmaker Takes On Hollywood blah blah blah" is the oldest Machinima, and indeed filmmaking, spin in the book. It also still works, provided you're local enough. If you're from somewhere that might genuinely get a bit of pride from a local boy/girl taking on the media moguls, go for it.

# Johnnie and Hugh's superlist of shameless spin suggestions (stupid sibilance — sorry)

Think hard enough, and you can spot the perfect spin for almost any story, but here are a few (Machinima-biased) ideas to get you started:

- **Local Boy Competes with Hollywood.** A chestnut so old that it's now grown roots, sprouted shoots, and has a variety of woodland creatures living happily in its branches. The old ones aren't always the best, but it's a good fall-back position if you really can't find anything better. You're simultaneously playing on David versus Goliath and local versus Everywhere Else with this spin.

- **X provokes fury within Y.** Controversy is always good, and it's the perfect opportunity to use any negative press you may have already received to your advantage. **For example**, in early 2007, Strange Company produced a series of advertisements for Fair Trade products. While most people gave us virtual back-slaps for our good work, our political message in a game engine made a few Fair Trade dissenters quite angry, and comments on message boards ensued. We were delighted by this event, as it gave us lots of free material for our next press release, titled Fair Trade Machinima Provokes Controversy Within Gaming World. Spin, spin, and more spin.

- **Ten Ways To Do Z.** What is it about the number ten? Comedy works in threes, but when imparting knowledge, ten seems to be the number to go for. (Just see The Part of Tens of this book.) Whatever the reason, a list of ten points feels concise but thorough and immediately lends a feeling of authenticity. Why not offer to write an article for a suitable publication entitled Ten Ways to Make Machinima, or Ten Things I Learned While Making My First Film? Just make sure that your movie's URL is all over it. It's not just free publicity — if you're lucky, *they* might even pay *you*.

- **You, Too, Could Have Your Own Jet-Pack.** Anybody can make Machinima, you know. It's fast, easy, and simple. Of course, if you've read any part of this book, you know that's not exactly true. That doesn't stop it from being a great angle to take, though. Heck, it's how we sold you the very book you're holding.

- **A New Type Of Movie-Making Called Machinima.** *Diary Of A Camper,* generally reckoned to be the first Machinima movie, was released in 1996. We've been making Machinima for quite a while now, but Machinima is still referred to as the "new way of making films on the Internet". Well, let 'em. It's a good angle, much as it may pain us to hear the same trite nonsense constantly repeated. A story pitched from this angle is basically aimed at your grandmother. (No offense to any l33t grannies who may be reading — we're generalizing unforgivably here.) Certainly, the target audience are people for whom voice-over-IP is a new concept, rather than your Warcraft guild-mates.

# Word-of-Mouth and Word-of-Mouse

If you've been on the Web for the last few years, you'll probably have gotten thoroughly sick of the phrase *viral marketing*. The idea is that you create a product (or an advertisement for that product) that effectively publicizes itself. The reason it's called *viral* is that each viewer has the potential to show the advert or product to someone else — effectively passing on the infection.

Imagine, for example, that you've managed to create a very funny 60-second video. It just so happens that the video advertises your new Machinima movie, but primarily, it's splutter-coffee-on-your-keyboard funny.

You put it up on YouTube, and it gets a few hits. Those people recommend it to their friends and put links to it on their blogs and their mySpace pages. Other people come across it, download it, and e-mail it to everyone in their address books, because they think it's funny and they want everyone they know to laugh at it, too. (There are the people who forward *everything* they find on the Internet to their entire address book, indiscriminately. Normally these people are a curse on society and are the reason that the Internet is so darned slow, but in this case, they're your new best friends.) Now an army of strangers are voluntarily sending your publicity material to everyone they can think of. You don't have to pay them. What's more, they'll probably recruit another volunteer out of the people they contact. The potential growth is, theoretically, exponential.

Most importantly of all, your movie is automatically given authenticity. You're more likely to feel positively toward a product if it's recommended by your Great Auntie Mavis than if you happen to see it on a random Weblog. And as if the benefits weren't enough already, all this publicity is free. The only tricky bit is setting the pebble rolling. Once you've managed that, you don't need to do anything other than watch the landslide.

If you want your work to be publicized by total strangers, there's something important you can do to help that process along. Ask them to do it. At the end of each episode you make, ask your viewers to tell their friends about your series. Put a post on your forum asking people to publicize your movie. If someone is impressed by your movie, they'll naturally assume that you're a total expert who's got it all under control. Unless you actually ask for help, it may never occur to your viewers that it would be useful.

# Can I Get a Second Opinion, Doctor?

Any publicity material you create, from an intricate two-minute video, to a carefully-worded written press release, to a hastily composed reply to a forum post, should be checked by somebody else. It's not too important who — just get somebody else to give it the once-over before you release it to the Great Intraweb. This small safety-check can save you a whole heap of trouble. It's all too easy for the intentions behind your words to be misinterpreted. What you meant as a throwaway comment may read as a personal attack to somebody else.

During the publicity drive for *BloodSpell,* Hugh gave an interview to Bioware (the creators of Neverwinter Nights), in which he tried to explain the professional approach that we'd taken with the production of the movie, rather than being — as he put it — two guys in a bedroom. Adam Freese & Tawmis Logue were working on a series called *Neverending Nights,* which was made in Neverwinter Nights by, well, two guys in a bedroom. They got a little worried that Hugh was making a snide criticism of their series. We quickly reassured them that we meant no such criticism — we love Neverending Nights — but it just goes to show how easy it is to misinterpret a statement. (*Neverending Nights,* incidentally, is well into its second season at the time of writing, and you can view it for free at www.neverendingnights.com. In a bedroom, if you want.)

# Online: The Key Sites

Online publicity is crucial, especially for a Machinima movie. Almost your entire audience is likely to be accessing your movie over the Internet, even if that's not where they first came across it. In order to make people aware of your movie's existence, you're going to need to shout about it in the cyber-virtual-userspace of the Mighty Internetweb.

Here are some of the key sites that, as of 2007, you really need a good excuse not to include in your publicity targets list:

- **Machinima sites** (www.mprem.com): Machinima Premiere, Sims 99, Machinima.com, the Internet Archive and more — you should let all the prominent Machinima sites know of your film. See Chapter 22 for our top picks from the Machinima world.

- **Engine-specific sites:** It's always worth looking for prominent fan sites for the game engine, or engines, that you've used for your movie. If the engine is popular enough as a Machinima tool, there'll be at least one site specifically dedicated to Machinima movies made using that engine.

For World of Warcraft, for example, there's `www.warcraftmovies.com`. The Movies has `http://themoviesgame.com`, and EA Games have a good listing *of The Sims 2 movies* on its site at `http://thesims2.ea.com/community/movies.php`. If you're using a dedicated tool such as Moviestorm or IClone, the software's official site is the way to go — it'll be almost as keen to promote your movie as you are.

## Cast your net wider

Although hardcore geeks (such as Yours Jointly) may sometimes forget it, there are sites out there about subjects other than Machinima or computer games. If your movie addresses a specific theme or specific subject matter, be sure that you bring the movie to the attention of the type of people who are interested in it.

Have you made a movie about two rival chess players? Find the top half-dozen chess community sites and make a post on each of their forums. Make sure that it's polite — some people won't be remotely interested in your movie and may well object to their forum being hijacked for what they view as an off-topic discussion.

Be certain that you emphasis why you're promoting your movie on this specific site. It's always a good idea to ask the forum members for their comments and criticism. People are much more likely to watch your movie if they feel that their professional opinion is being called upon. A slightly underhand tactic, we admit, but it works.

Incidentally, you should probably stay away from the "rival chess players" idea. Tim Rice and Abba already made a musical about it. Ah, Abba. We know them so well.

## Other sites

You can find a lot of Web sites that, even though they're not in our list, would be a good place to promote your film. Politeness is the key at all times here. Remember that you're a stranger on their territory. The last thing you want to do (or give the impression of doing) is to throw your weight around and be a general pain in the communal side of the site's regulars.

Several sites are dedicated to independent films and short movies. Try Indie Film Spot (`www.striketheset.com`), IndependentFilm.com, or UndergroundFilm.org. There are plenty more examples.

Be aware that these sites tend to have pretty exacting standards. They don't often feature animation of any sort, and — we have to be honest — can sometimes look down on Machinima as a genre.

You should also make sure that your film is available from as many of the dozens of video-sharing sites as possible. YouTube, DailyMotion, Revver, and soon TheVideoBay.org are among the top sites at the moment, but the online video world is changing fast right now. Also try some of the popular geek and tech sites. Being featured on BoingBoing.net, Digg.com, or Slashdot.org will give you so much traffic you'll probably kill your Web server. It's not easy to make it onto sites like these, though. A basic "I've just released my first Machinima movie" isn't newsworthy. You'll need an interesting (preferably fascinating and unique) angle to the story — see the earlier section on spin.

Be sure that your movie is available and widely distributed online. See Chapter 10 for more advice on how to properly distribute your movie.

## Create an RSS feed

Finally, ensure that you provide an RSS feed of your movies. An *RSS feed* is nothing more than a small text file attached to a Web site that provides details of the latest news from that site. By providing a RSS feed for your new Machinima series, your back catalog of Machinima films, or even just a single enclosure of your new movie, you're ensuring that your audience will always be up-to-date and will return to your site even if they've forgotten that it exists; they just need to subscribe to your RSS feed using a *feed reader* like Google Reader.

If you're reasonably technical, you can easily create your own RSS feed from scratch, but plenty of automated or semi-automated services are available to do it for you, too. For example, if you've hosted your videos on the video-sharing site YouTube, an RSS feed is automatically created for you. Here's a link to the RSS feed for Strange Company's YouTube video page: `http://feed://www.youtube.com/rss/user/strangecompany/videos.rss`.

You should also ensure that your movies are listed on the Channel Guide at Democracy Video (`https://channelguide.participatoryculture.org`). As well as enabling your videos to be listed on this popular site, your movies will be available to anybody using the fantastic Democracy Player.

# Offline Media

Web sites are great, but if you really want to go for it publicity-wise, you need to be thinking about offline media, too, by which we mean newspapers, magazines, and television.

You need to adopt a different attitude for offline media. You'll also have a lot more luck with offline media sources if you're willing to pick up the telephone and call them: While you'll still end up sending your press release out via e-mail, direct telephone contact with whoever you're trying to pitch your story to will massively improve your chances. Politeness is the key here.

Bear in mind also that an offline media publication is, by its nature, less likely to assume familiarity with Internet culture. If in doubt, define every unusual phrase, technique, technology, or terminology. You should certainly take care to define Machinima. At the time of writing, our genre is still a niche one, and it's only just started to emerge from underground status. In all likelihood, that will continue to be the case for the near future.

There are two types of offline media, and your approach should be different for each.

- ✔ **Technology savvy:** A publication with a technologically aware readership will probably be interested in the technical aspects of Machinima production: the games you used, the difficulties you faced, the fact that you're using the Internet as a primary distribution medium.

- ✔ **Nontechnology savvy:** Other publications will concentrate more on the human aspect of the story. Who are you, and why have you made this movie? What's the movie about, and why would it appeal to anyone other than the most nerdy computer-game obsessive?

All these considerations apply to online media promotion as well, of course, but offline media still tends to have a wider range of styles and approaches.

A final consideration for an offline media promotion is that of locality. Such a specification is effectively meaningless for an online promotion. The Internet is the Great Leveler when it comes to geographical location (as well as age, sex, and social status, to a lesser extent).

A printed publication, on the other hand, has a defined area of distribution. Your local free paper is distributed to a tiny percentage of the world's population, but it's an ideal target for a local-boy-makes-good story. A statewide or national publication has a much larger readership, but is still localized. You need to consider the localization of your target publication.

And how do you find offline media sources to target? A visit to your local newsagent will do it. Write down the Web addresses of any promising magazines or newspapers, have a quick flick through a TV magazine for programs that may find your work interesting, and then get home and start working through your list!

# Press Releases

If you're just sending e-mails to Web sites, all you need is a good, short e-mail. But if you're going to take the next step and talk to newspapers and magazines, you need a *press release*.

A press release has a limited number of objectives:

- ✔ Make the eventual reader aware of whatever it is that's being promoted.
- ✔ Give the publication all the information it needs.
- ✔ Be interesting enough that it will make it to print.
- ✔ Convince the publication's editors that the subject of the press release is totally relevant to the publication.

Anything that doesn't fulfill one or more of these aims has no place in your press release. Rip it out. You should ensure that the press release states clearly who you are, what you're doing, and why. Remember to include your contact details.

Writing a press release is easy. Writing a good press release is harder. Writing a good press release that will grab an editor's attention well enough to make it into print (virtual or otherwise) — well, that's the real trick.

## Writing your own press release

Your press release should start with a short headline, describing your story (this is Spin Central). From there, you should reiterate the key points in a longer, but still single, sentence, before going into the body of the text.

The closer to a publishable article you can make your press release, the better. Finally, remember to tailor the text to suit each specific publication. Will the publication want to hear about the technical details of your movie, or is it a magazine more concerned with the novelty factor of Machinima itself?

Oh, one more thing. Once you've written your press release, go through and ruthlessly eradicate anything that looks like hyperbole. Adjectives such as revolutionary, unique, or fantastic have no place in a press release and will just annoy journalists.

To give you a better example, here's a (by no means perfect) press release from the early days of the *BloodSpell* publicity drive, whole and unedited.

*FOR IMMEDIATE RELEASE*

*Indie film takes on Pixar — with the aid of an invisible badger.*

*Can one small film company compete with Pixar, with home PCs and no budget? Only if their film is shot by an invisible badger.*

*Edinburgh-based Strange Company have released the first part of 'BloodSpell', a computer-animated feature film. Thanks to computer games technology and 'Machinima', a new way of making animated films, they were able to complete their film in under three years, with a mostly-volunteer staff and a budget of less than £5,000.*

*'BloodSpell' is an action-adventure fantasy film, telling the story of a world in which some people carry magic in their blood — when their blood is spilled the magic is released. It follows the adventures of Jered, a monk of the magic-hating Church of the Angels, as he discovers he is one of the Blooded and has to flee for his life into the bizarre magical underworld.*

*'BloodSpell' was shot using the visual technology of the computer game 'Neverwinter Nights'. Using the game's graphics to create the visuals for the film, Strange Company were able to shoot their film for a fraction of the millions of pounds companies like Pixar and Dreamworks spend on their animated epics.*

*But in order to use the computer game as a film set, Strange Company's Executive Producer Hugh Hancock had to come up with some unusual workarounds. If a character in BloodSpell looks around for a reaction shot, it is because there's a dragon standing behind his co-star. If there's a low-angle shot that needs to be taken, Hugh's got the ideal cameraman — an invisible badger.*

*"Modern computer games have immense graphical capabilities, which we've harnessed for BloodSpell," says 28-year-old Hancock, who has worked on 'Machinima' films for the BBC and Scottish Screen. "But they're not really designed for filmmaking, so we have to find some bizarre ways to get the shots we need. If we need a low shot, for example, we use one of the in-game spells to make our cameraman into a badger, then turning him invisible and film the scene from his perspective!"*

*Although it has only been available on the Internet for two weeks, 'BloodSpell' has already attracted widespread attention, with articles in The Guardian and trendspotter Web site BoingBoing, and an appearance on CNN. Technology commentator and science fiction author Cory Doctorow, one of the founders of the BoingBoing Web site, said, "There's some damned fine storytelling and editing/production work here — Machinima is still finding its legs, discovering what it's for, and the Strange Company folks are at the forefront of using the medium for feature-length drama."*

*Some of the attention BloodSpell is getting may be due to Hancock's controversial decision to release 'BloodSpell' for free under the 'Creative Commons' project. At the same time that Hollywood is becoming increasingly desperate to curb movie piracy, Hancock's film is available free on the Internet for anyone to download — and under the 'Creative Commons' mantle, downloaders can also freely share the film with their friends, via the Internet or in person. Over 30,000 people have viewed the first part so far.*

*"It just doesn't make any sense for us to restrict what our viewers can do with BloodSpell," says Hancock. " I'm not convinced that it makes sense for anyone to do that, in fact. But for a small filmmaker, the struggle to gain exposure is a far bigger problem than that of piracy. I know of larger, more expensive films than ours which have never even been released, and have ended up sitting in their maker's basement. Thanks to our releasing BloodSpell free to download and share, that's never going to happen to us."*

*BloodSpell is available for free download from www.bloodspell.com.*

*Glossary:*

*Machinima: The technique of using computer games technology to create animated films for a fraction of the cost of conventional animation. Now a cult underground movement featured at the Sundance Film Festival and in the New York Times.*
*See: www.machinima.org*

*Creative Commons: Creative Commons is a nonprofit organization that offers flexible copyright licenses for creative works, offering alternatives to the traditional all rights reserved copyright. Controversial aspects to the licenses include the ability to freely distribute works offered under Creative Commons, provided no commercial transaction takes place.*
*See: www.creativecommons.org*

*Neverwinter Nights: Bestselling computer game produced by Canadian developers Bioware. A fantasy adventure game, it achieved success partially through the revolutionary tools distributed with the game, allowing players to make their own games within the Neverwinter Nights 'engine'.*
*See: nwn.bioware.com*

*Contact:*

*Strange Company*
*Name: Johnnie Ingram*
*Position: Media Coordinator*
*Telephone: 0131 555 ####*
*Email: info@bloodspell.com*
*Website: www.bloodspell.com*

Johnnie isn't the Strange Company Media Coordinator — we don't even have such a person. Using a title like this just sounds more professional than "Guy who makes the coffee."

Notice that we deliberately chose not to list Hugh as the contact — releasing a press release about yourself and listing yourself as the sole contact makes you look amateur and suspiciously agenda-driven.

The press release starts with an attention-grabbing strapline (*Indie film takes on Pixar — with the aid of an invisible badger*), which begs further reading for clarification. It's also worth noting that the strapline is one of those lies that we were talking about earlier in this chapter. We're not really trying to take on Pixar as such, but it's an easily understood comparison and gets the reader into the right frame of mind.

*BloodSpell* wasn't really entirely shot using invisible badgers, but we did use that technique a couple of times — and it gives a great tag-line to invite our audience to read more. This is more hot spin action.

We list a contact in a prominent place and give details of how to contact us by telephone and by e-mail. We also give a short glossary at the end of the press release, clarifying any terms that may not be familiar to the casual reader (and, more importantly, to the editor responsible for plowing through our press release). Each item in the glossary is accompanied by a URL at which an interested reader (or editor) can find out more information.

The bulk of the press release reads as if Hugh's being interviewed. He actually wrote most of that section himself, with Johnnie acting as proofreader and idiocy-filter; phrasing it in this way means that it can be lifted verbatim and used in whatever publication we've sent it to. Less work for the editor or journalist means more chance that your article will make the cut.

Whether your press release is aimed at a printed publication or an online site, be prepared with a selection of high-resolution images from your movie. We offered a `.zip` file full of images to anyone who wanted them. Machinima is still a new concept for most people. First and foremost, they want to see what it looks like.

It's an old saw that images sell a film, and that's very true. Spend a lot of time choosing the best images you can, as they may well make the difference between a full-page article and a boxout on page 37.

In general, limit your body text to short paragraphs of one or two sentences each. Each paragraph should cover a single point of information and no more.

This leads to the sort of prose that would make your old English teacher weep, with copious over-employment of paragraph breaks, but it's easy to read, and that's the important thing. Keep the whole thing quite short; under no circumstances should it spill over to more than two pages, and one page only is far more preferable. The *BloodSpell* press release is, to be honest, far too long.

It's particularly important to check press releases such as this one thoroughly. Check, double-check, triple-check, and then check once more just to be sure. Nobody's perfect — not even us. We made a slight mistake in this press release, which we only spotted after re-printing it here. We've left it in to show humility and to help us identify with the common man. Oh, and also because we only spotted it when our editor very politely pointed it out.

## Hiring a PR agency

A proper PR agency is, to be quite frank, probably outside your budget. To get the likes of Bubble and Squeak in London to run your PR will cost you, at least, a few thousand dollars, and probably more like $10,000 to $30,000 — peanuts for a million-dollar budget film, rather more of a problem for us. Having said that, it's worth sitting down and chatting with a big-name PR agency anyway — you might get some good tips for the price of lunch, and you never know when someone may take a liking to you and offer a discount!

## Trying a PR distribution agency

A PR distribution agency, on the other hand, is a great deal. We recommend PRWeb (www.prweb.com). For $80, it gets your press release onto Yahoo! and Google News, as well as a whole bunch of lesser known places. A distribution agency is a very random approach — you may get nothing out of it, or you may get interest from a smaller or larger media organization. At the very least, though, an appearance on Google News is a good boasting point and something to link to from your Web site.

Don't use services like these as a substitute for personal contact. Instead, use them as a backup to hit publications and Web sites you've missed.

# The Life-Cycle of the Lesser Spotted Publicity Machine

Publicity for any film usually follows a predictable path. Here are the different stages of publicity, and a few suggestions as to what you should be doing at each point:

## Before you start

It's counterproductive to send out a lot of publicity at the start of a project. By the time you release your movie, the chances are that anybody who read this first batch of publicity will have forgotten about it.

The Web sites, magazines, and newspapers that you hit won't have, though. They probably won't give you any more column inches (or screen space), because to their minds you are now old news.

Online publicity is the only slight exception to this rule. Getting your own Web site up and running at the start of the project is a good idea. Keep the site updated and let people know how the project is progressing. Invest a little time each week into publicizing your Web site, but only hit those sites that you know will be interested. It may seem like a waste of time, but keeping your project publicity simmering quietly will pay off in the later stages, as you get the reaction, "Ooh, I've heard of that," from all the people you've been quietly bugging up to now.

Don't try anything too complicated. The only purpose of this sort of publicity is to make people aware of your project and keep them aware of it.

## Right in the thick of it

Once your project is firmly underway, step up the publicity that you've been employing. Of course, the problem is that you'll be working flat-out on your project. Finding time to keep up with this sort of publicity will feel like an impossible challenge.

Going into seclusion for a few months, effectively disappearing from the community, and then reappearing, blinking in the sunlight, with a finished movie under your arm is rarely a good plan. Aim to maintain a certain level of visibility — merely commenting on other people's work or joining in online discussion can serve as viable publicity.

Remember to mention your current project in your forum signature! And if you can find a keen marketing student from your local university who wants to work as a marketing guy for your film, now's the time to grab 'em.

## Almost done

Start the countdown! When you enter the final furlong, and your movie is almost ready for release, that's the time to turn the publicity machine up to 11. Ideally, by the time you actually release your movie, you want people breaking down your virtual front door to get a peek at it. It's unlikely that even your mom will be quite that excited, but it's still a good state to aim for. In these final stages, you should be releasing progress updates, teaser trailers, or press releases every single day. Yes, we mean it. Clusterbomb anyone and everyone you can think of.

You'll upset a few people with this technique — eventually, even you will be sick of the sound of your own voice — but stick to your guns. Do be aware of just how annoying you're being. If a couple of people get upset, that's okay, but you want to dial it back before you annoy everyone.

The final furlong stage is the one most likely to cause the breakdown of your marriage, career, and mental health. The amount of work that you'll have to do for even a medium-sized project is considerable. Remember that, as well as flicking the Nitro switch on your publicity sports car (don't judge us — we're running short on metaphors), you've got the minor side issue of a movie to finish. Please, please, don't work so hard that you damage yourself. We've both been there, and we can tell you: It ain't pretty.

## Release day

Or, as it's known at Strange Company Towers, the Annual Bring-A-Buddy SpamFest. The official release of your movie definitely warrants a dedicated press release, both on- and offline.

You'll also want to make a prominent post on every relevant forum, submit to the news page of any relevant site, and contact prominent reviewers and commentators. Make sure that you've got a full list of reporters who may be interested and get them on the phone.

Get your movie online and ready to download or stream the night before so that you can just flick a switch to make it live. Dedicate the whole day to publicity. You'll need it, and more besides.

## About a month later

To a certain extent, once your movie is released, it's out of your hands. People either like it, or they don't. It will either be viewed a lot, or it won't. Now is the time that you can have a well-earned rest and remind your family and friends what you look like. You do have one more round of publicity to go through, though.

When the movie's been out for a little while, and you've accrued some feedback (good and bad, in all likelihood), you'll reach a moment when interest in your movie will fade away quite rapidly. This is only to be expected. There's always something new on the horizon, and your beloved audience is a fickle gestalt at heart.

You can get some extra mileage from your movie by creating publicity based on the reaction to (and success of) your movie. Now is the time to write, "What I learned from making this movie"–type articles, as well as to tailor press releases around any positive feedback and reactions you may have had. Talk about whether the movie has had the reception you anticipated and about what you plan to do next.

## Scraping the bottom of the barrel

"It's two years to the day since we released *Romeo & Juliet 2: Back From The Grave!*, and we're celebrating with a competition to win your very own Elizabethan ruff!"

If you've still got some self-respect left after plowing through this chapter we're not doing our jobs properly. The horse may have shuffled off this mortal coil, run down the curtain, and joined the choir invisible, but that's no reason not to flog it until your flogging equipment snaps.

Seriously, though, returning to an old movie after a little time can sometimes reap rewards. You can find a new audience, or at least remind people of why they loved it in the first place.

# Chapter 15

# You're Nicked, My Son: Machinima and the Law

**M**achinima has many strengths, but being legally uncomplicated isn't always one of them. Technically, 90 percent of all the Machinima out there could be considered illegal. It uses unlicensed music and unlicensed art, it breaks End-User License Agreements (EULAs), and it's just plain wrong.

Of course, Mr. Common Sense interjects at this point, and fortunately, believe it or not, U.S. law and Mr. Common Sense are quite close buddies. There's a lot more protection for Machinima under U.S. law than most people think.

And in an even more amazing turn of events, most games companies are also on reasonably good terms with Mr. Sense (or the Guvnor as he's known around these parts) and aren't going to sue people who are creating work that publicizes their game.

So, luckily, 90 percent of all Machinima creators will never really need to read this chapter. But for those who do, get yer lawyerin' hats on. We're going in.

Using Moviestorm, Second Life, or IClone? You can pretty much skip this chapter. However, if you're using Second Life props or anything similar created by other users in any game, be aware that your fellow gamers may get upset if you film their buildings and clothes without permission.

# The Lawyers Made Me Do It

Before we get going, we need to make a few things clear:

- ✔ We're not lawyers in any sense of the word. Our understanding of this subject comes from practical experience and may be partial, erroneous, or just plain dumb. We don't think so, but we're wrong on a pretty regular basis.

- ✔ None of this chapter should be construed as legal advice. If you have any doubts over your legal status or questions about legal issues related to Machinima, you should speak to a lawyer — and we've got a couple of contacts later in this chapter.

- ✔ A lot of the advice in this chapter is specific to country and state law and may vary according to your place of residence. We point that out where we can, but as we said, if in doubt, find a good lawyer.

- ✔ Please don't sue us. We're poor. And English.

# Get 'im, Guvnor!

So, do you even need to read this chapter? Well, obviously, we'd like you to, because we slaved away on it for literally hours. And by slaved away, we mean drank coffee, played World of Warcraft, and eventually got around to writing it.

But, as we said, 90 percent of all Machinima creators will never be within spitting distance of a lawsuit. The games companies are, to a man/woman/child, supportive of Machinima made in their engines. Even the mighty Microsoft has allowed the Halo 2 Machinima creation scene to flourish unchecked (although that company wasn't so keen about Halo being written about in this book. Oh, well.). And, frankly, the music companies generally have more profitable fish to dubiously sue.

This chapter applies to Machinima as it stands at the time of writing (mid-2007). These things may change suddenly as Machinima gets more popular, particularly if there's one high-profile case. If you're involved with Machinima at all, keep an eye on the prevailing legal weather.

You should probably not worry about the legal implications if:

- ✔ **You're using an open-source or dedicated Machinima package, and you're using all your own art, sound, and music.** You're free and clear then.

- ✔ **You're using your own sound and music, you're not making money, and you don't think you'll be an overnight hit** — although watch out, because you may be wrong. But games companies don't have a history of prosecuting their fans – unlike some industries we could think of.

- ✔ **You're working for a games company, and they're providing all your assets.** Duh.

You want to be aware of this stuff, and potentially have a free introductory chat with a lawyer, if:

- ✔ **You're using major-label music.** At all. The major labels and the lovable people at the Recording Industry Association of America (RIAA) haven't sued for the use of their work in Machinima yet, but they might. The good news is it isn't an open-and-shut case under U.S. law thanks to transformative use protections. The bad news is that the RIAA has more lawyers than you. And even if it doesn't sue you, RIAA can pepper hosting services with takedown notices that can effectively chase your film off the Internet.

- ✔ **You've got an offer from a TV company, or a film festival, or a major online film promoter, or you think you might.** Be aware that you can move from "I don't think this will be a hit" to "Please stop calling me, Miramax!" in a matter of days. In any event, you should always talk to a lawyer before signing over your soul to any of these guys.

- ✔ **You want to make money from your Machinima.** At all. Making money with Machinima without knowing the law is risky, to say the least.

- ✔ **Your film covers sensitive themes: sexual, political, religious, any of that stuff.** Believe it or not, there have already been U.S. government hearings about some political Machinima. If you make Machinima that defames or belittles the game in which it is made, makes strong religious or political statements, or would commonly be considered pornographic in nature, in particular, make sure that you've got your bases covered.

Fall into Category A? Then it's off to The Final Frontier (Part IV) for you. Fall into category B? Welcome to Machinima Law 101.

# Get Your Knickers On, Love — You're Nicked

Machinima faces three obstacles on its course to legal freedom:

- **The End-User License Agreement:** Or Intensely Dodgy Shrink-wrap Contract, as we like to call it — but IDSC is harder to pronounce than EULA, so we'll stick with that. The EULA is the agreement that by now you should know better than to just scroll through and sign, but you do anyway. It appears at the installation or registration phase of your software and sets out a whole bunch of things you can and can't do. These limitations can include commercial usage (no cash for you!) and derivative works (technically, that means no Machinima at all, sonny!). There's still a lot of debate over the legality of EULAs, particularly as they become more and more abusive. Courts in several jurisdictions appear willing to treat them as legally binding, so watch out, although there have also been recent legal developments on this front. (See the upcoming section "EULA-reading: The fine print" for more details.)

- **Copyright law:** All the art inside your chosen game is copyright to some-one — usually the games developer or publisher. That means that you can't redistribute it without permission, and that any works you produce using it are technically derivative works, which require the permission of the original copyright holder to redistribute. In the U.S. there's an exemption for *transformative use,* which may put Machinima in the clear (see the upcoming section "Copyright: It's back"), be aware that if you're using the games companies' art for all but the most transitional things, they can force you to stop distributing your film. (Again, see the upcom-ing section "Copyright: It's back" for more details.)

- **People:** All the theory of the law is fine, but the fact remains that if you have any legal trouble, it'll be because a person decided that she didn't like your work. Hence, the most important aspect to navigating dodgy legal waters is to keep aware of the people involved. If you're using a band's work, ask first; if they're cool, you'll probably not have any trou-ble. If you want to do a big project in an engine, ask the developer nicely; we've had huge developers like EA and Bioware fully support our work.

## EULA-reading: The fine print

Yes, the End-User License Agreement is a pretty scary piece of work, but it's a good idea to read it. Some games have more disastrous consequences attached to breaching the EULA than others.

Here are three phrases you should look for:

- **Noncommercial usage or commercial usage:** Usually attached to the phrase *Only for* and *Not for* respectively. World of Warcraft goes further by specifying noncommercial *entertainment* purposes only, which presumably means that if you're not enjoying the game any more, you're legally obliged to stop playing.

  Virtually every commercial, major publisher game will have these clauses in its EULA. They're designed to stop . . . well, pretty much anything that makes money. So, if your game includes these clauses in its EULA, and you sell a DVD of your work, you're in breach of contract and may be sued.

- **Create derivative works:** Usually attached to the phrase *You may not.* Not all games have this clause in their EULA. For those that do, however, you're essentially forbidden by contract from making Machinima at all using that engine, unless you use none of the existing art, sound, or music assets.

  A number of games seem to have put this phrase in their EULA and then forgotten about it — notably Blizzard Entertainment, who has supported a number of official Machinima contests despite having a clause banning Machinima production in its EULA!

  If you see this clause in a EULA, therefore, you're left in a quandary. You could contact the company and ask politely whether it, er, really means it. Of course, that risks a "Don't you dare" in response. After all, it's easier for a company to ignore things than to give.

- **The prevailing party in such litigation shall be entitled to recover from the other party all the costs, attorneys' fees, and other expenses incurred by such prevailing party in the litigation:** This one won't always be phrased quite like this — you're looking for similar words meaning the same thing. This is bad. Essentially, it means that if the games company sues you and wins, it's entitled to force you to pay all its expenses, which are likely to be reaching into the hundreds of thousands or even millions of dollars. That removes the option of having a pro-bono organization, such as the Electronic Frontier Foundation, do your legal work and thus save you legal costs — if you lose, you'll still be on the hook for huge amounts of money. If a games company with this clause in its EULA sues you, be aware that if it wins, you'll be paying out a *lot* of money.

  Otherwise, if you've got pro-bono legal representation (and it's quite likely you'd be able to find that for such a new, exciting cause as Machinima), you'll have to pay only damages, which are likely to be a lot smaller assuming that you weren't making millions off your Machinima work.

Looking around for these phrases in an EULA lets you know just how much trouble you could potentially be in.

Keep your eye on the legal EULA scene — it's a moving target. As we were going to press, a federal court in Pennsylvania ruled that portions of the EULA for Second Life were "unconscionable" due to "lack of mutuality". The entire situation with shrink-wrap licenses could change dramatically.

## Copyright: It's back

Okay, so you can't use other people's copyrighted works in your own, right? Well, no. It's a bit more complex than that. Here's what you need to know:

- **Derivative works:** In order to distribute — technically, in order to create — a work containing another artist's work, you must obtain permission for that usage from the artist. Pretty cut-and-dried so far. One point to note, though: The copyright owner or his representatives are the only ones who can pursue you for that infringement. So if they don't care, you ain't getting sued. But sometimes the artist is no longer the owner, so be sure that you're getting permission from the right chap.

- **Transformative Fair Use:** U.S. laws contain exemptions for fair use of copyrighted materials. One criterion that weighs very heavily into the decision as to whether a use is fair use is whether a work is *transformative* — that is to say, if it transforms the works it uses into a different form. For example, a film that uses graphics from computer games is transformative.

  These exemptions provide what the Electronic Frontier Foundation believes may be a suitable defense for a Machinima creator using copyrighted game assets or even major label music. Unfortunately, though, no one knows for sure until there's a test case!

  In more bad news, this exemption is only present in U.S. copyright law; UK copyright law, for example, has no such defense.

  Watch out if you're making a fan-film set in a popular universe. If you're making a film set in the world of *Lord of The Rings, Star Trek,* or *Buffy The Vampire Slayer,* you're automatically making a derivative work, and the media companies that own these franchises can be touchy about unauthorized uses. Projects have been shut down for this reason in the past.

- **Incidental use:** Most copyright laws also provide protection for brief or incidental use of copyright items. Quite how brief this use has to be is a matter for the courts, but if you see game assets for only three or four frames, or a few seconds in a longer film, you're probably okay.

# If You May Be Infringing . . .

For whatever reason, you've created a work that may be infringing — you've followed our chapter on World of Warcraft movie-making, for example! What happens now?

- ✔ **Nothing.** Most likely, you'll be fine. Games developers and music producers alike are busy people, and they all see the sense in not suing people who love their games.

  Even if you're selling your film for hard cash, you may slip under the radar (although we *really* don't recommend this!). Chances are you'll get a slight sense of panic from reading this chapter, and then you'll be fine.

- ✔ **C&D.** If you manage to draw the 1 in 100 short straw, and you've managed to upset someone, chances are she'll open up with a Cease and Desist letter. This legal letter says, in essence, "Stop that right now, take it all offline, or we sue you into a smoking pile in the ground." These letters have one function — to make you void your bowels in sheer legal terror and do what they say.

  If you've received a C&D, you need to go chat to a lawyer, right this second. We recommend talking to the Electronic Frontier Foundation (www.eff.org) as a first step. In the UK or Europe, you should go find a lawyer recommended by TIGA (www.tiga.org). It'll let you know if you can ignore the letter, if you have the option of pro bono (For good — meaning free) legal defense, or if you should roll over and say Uncle.

  If you really can't be bothered or don't care that much, just take the project down, and that'll almost certainly be the end of it.

- ✔ **DMCA Takedown Notice:** If you're in the United States and someone's really upset, she might serve your ISP or other hosting provider with a takedown notice under the US Digital Millennium Copyright Act (DMCA). That means that your video will likely be taken down immediately. You then have to file a counter-notice on your hosting provider to have your material put back up, assuming that the taker-down doesn't start a lawsuit. DMCA takedowns cost very little, meaning that they're sometimes used by random individuals who want to censor information. Again, go see a lawyer and ask him what to do now. You can file a counter-notice to have your work put back up if the claims are not legitimate, and this is both cheap and easy.

- ✔ **Lawsuit:** If you've managed to upset someone really ornery, or if he thinks he can make money out of suing you, then you may go straight to court. This scenario is, frankly, blisteringly unlikely unless a test case happens between when we write this book and you read it. No one has been sued for Machinima yet.

Machinima is a very grey area legally right now. No one wants to walk into an expensive lawsuit without knowing she's going to win — particularly when she may be forced to pay damages and fees for both sides! Even the RIAA, busily suing file-sharers, has so far stayed clear of Machinima videos made to a RIAA piece of music. And most importantly, the games companies and publishers have, thus far, not aimed any lawsuits at Machinima creators.

If you are hit with a lawsuit, hie thee to a good lawyer, once again, and do whatever she says, basically. Good luck.

# Finding a Lawyer

So it's all gone horribly wrong. How do you find a lawyer?

The first thing you need to know is that you need a lawyer with a very specific field of knowledge. Your family lawyer will be quite literally worse than useless if you're getting sued over Intellectual Property (IP) issues in Machinima, unless he happens to also be an IP lawyer with a games background.

First port of call, more or less regardless of where you are, should probably be the Electronic Frontier Foundation (www.eff.org). It can give you basic advice and point you in the right direction. If you're in the United States, it may even be able to officially act as your attorney in any court case.

If you're in the UK or Europe, TIGA (www.tiga.org) are the people to go to. Unlike the EFF, this group can't offer pro-bono assistance, but it can point you to a good lawyer with the expertise you need. You should also consider contacting the Machinima community to see whether anyone with prior experience in this area can recommend anyone.

If you absolutely have to go looking for a lawyer yourself, you probably want to look for someone with entertainment industry knowledge specializing in intellectual property issues if you're being sued on copyright grounds, or software contract law if you're being sued under an EULA. That's quite a tough mix to find, and it may be expensive if you end up hiring this kind of lawyer.

Regardless, pretty much any lawyer should meet with you initially at no cost to you. This is your chance to evaluate her and also your chance to get as much free information as possible! With any luck, you'll never have to go beyond the first free meeting into actual paid-for time until you've got Machinima-related money coming in to pay for it!

# Making Legal Machinima

Well, if you're wondering how you make legal Machinima, it depends on your goal:

- ✔ **I just want to avoid being sued!** This one's simple. Don't use big-name band music, because the RIAA is by far the most unpredictable element in this equation. Don't set your film in a fictional world written by someone other than you or the games company, because big-name IP holders sometimes shut people down, too. Don't sell your film. And credit the games company in your film. The chances of the games company getting upset then are tiny, tiny, tiny. Oh, and if for some bizarre reason they C&D you, shut your work down immediately and then write about it on ChillingEffects.org.

- ✔ **I need to be clear, but I don't want to make money.** You should contact the games company that produces the game you intend to use — ideally through e-mail so that you have some kind of written record. Emphasize that you're a fan, that you want to make a film on a nonprofit basis using its game, and that you're happy to promote the company in your film, and ask whether that's okay. If it's okay with that, you should be free and clear for most usages that don't involve cash — although you should probably contact the company if you're going to Sundance with the film, for example!

  Other than that, don't set your film in another world aside from the game world and make sure that you've got permission in writing from your musicians and any other artists on the project, and you should, again, be fine.

- ✔ **I want the moolah!** This one's harder. Your best bet is to use a dedicated Machinima package, such as IClone, VirtualStage, or Moviestorm. All these packages are specifically licensed for you to make commercial Machinima with them. A few games and virtual worlds have similar licenses — for example, you can license the Torque engine for commercial use and use the Second Life virtual world to make commercial Machinima.

  Make sure that you've got permissions for your music, your sound, your actors, and your world background. All these permissions should be in writing and preferably using a legally binding release form (which you can find in a number of places online depending on your location).

  If you really have to use a game engine that usually isn't licensed for commercial usage, put on your best sales voice and either e-mail or call the company who develops it. Whoever is paying for you to make or distribute your film will require that you do this anyway, sooner or later.

It'll probably take some time to find the right person to speak to — if you know anyone who has done commercial work with that company, call her! Or, if you e-mail the Academy of Machinima Arts and Sciences, it will try to put you on the right track.

You may be able to negotiate a license, or you may not. Some companies will be fine with your work provided you're not making a lot of money, some will have a prewritten contract for this sort of thing, and some will be interested only if there's a few thousand dollars minimum in it for them.

# Checking into Creative Commons

You need permissions for music, art, and so on, but you do have an alternative: Look for an appropriately licensed piece of artwork or music shared under the Creative Commons license.

*Creative Commons* is an international charitable endeavor aiming to reduce the damage that existing copyright law is doing to the commons of creative material available. Artists can license their work under a variety of Creative Commons licenses, which allow other users to redistribute, modify, or use their work under a set of guidelines aimed at being fair to all. You can find out more at http://CreativeCommons.org.

From your point of view, Creative Commons-licensed material is a great way to find fantastic music and art that isn't tied up in restrictive copyright.

Here is a partial list of useful Creative Commons distribution sites. More sites are appearing all the time as Creative Commons grows!

- ✔ **Magnatune.com** offers Creative Commons-licensed music from a variety of really cool artists.

- ✔ **Archive.org** offers a huge range of Creative Commons-licensed work, from stock footage to music to Machinima!

- ✔ **Flickr.com** has a Creative Commons section with literally millions of Creative Commons photographs.

- ✔ While it doesn't have an official Creative Commons section, **Deviantart. com** has thousands of pieces of Creative Commons artwork.

If you're using Creative Commons work, it's only polite to release your own work under Creative Commons. In fact, we recommend that you release your films under Creative Commons anyway, unless you've got a good reason not to. It's a great way to free your fans from copyright worries, make yourself look good, get some free publicity from all the Creative Commons sites out there, and do some good at the same time!

# Part IV

# The Final Frontier: Pro Machinima

The 5th Wave      By Rich Tennant

THE NEW HOLLYWOOD

@RICHTENNANT

CUT! PASTE!

# In this part . . .

In Part IV, we look at ways that you can use 3D modeling packages to create custom objects for your movie and how to import these objects into your game of choice. You also explore Moviestorm — a self-contained Machinima production toolkit. We show you how Moviestorm can do everything from character and set design to filming and editing, all in one single software package. If your needs are individual enough that you're still not satisfied, we discuss how you can make your own custom tools.

# Chapter 16

# Making Things That Don't Exist: 3D Modeling and Animation

. . . . . . . . . . . . . . . . . . . . . . . . . . . . . . . . . . . . . . . . . . . . . . . . . . . . . . .

. . . . . . . . . . . . . . . . . . . . . . . . . . . . . . . . . . . . . . . . . . . . . . . . . . . . . . .

**M**odern-day game engines rock, but they're also constructed from a limited palette. At some point, your imagination will outstrip the available characters, sets, or props, and you'll be forced to do one of two things: Change your story to fit the game or change the game to fit your story.

Creating 3D objects from scratch is time-consuming and difficult, both on a technical and artistic level. To create anything sophisticated — a new character, say, or a complex piece of machinery like a train — you need skills as a sculptor and fine artist, and teaching you those is really more than we can do in a chapter. We're good, but we're not that good.

But often you don't need something complicated; you just need a different picture above the fireplace or a new statue on the mantelpiece. Those sorts of alterations are well within anyone's capabilities.

In this chapter, we tell you how to perform simple 3D modeling tasks. We also show you how to get your 3D assets back into the game once you've modified them.

# Figuring Out Whether You Need to Model

3D modeling is a fascinating and rewarding artform, but it's also a complex one. If you don't have to change the 3D data in your game, don't. And if you do have to create a new model, alter an existing one if you can.

If, for example, your lead character doesn't have a beard and he needs one, you may think about re-modeling his head. But there's really no reason to do that unless you're working with some new, frighteningly high-detailed engine that individually models character hairs. And if that's the case, you're reading this in 2025 or something, and should go out and buy *Machinima For Dummies,* 14th Edition, in which we cover Holodeck technology.

There's no real reason to remodel a character's head to add a beard, unless it's an enormous, bushy thing. Instead, you can simply recolor the texture (see Chapter 7) and produce quite an acceptable beard texture. A short beard doesn't change the shape of the character's head enough to require a full retexture.

Strange Company did this for the Matrix 4x1 series, re-texturing the Half-Life GMan model.

Likewise, many modern engines now allow users to make sophisticated changes to clothing by simply altering transparencies on textures and changing colors. And you can add fairly large details — planks on walls, rafters on ceilings — to sets with textures, particularly if your engine also supports bump-mapping to enhance the effect.

# Exploring 3D Packages

Most 3D engines (with Second Life an honorable exception) don't include any 3D modeling facilities. So, if you want to produce or edit 3D models for your games, you'll need a 3D package with which to do it.

3D modeling software has a reputation for being horribly expensive. 3D Studio Max, the most commonly used 3D modeling package in the games world, retails for $3,495. However, a few products have started to come down to prices that Machinima creators can afford:

# Blender

Originally a commercial product developed by Dutch animation studio NeoGeo and Not A Number Technologies, Blender was released as open-source in 2002, when NaN went bankrupt. Since then, the open-source community has developed, extended, and improved Blender until it is now a viable competitor to pro 3D packages.

At present, Blender is probably the most attractive option available to Machinima creators who want to create or modify 3D objects for their movie. For starters, it's free.

Blender is a very full-featured application. It includes an extensive plug-in architecture, so exporters are available for many game engines, including Unreal Tournament and Half-Life 2. And while Blender's user interface is infamously difficult to learn, a wealth of documentation is available on the Internet. We use it in this chapter.

# Milkshape

Hugh remembers working with Milkshape back in 1999, just after the release of his second film, *Eschaton: Nightfall.* Originally developed for Quake II, Milkshape is the oldest of the successful, low-cost 3D packages for games, boasting support for an enormous range of games engines, from Quake II to The Sims to Half-Life 2.

Currently, Milkshape retails for $25, as it has for the last 8 years. For that, you get a reasonably usable, but slightly basic, modeling package, which is primarily useful for conversion between 3D formats. If you're doing your modeling or animation work in another package (Softimage, for example) Milkshape's an excellent way to get your 3D models into a game. As a stand-alone package, you may find it a little limited for complex work.

# GMax

GMax is essentially a cut-down version of 3D Studio Max, released for free. GMax is a very powerful modeling and animation package, with most of the features of 3D Studio Max. It doesn't have the manuals that 3D Studio ships with, meaning that learning the basics of the interface is an uphill struggle. It also doesn't come with 3D Studio's Character Studio, so its animation capabilities are slightly limited. GMax's most severe restriction is an almost total lack of official exporters to game engines. Originally, GMax was released with the intention that games developers would pay to write exporters for their games, in order to support their modding communities. It hasn't quite worked out that way. Games developers don't seem willing to pay out to support their modding communities in this way. Whilst various teams have hacked GMax to export 3D data (notably to Neverwinter Nights and Doom 3), it's a lot of work, and hence there are only a few engines to which it can send its data.

# Getting Your Model into Your Game

You'll probably be surprised to learn that the hardest part of making a 3D model, at least the first time you do it, will be getting your model to appear inside your chosen game engine.

Game engines are huge, complex beasts, and their designers rarely give much thought to simplifying the complexities of adding data to them.

In addition, a 3D game model is meant to represent some part of the world and will have data attached to it, whether that data is artificial intelligence, hit points, or simply a reminder that the player can't walk through it! Hence, you'll have to find some way to add this data to the game, often using pretty technical tools.

## Do the tools even exist?

Before you can add a model, you need to find out if tools are even available to do such a thing. If you can't find any information on these tools after a thorough search, chances are that they don't exist.

Unfortunately, no standard format exists for 3D game models; there's no .doc equivalent for modelers. In order to add a model to a game, you need an exporter that will take the 3D information from your authoring package and translate it to

something the game you're using will understand. If the game developers haven't produced one, and the modding community hasn't hacked one, then you're basically out of luck.

Check Chapter 5 to find out whether the engines we discuss there support model importing. If you're using a newer engine, try www. machinimafordummies.com; we'll do our best to keep up with new engines as they come out and update you on what you can and can't do.

The simplest way to get a new or modified 3D object into a game is nearly always to simply overwrite an existing model. We don't mean literally copying over a file, but persuading the game that a new file you've added is a replacement for something that's in the game.

That won't always work. If you replace a model of a truck with a model of a toy truck, characters may still refuse to walk inside the original truck's volume, or even be crushed by your toy truck as it moves! Here are the four stages to getting a model into a video game:

1. **Figure out how you do it.**

   Getting a model into a game is invariably a highly idiosyncratic, slightly odd, rather kludgy process — and that's if the game is well-supported by its developers. Hence, before you even start working on your model, you should spend a little time searching the Internet for information on how to add models to your game. (See the sidebar "Do the tools even exist?" before you start this search.)

   Fortunately, exporting a model is one of the most common and popular pursuits for game modders. (Chapter 18 contains a list of modding sites for all the engines we cover in Chapter 5.)

   You should always try to find at least two, and preferably three, different tutorials or sources of information on adding models to your chosen engine. Internet tutorials are often incomplete, obscure, or badly written, and having several to compare means that you'll have more luck getting over the humps.

2. **Add game information to the model.**

   The game needs to know a lot of things that may appear obvious, but aren't. For example, if you're creating a tree, the game engine may need to know the volume around the tree into which game characters can't walk. If you're making a gun or indeed a newspaper, the game will need to know how a character should hold it, which may be a single attachment point or an invisible hand (economists would love 3D modeling).

   How you add this information will vary game to game. This is where you'll need the exporting tools for your game, which usually include tools to mark up your model for the game engine you're using. Normally, this process involves adding modifiers to your various 3D objects, and sometimes to the points or surfaces of the objects. It may also involve adding null objects (invisible points) to the model to represent lights, special effects, or attachment points for characters or other in-game objects.

   For example, in The Sims 2, objects that interact with characters require animation targets to tell the game where a character can sit, grab, or interact with the object.

3. **Export the model.**

   Theoretically, after you've added all the information the game engine needs about your model, you can simply click Export (or Save As, or whatever your particular game engine requires), and the model is exported in a format the game engine can understand.

   Once you press the button, the model either exports or doesn't. If it doesn't, or your exporter throws out a whole pile of errors, or the entire screen goes green and starts repeating an animation of a dancing duck, now's the time to dive back into all the modding information you've found (see Step 1). Googling the error text, if any, is a good start. You'll find that many game engines have very specific requirements for their modeling, and it's easy to create a model in a 3D package that doesn't fulfill those requirements. For example, the exporter to Half-Life 2 from Softimage XSI fails if any textures have spaces in their names.

   You can avoid a lot of problems by remembering to use simple tools in your 3D package. Very few engines will handle a model made out of anything but simple polygons. Unless you know for sure that your engine supports layered textures, use only single texture maps on surfaces. And try not to use Boolean tools (subtractions between one model and another), as they're infamous for causing up-all-night-with-a-debugger-and-Google problems.

4. **Add the game data.**

   Now you'll almost certainly have to provide the game with additional information it needs to incorporate the model. Exactly what this game data consists of varies hugely between engines and between model types.

   If you're adding a model that you can place using the game's editor, you'll usually have to add it to a list of such models held somewhere in the game's data files. If you're creating a new weapon model for a first-person shooter game, you may need to edit some game code to tell the game to use this new model. (See Chapter 18 for more on editing game code.) In short, follow the tutorials that you've found for adding models to your games and edit the files they tell you to edit.

   Finally, you'll most likely package all the files you've created into a single collection file, in the game's preferred format.

   For most games, you can get away without packaging your model, but simply leaving hundreds of files lying around on your hard drive with no indication of their purpose is a bad idea. Unless your movie is very short and simple, mod files can easily get out of control, and package files are good ways to keep your movie in check.

   Using Doom 3, you can simply package your file as a standard .zip file. Using Half-Life 2, you write a .qc file, which acts as a guide for the engine for each model you produce and references all the other model and texture files you use for that model.

# Creating Your First Model

Assume that you've decided that you need a custom model. In fact, assume that, for some reason best known to yourself, you've decided to use The Sims 2 to make an advert for this very book. Hey, it could happen. But, for some reason, when Will Wright and his team crafted this multi-million selling game, they failed to include a framed picture of the *Machinima For Dummies* front cover. How inconsiderate.

## Working with Blender

You can find a copy of Blender on the DVD. Install it now, run the program, and take a look around. Yikes. It's safe to say that Blender, shown in Figure 16-1, looks a little intimidating. But really, it's not as complicated as all that. You won't be using most of its advanced features, which makes your job a whole lot simpler.

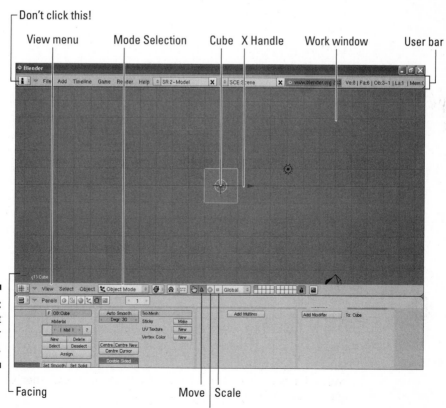

**Figure 16-1:**
The default
Blender
screen.

Here are the basics:

- ✔ **Up at the top of the screen,** you've got your user section, which includes all the menus you'd expect (Save, Load, and so on), as well as information on the existing scene (Fa:6, for example, means Faces: 6, meaning that your current scene contains six polygons) and shortcuts to add elements to the scene. At the top left, you've got a selector for the type of menu shown here.

- ✔ **The center of the screen** contains your work window. Currently, Figure 16-1 just contains a simple cube right in the middle of the screen. The arrows are handles for that object. If you left-click and hold the right-facing arrow, you can move the cube left and right. The little axis at the bottom left of this window shows your facing. Try holding down your middle mouse button and dragging to turn your view, and notice how the axes change.

    You select items in this window with the right mouse button. That's very counter-intuitive for most people.

- ✔ **The line below the work window** contains a bunch of modeling tools. For now, just try clicking on the circle next to the red triangle and notice how your handles change. You're now in rotation mode and can rotate your cube by, again, clicking and dragging. Note that the View menu is in the bottom right here.

- ✔ **The bottom pane** contains an enormous pile of additional tools. The six buttons over to the left change the mode of this pane. Because you're just using Blender to construct simple game objects, you won't use most of these functions, but an animator working with Blender can use these settings to assign sophisticated material functions, write logic functions to make elements of the scene run automatically, animate his scene, and render it to visual standards up there with Hollywood.

To get a clean scene, choose View⇨Front. Right-click the cube, press the Delete key, and choose Erase Selected Objects.

## Creating a simple cube

After you have a clean scene (see preceding section), you're ready to create your model. Here's how you can create a simple cube.

1. **Choose Add⇨Mesh⇨Cube.**

    A cube appears wherever your crosshairs are currently set.

2. **Select the small blue cube (the Scale tool) next to the Rotate tool.**

3. **Drag the two scale handles until you've got a larger rectangular shape (see Figure 16-2).**

   If you want a framed painting, for example, you need it to be rectangular and thin.

4. **Choose View⇨Top to view your object from the top.**

5. **Drag the green handle down to make it thinner, rotate the view around a bit to check that it's the shape you want it to be, and then choose View⇨Top.**

So far, this is all pretty obvious stuff. We've been editing on what we call the primitive level. By that, we don't mean we're editing like cavemen, although people have certainly made that statement about Hugh's 3D modeling skills. We mean that we're working with a primitive object — in this case, a cube. Nearly all modeling jobs start with one or more primitive objects, which you can then rescale, deform, and generally craft like a potter works with clay.

Basic scaling tools let you do some of that, but in order to really mold your 3D object to your will, we need to deal with the very building blocks of a 3D model: its constructing points or vertexes.

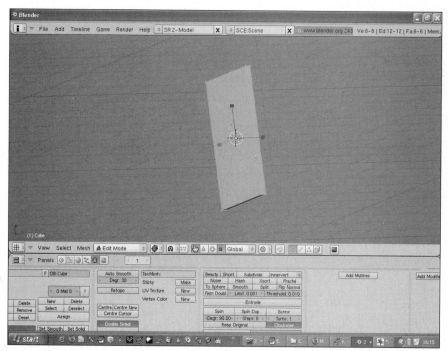

**Figure 16-2:**
Scaling
the cube.

## *Editing model points*

If you've read Chapter 6, you know that there we told you that all elements in a 3D world are created from 2D polygons. (If you've not read Chapter 6 yet, it's a good basis for this chapter.)

Well, that's true. But just like the little fleas and lesser fleas, polygons are themselves constructed from lesser particles. And these subpolygon particles are called *vertexes*. Sounds very technical, doesn't it? Well, there's a simpler name for them: dots.

How do you create a polygon? You place a series of dots in 3D space and then tell the 3D engine to connect those dots using lines (called edges), until those lines finally close up. Then you've got a 2D shape sitting in 3D space. And if you take, say, six square 2D shapes, all composed of the same eight dots, and put them together in the right order, you've then got a 3D cube. Essentially, the magic of the most complicated 3D scene boils down to a join-the-dots puzzle.

In the following steps, you're going to grab one of the lines between the dots on your model and put a new dot halfway along it, which you can then use to change the shape of your soon-to-be painting:

1. **Choose View⇨Front.**

   Your view changes so that you're now viewing the front of your object.

2. **Using the middle mouse button or Alt+click, rotate your view until you can see the top surface of your object.**

   You need to be in 3D space here so that you know which edge you're dealing with.

3. **On the menu bar below the work window, select the line icon next to the triangle.**

   This icon is the Edge Select tool. If you're confused, hover your mouse pointer over the icon until you find the Edge Select tool.

4. **Select the back, top edge of the object**

   Remember, right-clicking selects.

5. **Choose Mesh⇨Edges⇨Knife Subdivide⇨Exact Line.**

   You're going to chop this edge in half with your Knife tool, thus giving you an extra point in the middle of this edge.

6. **Left-click just above the middle of the selected edge and then left-click just below it.**

A line appears between these two points.

7. **Press Enter.**

You've now subdivided the edge into two halves. Notice that the Knife subdivided only the edge you had selected, not every edge it intersected.

8. **Switch to Vertex mode by pressing the Dots button next to the Edge Select tool; press A.**

This step deselects everything on the screen (and selects everything, if you press it again). You now have a new dot in the middle of the edge that you used the Knife tool on.

9. **Select the new vertex, choose View⇨Front, choose Translate Manipulator Mode (or the red triangle, as we like to call it) and drag the vertex up using the handles to form a triangle shape.**

If you turn your view with the middle mouse button, you see that your shape now looks something like Figure 16-3.

10. **If the point moves without changing the shape of the object, delete the vertex that you're moving and re-do Steps 1 through 9.**

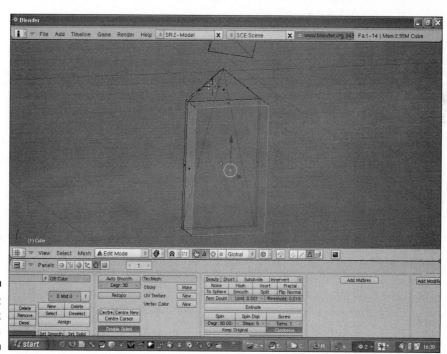

**Figure 16-3:** After vertex editing.

The preceding steps walked you through changing the shape of an object by moving a single vertex. But that's very time-consuming if you're editing a shape with a lot of vertexes. Fortunately, certain tools make this process easier. In the following steps, you select the front face of the object and extrude it backward to create the surface that you'll put your image on.

1. **Select the Face mode by clicking the triangle next to the Edge Select tool; right-click the front face of your object.**

   It should turn pink, indicating that you've now selected it.

2. **Choose Mesh⇨Extrude.**

   As your mouse moves, the front face of your object moves forward or backward. Move it a little bit forward for now, so that it looks like the object in Figure 16-4.

3. **Left-click to finish extruding.**

4. **Select the Scale tool and rescale the selected face so that it's slightly smaller than the original face.**

5. **Select the red triangle (the Translate Manipulator Mode, which lets you move things) and move the face you're editing backward until it's sunk into the object's front.**

   You should end up with something like Figure 16-5.

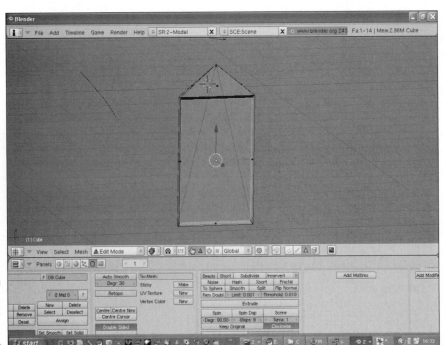

**Figure 16-4:** Extruding an object.

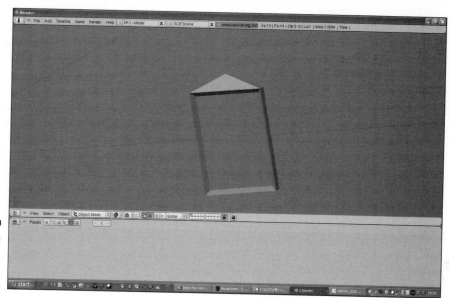

**Figure 16-5:**
The finished
model.

You've done it! Or at least, you've done the first stage.

## Adding texture to your model

Translating a flat 2D image onto a 3D object is a hard problem, and it took
quite a few years for 3D modeling packages to settle on a standard approach.
Nowadays, most game objects use an approach called *UV mapping*.

UV mapping makes perfect sense if you've ever assembled one of those cardboard models that arrive flat and you then bend along the pre-applied lines
and glue together to make a 3D object. Essentially, it's the reverse process;
rather than assembling a 3D model from a 2D skin, you're unwrapping the
3D model to a 2D representation, onto which you can then paint textures.
This is a pretty hard concept to get your head around, but it becomes easier
as you do it.

And why's it called UV mapping? Well, because what you're doing here is
assigning 2D coordinates for each face, and you're then applying the coordinates to the texture. So as not to confuse these coordinates with the 3D coordinates of the model, these 2D coordinates are referred to as U and V rather
X, Y, and Z.

First, you need two 3D windows for this process.

1. **Move your mouse pointer below the work window until it becomes a Windows resize pointer; right-click and choose Split Area.**

2. **Click in the middle of the work window.**

   Lo and behold, you have two windows!

3. **Click the Grid icon at the bottom left of the left work window.**

   A huge list of other window types appears.

4. **Choose UV/Image Editor.**

   You now see a 2D grid in your left work window.

The actual UV unwrapping process is really simple because Blender does it automatically! If you were super-advanced modeler types you'd do this manually, but for now, automatic is fine.

To unwrap the 3D model:

1. **In the right work window, where it says Edit Mode, click and choose UV Face Select from the list of options.**

2. **Right-click anywhere on the model and press A twice.**

   This step selects all the faces of the model.

3. **At the bottom of this window, choose Face⇨Unwrap UVs.**

   A pop-up window appears.

4. **Choose Unwrap (Smart Projections).**

   This step tells Blender to unwrap your model in the smartest way it can. The left window changes to show the UV Map that it unwraps.

   You may see one more screen, giving more options. Just click OK. You may also find that your UV map doesn't look like the one in Figure 16-6 — that's fine!

   What is this? Well, it's a guide for you to create a 2D texture image. Each polygonal area on this image represents a face of the model. To see how this works, press A again to de-select all the faces. Now, select one of the faces of the model in the right work window. See how a single polygonal shape pops up on the left window? That's the part of the unwrapped image that represents that polygon. When you assign a texture to this model, Blender will wrap up the model again. The bit of the image that is within the area of that shape is the bit that will be assigned to the face you have selected.

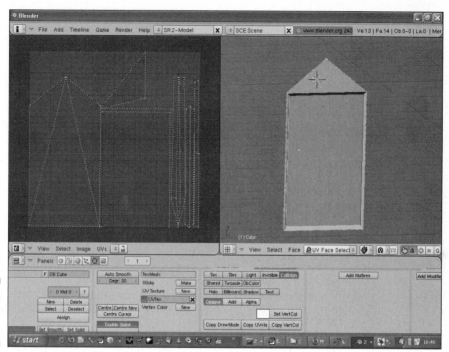

**Figure 16-6:**
Unwrapped
UVs.

You can alter this UV map if you need to — for example, if you find that an important face is really small (and hence won't have room for much texture detail), you can juggle the shape of the map to make the area larger. You can play with that if you like, but you'll notice it can be quite complicated to persuade the map to do exactly what you want it to!

5. **Select the rectangular sunken face you created with extrude and remember where this face is on the UV map.**

   That's where you're going to place your front cover image.

6. **Press A twice to select all the faces; in the left work window, choose UV⇨Scripts⇨Save UV Face Layout and click OK.**

   The lower pane turns into a file browser.

7. **Change the filename to something you can remember and save the image.**

8. **Load the image that you just saved into any image editor.**

9. **Load the `MfD.tga` image from this book's DVD and paste it onto your UV image; move and scale it so that it fits on the area corresponding to your canvas.**

   That's the area we asked you to remember in Step 5.

10. **Save the resulting image as a PNG.**

    You can remove the black lines if you like, but for this rough work, we won't do that. If you want to remove those lines, texture the other polygons with a nice wood texture, or whatever you fancy, you can do that now, too!

11. **In Blender, choose Image⇨Open and open the image you just saved as a PNG.**

    And, as if by magic, the cover appears on the canvas of your painting, as shown in Figure 16-7.

And that's it! That's all you need to do to create a game-worthy basic model.

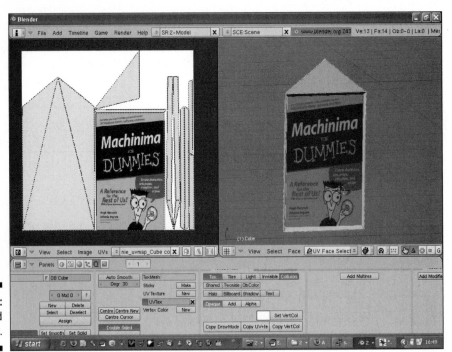

**Figure 16-7:** The finished portrait.

# Importing into The Sims!

The Sims 2 is a pretty complicated game, and getting objects to work with it is a pretty complex process. Fortunately, it's made a lot easier with tools that The Sims 2 community have developed, notably the Package Editor, SimPE. You can find it on this book's DVD. Install it now.

## Cloning a package

Rather than create a package from scratch (an intimidating task), the following steps show you how to copy an existing item and alter the properties and model file of the item for your own ends. This is the standard approach in The Sims 2 community to creating a new object.

1. **In SimPE, click the Object Workshop tab at the bottom of the screen.**

2. **Press Start.**

   SimPE loads all the existing Sims 2 objects, which may take a while.

3. **From the tree list of objects, choose Decorative⇨Wall⇨In The Beginning and click Next at the top of the pane.**

4. **Select Clone from the Task drop-down menu and select Next.**

   You're cloning this painting and replacing it with your own.

5. **Change the Title and Description to whatever you feel like — we chose MfD Picture — and set the price to 1 (so that you can easily afford to put it up in your Sims 2 set!).**

6. **Click Finish.**

   The Scenegraph Rename wizard appears.

7. **Replace** `paintinghorizontalapplehead` **in the title with** `MfDPicture` **and click OK.**

   A Save dialog box appears.

8. **Save the package in your** `My Documents/EA Games/The Sims 2/Downloads` **directory.**

   You've now cloned the package.

## Modeling on

While we show you only a very basic bit of modeling in this chapter, you can use the same skills to achieve some extremely complex results. For example, if you export a character model from your game, you can use the same vertex editing to heighten his cheekbones, make his jaw stronger, or even, with a bit of time, change him from a man to a woman!

Animation is a different kettle of fish altogether. Only a few engines support new animations, and there is an entire artform in just animating characters. If you want to work on new animations — and they are very useful in really making your

Machinima stand out — we recommend picking up a book on the subject — *3D Game Animation For Dummies* by Kelly L. Murdock (Wiley Publishing) is a good place to start.

But even if you can't change animation, you can do amazing things with modeling, lighting, texturing, and clever camerawork, from adding a simple prop to your scene to completely re-imagining your game in an alternate setting, as several people have done for The Sims 2. (See Britannica Dreams' *A Mermaid's Tale,* for example.) However you change your world, have fun doing it!

## *Checking the scale*

After you clone the package, you need to check the scale of our model and export it ready for importing to The Sims 2.

Scale is a big problem in 3D modeling. In general, you shouldn't start modeling without some kind of reference for the scale that the game uses, or you'll end up with telephones the size of houses and spaceships the size of mice. You need to check that your painting isn't scaled insanely.

To check the scale:

1. **Under the Resource Tree, select Geometric Data Container; in the Resource List, select** Paintinghorizontalapplehead.

   We're choosing an item that should be approximately the same size as the item we're creating. If you were making something else, you'd choose a different object — a food carton if you were making something small, for example, or a car if you were making something bigger.

2. **At the bottom of the screen, click Plugin View.**

   You return to the standard SimPE view, which allows you to export and import objects.

3. **Click Export and save the object anywhere you want.**

   We're exporting The Sims 2 model for reference so that we can see that our painting is roughly the right size!

4. **In Blender, choose File⇨Import⇨Wavefront (.obj) and then select the object you just saved.**

   The object appears in your Blender scene. You'll probably see that your painting is far larger than The Sims 2 painting (or whatever you're checking).

5. **Change from UV Face Select to Object Mode in the right window and rescale your painting using the Scale and Move tools.**

   It should end up approximately the same size as the other painting, (although taller than it is wide) and at the same point in space.

   To scale the object on all axes at once, select Scale mode, go to Face Select mode, select all faces, and then drag the white circle at the center of the "handles".

6. **Right-click The Sims 2 object to select it and delete it.**

7. **Right-click your object to select it, choose File⇨Export⇨Wavefront(.obj) from the top menu, select a place to export it, and click OK.**

   We're exporting using the *.obj format, which is one of the more standard 3D formats for simple models. SimPE can export and import in this format, which is the only reason we're using it.

8. **On the screen which appears, click Normals and then click OK.**

   Normals tell The Sims 2 which way our object's faces are pointing so that the painting doesn't end up inside-out!

## Adding the model and texture to your game

After you check your model's scale, you just need to add the model and its texture to our package, and you're done!

1. **In SimPE, click Import and select the model you just saved.**

2. **On the following screen, under Group settings, change Add to Replace and select the model you want to replace.**

3. **Click Commit to finalize the changes you just made.**

4. **Under Resource Tree, select Texture Image; under Resource List, select the top image.**

   A lovely painting of an apple-headed woman appears. You'll be replacing that, too.

5. **At the bottom of the window, select Build.**

6. **In the popup window that appears, set the dimensions listed to 512 x 512.**

   This is the size of the UV Map texture Blender creates.

   Your texture doesn't have to be this size, provided it's these dimensions. If you wanted to create a higher-resolution texture, you could create a 1,024x1,024 or even 2,048x2,048 texture and use that, provided everything was still in the same relative position on the texture. Make sure that you tell The Sims 2 the correct size for the image, or hilarity will ensue.

7. **Select Image 512x512 from the list above Build, right-click the checkerboard that appears, choose Import, and select the texture you created for your object.**

8. **Right-click the image when it appears and choose Update All Sizes.**

   We're replacing the existing texture map for our object and converting our image to The Sims 2 format.

9. **Click Commit.**

10. **From the Resource Tree, select Object Data; in the Resource List, select the top resource.**

   Now you've got to input data that tells your game engine that this is a unique object and where it should be placed in the game.

11. **Click Get GUID.**

   You have to create a custom ID for your object that's different to any other registered object. This ensures that your object will never conflict with something else you've downloaded from the Internet. It's really quite neat!

12. **Make up a username and password and enter them in the pop-up window; click Register New User.**

13. **Click Register Object; in the main SimsPE screen, check the box marked Update All MMATs and click Update.**

14. **Choose File⇨Save.**

   And you're done! If you load up The Sims 2 and start a set (see Chapter 8), you'll now see that there is a painting with a snowflake next to it in the decorative Buy menu. If you place that on your lot, you'll see your beautiful *Machinima For Dummies* picture for all your Sims to admire.

# Chapter 17

# A Storm Is Brewing: Moviestorm

. . . . . . . . . . . . . . . . . . . . . . . . . . . . . . . . . . . . . . . . . . . . . . . . . . . .

### In This Chapter

▶ Introducing Moviestorm, the professional Machinima toolset

▶ Creating sets and characters

▶ Using Moviestorm's Director tools to make a film

. . . . . . . . . . . . . . . . . . . . . . . . . . . . . . . . . . . . . . . . . . . . . . . . . . . .

*A*fter a while of creating Machinima, you'll start to get frustrated with the limitations that are imposed upon you by your chosen game engine. We guarantee this. You'll get frustrated with the odd things that you can't change in the engine, tired of the art assets that aren't designed for close-up camera-work or wide-angle shooting, and depressed by the fact that you can't sell your work.

Now, for the first time in Machinima history, you have other options. You can use game-type engines to make commercial work. There are tools specifically designed for Machinima. And there is Moviestorm, which creator Short Fuze describes as Photoshop for movies — a tool that will let anyone, anywhere, make the movie he wants to make, using Machinima technology without many of the common Machinima frustrations.

Oh, yes. And Moviestorm is free. In fact, you can find a copy of it on the DVD that comes with this book.

## Using Moviestorm

In many ways, Moviestorm is the sort of package that long-term Machinima creators have longed for. In addition, the creators of Moviestorm are so receptive to user comment that by the time you read any cons we list here, they may well have fixed them.

Pros:

- ✔ **It's a dedicated Machinima package.** If you're using Moviestorm, you won't have to make sure that your actors don't get hungry and die. You won't have to spend 15 minutes running through a game world to get to where you need to go. You won't have to avoid irritating game behavior that just gets in the way when you're making Machinima. Because Machinima is all Moviestorm does.

- ✔ **It's written by Machinima creators.** Moviestorm's development is led by experienced Machinima creators, and they've hired from within the Machinima community. That means that, unlike other tools we've seen in the past, very few features look great but just aren't useful in practice.

- ✔ **It's free.** No, really. Free. No cash. In fact, you already own it — there's a full version on the DVD inside the cover of this book. Yours to keep forever and ever. You really can make a film for nothing.

- ✔ **You can sell your work.** Moviestorm is commercially licensed, which means that the glass ceiling of other Machinima engines isn't a problem here. Accidentally make a hit and get contacted by a big movie studio? Great. You don't need a lawyer, you don't need to know a lawyer. You never even need to see a lawyer, at least until Miramax dumps a contract an inch thick in front of you. At which point, you're on your own.

Cons:

- ✔ **Wide but shallow.** Moviestorm has no specific genre or style. The setting of your movie is up to you, as are the costumes, props, and characters that you may want to use. Unfortunately, because Moviestorm is trying to cover so many bases, Moviestorm may not include the exact props you want for any one setting. This limitation will become less of an issue as Moviestorm matures and the amount of content available increases, but it's still an unavoidable side effect of such an ambitious platform.

- ✔ **Add-on packs cost money.** There's no such thing as a free lunch — unless you work in marketing. The various Moviestorm add-on packs (of which many are planned) will indeed cost money. Probably not as much as a copy of any recent Machinima-capable game, but you're still going to have to spend money if you want content.

  The default props and characters that are provided with Moviestorm for free won't last you forever. If you get serious about Moviestorm, expect to have to splash out on a couple of add-on packs at least.

- ✔ **Money can't buy you lovely costumes.** At the time of writing, it's very early days for Moviestorm. Only time will tell what success and longevity it will enjoy. Short Fuze is promising more add-on packs and additional content than we can eat, eventually, and you can be sure that modders will soon start to create their own content.

✔ **It's not finished.** When we wrote this book, Moviestorm was still in testing. The version that's current as you read these words will probably be substantially improved from the version we used to compile this chapter (and Chapter 3 as well). At the moment, we can't import models, there are still a bunch of crash bugs, and a lot of features are "coming soon." What we've seen is very encouraging, but there's still a way to go. We'll update news on Moviestorm as it develops on the *Machinima For Dummies* blog at www.machinimafordummies.com.

# Movie-Making in Moviestorm: The Basic Principles

In many ways, movie-making in Moviestorm is like movie-making in The Sims 2, but much less annoying.

1. **Write your movie script.**

2. **Design your set or sets by dragging out walls, floors, and ceilings and then dropping in props from a huge library.**

3. **Create your cast in the Puppet Shop by choosing and modifying body parts and textures.**

4. **Block out your characters' large-scale movements in the Director's View.**

5. **Add gestures, lines of dialogue (complete with automatic lipsynch), and facial animation using the timeline in the Director's View**

6. **Set up cameras and lights to cover the scene.**

7. **Use the Director's View to set up cuts between cameras.**

8. **Render your movie, edit it, and produce the final movie.**

If you need to change art in the movie, you can also use the built-in Modder's Workshop to alter whatever you fancy.

If you want to create models or animations, Moviestorm uses the cal3d model format, which will hopefully be supported by Blender (see Chapter 16) in the near future.

# Creating Your Set

Chapter 3 shows you how to create a Moviestorm movie using a pre-created set. In this section, we show you how to create a new set in Moviestorm. For the following steps, we decided to create a Sherlock Holmes story in Moviestorm, using some of the old Sherlock Holmes radio plays from www.archive.org.

1. **Install Moviestorm from the DVD, if you haven't already; start it up and choose New.**

   Moviestorm opens the New Movie Wizard.

2. **Choose a name for your movie.**

3. **Leave the other options as they are and click the check mark.**

   The Director's View appears.

4. **Move your mouse pointer to the top of the screen and click the Set Workshop button.**

   The Set Workshop appears (see Figure 17-1.).

If you'd like to have a closer look at the set you've created, you can move around by clicking, holding, and dragging the middle mouse button; zooming in and out by using the mousewheel; or looking around by clicking, holding, and dragging the right mouse button.

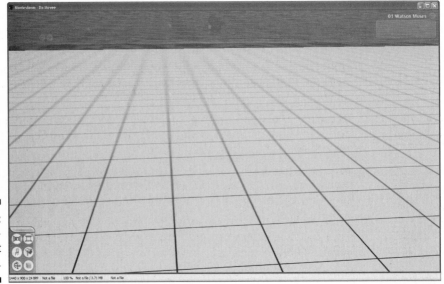

**Figure 17-1:** Movie-storm's Set Workshop.

5. **Start by putting down the basics: walls, doors and windows, and floors and ceilings, in that order.**

**To add walls,** click the Work On The Wall button on the menu. Click Add A New Wall from the menu that appears. Click a corner of one of the ground squares and then drag. You see a wall drag itself out behind your cursor — unlike The Sims 2 walls (see Chapter 7), you can place this wall at any angle you want. For now, though, drag it out straight as the back wall of your set, for about 10 squares. Then drag out another three walls to form a square.

There's no need to keep your walls parallel to each other if you don't want to. Moviestorm allows you to define a polygon of any number of sides and any crazy internal angles you might want. Only do this if you really need to, though.

**To add a door,** click the Work On The Wall button and then the Add A Door To A Wall button and choose a doorway from the available choices by left-clicking. Hover the cursor over a wall, and a doorway appears. Select where you'd like your doorway and left-click to place it.

**To add windows,** click the Work On The Wall button and then Add A Door To A Wall button. The windows appear on the same panel as the doors. Choose a window, select and place it in the same way as you placed a doorway. Light shines through the windows and changes the shape of the shadows on the ground — nifty!

6. **To paint a wall, click the Work On The Wall button, select Paint A Wall from the buttons that appear, choose a texture, and click a wall to place the texture on it.**

Depending on your particular screen set-up, you may find that the ToolTip for some of the buttons is displayed below the bottom edge of your screen. If you're in doubt, refer to the images we included in the margins.

There's no need to add floors or ceilings. They're already in place, but invisible. If you want them to be visible, just paint on a floor texture or a ceiling texture.

**To create a floor or a ceiling,** select Work On The Floor And Ceilings from the left menu, select Paint The Floor or Paint The Ceiling from the buttons that appear, and select a texture.

You can find more specific categories of floor texture by clicking the drop-down arrow at the top right of the floor texture window. Click and drag across the floor or ceiling to place the texture.

If the ceiling is getting in the way, you can temporarily hide it using the Hide Ceiling button on the Work On The Floor And Ceilings menu.

You can choose Edit The Lighting from the buttons that appear if you want to alter the lighting in your set. In future versions of Moviestorm, Edit The Sky will allow you to choose different skies for your movies.

Making sets in Moviestorm is very fast. Once you've gone through these processes a couple of times, you can probably create a simple room in less time than it took you to read this section.

# Adding Props to Your Set

After you create your set, you'll want to add some props to fill it out.

1. **Choose Add Objects To The Set from the left menu.**

   We bet you didn't expect that! A huge menu of different types of props appears. Browse around and see the sheer variety of things you can deploy in your movie.

   If, for example, you want to add a chair to your set, from the drop-down list at the top of the props window, select Seating, choose the type of seating you want, and click the floor to place the item.

   For this step, we chose the Antique Armchair. (Names of the props appear when you mouse-over the pictures.)

2. **Start by placing a couple of the overstuffed armchairs that Watson almost certainly has sitting around.**

   However, notice that the item always appears facing the same direction.

3. **Once you have placed your prop, press Ctrl+click and hold on the prop.**

   The cursor changes to a Rotation tool, and you can now drag to rotate the prop. Unlike The Sims 2, you can rotate it to any angle you want.

4. **Place another couple of props and rotate them as you like.**

   For this example, we placed one chair at the window and the third across from the first chair we placed so that two old friends can sit and talk while smoking a pipe. Or, preferably, two pipes. One for each.

   There are lots of other props that you can add to decorate your set. We added a rug underneath our armchairs to give some detail to the room.

But what happens if you decide that that you've placed your prop too close to the wall? Simply click the prop and hold. You can now drag the prop farther back. Repeat with other props if you feel so inclined.

If you want to get rid of a prop altogether, click the Move/Rotate/Delete button (at the bottom left of the screen). Then click the Wrecking Ball icon from the buttons that appear. Now, you can click anything — wall, window, or prop — to delete it. You can tell what you're about to demolish because it will highlight as you move the mouse pointer over it. You can also add detail to the walls — for example, we want to give Watson's study the wallpapered-with-books feel we know from the movies and Hugh's living room. Manually rotating everything against the walls is very time-consuming, but fortunately, you don't have to do that. Just click the object you want to align to a wall (one of our armchairs, for example) and drag it against a wall. It will align with the wall automatically.

  Once you're happy with your set, move your mouse pointer to the top of the screen and click Return To Director's View. Save your movie file using the Save button on the top menu.

---

# Fence it!

Aligning several props to form a row (to create a line of fences, for example) can be quite a time-consuming process. Fortunately, there's a way to use wall alignment to make this sort of work very quick and easy.

Say that you want to place a hedge outside your windows, but running at an angle to the window rather than straight on to it. Do you have to manually place and rotate each piece? You do not. Just follow these steps:

1. **Click the Work On The Wall button on the main menu and select Add A New Wall; place this wall outside your window, viewable from the window, at a slight angle to your existing wall.**

2. **Click the Add Objects To The Set button, select the Fence category, and then select Hedge — Very High.**

3. **Place the hedge next to your new, skewed wall.**

   It automagically aligns itself to the wall.

4. **Repeat Steps 2 and 3 a few times, placing hedge parts next to each other.**

   Carry on placing hedges until you've really got that suburbia feel down.

5. **Choose Move/Rotate/Delete from the main menu and then click the wrecking ball icon; hover the cursor over the wall next to your hedges and click to delete it.**

   You've now placed a nicely aligned hedge, with no trouble at all!

6. **Press Esc to get out of demolish mode before you break anything!**

# Creating Characters in Moviestorm

The Moviestorm character creation tool isn't yet quite as flexible as that of, say, The Sims 2 (see Chapter 7). At the time of writing, character meshes were not deformable through morphs — something that gives The Sims 2 a major advantage over Moviestorm.

The *morph facilities* in The Sims 2 are the things that let you define the exact length of your character's nose, or the shape of her chin. Moviestorm allows you to choose from a number of predefined head shapes. After that, the only customization you can apply is in the skin texture that's applied to that mesh.

We're assured that morph deformation is on the cards for Moviestorm eventually. By the time you read this book, it may even be part of the software already. For the time being, though, you're limited.

The tools we do have give you a surprising amount of flexibility, though. Two radically different skin textures applied over the same mesh can produce two characters who — as far as the viewer is concerned — couldn't be more different. And you can add different hairstyles and accessories to further distinguish your cast.

The following steps walk you through character creation in Moviestorm:

1. **In Moviestorm, load your project and then, in the Director's View, hover your mouse over the left side of the screen.**

   A blue menu appears. There are some very small buttons at the top.

2. **Click the New Character button at the top right of the blue menu.**

   Moviestorm asks for a name for your character.

3. **Name your character, and click the check mark.**

   For this example, we call our character Watson. Your character appears, as shown in Figure 17-2. There's your character, in his (or her) elegant upper-class underwear.

   You can put some clothes on him in a second, but first of all, take a look at your character's body. (Settle down at the back!)

   You can rotate your character by dragging with any mouse button.

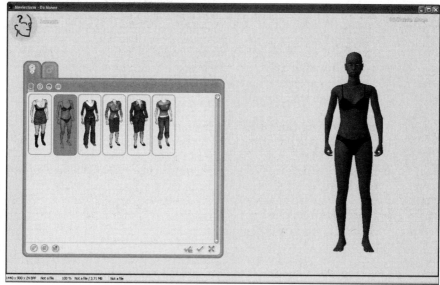

**Figure 17-2:**
The
Moviestorm
Puppet
Shop.

4. **Choose your character's sex by clicking either the male or female gender buttons.**

   These tabs have ToolTips of either Male01 or Female 01. Because we're planning to be reasonably faithful to poor old Arthur Conan Doyle, we chose Male01 for this example.

5. **Click Clothes and give your character some clothes.**

   For this example, we gave Watson a suit (closed). You can right-click the suit on your character to choose from a number of different textures. We went for texture number 4, but you can choose any that seem appropriate. Notice that you can choose a different texture for his jacket and for his pants/shoes.

6. **Click Face.**

   Moviestorm provides a few different heads for you to choose from. We went for Head (Euro01). He's starting to look a little more like Holmes' faithful biographer, but there's still a fair way to go.

7. **Right-click your character's face and choose an appropriate facial texture.**

   We chose texture number 12.

**8. Select Beard and select some facial hair.**

We selected a big moustache. Now you're getting somewhere. We can feel his upper lip getting stiffer as time goes on.

**9. Click Hair.**

Another range of options appears. We left Watson bald, but you can add hair to your character if you prefer the full-pate look.

**10. Pick your favorite hair texture.**

**11. Select Accessories.**

All you have to choose from here is two pairs of equally inappropriate sunglasses. If you really want a cool Watson who's down with the kids, then slap a pair of Aviator Glasses on him. We chose not to. We're happy with Watson now.

**12. Select Edit Character Sheet.**

This is second from the left at the bottom of the window. The Character Sheet appears. Now you can give him a few props to work with.

**13. Choose the Inventory tab from the bottom of the character sheet.**

**14. Press the + button at the bottom right of the screen and select a prop from the menu which appears.**

The only prop available with the base Moviestorm installation is a cellular (or mobile) phone. That's not really appropriate for Watson, but you can add it to your character now if you choose.

**15. Close the Character Sheet and select Keep Changes (the green check).**

You now go back to the Director's View, ready to make a movie.

# Creating a Scene

Moviestorm allows you to create any number of scenes. A scene represents one segment of action, all of which takes place in the same location.

If you later want another scene in the same location, that's not a problem. Each set can be assigned to as many scenes as you want. Here's how to create a scene:

1. **In the Director's View, hover your mouse pointer at the top of the window and click the Edit Script button.**

   The Director's View is the view that appears when you start Moviestorm, or when you exit the Character or Set Creation Screens. When you click Edit Script, the Script Editor window appears.

2. **Right-click the highlighted Scene in the Script Editor window and choose Rename; give the scene a descriptive name.**

   We chose `Watson muses`.

3. **Click the check and then close the Script Editor window, and you return to the Director's View.**

   If you've created a set already, you see the set in the Director's View, but you're probably wondering, "Where the heck are the walls?" Relax, they're still there. This is the Director's View, which allows you to easily move around your set and experiment. Moviestorm automatically hides any walls that may get in your way while you're in this view. After you add a camera and start to view the set through it, the walls will be nice and solid once again.

   To follow along with the rest of this section, you must have created a set and a character. See the earlier sections "Creating Your Set" and "Creating Characters in Moviestorm."

4. **Move your viewpoint so that you're close to one of the comfy antique chairs.**

   The camera controls here are just the same as in all the other Moviestorm views.

5. **Select your character from the left side of the screen.**

6. **Right-click the ground near the chair and select place here from The-Sims-2-like menu that appears.**

   Watson appears on set as if by magic, ready to muse at your command.

7. **Move your mouse pointer over the chair.**

   A helpful blue hand appears over the chair, intimating that Dr Watson may, if he chooses, alight on this chair for his future repose.

8. **Right-click the chair and choose Sit Down.**

   Watson moves to the chair and sits down.

Watson musing alone in his room may be very interesting, in a pretentious art-housey way, but we'd really like to introduce another character, with whom he can have a nice chat. The problem is that we forgot to create any other characters. What to do? Well, as you have probably predicted, Moviestorm has a solution.

1. **Navigate your viewpoint to outside the door.**

2. **Hover your mouse pointer over the left side of the window.**

   A panel with a blue background appears; this is the list of your characters.

3. **Click the New Character button and name him what ever you want.**

   We called him the Narrator. Very Rocky Horror.

   What do you know? You're back at the Character Creation window.

4. **Create a narrator for the scene; once you're happy, click the Keep Changes button to return to the scene.**

   If you're following along with our Dr. Watson example, make sure that your Narrator character has Hair (Medium). You can see why in the upcoming section "Changing A Texture."

   If you're not sure how to create a character, see the section "Creating Characters in Moviestorm," earlier in this chapter.

   Your new narrator character is now selected on the Cast List panel, although he isn't in the scene yet.

5. **Right-click outside the door and select Place Here to introduce your character to the scene.**

6. **Right-click inside the room and select Move Here to tell the new character to move into the room.**

   Don't worry about the door; he's clever enough to open it himself.

That was pretty easy. With just a few clicks, you've added a new character, positioned him in the scene, and given him his first bit of blocking. Your first character — Watson, for us — doesn't seem to have noticed his visitor, though.

# Blocking with the Timeline

What we're about to show you in this section is tremendously exciting. Well, it is for us, anyway. As professional Machinima creators, this next section has us bouncing up and down in our chair making little squee! noises. Yes, ladies and gentlemen, the rumors are true: Moviestorm has a fully editable timeline, shown in Figure 17-3.

Figure 17-3:
The
Moviestorm
timeline.

What's a timeline? Well, if you've ever seen a history documentary, you probably know what we're talking about. Put simply, a *timeline* is a list of events, organized in, well, a line, which represents a chronological order. On a history documentary, all you can do is look at the line. In Moviestorm, though, you can scroll your line of events back and forward and change anything you like, any time you like. All without a blue police box. (This timeline is very similar to the Medieval II: Total War Curve View — see Chapter 12.)

Once you've issued a command to one of your characters, that command is stored on the timeline at the scene time it was issued. Because the timeline is editable, you can drag this action around to change its start time and duration. You can also add new actions directly to the timeline:

1. **Select your first character by clicking his icon at the left of screen.**

   The timeline changes, but that's okay: Each character has his own personal timeline.

2. **Click and drag the time marker on the timeline.**

   It's the vertical white bar with a dot on top. You'll probably find it all the way over on the right side of the timeline.

   If it won't move, try using the Rewind button at the far right of the screen to rewind to the start of the scene and then try dragging it again.

3. **Drag it to the left.**

   Notice that time effectively rewinds as you do this step. In our example, Watson's visitor walks backwards through the open door, closes it behind him, and waits patiently outside. Stop the action there; don't rewind to the very beginning of the scene.

4. **Right-click the new character and choose Look At to tell your first character to look up and around as the new character comes through the door.**

   A new-look-at action is added to the timeline. In our example, because we rewound to this specific point, Watson (or whoever) looks up as his visitor walks through the door. Drag the time marker forward a bit to see.

**5. Click the Fast Forward button (at the right of the timeline window) to move the position indicator right to the end of the scene.**

A scene lasts only as long as the events within it. So, at the moment, the last event in this scene is Watson looking around. The scene therefore finishes once he's completed that action. If you add any other actions after this one, the length of the scene is automatically adjusted to compensate.

Watson is a genial host and is unfailingly polite, so we're going to have him greet his visitor as he comes through the door.

**6. Make sure that your first character is still selected, right-click him, and choose Say.**

In our case, Watson is our first character. The Record Line dialog box appears.

**7. Click the Load Audio File button at the bottom of this window and load the** watson01.wav **audio file from the book's DVD.**

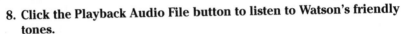

**8. Click the Playback Audio File button to listen to Watson's friendly tones.**

If you've got an idea for a line for Watson, you can also record your own line here, using the red Record button.

**9. Type the line in the white box.**

In our case, the line is "Ah, good evening. Horrible day to be out, I must say."

**10. Click the green check to accept the audio file.**

If you move your viewpoint a little closer to Watson and press Play at the right-hand side of the screen, you can see Watson's lips move as he talks. Notice how the narrator automatically turns his head to look at Watson when he speaks: Moviestorm always has listeners look at the speaker in the room unless instructed otherwise.

Don't be confused when two versions of Watson's line appear on the timeline, one above the other. One triggers the audio file itself. The other represents Watson's mouth movements.

**11. Select the new character at the top left and move the timeline to the end of your character's line.**

**12. Right-click the second character and choose Say to add another line.**

This time, use the narrator01.wav file. This time the line is "Yeah, it's a regular pea-souper, as you Londoners say."

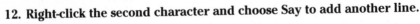

13. **Give the new character a command to look at the first character when he speaks his line.**

    Remember, you do this by right-clicking your original character and clicking Look At.

14. **Play through the timeline a little, so that the narrator has spoken the first part of his line, and then give him a command to Sit Down in the other chair.**

15. **Right-click the narrator's new movement action in the timeline and select Sit Down and then Customize.**

    You can now choose different gaits and moods for the narrator to adopt while he's walking from the window that appears.

    Make sure that you know which character you have selected before you issue any commands. It's all too easy to tell the wrong character to move. Thankfully, Moviestorm makes rectifying these mistakes simple (you just delete the action from the timeline), but it can still get both frustrating and confusing.

16. **Once he sits down, give your first character another line.**

    Throw `watson02.wav` in there with the Say command. Remember to select Watson first! Watson's line here is "Hmph, yes, quite. This reminds me of the Adventure of the Foggy Armadillo. It was a dark night, and Holmes had been quite ill at ease . . ." Watson is starting to wax lyrical now, so give him a gesture to accompany his tale.

17. **Move the timeline to the start of your original character's second line, right-click him, and choose Gesture.**

    The Gesture window appears.

18. **Give your gesture a name — we chose wag finger — and then click the Add Gesture button; choose Right Hand⇨Wag Finger.**

    The Gesture window has a mini-timeline within it.

19. **Move the Gesture window timeline to about halfway through the Wag Finger animation and add another gesture by choosing Head⇨Mouth⇨Quick Smile.**

20. **Play through the animation to check that everything looks fine.**

    If not, you can move the Quick Smile animation back or forward along the Gesture window timeline. Watson should smile briefly about half way through wagging his finger.

21. **Close the Gesture window.**

You can layer different gestures on top of one another to create quite complex character behavior. Be sure to review the overall gesture each time you add another animation; some of them can conflict with each other.

# Creating Camerawork

Cameras — usually a good idea if you want to make a movie. Fortunately, Moviestorm lets you add cameras with gay abandon, which means that this chapter isn't going to be cut summarily short.

1. **Right-click the ground somewhere outside your set and choose Place Camera Here from the menu that appears.**

   Don't worry about pixel-perfect accuracy. As you'd expect, you can move the camera once it's placed.

   Moviestorm moves to the Camera View, at which point you'll be looking through the lens of your virtual camera.

2. **Rewind to the start of the scene and click the Set Up A New Shot button at top of the left menu to create a new shot.**

   The New Shot screen appears. By default, Moviestorm creates this shot as a Free Shot. That's fine for our purposes, so keep that.

3. **Move the camera around now to get the perfect opening shot (see Figure 17-4) through a window onto the scene you've been creating.**

   Right-click and drag to rotate, click the middle-mouse button and drag to move the camera, and use the mouse-wheel to move up and down.

4. **Drag the Lens To Use (field-of-view) slider left a little to pull the lens out; click the check mark to accept the shot when you're happy with it.**

   The slider is just below the bottom of the center of the shot.

5. **Drag the timeline to about three seconds after the start of the scene and click Set Up A New Shot at the left of the camera view to add another shot.**

   For our example, we dragged the timeline to just before Watson sits down. Now we're going to set up a zooming camera.

6. **Change the lens-length until you can just see the window frame at the edges of the shot (turn your camera if necessary) and click the check mark to accept this second shot.**

**Figure 17-4:**
Our opening
shot.

7. **Rewind and then play back your scene.**

   The camera slowly zooms in on the window. You can create a moving camera in the same way.

## Editing your shot

When we played back our example from the earlier section "Creating Camerawork," we noticed that there's a big section during which Watson stands around looking useless. We don't want that in your masterpiece. To edit the shot we created in that section to better suit your purposes:

1. **Click the first keyframe — it looks like a little flag — and drag it along the timeline until just before your first character starts to sit down.**

2. **Drag the second keyframe to a point after your first character sits down, thereby providing a nice establishing shot to start your movie.**

3. **Click the Back To Director's View button to go back to Director's View.**

# Adding a camera on a character

To add a camera on a character:

1. **Drag the timeline along until just before your second character walks in the door.**

   Once you've created a camera, Moviestorm creates a small preview window at the bottom right of the Director's View. You can check the view through your new camera here at all times, and the image updates as the timeline moves along — although not while it's playing back. Believe us, you'll be stunned at how useful this preview proves to be.

2. **Make sure that your first character is selected and right-click him.**

3. **Choose Put A Camera On Me to set up a brand new camera pointing right at your character.**

4. **Click the Set Up A New Shot button.**

   You're using a one-shot camera here. Whereas the free-shot camera allows you to move your camera as you please, a one-shot camera is designed to always focus on one specific character, no matter where he or she moves. In our example, the focus is on Dr. John Watson of the University of London Medical School. As you maneuver your camera, Moviestorm will always try to keep the focus on Watson.

   You see two horizontal and one vertical blue line on-screen now. The top horizontal line represents Watson's eyeline: Move it higher, and his eyes are placed higher in the shot. The bottom horizontal line usually is focused on Watson's hips, but you can change this. By clicking the + or – buttons, you can move to a closer or more distant framing.

   Roughly speaking, these lines move the focus of the bottom line from Watson's mouth, to his chest, then his hips, and finally his feet at the most distant framing. The vertical line controls the position of Watson's head in frame (left or right).

   You can rotate the view, as usual, by clicking and holding the right mouse button. You can also rotate using the little blue triangles, one on each side of the frame.

5. **Adjust the shot until you have a nice close-up. Confirm it.**

6. **Return to Director's View by clicking the Return To The Director's View button.**

For this shot, you'll probably want to pull the lens-length in quite a bit, to about 35 to 37, to give your shots a more filmic look.

You may want to continue through the timeline and set up another few shots. Use a mixture of Free Shots and One Shots. Remember, One Shots will turn to follow a character as he moves. After you have your shots set up, you can switch to the master view and choose which camera you want to use and when.

# Editing Camera Sequences with the Master Monitor

After you create your individual shots with Moviestorm, you need to set up the cuts between them. Advanced users would probably render each camera out separately and use an outside editing package, but it's also possible to set up all your camera cuts within Moviestorm to render out a fully edited sequence. Here's how:

1. **Click the Moviestorm logo at the bottom right of the screen to switch to the Master Monitor.**

2. **Select Free cam 01 and rewind the timeline to just after your first keyframe.**

3. **Click the Insert A Cut To This Camera button to insert a cut to this camera at this point in the timeline.**

   Now, the movie starts with a view through this first camera.

4. **Drag the timeline along until about three seconds before the first character looks around at the second character and use the button on the top right to go back to the Director's View.**

5. **Double-click the camera on the first character and, again, insert a cut to this camera.**

6. **Click the monitor in the bottom right of the screen. Rewind and press Play.**

   The scene now cuts from the first camera to the close-up where you placed your cut. You can now keep adding cuts to cameras to cover the rest of the scene.

# Adjusting Your Set While Filming

Moviestorm is pretty forgiving if you forget to add something or want to change part of your scene halfway through filming. Here's how to perform a few small adjustments:

1. **Open your movie and scrub through the timeline in the Master Monitor to find a shot that seems to need to some background detail.**

   We chose the shot of the narrator as he walks into the room; the wall behind him was pretty bare in our set.

2. **Switch to the Director's View and then click the Set Workshop button (the hammer and spanner icon at the top of the screen).**

   You can now edit your set. Be careful here. You can delete the entire set if you really want to, so . . . don't.

3. **Find the wall that featured so unfortunately in your earlier shot, select the Work With Props button, and add something suitable.**

   Maybe a picture on the wall, or an interesting bookcase (see Figure 17-5)?

4. **Move your mouse pointer to the top of the screen and click the movie camera to take you straight back the Director's View.**

**Figure 17-5:**
We added this painting after we set this shot.

5. **Click the preview of your shot (at the bottom right) to see whether it's improved.**

In our case, it has, most certainly.

# Using a Matte Backdrop

The view out of our window is pretty bare, but you can fix that. We're going to use a Real Filmmaker's trick now and add a 2D background a little way outside the window, on a 3D image, to give the impression that there's something outside the window. We chose a static image of a Victorian street, but you can use whatever you like. It'll be visible through the window that occasionally appears in shot (see Figure 17-6).

1. **Open the set workshop again, click Add Objects To The Set and select the Simple category; place simple backdrop 02 about ten feet outside the window.**

It looks like an ugly gray block at the moment, but that's okay.

2. **Right-click your backdrop.**

A menu appears with a Scale slider.

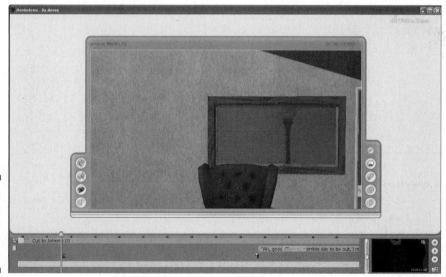

**Figure 17-6:** Viewing our matte through the windows.

A number of props in Moviestorm are re-scaleable: trees, simple objects and, outdoor objects, in particular.

3. **Rescale your backdrop until it's all that is visible from your windows.**

   Rotate the backdrop at this point so that it faces the window, if you need to.

4. **Go to the DVD and select** backdrop.jpg **from the Tutorial/Moviestorm folder.**

   Have a quick look at it in an image editor. It's a (very) foggy street scene that will be only just discernable outside Watson's window — perfect for our movie.

   If you want to use your own image, paste it into this backdrop and resize it appropriately.

5. **Go back to Moviestorm, right-click your simple backdrop and choose Change Image.**

6. **Select** backdrop.jpg **from the DVD, exit the Set Workshop, and go back to the Director's View.**

   If your backdrop appears to be unnaturally dark in Moviestorm, try adjusting the scene's default lighting position. You can find a slider for that under Edit The Lighting Setup, in the Set Editor.

7. **Create a new camera and use it to frame a shot containing at least one window, with something from the rest of the room (a chair or something similar) in foreground.**

   Looks pretty good, doesn't it?

You can use background images like this — known in the film industry as *mattes* — for all kinds of effects, particularly where you require a complex background shot. They can often save you days or weeks of modeling a scene in 3D.

# Changing a Texture

As with most of the other game engines, Moviestorm includes tools that support modification of the existing art. Unlike many engines, these tools are both user-friendly and bundled with the game itself. (It's worth noting that they're still not officially supported by Moviestorm Ltd., so please don't shout at them if they don't work!)

Say that you're tired of your character's hair. In our movie, it's a big, floppy red haircut, and frankly it's getting a bit much. We want to change it.

1. **Save your project, close it with the button at the top right, and then select Go To Main Menu from the window that appears.**

   Go all the way back to the Moviestorm Start screen where you initially created a movie.

2. **Click Settings.**

3. **From the Settings window, select the tab marked Modder's Workshop; read the scary warning, take a deep breath, and click Go To Workshop.**

4. **In the Select A Model window that appears, click** Male01.

   We make this selection because we want to alter an asset — in this case, some hair — that is normally used by the Male01 model.

5. **From the drop-down box that currently says Tile Editor, select Body Parts.**

   Now you're into hot body-part-editing action.

6. **Scroll down the window with pictures of body parts until you find the one that looks like the hairstyle you selected for your narrator and click it.**

   It will have the same name as it did in the Puppet Shop — in our case, Hair – Medium.

   You see a whole bunch of information about this model, over on the right side of the window with the body parts in it. You could, for example, reassign this hair as a prop so that characters could carry it around like a toupee! You can also change the 3D mesh here if you've made a new model (see Chapter 17 for more on 3D modeling). But right now, you're going to alter the textures under Materials.

7. **Drag the window you're working on further down your screen.**

   Behind it, the model you currently have selected appears in the 3D view.

8. **Click the Material listings until you find the hair color you used.**

   The 3D model changes as you select each color.

9. **Click Edit Material below the Material listings.**

   Yikes! More information. Fortunately you need only one piece, and that's the name of the Diffuse material. (Diffuse Map is the term Real 3D Artists use to refer to the base texture map for an object.)

10. **From the Diffuse Map section, copy the name of the Diffuse Map texture used.**

    You want the bit after all the slashes, obviously. It'll be called something like `Male_Medium_Hair_Redhead_Diff.png`.

11. **In Windows, go to your Moviestorm folder and search for the name of that texture using Find Files.**

    There are other ways to find the texture, but this method is the easiest.

12. **Load the texture up in an image editor.**

    It's just a standard PNG, which most image editors should be able to read.

13. **Convert the texture to grayscale and decrease the brightness on the texture.**

    Or do whatever you want! We're altering the texture — you could make it green, you could scribble all over it. Go wild.

14. **Save the texture in the same directory that you loaded the original from.**

    This directory is likely to be somewhere in `Moviestorm/Addon`, but beyond there, it could be anywhere! Just make sure to save in the same directory you loaded from, and you should be okay. Make sure to save it with a new filename — you don't want to overwrite the original texture — and make sure that it's a PNG.

15. **Back in the Modder's Workshop, click Copy Materials.**

    This step creates a copy of the material, to which you can then add your texture.

16. **Select the new material in the list.**

    Now change the name of this new material.

17. **Edit the Diffuse line, replacing the name of the old texture with the name you saved your new texture under. Now click Save at the bottom of the Edit Material box.**

    You should see the 3D model in the 3D view change to use your new texture.

18. **Re-load your movie, go to Cast, select your narrator, and click Go To The Puppet Shop; select Hair and select the style you edited.**

    You now find your edited texture style available to use.

# Rendering Out the Final Version

After you've set up your movie, your characters, and all your cameras, as well as tweaked every bit of the movie to your exact taste, it's time to render out the final version so that it can be enjoyed by everyone. Go on, send your mom a copy. She'll be so proud.

1. **Go to the Director's View and click Wrap And Render This Scene.**

   The Render Settings window appears.

2. **Choose the directory you'd like to render to using the Browse button and then choose a filename to save your movie as.**

3. **Click the green check to start the rendering process.**

   Don't move the window or do anything else with the computer, unless you want your e-mail memorialized in virtual celluloid.

   The final version of the movie is rendered, and Moviestorm switches between cameras as you've commanded it to. Depending on the speed of your computer and the length and complexity of your movie, this process can take a few minutes — a progress bar keeps you updated. Put the kettle on. Black with no sugar for us — we *are* hackers, after all.

A shiny new video file appears in whichever directory you specified. You can now edit that movie in whatever movie editor you please. Chop it together, delete the slow bits, slap some titles in, and you're done, done, done!

# Going Further

We think Moviestorm is going to be huge. And whilst we've covered many of its features, we've really only scratched the surface of what it can do and what you can achieve with it.

If you want to find out more and interact with other Moviestorm users as everyone learns how to use and exploit this tremendously exciting tool, your best bet are the official Moviestorm Web pages and forums, at www.moviestorm.co.uk.

# Chapter 18

# Build a Better Mousetrap: Going Beyond Engine Limitations

**M**achinima is great. (If you don't agree, according to the invisible shrink-wrap license you signed when you opened this book, large men will now be traveling to your door to do you injury.) But sometimes, you'll just hit a brick wall: Either your chosen engine can't do what you want, or there's something about it that's just constantly irritating. Well, we're here to relieve the irritation, like a brand-name nonprescription drug we can't name for fear of a lawsuit.

There are a whole bunch of things you can do to improve your engine's utility for Machinima. You can create new content for it, of course. You can also write tools and extensions to make it a better Machinima platform. And, if all else fails, you can pull on your elite, ninja black-hat outfit and hack the engine until it finally breaks and agrees, sobbing, to do your bidding.

## Improving Your Engine's Utility

There are a lot fewer limitations on your Machinima creation than you may think:

- ✔ **New tools:** You don't know how much a new tool can improve your Machinima production until you build one. No matter what task you're trying to accomplish, the chances are that you can do something with your engine to make it easier.

- ✔ **New stuff:** And by stuff, we mean actual, physical stuff. New, funky mice. New keyboards. New input devices. Entirely new PCs. All these things can make your Machinima work easier, at the cost of mere cash.

✔ **New limits:** Game developers have a tendency to hard-code certain limits into their games — *by hard-code,* we mean include in the source code for the game. But that's not as insoluble a problem as you'd think. Want to make your camera go out further? Or reduce the size of a character's bounding box? You can (probably) do it.

✔ **New angles:** And there are more ways to skin a cat, Horatio, than are dreamt of in your philosophy. Or something. Your game isn't running in a vacuum: There's a whole bunch of underlying code and hardware, from the operating system to the monitor, that makes it go. You can turn these dependencies to your advantage.

But is it worth going to all this effort? It's worth remembering that time you're putting into hacking your engine, investigating obscure memory exploits and coding new user interfaces, is time you're not spending making your film.

In general, it's probably *not* worth getting with the hackery if:

✔ **You're working on a very small project.** If you're only making a minute-long Machinima film, it's not worth spending a week customizing the game's user interface.

✔ **You're hacking in expectation of likely needs.** It's easy to say "Oh, we'll definitely need lipsynching/larger characters/whatever". Don't hack until you're sure.

It definitely, definitely *is* worth looking into hacking at your engine if:

✔ **You're losing time or patience to a problem.** If there's something that's significantly slowing down your shooting, and if you're going to be spending more than a few weeks on your movie, find a way to fix the problem.

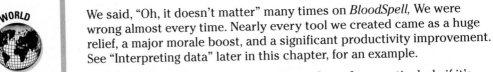

We said, "Oh, it doesn't matter" many times on *BloodSpell,* We were wrong almost every time. Nearly every tool we created came as a huge relief, a major morale boost, and a significant productivity improvement. See "Interpreting data" later in this chapter, for an example.

✔ **It will make a huge difference to the end result** — particularly if it's going to meaningfully differentiate your movie from other Machinima work. Visual quality and cool tricks are both excellent ways to get noticed. It can be worth spending weeks or even months to achieve the extra 5-percent quality that will make the difference between a user-page on YouTube and the front page of YouTube.

# Fiddling with Tools

So, how do you get in there and make tools? First figure out how much lati-tude your chosen game gives to new code and modifications.

Some games feature a very limited scripting language, through which it's possible to alter the on-screen user interface (UI), but not much else. Other games have entire programming languages available to modify their game play. Still others expose chunks of raw C++ or other code, with which you can write the functions you want to use. And, of course, some game engines offer absolutely nothing at all. Table 18-1 describes the tools of the engines we cover in this book.

| Table 18-1 | Potential for New Tools |
|---|---|
| *Engine* | *Tool Development* |
| The Sims 2 | Extensive scripting language covering interactions between char-acters and objects. Some odd limitations based on The Sims 2's basic architecture. |
| The Movies | No scripting language. No tool programming. |
| Half-Life 2 | Huge SDK (software development kit) based on the C++ code from the game. If you want it, you can build it, but you'd better be a fully fledged C++ programmer to do so. |
| Halo 2 | No accessible scripting language. |
| Unreal Tournament | Uses its own programming language, UnrealScript. Like Half-Life 2, huge, extensible, and very complex, but doesn't require as much existing programming knowledge. |
| Neverwinter Nights | Easily accessible scripting language that ties neatly into the game via in-game items like Wands. Our No. 1 choice for quick tool devel-opment. More limited in the long run than Unreal Tournament or Half-Life 2. |
| Neverwinter Nights 2 | Extends the scripting available in Neverwinter Nights 1. Because it's a newer game than NWN1, less information at the time of writ-ing, on NWN2 scripting and tool development. |
| Medieval Total War 2 | No available tool scripting. |

*(continued)*

### Table 18-1 *(continued)*

| Engine | Tool Development |
|---|---|
| DooM 3 | Like Half-Life 2, an SDK is available opening large segments of the game code. Nontrivial to modify, but very powerful. |
| Grand Theft Auto series | Some scripting and tool development available. Less powerful than UT and less accessible than NWN, but usable. |
| Moviestorm | No scripting language yet, but it's promised toward the end of 2007. |
| IClone | No scripting, reprogramming, or UI modification. |
| Second Life | The sky's the limit! Huge array of programming functionality, using Second Life's proprietary scripting language, LSL. |
| World of Warcraft | Extensive modifications possible, using the LUA scripting language. However, modifications are limited to interface customization only — nothing that would modify other players' experience. |
| Battlefield 2 | Some modifications possible with built-in scripting language. |
| Company Of Heroes | No real tool development possible at present. |

Any game that uses C++ or another programming language that requires an external compiler — notably DooM 3 and Half-Life 2 — is likely to be very complex to modify. The complexity of the programming languages they use, plus the fact that you'll need a separate compiler (like Microsoft Visual C++) to even start work, means that you really need to be an experienced programmer to modify these games. Table 18-2 describes the level of expertise each game requires.

### Table 18-2    Potential for Third-Party Tools in Different Engines

| Easy to Write | Moderately Tricky To Write | Hard to Write Tools |
|---|---|---|
| Neverwinter Nights | World of Warcraft (in-game UI) | DooM 3 (requires a C++ compiler) |
| Neverwinter Nights 2 | Battlefield 2 | Half-Life 2 (requires Visual C++) |
| Second Life | Unreal Tournament | |
| World of Warcraft (console commands) | | |

You can do some tool development in the editor of a game, without touching code. It's possible to set up triggers, scripted sequences, camera moves, and special effects in the editors for Half-Life 2 and Unreal Tournament, in particular, without ever having to touch a line of code.

# What Can You Do with Tools?

Most tools automate a task that you can do manually, but that would be wickedly hard, frighteningly repetitive, or both. Sometimes you'll use a tool to access an aspect of the engine that you otherwise couldn't. For example, you can trigger a special effect that's normally played randomly or remove a feature that the game enables by default.

Here are a few tools that you can create for most engines:

- ✔ Store a character's position and teleport him back to it.
- ✔ Store a character's position and have him walk there.
- ✔ Store a camera location and orientation.
- ✔ Trigger an explosion special effect.
- ✔ Play a simple camera script, such as a circling shot or a zoom.
- ✔ Set up several characters in a formation and have them hold that formation when walking.
- ✔ Have two characters fight.
- ✔ Have two characters walk to positions as if to fight — but then don't — very, very useful.
- ✔ Make characters ignore in-game health rules — because there's nothing more annoying than spending ages setting up for a shot, only to have one of your principal actors finally run out of hit points and die.

Some things aren't possible in a game where you're not allowed to modify the server. In World of Warcraft, for example, you can't make your character invulnerable, for obvious reasons. And while you can make computer-controlled actors in Second Life, it's not easy, and the people who run the game aren't very fond of you doing it!

The approach we're taking here is, in some ways, very similar to the way that you can create scripted movies. Tools can indeed include Machinima scripts. If you need a particularly complex camera movement in Neverwinter Nights, for example, you can write it in a script and then cue it from a wand in-game.

# What about World of Warcraft?

World of Warcraft is clearly the odd engine out. You can't control monsters, and you can't change the game, so what use are tools? Well, here are some things you can do:

✔ Set up tools to give smooth, pre-set camera movements.

✔ Save your favorite shooting locations — even direct yourself back to them if you get lost!

✔ Set up commonly used chat commands (Ready . . . Action!) to use automatically.

✔ Track the locations of your cast and crew in a window so that you know when they're going to arrive for a shoot.

You can do less in World of Warcraft than other games in which you have more control, but tool scripting is still useful.

---

You also need to choose how your tool is activated. Most games have three basic options:

✔ **Console command:** The simplest way to trigger a tool, in most games, is by using the in-game console. Most games include a developer's console, like a command prompt, originally intended for the game developers to input commands to help them test and design the game. Adding commands to the console to do your evil bidding is usually pretty easy. If you want an example of using console commands, check Chapter 9; we use console commands in The Sims 2 to set up our filming environment.

✔ **In-game item:** You can tie a tool to an in-game item. Often, this option allows you to select the thing you want the item to operate on, by shooting it with a gun or clicking it as if you were going to cast a spell in the game. You can even re-purpose existing items in the game that you're not using for your film, which saves on the coding you'll have to do. In Chapter 9, we use the Pawfect Films Sims 2 Studio item, which uses the logic of Sims 2 items to do its work.

✔ **UI:** You can access the same tools that the game developers use to build the game's user interface. The most user-friendly option, it's also the most work. In Chapter 12, we use CameraPlus, a World of Warcraft add-on that extends the World of Warcraft UI.

# Scripting in Your Engine

We can't cover all the engines here, thanks to lack of space, but fortunately we don't need to. Thousands of resources on the Internet can show you how to script add-ons for any game you care to mention. Table 18-3 provides a quick list of the top resources for the games covered in this book.

| Table 18-3 | A Resource Guide to Scripting Add-Ons |
|---|---|
| *Game* | *Site* |
| Neverwinter Nights | `http://nwvault.ign.com/dm/scripting/course.` Step-by-step guide to learning to code in NWN. |
| | `http://nwn.bioware.com/forums/viewforum.html?forum=47`. The official NWN coding forums. If you have a question, chances are it's been asked here. |
| Neverwinter Nights 2 | `http://nwn2forums.bioware.com/forums/viewforum.html?forum=114`. The official NWN2 coding forums. Still quite new, but filling up nicely. |
| Second Life | In-game resources. Second Life itself includes extensive scripting tutorials that can get you started on tool development in SL. |
| | LSL Wiki at `http://lslwiki.net/lslwiki/wakka.php?wakka=HomePage`. |
| World of Warcraft | `www.wowwiki.com/Interface_Customization`. Everything you possibly need to know about World of Warcraft scripting. |
| | `http://forums.worldofwarcraft.com/board.html?forumId=11114&sid=1`. The official World of Warcraft UI development forums. |
| Battlefield 2 | `http://bfeditor.org/forums`. Extensive discussions on Battlefield 2 modding. |
| Unreal Tournament | `http://udn.epicgames.com/Main/WebHome.html`. The Epic Megagames guys love and support UT modding like doting parents. There's more info here on the various Unreal engines than you can shake the proverbial stick at. |
| | `http://wiki.beyondunreal.com/wiki/UnrealScript_Lessons`. Part of the generally useful Unreal Wiki; a series of lessons on UT scripting and development. |
| The Sims 2 | `www.modthesims2.com`. The tutorials at MTS2 are fairly comprehensive, beginner to advanced. |
| | `www.sims2wiki.info/wiki.php?title=Sims_2_Modding`. Tons of specific info on all aspects of Sims 2 editing. |
| DooM 3 | `www.iddevnet.com/doom3`. Not terribly organized, but chock-full of DooM 3 information. |
| Half-Life 2 | `http://developer.valvesoftware.com/wiki/SDK_Docs`. A bit thin given the depth of the engine, but still a good resource for HL2 modding. |

Many more resources are available than the ones we list, particularly for the popular games. Google is your friend.

# Developing Tools: An Example

On *BloodSpell,* we noticed that our shooting script featured a whole lot of characters gushing blood for various reasons. However, there was no easy way to cause our characters to do that. A few experiments with hitting them with sticks, swords, and broken bottles proved unsuccessful (no, we're not joking), so we decided to investigate the world of tool development.

Fortunately, we were working in Neverwinter Nights, which makes it easy to set up tools to control characters, using its in-built scripting language. Because Neverwinter Nights already has in-game items called *wands,* which perform an effect on a target, we knew we would be creating this tool as a Blood Wand. We started by opening up the Neverwinter Nights Editor. We wanted our wands to be available to us in-game as inventory items, so we created an item called Blood Wand (see Figure 18-1). Our investigation of the available item properties didn't show us a way to link the item to a script, so we Googled for *how to tie wand to script nwn.* The results from that search led us to the Neverwinter Nights scripting forums. Posts there told us that we had to give the item a Use Unique Power ability and a distinctive tag to trigger a script. We decided on a tag of `bs_blood`.

**Figure 18-1:**
Creating an item in Neverwinter Nights.

Then, we had to activate a script in OnActivateItem, according to http://
nwn.bioware.com/forums/viewtopic.html?topic=81523&forum=47.
We Googled the term OnActivateItem: The first result told us we needed
something called tag-based scripting. Go go gadget Google!

The second Google result led us to a detailed explanation of what this mystic
term meant and how it worked (http://nwn.bioware.com/forums/
viewtopic.html?topic=480881&forum=47). This forum post and its
links told us to check that we had the script x2_mod_def_act set up for
OnActivateItem (aha!). It turned out the script was set already, as was the
module variable another tutorial mentioned. The NWN editor had been
updated since that tutorial was written and, handily, had set these things as
defaults!

Now all we had to do was to write a script, with the same name as the tag of
the item. So, to the script editor we went. The script from that tutorial looked
a bit frightening, so we Googled around a bit more and found a NWN tool
called LilacSoul's Script Generator: Perfect for us.

We clicked through the Unique Item Script dialog options in LilacSoul's tool.
It all looked good, aside from the fact that it didn't have the option to generate a script that would spew blood — not a big surprise! But we figured, with
considerable optimism, that we could adapt it easy enough, so we chose
something that looked similar: the Add Effect script. The tool produced this:

```
/* Script generated by
Lilac Soul's NWN Script Generator, v. 2.3
For download info, please visit:
http://nwvault.ign.com/View.php?view=Other.Detail&id=4683&id=625
*/
void main()
{
object oPC;
if ((GetObjectType(GetItemActivatedTarget())!=OBJECT_TYPE_CREATURE)
){
return;}
object oTarget;
oTarget = GetItemActivatedTarget();
effect eEffect;
eEffect = EffectDeath();
ApplyEffectToObject(DURATION_TYPE_TEMPORARY, eEffect, oTarget, 60.0f);
}
```

Then we had to figure out what we should change to make blood, not war. An
obvious candidate was the EffectDeath thing. We didn't know what it did,
exactly. Reading the script editor's documentation, we learned there were a
bunch of Effect functions, including EffectVisualEffect, which apparently created a visual effect. That sounded like what we were looking for.

The text for that function talked about a Visual Effect ID. We didn't know what one of those was either, but a bit more Googling led us to believe that we needed a special number from a `VisualEffects.2da` file, which is a data file for Neverwinter Nights.

We opened a copy of `VisualEffects.2da` from our Neverwinter Nights directory, and lo and behold, found a massive list of potential visual effects. Number `115`, `VFX_COM_BLOOD_CRT_RED` sounded good — a Critical Red Blood effect. We modified `eEffect = EffectDeath();` to read `eEffect = EffectVisualEffect(115);` and saved our set.

We loaded our game, created a Blood Wand, clicked a creature with it, and lo, did spurting of blood ensue.

As you can see, we didn't know how to create our tool, or indeed any tool, in NWN, before we began. You can use a similar process with most games to cobble together some code into a tool you can use. Your code may not be pretty. It may be something real programmers would laugh at. But if it does the job, that's all that matters.

# Considering Hardware Add-Ons

Surely a new mouse can't improve your Machinima production? Well, actually, yes, it can, if it gives you a smoother action for better camerawork, or more buttons to fire actions easily. Table 18-4 describes a few add-ons that can improve your Machinima experience.

| Table 18-4 | Add-Ons to Consider |
|---|---|
| **Add-On** | **Description** |
| Dual-Core CPU | If you're using FRAPS or another real-time video capture solution, this one's a must. Essentially, it gives you two PCs in one box. With this and a second hard drive, you can record video using FRAPS at up to high-definition quality. |
| Nostromo keypad | As used by the ILL Clan of New York for its live performance Machinima. The Nostromo is a programmable, palm-sized keyboard replacement designed for gaming, but very useful for Machinima, giving you dozens of commands at your fingertips. |

| Add-On | Description |
| --- | --- |
| Bigger monitor | One of the best investments you can make for your Machinima. A larger monitor allows you to work faster and more efficiently when editing. It also gives you a better view when filming, and if you buy a wide-screen model, you can easily shoot in 16:9 resolution. |
| Steering wheel | A lot of the time, a mouse is absolutely the worst input device for, say, smooth camera movements. A lot of people automate or script their pans, tracks, and so on for exactly this reason. But there's another way: Control your pans exactly the same way that film cameramen control their cameras, by using a wheel. Tied to the appropriate controls, you can easily achieve smooth pans and tracks. Make sure that you get one with full rotation. |
| | If you don't want to shell out for a wheel, many Machinima creators also swear by a good joystick for smooth camera control. |
| Another PC | If you're filming using a multiplayer game over a network, here's a very simple rule: You want as many PCs available as possible. On *BloodSpell*, we routinely worked with two PCs for each person in a two-man crew, which allowed us to run a lot more characters simultaneously. With more PCs, you can run your game server (if it's a game that has a server) on a separate machine, giving you the best performance possible, and if necessary control multiple characters at once. |
| External storage | If you're working on a project that takes you more than a few days, some kind of backup is not optional. Fortunately, you can buy huge external hard drives for very little money these days: a 500 GB drive, at the time of writing, sets you back about $200. Make sure to back up your footage using a lossless codec (we use HuffYUV) every day after shooting. |
| Nintendo Wii | The Wii console has intriguing possibilities for Machinima. You can adapt its motion-sensing controller (the Wiimote) to work with a PC using standard Bluetooth drivers. Once you've done that, you've got the best possible controller for hand-held Machinima shooting and an excellent controller for Machinima camerawork in general. |
| Motion Capture equipment | Now we're getting a bit futuristic. But, as the Wii shows, motion capture is coming to the home, and it's coming fast. You can already buy mocap-capable cameras from NaturalPoint (www.naturalpoint.com) for about $200 each, and they're promising a full motion-capture solution using these cameras by the end of 2007. You need to do quite a bit of processing with a 3D package to get the best use out of mocap right now, but the potential is absolutely fantastic. |

# Removing Limitations

It will take you about, ooh, five or ten minutes to find some programmed limitation in your Machinima software that will really annoy you. Tops. Probably less. Whether it's a character who won't quite turn his head far enough or a doorway that's somehow mysteriously too small for your characters to get through, it'll irritate the heck out of you.

Fortunately, you can investigate a whole pile of options to fix or remove your problems by changing data in the game:

- ✔ **In-game menus:** Before you go mad with the hacking tools, check that the thing that's annoying you isn't accessible through the in-game menus. In World of Warcraft, for example, the weather effects can really interfere with your filming. You can hunt for the shaders responsible inside the World of Warcraft data files, but it's probably easier to just use the various sliders under Video Settings to turn them down.

- ✔ **Key bindings:** Make sure that a key isn't already available that does what you want. Many games don't list their keyboard commands anywhere but in their bind keys menu. For example, World of Warcraft's keyboard bindings include Hide HUD (to hide all the in-game menus and just show the 3D view), Sit/Stand, and Draw Weapons, all useful for Machinima.

- ✔ **Console commands:** Many games have a developer console hidden within the game, from which you can access all sorts of useful options. The simplest way to find out what you can do with this console is likely to be to Google "console commands *NAME OF GAME*": *Console Commands Half-Life 2,* for example.

    Before you start filming with any new engine, find out whether your engine has a console, and if so, what you can do with it. For example, Half-Life 2 has literally hundreds of console commands, allowing you to hide the HUD, hide your weapon to give a full-screen camera, execute an in-game script file, and more.

- ✔ **Command-line options:** Different to console commands, these commands are given to the game at the time you run it. In general, they deal with setting the game to a specific mode, such as developer mode, dungeon master mode, or a mode where intro movies aren't played. You normally add a command-line option by editing the shortcut you use to run the game and changing the program name or target from, say, `C:\Program Files\EA Games\Battlefield 2\BF2.exe` to `C:\Program Files\EA Games\Battlefield 2\BF2.exe +menu 1 +szx 1280 +szy 1024'`.

    For example, in Neverwinter Nights, you can run `nwn.exe -dmc` to start the game up with the DM Client active.

✔ **Configuration files:** Virtually every game has a series of configuration files in which the settings for that particular game are stored. These configuration files also often affect additional settings that you can't access from the game. You can most easily find out where and what the configuration files for your game are with a quick Google search, à la Neverwinter Nights 2 configuration files. You can also simply open your game's folder and look for either directories or files named something like Config or .cfg. For an extensive example of using configuration files in a game, see Chapter 9, where we use The Sims 2 config files to change camera speeds.

✔ **Data files:** Ah, now we're getting hardcore. All game engines have to store a wide range of data about the game they're currently running. This data may be model texture names, values for the size of collision detection boxes, or the maximum angle a character can turn his head. If you change this data, you can change the way your game engine works — to the better for Machinima.

Again — and we're sure you're sick of us saying this — how you access this data depends on the game engine you're using. Most likely the data will be sorted in individual files, probably text files, packaged up inside a larger file called a package file. You need to find a program to let you extract these text files. (See the sidebar "Package extractors" for more on this topic.)

## Interpreting data

After you've extracted your files, you'll probably be looking at a big pile of data in a text file. You'll have to figure out what that data means! Search through modding forums and sites for your game to see whether anyone has already decoded the format of these files.

Ideally, try searching on terms you find inside the files to get more information. Other than that, try making your best guess as to what any value is used for and then change it, run the game, and test to see whether the change you predicted has occurred. This sounds like a painful process of trial and error, but the results can be hugely beneficial for your Machinima.

In *BloodSpell,* production was plagued for over a year by a blue halo that appeared around any character over which a mouse pointer was hovering. As we discovered late in production, this apparently insoluble behavior was controlled by a single line in Neverwinter Nights' appearance.2da file, which governs creature behavior. Five minutes with a text editor allowed us to eliminate a problem that had frustrated us for months.

## Hex editing

If all else fails and you really want to change a specific detail in your game, and it has a number associated with it that you're fairly sure of, then you have one final option: Hex edit your game's executable program file.

This approach is pretty technical. You take the compiled program that runs your game and edit it at the machine-code level to change your chosen value to a different one. Don't try this unless you're reasonably comfortable with code.

Hex editing is another trial-and-error process. You search through the hex code of the program and change all the instances of your chosen number until one works.

## Package extractors

Handily, uber programmers like to write package extractors for the games they play. For the games in this book, you can use the package extractors described in the following table:

| Game | Package Extractor |
|---|---|
| The Sims 2 | SimPE, available from `http://sims.ambertation.de`. |
| The Movies | PakPoker, available from `http://themovies.filefront.com/file/Pak_Poker;54205` (doesn't work with downloaded versions of the game or expansion). |
| Half-Life 2 | VTF Explorer, available from `http://www.hl2source.com/?content=projects&id=vtftool`. |
| Halo 2 | Ch2r, available from `http://sourceforge.net/projects/ch2r` (Halo 2 is very unfriendly to edit, and so this isn't a complete solution). |
| Unreal Tournament 2003/2004/2007 | Doesn't have an unpacker as such, although you can view most of the data files in the editor or online. |
| Neverwinter Nights | NWNExplorer, available from `http://nwvault.ign.com/View.php?view=Other.Detail&id=248`. |
| Neverwinter Nights 2 | NWN2Packer, available from `http://nwvault.ign.com/View.php?view=NWN2Tools.Detail&id=9`. |

| Game | Package Extractor |
|---|---|
| Medieval Total War 2 | Comes with an unpacker program, found in `Medieval II Total War\ tools\unpacker`. |
| DooM 3 | DooM 3 uses the `.pk4` package format, which is identical to a `.zip` file. Use any `.zip` file extractor to extract files. |
| Grand Theft Auto series | A selection of unpacking tools are available from `www.thegtaplace. com/pafiledb.php?action=category&id=3`. |
| Moviestorm | No unpacking tool needed. |
| IClone | No unpacking tool needed. |
| Second Life | No unpacking tool needed. |
| World of Warcraft | MyWarcraftStudio, available from `www.wowmodelviewer.org/index. option=com_remository&Itemid=35&func=fileinfo& id=12`. |
| Battlefield 2 | The Battlefield 2 Map Editor works in a similar way to an extractor — `www.ea.com/official/battlefield/battlefield2/us/ editorial.jsp?src=mod_editor`. |
| Company Of Heroes | The Company of Heroes Mod Studio, available from `http://wiki. reliccommunity.com/Modding:Mod_Studio_Usage_Guide`. |

If you're looking for an extracting tool for other games, start by searching for something like `NAME_OF_GAME file extract`. If that doesn't work, search for `NAME_OF_GAME` `modding information` and look for modding utilities. These utilities usually include some kind of file extractor.

A huge number of hex editors are available on the Internet. We recommend HxD from `http://mh-nexus.de/hxd` (on the book's DVD). It includes a useful Find/Replace function that automatically translates floating-point numbers to and from hexadecimal notation.

To hex-edit your game into submission:

1. **Find the number that you want to edit.**

   It is, practically speaking, only possible to change hard-coded single numbers or text strings using this process. Usually, you're changing something like a camera constraint. We used this method to hex-edit Neverwinter Nights to allow us to move a camera all the way above our characters.

2. **Learn or guess the number that you need to change.**

   For example, we knew from patch notes from the game that the engine was locked to 60 degrees above the horizontal.

3. **Copy the main program file (almost always a** .exe **under windows) and save the copy somewhere safe.**

   You'll be reverting to it if it all goes wrong.

4. **Open the main** .exe **file for the game in your hex editor.**

5. **Open the Find/Replace function, find the first instance of the value you're trying to change, and replace it with the value you'd like to use.**

   In this case, we replaced 60.0 with 90.0.

6. **Run the game to see whether the value you were hoping to change has indeed changed.**

   If it has, great! If not, go to Step 7.

7. **If necessary, delete the** .exe **you modified, replace it with another copy of your pristine** .exe **file, and try the process again, this time only changing the second instance of that value.**

   If that doesn't work, try the third instance. And so on.

As you can see, this technique is pretty limited. It also works better for more unique values. Finding an instance of 69.5 inside an .exe should be fairly easy, but if you're trying to change a value of 1 or 0, you'll be there for a while. But sometimes it's the only way to get the game to do what you want it to do.

# Trying New Angles

You can almost always make a game engine do what you want. It's just a case of how much time and effort you're willing to spend and how creative you can be.

Your game doesn't run in a vacuum. It depends on a whole ecosystem of other programs to function, from the OpenGL or DirectX drivers that run your graphics card, to Windows or Linux's network code, to the ultra-low level programs that change a sound file into voltage in a wire. You can employ all of these programs, if necessary, to make your game do what you want.

## TOGLFaces: Going beyond the engine

On Strange Company's first feature film, *BloodSpell,* we were facing a critical problem early in production. We needed our characters' lips to move when they talked, but Neverwinter Nights didn't have any such functionality. This was a complex feature — not something we could data- or hex-edit. So we turned our attention to the stream of information that the game sends to the video card via the OpenGL driver on the machine. This data includes names of the 2D images that the game uses as textures.

We wrote a program called TOGLFaceS *(Take Over GL Face Streams).* This program intercepted the OpenGL calls Neverwinter Nights made to our graphics card, replacing the face textures of our characters with different images. We then tied different images to different keyboard functions, depending on whether we needed our characters' mouths to be open or closed. Finally, we instructed TOGLFaceS to pass the modified OpenGL stream to the graphics card. And, thus, we were able to produce a lip-synched movie using an engine with no such feature.

Likewise, don't forget that you have plenty of options after you've recorded your footage. If you really need to, you can use all sorts of conventional video tricks to apparently break the rules of the game — see Chapter 12.

If you've got a problem, and you absolutely have to fix it, grab the best programmer you can find and brainstorm ways around it.

Absolutely need a cast of dancing orcs inside World of Warcraft? Perhaps you can intercept the network traffic from the game and convince your engine that it's seeing orcs where there should be none. Need a Terminator 2–style morphing shot in The Sims 2? Why not use a 3D-capture program to capture a static frame of a close-up of your character, take that into a 3D modeling program, and morph it there?

The sky's the limit — but only until you hex-edit a way to move your camera higher than the default skyline.

# Chapter 19

# Pro Machinima?

● ● ● ● ● ● ● ● ● ● ● ● ● ● ● ● ● ● ● ● ● ● ● ● ● ● ● ● ● ● ● ● ● ● ● ● ● ●

### In This Chapter

▶ Going pro with Machinima

▶ Getting a job as a Machinima developer for a games company

▶ Starting your own production company

● ● ● ● ● ● ● ● ● ● ● ● ● ● ● ● ● ● ● ● ● ● ● ● ● ● ● ● ● ● ● ● ● ● ● ● ● ●

*Y*ou may be perfectly happy just making Machinima in your spare time — and that's great! In fact, it's what we're most excited about: Machinima as a way to make films without devoting your life to the process.

But you may enjoy Machinima so much that you want to make it your day job. A few years ago, that would have been virtually impossible, but these days, it's possible, if still far from easy.

Even if you try, you may not succeed — there's still not a lot of space for full-time Machinima creators. If you want to give it a try, then this chapter is for you.

# Getting Hired by a Games Company

It used to be the case that finding a game with good cinematography or great cut-scenes was a rare occurrence. These days, thankfully, most game developers realize that a game is a story as much as a puzzle, and that having a good cinematographic vision can benefit their game immensely. Somebody has to be employed to create these cut-scenes. If you're an experienced Machinima creator, you've got the CV for the job.

A lot of top-class games companies have hired talented people from the Machinima community, often on a permanent basis. We know of Machinima enthusiasts who have been hired by Bioware, Shiny, Blizzard, and other prominent companies. Strange Company has contracted for games companies at various times as well.

The competition is tough — no matter how talented you may be, we can't guarantee you'll get anything other than rejection upon rejection — but this path can be a very rewarding way of getting paid to do what you love.

Making Machinima for a living has some obvious benefits:

- **Job security:** No job is 100-percent secure, obviously, but you can rely on employment by a major games company to pay the bills more reliably than the income from your self-financed short movie. Pay scales can vary for this type of job, depending on your expertise and the exact nature of the work that you're doing, but they're usually pretty competitive. Also consider the added security that a regular, salaried job brings in terms of benefits such as pensions, dental plans, and so on.

- **Company car (or maybe not!):** You probably won't get a company car, actually, but you will get access to the kind of tools that you probably wouldn't be able to afford otherwise. As well as an expensive PC workstation with a huge flat-screen monitor, you may even be lucky enough to be allowed to play with things like motion capture suites, high-end animation packages, and editing tools worth thousands of dollars.

- **An opinion that matters:** Your input counts and will affect the final product that you're working on. Perhaps the only decision you get to make is the color of the lead character's socks, but you might find you can significantly influence the areas you're working on.

- **Great colleagues:** You'll be working with other talented people, from whom you're sure to garner inspiration. We can't promise that you won't find yourself working with obnoxious idiots, but in general your work colleagues are likely to think the same way as you and be able to teach you lots of impressive things.

It's not all roses, though:

- **Not your baby:** Whatever you're asked to work on, you'll be following somebody else's directions and attempting to realize somebody else's vision. If you're the sort of person who has to run the show, this job may not be for you.

- **Busman's holiday:** It's 8:00 in the evening. You just got back from a hard day at the office, mainly spent trying to force a buggy and undocumented game engine to do what you want it to do. Do you really want to boot up your own computer and open the editor for a different, equally buggy, equally undocumented game? If you make Machinima all day, you'll probably not want to make it all night as well. Expect your own projects to suffer because of it.

✔ **This isn't what I signed up for:** Even though your Machinima skills may be the thing that gets you hired in the first place, don't expect to be allowed to just make Machinima all day. You're going to have to develop other skill sets, too, especially in a smaller task force.

✔ **Stick it to the man:** If you're making your own movie, you can prioritize your artistic vision over anything else. A company producing a game, though, has a bottom line and certain targets that it has to meet. You'll be asked — nay, told — to make a lot of fairly hefty compromises; and you won't like many of them.

If, after reading the pros and cons, you still want to get a job working for a computer games company, here are a few quick tips to increase your likelihood of success:

✔ **Keep watching the skies.** Keep an eye out for vacancies. Most games companies have a page on their Web site dedicated to current job vacancies. Check them all regularly.

✔ **Cold call.** Don't bother e-mailing identical begging letters to every games company whose URL you can remember. They won't even be opened. If you're going to make unsolicited contact (and you probably should), treat every application as a separate project. Find out the name of the person responsible for hiring and do some research into the company itself — then contact him with your best foot forward.

✔ **Here's one I made earlier.** If you've never made a Machinima movie, there's no way you'll be hired as the Machinima consultant for Blizzard Entertainment (or wherever). Get some experience under your belt, preferably as varied as possible, and then put together a portfolio. Virtually every Machinima maker hired by a games company was picked up on the back of a movie he made.

✔ **Make your presence known.** If you want to convince your prospective new employers that you're one of the world's top Machinima makers, you'll have to provide some evidence. Any employer worth his salt is probably going to hit the Internet to see how much the rest of the community respects your opinions and looks to you for advice. Anticipate this action. Start a blog. Answer some of the newbie questions on your favorite forum. Post on other Machinima maker's sites and try to start some interesting discussion. The more times your name appears, the better your profile will look.

# Starting Your Own Machinima Company

But what about starting your own Machinima production company full-time, and following in the footsteps of Strange Company, the ILL Clan, Rooster Teeth, and, er. . . .

Well, that's the thing. There aren't a lot of professional Machinima production companies out there, and there's a reason for that. And the reason, basically, is that you've got to be a bit mad to try to turn this particular activity into a full-time profession right now.

Having said that, Hugh did it. And it's certainly possible for other people to do the same thing.

Hugh thinks he has one of the best jobs in the world:

- ✔ **If you're running the company, you're your own boss.** No one can dictate what you're working on. If you want to dedicate the next two years to making a Machinima feature film, for example, you can.

- ✔ **If you're the boss of the company, you get the profits.** You'll have to be smart and lucky, but being a business owner is basically the only way for your company's success and your success to be the same thing.

- ✔ **Want to lead?** If you're working for yourself, you have to stay ahead of the pack. Because you're in charge of the schedule, you can start projects purely to test new techniques and advance your Machinima.

Most of Hugh's friends and relatives think Hugh's a bit mad:

- ✔ **Even if you're *Red vs Blue*, there's not a lot of money in Machinima.** Rooster Teeth is probably the most profitable Machinima company right now (they're not saying for certain), but even it isn't making a lot of cash — $100,000 a year or more may sound like a lot, but split between four or five people, it doesn't go very far.

- ✔ **Running a Machinima company is very, very hard.** In addition to the huge range of skills you need just to be a Machinima director, you also need to be able to project manage, sell projects, handle investors, write presentations, do bookkeeping and financial projections, meet with lawyers, argue with bank managers, chase bills, and more. Hugh learned the hard way, and things went off the rails more than once.

✔ **It's very tricky to come up with a steady income.** In addition to the usual problems facing any media company (which are tough, tough, tough — ask anyone in the comics industry), you've got the added legal hassles presented by Machinima. Strange Company has survived by spending very little money, pulling in some big contracts, and generally being fast and light on its feet.

If you want to go ahead and start your own company, you're either mad or brilliant. As Captain Jack Sparrow said, it's remarkable how often those two traits coincide.

✔ **Don't spend money.** This is Rule No. 1 — if you've got $40,000 to start, you've either got 1 year to get things going at $40k a year, or 4 years at $10k a year. Certainly at the start, if you really want to jump in with both feet and go pro right away, you need to be prepared to live on Ramen noodles and baked beans.

✔ **Don't quit the day job.** That applies doubly to Machinima. If you have any minimum income that you *must* have, be very careful about starting up pro Machinima full-time. There's nothing wrong at all with running a business part time, whether that's two days a week or in the evenings.

✔ **Talk to everyone.** Absolutely everyone. We've not even begun to explore the avenues that Machinima opens in terms of business yet — there are a huge number of potential clients for a Machinima company. Talk to estate agents and architects (3D walkthroughs), talk to training organizations, and talk to universities.

✔ **Make sure that you charge enough.** At the beginning, in particular, it's very tempting to charge the minimum you think you can get away with, to ensure business. Remember these two rules: People value what they pay highly for, and the project will always take three times as long as you expect.

✔ **Get paid.** You will deal with slow payment, late payment, or complete absence of payment on a frequent basis. Make sure that you have a signed contract specifying how much you're being paid before you do any work at all, and don't be afraid to send out lawyer's letters if you're not getting paid. No money coming in will kill a business for certain. Try to get the money by being nice first, but if you're coming to 30 days after agreed payment, it's time to talk to lawyers.

✔ **Enjoy the experience.** Very few people will have the guts to start a business like this. Very few people will ever experience the joy of doing what they love as their working day. Remember to have fun. Even if it all goes horribly wrong, it'll still be a great experience, and it'll give you dinner-party stories for years to come.

# Part V
# The Part of Tens

## In this part . . .

This part contains three chapters, and each chapter has ten sections in turn. It's like little fleas and lesser fleas, only without the Black Death.

Want to learn which Machinima films are at the top of the game right now? Or what sites on the World Wide Web are the places to go to discover more about Machinima? Or why the top Machinima creators work in this artform? Then you're in the right place.

# Chapter 20

# Ten Machinima Films
# You Must Watch

*In This Chapter*

▶ Catching inspiring, must-watch movies

▶ Viewing the classics that made Machinima what it is today

**Y**ou wouldn't write a book without reading one. You wouldn't join a rock band if you'd never listened to a band with long hair and guitars. Likewise, if you want to get some serious inspiration for your own Machinima movies, you can start by watching the classics that have gone before. We think the movies listed here represent the best that Machinima has to offer. Most of them have won awards, and all are state of the art, or as the case may be, state of the Machinima.

Oh, and they're also all really good fun to watch.

You can watch a lot of these movies straight from the DVD that comes with this book. We also have links to all of these movies at www.machinimafor dummies.com.

# Anna

You'll probably find the movie *Anna* on the top-ten list of every prominent Machinima maker in the world.

*Anna* tells the story of a flower, from birth as a seed to growth as a flowering plant, and beyond. This leisurely, visual-led movie has a wonderful aural backdrop and a richly detailed visual world that is entirely custom content created by Fountainhead Entertainment, the team behind the movie. Astonishingly, the engine behind it is the aging Quake III.

*Anna* plays to the strengths of Machinima very well. With one very brief exception, the move contains no human characters, so Fountainhead is free to imbue its central character with the emotive flexibility that a human game character often lacks. The fact that the central character is a flower doesn't seem to deter the company; Anna succeeds as a moving and an elegant fairytale.

When you're picking a few sample Machinima films to show to the type of people who ask you, "So, what is this *mashy cinema* thing, then?", *Anna* has got to be on the list.

# *Hardly Workin'*

The ILL Clan, a New York improvisation comedy troupe with backgrounds in animation, programming, and music, turned to Machinima thanks to the gaming interests of several of its members. Back in 1998, the group released a riotously funny first Machinima film called *Apartment Huntin'*, which instantly elevated the ILL Clan to the top rank of Quake Movie producers. *Hardly Workin'*, the hotly awaited sequel, is one of the two films on this list directed by Paul "ILLRobinson" Marino.

*Hardly Workin'* was one of the first Machinima films to use entirely custom-created sets, textures, and character models. The movie tells the story of Larry and Lenny the lumberjacks' quest to find a job, but the plot isn't really the point. The movie features the kind of physical and slightly surreal, entirely improvised humor that the ILL Clan love. Much of the filming was shot live and in real-time.

*Hardly Workin'* is a movie from the Good Old Days of Machinima's infancy, and it showcases the potential of this emerging new medium (as many technology journalists still insist on referring to it). If you want to see why the potential of Machinima got people excited in the first place, *Hardly Workin'* is the movie to watch.

# *The Internet Is For Porn*

*"Ready, normal people?"*

*"Let me hear it!"*

*"The Internet is for porn! The Internet is for porn. . . ."*

We're occasionally asked to give a talk or a lecture about Machinima to a group of unsuspecting people. We've taken to finishing these talks with an audience-participation, sing-along version of *The Internet Is For Porn,* pantomime-style. We know all the lyrics, and it makes us laugh every time. And to think — we're old enough to vote.

*The Internet Is For Porn* is a music video lovingly made in World of Warcraft to the song of the same name, which was originally written for the cult Broadway show *Avenue Q*. This version of the song, by Evilhoof & Flayed, spread across the video-sharing sites and the blogosphere like wildfire in 2005 and is still a firm favorite in the Strange Company offices.

If you want to hear a distressingly catchy song in praise of pornography or see how an incredibly simple idea, realized by first-time filmmakers in Machinima, can take the Internet by storm, give this movie a try. Just don't show it to your mom.

# BloodSpell

Okay, we made this one. Hugh directed, wrote, and produced *BloodSpell*, and Johnnie was 1st Assistant Director. And we've been talking about it all through this book. We have to admit to a slight degradation in our journalistic impartiality at this point. But we're told *BloodSpell* is important, so here goes.

*BloodSpell* is a feature-length fantasy epic that tells the story of a world where people are infected with magic in their blood. Three years in production, *BloodSpell* is probably the largest and most complex Machinima project ever, at approximately the scale of the first *Star Wars* film in terms of sets, characters, and action sequences.

We can't really speak to its quality, but *BloodSpell* has been praised by some of the biggest names in Machinima, so it can't completely suck. Taking a post-Buffy, punk attitude to heroic fantasy films, and scored not with orchestral music but with aggressive punk and some of the weirdest indie music out there, it's certainly a project that couldn't have been made any other way.

If you want to watch some ambitious Machinima on an epic scale, or if you just want to hear Hugh and Johnnie pretending to be, respectively, a monstrous, squid-like butler and what one of our preview audience described as "a jelly-hatted pimp priest," then watch *BloodSpell*.

# The Snow Witch

Another movie in a fairytale style, *The Snow Witch* leans more toward the dark and sinister than *Anna* does. (See the section on *Anna,* earlier in this chapter.) Based on an old Japanese ghost story, *The Snow Witch* tells the story of Minokichi the woodcutter's encounter with a mysterious pale woman during a snowstorm.

Britannica Dreams possess an uncanny ability to make The Sims 2 look fluid, high-resolution, and gorgeous; *The Snow Witch* is perhaps its most aesthetically beautiful movie. Most of the dialogue is actually a narrator's voice (thereby cleverly avoiding the problem of lipsynching in The Sims 2). High-quality editing and post-production work is apparent on this movie, and a number of video composites and fades are used without becoming too intrusive.

The real highlight of the movie, though, is the set design. Many of the scenes are outdoor scenes, often featuring snow-covered forests and low sunlight bouncing off icy rivers. The attention to detail here is unsurpassed. Hours upon hours must have been spent preparing these sets, and the eventual movie is all the better for it.

*The Snow Witch* is a great example of a Machinima movie in which every aspect is of painstakingly high quality.

# Red vs Blue

What can we say? It's *Red vs Blue,* for pity's sake! If you're reading this section, there's about a one in four chance it's because of those wacky Texans.

Okay, for the, ooh, two of you who don't know what the heck we're talking about — *Red vs Blue* is the show that has done more to raise Machinima's profile than just about anything else. It's a sitcom, set in the game Halo 2, made by production house Rooster Teeth. Our heroes bemoan their situation, wonder about the illogicalities of their world, and engage in unsuccessful adventure.

*Red vs Blue's* first episode is a simply superb piece of writing and would hold up against the finest work in television sitcoms. That's doubly impressive considering it was shot using totally vanilla Halo 2 — no mods, no nothing.

From there, the series has sprawled out to (at time of writing) four feature-length seasons, of slightly uneven quality. However, the team's acting and production values are consistently superb, and this sitcom is a must-watch for an example of how to exceed your limitations.

If you're planning on making Machinima, or you're at all interested in the medium, you really can't afford to miss at least the first few episodes of this most iconic Machinima production.

# Still Seeing Breen

Paul "ILLRobinson" Marino, president of the Academy of Machinima Arts and Sciences, is, as you may gather, far, far too talented.

Not only was he one of the pioneers of Machinima. Not only is he a visual artist with a track record as long as your arm and an Emmy sitting on his shelf. But when he makes a simple test film to learn a new engine, the so-called "test film" is so accomplished and successful that it's subsequently picked up by MTV.

*Still Seeing Breen* matches *Breaking Benjamin's* track "So Cold" with the visuals of the game Half-Life 2, juxtaposing the two to brilliantly head-banging effect. Its piece de resistance is the stunning lipsynch and facial animation work that let Paul cast the G-Man, a character from the game, as lead vocalist. (He makes a surprisingly good heavy-metal singer, suit and all.) But the hidden backup singer is the stunning editing work, distilling the most emotive moments from all of Half-Life 2 into a whole that has been described as "the trailer Half-Life should have had."

Paul originally created *Breen* to learn and test Half-Life 2's facial animation systems and released it onto the Internet with very little fanfare. But within weeks, it had become an Internet sensation, and he received an offer from MTV, who wanted to take his "test film" and screen it on its Video Mods show.

In a medium filled with attempts at music videos of varying quality, from poor to superb, *Breen* is head-and-shoulders the one to watch.

# The Journey

We're looking down on a pencil-sketch scene, simple and abstract. A figure — it might be a man, might be a woman — walks with a crowd of hundreds of others down a scratchily painted valley. But this one figure, alone, steps away from this crowd and sets out to explore the abstract, artistic world he inhabits. Oh, yeah. And it's made in Unreal Tournament.

Friedrich Kirschner, director of *The Journey,* may be one of the few Machinima creators who can genuinely be described as a genius. Where other filmmakers — and both Hugh and Johnnie would include themselves in this description — use Machinima to mimic existing art forms, Friedrich continues to press forward to develop work that's totally new.

*The Journey* isn't just a technical exercise, although it brilliantly realizes a style that's almost impossible to differentiate from classical, pencil-drawn cel animation. It's also a great film and a great story, with some genuinely moving moments that make it one of the showcases for Machinima. If you want to explain to an aged but artistic relative why you're spending all this time playing with computer games, show them *The Journey.*

# Edge of Remorse

*Edge of Remorse,* directed by Jason Choi, may be the most visually sophisticated Machinima production yet released. It's made in World of Warcraft, or at least using World of Warcraft characters; in actual fact, the production was a marvel of sophisticated compositing and 2D effects. But the story and style owe less to Tolkien than Kurosawa.

The plot is simple. Two brothers love the same girl. One turns to good and wins the girl. The other turns to evil. Tragedy ensues. But the strength of *Edge of Remorse* is in its beautiful cinematography, the sophistication of its wordless, interleaved storytelling, and the emotive power of its imagery. Several shots from the film — a brother's face wreathed in shadow, the iconic dueling shots — seem destined to become classic images of the medium as a whole.

If you want to see an amateur filmmaker compete with the best art directors of Hollywood, see *Edge of Return* now.

# The Return

*"Today we fight! We fight! For those who have fallen, for those who we love, for the sons and daughters, mothers and fathers, who watch over us now!"*

Machinima's really unique, killer selling point is that it allows filmmakers with no money to compete on scale with the Peter Jacksons and George Lucases of this world. But before 2005, there really weren't any Machinima films that had achieved both scale and quality. Enter *The Return*.

Made by the collective known as Rufus Cubed, *The Return* is a tale of a man returning from war to find that the same war has touched his home. It's short, it's near perfect in its filming and realization, and it boasts possibly the best vocal performance ever in Machinima, from Ezra as Voldegar, the lead character.

We've been going on about how Machinima can let you compete with the *Lord of the Rings* films. Want proof in five minutes? Go see *The Return*.

# Chapter 21

# Ten Ways to Ruin Your Machinima Movie

*In This Chapter*
▶ Ensuring disaster with poor planning
▶ Sabotaging your movie by ignoring the details

**W**hat's that you say? You're allergic to success, and you're determined to make the worst Machinima movie in the history of the medium? Well, that's quite a challenge — there is some real junk out there — but we're here to help.

In this chapter, we give you a list of guaranteed death-blows for any Machinima movie. Follow along, and your masterpiece will be a stinking disaster before you know it.

# Don't Plan!

You don't want to lose that spark of impromptu creativity. All the greatest geniuses winged it — why be different? After all, it's not like Machinima requires a whole bunch of different disciplines to come together at once, or there's a complex preproduction stage that you need to get right.

Don't plan and don't think about what you'll need to do to make this movie, and you can guarantee that:

 ✔ You'll discover your production is five times as hard as you thought it was.

 ✔ You needed that set finished yesterday, or you can't do any work today, and the guy who's making it is away in France for the weekend.

 ✔ Your volunteer crew is getting fed up making things that you send back because you didn't plan what you really needed.

Distaining any form of contingency planning or forethought will probably doom your venture to failure. Yay!

# Don't Spend Time on Your Script

You're all enthused about making this Machinima stuff. You want to make the best movie evar on the interwebz. You're ready to get started!

Script? You don't need a script. Sure, if you've got a dull story, characters who don't engage (or indeed exist), or accidental lines so bad that no one can listen without laughing, your movie's doomed from the start. Sure, no matter how long you spend on your script, it'll still be a tiny fraction of the time you spend on actually filming the piece of drivel you scribbled in five minutes. Sure, every Hollywood expert tells us that the script is the most important part of your movie.

The greatest filmmakers struggle to make something tolerable out of a dire script. Neither we, nor you, are as talented as they are. If your script stinks, you'll spend weeks or months slaving to realize your original artistic vision, only to conclude that your original vision was a view out of the hotel window onto an alley full of garbage cans.

# Get Your Friends to Act

My friend Dan is so funny! He'll be great in this movie!

Actually, Dan's only funny when he's hanging around with you and the rest of your clique, cracking jokes. Dan's not an actor. He has terrible diction and an absolute inability to emote. Anyone who doesn't know him won't be able to understand a word, let alone enjoy his performance.

You can find an actual actor— someone who will speak your carefully crafted lines well. Somebody who may actually be able to deliver comedy. Somebody who's spent several years training to do exactly this, and who is as passionate about being an actor as you are about being a filmmaker. Someone who can deliver your script even better than you'd imagined.

Bad plan. You can count on Dan.

# *Ignore Camerawork*

There's a complex language of cinematography, and in order to use it properly, you have to do a lot of learning. You have to watch a lot of movies, and you have to do some brain-melting visualization of your finished movie. In fact, the best Hollywood cinematographers try to compose *each and every shot* to look like an oil painting.

That sounds a bit like hard work; Machinima is supposed to be easy. Aside from the occasional funky flying camera shot to show off your cool set with the sparkly bits, you've just got to make sure that your audience can see your characters, right? No need for this camerawork nonsense.

Of course, if you don't worry about camerawork, your movie will look really, really ugly, and your characters will just stand there and look like planks of wood, but that was true of your high-school play, too, and your parents said that was wonderful.

# *Don't Cut It Down to Size*

Feature movies get more respect than little YouTube efforts — which proves that when it comes to movies, longer is better. So, when you're making your movie, just shoot it, string all the shots together, and call it a movie. Twenty-two minutes and eight seconds of the two leads walking down a corridor? Great plan! Gives the audience more time to watch their trench coats swish in a cool way.

Those small-minded, so-called "professional" filmmakers will insist on editing pass after editing pass. They'll tell you that to get to a well-edited movie, you have to keep cutting and juggling long after you think it's as tight as it can possibly be. You may even have to listen to some idiot scriptwriter pointing out the parts of your story that aren't needed, or that just don't make sense.

These morons will do their best to convince you to chop and rearrange your movie, then show it to other people and have them chop out bits too, until it's a slick, fat-free ninja of a movie. Stick to your guns. What do they know, eh?

# Don't Get Help

If we wanted to talk to people, we'd be doing theater.

The great thing about Machinima is that you can do everything you need to do to make a movie by yourself. You can create the sets — you're not an artist, but they look OK. You can make the characters — you don't know anything about costume design, but they look all right. You can do the sound, find the music, and record your own voice. All this stuff is easy. It's not like anyone dedicates her life to one element of it.

It's quite easy to find people who want to help with your movie. If you just place a couple of adverts in the right place, they'll practically come begging. And with more people helping, you can split the workload so that you don't have to make 20 sets all by yourself. You'd have people to review work and bounce ideas against, and you'd be able to find people who are genuinely expert and passionate in the things you need. You'd also find it more fun working with people than sitting in your basement alone.

But that would involve talking to people. And we don't want to do that.

# Copy Existing Machinima Movies

When you start making movies, you'll probably be doing it because you're inspired by other movies and film-makers. Perhaps you saw that great *Red vs Blue* series and figured you could do the same thing, but starring your friend Dan. (See Chapter 20 for more on *Red vs Blue.*)

Whatever you do, don't analyze why you liked the thing that inspired you. Don't think about how you can make something that has the same elements as the movie you like, but is original in other ways. Absolutely do not think about what the mechanics of that thing are, or why it works, and try to take those lessons to another movie that reflects other things you like or care about, too.

Just turn on your X-Box, sit down, and make another comedy about computer game characters saying funny things. Because that's obviously what made the original so successful.

# Don't Read About Filmmaking

No matter what mistake you're about to make, some poor fool of a film-maker has already made it. No matter how obscure the scene or how complex the sequence you're about to attempt, someone's done something similar and has useful advice on how to make it better.

And what's worse, not only have they done these things, but the evil, evil people have even written about it! They've written entire books full of mistakes they made, and things they've learned about making better movies! Some of them have even written on the Internet so that you don't even have to spend money to learn from them!

Clearly, it's vital that you don't read this stuff. Use whatever excuse you like. Say that you don't believe you can learn to make "art." Say that "old" moviemaking has nothing to teach the Internet generation. Just stick your fingers in your ears and go "la, la, la."

# Don't Release Unless It's Perfect

This movie is your masterpiece; it's the visual personification of your heart and soul. This movie is like a lover to you. Just like a lover, you want to change, fix, or just outright get rid of certain little irritating aspects. Until it's absolutely, exactly the movie you have in your head, there' no way you're going to be seen in public with *that* on your arm, so lock it in the basement until it puts the lotion on its skin, or else it gets the hose again.

Your movie is never going to be perfect. The best thing to do is to keep tweaking it. Constantly. Unendingly. That way, there's no danger that anybody may ever get to see it.

# Don't Tell Anyone about It

If you build it, they will come. A quiet, understated release is what's called for.

How about just putting it up on your blog (three dedicated readers and eight people selling "V1agra"), and seeing what happens? Maybe you can e-mail a few friends? You know, the ones who helped with it anyway and already know about it. Send Dan an e-mail, for starters.

Unless you let people know that you've made a movie, they won't watch it. Not because they don't want to, but because they don't know it exists. So, don't announce it on the major Machinima sites. Don't upload it to any video-sharing sites. For goodness' sake, don't let anyone hear about it.

# Chapter 22

# Ten Machinima Sites to Bookmark

*Y*ou're not alone. Thousands of other Machinima creators are out there, discussing the topics in this book and much more. You can get help, advice, criticism, and friendship if you know where to look.

Here's a list of the top-ten Machinima sites, in our opinion, as of May 2007.

## Machinima Premiere

www.mprem.com

The premiere (no pun intended) Machinima community site, Machinima Premiere, boasts active discussions and up-to-the-minute news covering a wide range of Machinima-related issues. It's a must-read and must-subscribe.

## Sims99

www.sims99.com

There's a thriving community of Machinima makers using The Sims 2 as its engine of choice, and Sims99 is the hub of all this activity. Machinima makers of all hues can benefit from a visit to this huge and informative site, which covers much more than just The Sims 2 Machinima. As of May 2007, Sims99 listed more than 5,000 movies. Sims99 offers great forums, too.

# Machinima.com

`www.machinima.com`

Over the last few years, Machinima.com changed hands, and its development since has been the source of some controversy. Critics point to lack of development, a very limited community, frequent PR disasters, and slow updates of anything other than movies. However, its advocates point out that it still has a massive archive of forum posts and articles, and one of the largest and most actively updated archives of Machinima films on the Net. We debated long and hard about how and whether to include Machinima.com in this list, but in the end, we certainly recommend that you check it out and decide for yourself.

# Machinima Film Festival

`festival.machinima.org`

Machinima has its own film festival, you know. If you get a chance to attend, you absolutely must, but the Festival's official site is a good place to get your fix meanwhile. You can also get updates on the competition for the Mackies — Machinima's equivalent of the Oscars. This site has links to all the nominated movies each year, too, for a quick peek at the best of Machinima.

# Thinking Machinima

`www.machinima.org/paul_blog`

Paul Marino is the President of the Academy of Machinima Arts and Sciences. He's one of the pioneers of Machinima. He directed two of the vids on our top-ten list in Chapter 20. Oh, and he won one of those Emmy things. And now, he's blogging about Machinima. Go sit at his virtual feet and learn.

# Machinima For Dummies Blog

`www.machinimafordummies.com`

This site is the blog for the book you're currently holding. We're already blogging extensively over there, adding more tips, comments, and any errata, as well as freely downloadable content (also known as "all the stuff we couldn't fit into the book but really wanted to").

# Machinifeed

www.machinifeed.com

We spent several months trying to decide which Machinima blog to mention in this spot. Should we mention Peter Rasmussen's Nanoflix blog? Shattered Keyboard, known for insightful commentary and discussion? Well, we don't have to choose. Machinifeed, maintained by Phil "Overman" Rice, is an aggregation of every blog feed on the Interweb relevant to Machinima. It's a vital resource for any Machinima filmmaker.

# The Overcast

www.theovercast.com

Phil "Overman" Rice was a prominent figure in the early days of the Machinima scene and made a triumphant return to the scene in 2004. Phil writes and records a Machinima-themed podcast called The Overcast, which is simply essential listening. He's also the maintainer of the Machinifeed, the director of *Male Restroom Etiquette,* the sound editor on *BloodSpell,* the general reviewer on this book, and an inhuman robot of productivity. We mentioned he does all this stuff in his spare time, right?

# The Internet Archive Machinima Section

www.archive.org/machinima

In this world, you find very few out-and-out Good Guys. Brewster Kahle is one of them — the guy who founded the Internet Archive, dedicated to, well, archiving everything from the Internet. The Archive runs a Machinima section, administrated by longtime Machinima supporter Henry Lowood, offering a huge and varied collection of Machinima videos.

# WarcraftMovies.com

www.warcraftmovies.com

In the UK, we have an expression stolen from a series of incredibly successful ads: "Does exactly what it says on the tin." WarcraftMovies.com — well, it has lots of movies made in Warcraft or World of Warcraft. People talk there, too, about Warcraft and making movies in Warcraft. So if you want to make movies using World of Warcraft or watch movies in World of Warcraft, you want to visit this site.

# Appendix

# About the DVD

*I*n this appendix, you find out everything you need to know about the DVD that accompanies this book.

## System Requirements

Make sure that your computer meets the minimum system requirements shown in the following list. If your computer doesn't match up to most of these requirements, you may have problems using the software and files on the DVD. For the latest and greatest information, please refer to the ReadMe file located at the root of the DVD-ROM.

- ✔ A PC running Windows 2000 or Windows XP. Windows Vista may have problems with some software.
- ✔ A Macintosh running Apple OS X or later will run some of these programs.
- ✔ A PC running a version of Linux with kernel 2.4 or greater will run some of these programs.
- ✔ A broadband Internet connection is required for some files

If you need more information on the basics, check out these books published by Wiley Publishing, Inc.: *PCs For Dummies,* by Dan Gookin; *Macs For Dummies,* 9th Edition, by Edward C. Baig; *iMac For Dummies,* 4th Edition, by Mark Chambers; *Windows XP For Dummies* and *Windows Vista For Dummies,* by Andy Rathbone.

# Using the DVD

To install the items from the DVD to your hard drive, follow these steps.

1. **Insert the DVD into your computer's DVD-ROM drive.**

   The license agreement appears.

   *Note to Windows users:* The interface won't launch if you have autorun disabled. In that case, choose Start⇨Run (For Windows Vista, choose Start⇨All Programs⇨Accessories⇨Run). In the dialog box that appears, type D:\Start.exe. (Replace D with the proper letter if your DVD drive uses a different letter. If you don't know the letter, see how your DVD drive is listed under My Computer.) Click OK.

   *Note for Mac users:* The DVD icon will appear on your desktop. Double-click the icon to open the DVD and double-click the Start icon.

2. **Read through the license agreement and then click the Accept button if you want to use the DVD.**

   The DVD interface appears. The interface allows you to install the programs and run the demos with just a click of a button (or two).

# What You'll Find on the DVD

The following sections are arranged by category and provide a summary of the software and other goodies you'll find on the DVD. If you need help with installing the items provided on the DVD, refer back to the installation instructions in the preceding section.

*Shareware programs* are fully functional, free, trial versions of copyrighted programs. If you like particular programs, register with their authors for a nominal fee and receive licenses, enhanced versions, and technical support.

*Freeware programs* are free, copyrighted games, applications, and utilities. You can copy them to as many PCs as you like — for free — but they offer no technical support.

*GNU* and *open-source software* is governed by its own license, which is included inside the folder of the GNU software. There are no restrictions on distribution of GNU software. See the GNU license at the root of the DVD for more details.

*Trial, demo,* or *evaluation* versions of software are usually limited either by time or functionality (such as not letting you save a project after you create it).

## Tutorial material

*Freeware for Windows and Mac.*

All the examples provided in this book are located in the Tutorial directory on the DVD and work with the Machinima platforms listed in the book. These files are included:

- **Tutorial/Medieval:** Batch and configuration files for Medieval II: Total War
- **Tutorial/FirstMovie:** Files for Chapter 2
- **Tutorial/Moviestorm:** Files for Chapter 17
- **Tutorial/MfD.tga:** TGA file for Chapter 16

## Moviestorm

*Full software for Windows.*

A fully-working copy of this dedicated Machinima tool. Any movies you make using this software are licensed for commercial distribution. You'll also find a basic demonstration movie already assembled for you and ready to film — "your first Machinima movie." See Chapter 2 for where and how to use this. The demonstration movie will be automatically installed when you install Moviestorm.

## Our top films

*Not system- or software-specific.*

As listed in Chapter 20, some of our top ten Machinima films are included on the DVD. Sadly, we couldn't include all of them on the DVD; but you can find links to the ones that are absent at www.machinimafordummies.com.

## Open-source utilities

The following open-source utilities make your Machinima creation easier:

- **VirtualDub:** For Windows, an excellent AVI compression and processing package.
- **Audacity:** For Windows and Linux, one of the best audio-editing programs available.
- **Celtx:** For Windows, an excellent scriptwriting tool. Not covered in the book.
- **GIMPShop:** For Windows, a high-end art- and image-manipulation package.
- **Blogbridge:** For Windows, Mac, and Linux, an excellent RSS feed reader.
- **Democracy Player:** For Windows, Mac, and Linux, a revolutionary video player.
- **VLC:** For Windows, Mac, and Linux, a powerful video player.
- **Warcraft Model Viewer:** For Windows, software to allow easy filming of World of Warcraft character models and animations.
- **Blender:** For Windows, Mac, and Linux, full 3D modeling and animation package.
- **SimPE:** For Windows, the Sims 2 package explorer and editor.
- **7-Zip:** For Windows, one of the best `.zip` and `.rar` compression and decompression packages.

## Freeware utilities

The following freeware utilities make your Machinima creation easier:

- **Warcraft Map Viewer:** For Windows, software to allow easy filming of World of Warcraft maps.
- **HxD:** For Windows, a highly capable hex editor.
- **HuffYUV codec:** For Windows, an excellent lossless video codec.
- **Decorgal's Lipsynching Tools:** For Windows and Mac, lipsynching tools for The Sims 2.

## Trial software

The DVD also includes a trial version of FRAPS, video-capturing software for Windows.

## *Trial software*

The DVD also includes a trial version of FRAPS, video-capturing software for Windows.

# *Troubleshooting*

We tried our best to find programs that work on most computers with the minimum system requirements. Alas, your computer may differ, and some programs may not work properly for some reason.

The two likeliest problems are that you don't have enough memory (RAM) for the programs you want to use, or you have other programs running that are affecting installation or running of a program. If you get an error message such as `Not enough memory` or `Setup cannot continue`, try one or more of the following suggestions and then try using the software again:

- ✔ **Turn off any antivirus software running on your computer.** Installation programs sometimes mimic virus activity and may make your computer incorrectly believe that it's being infected by a virus.

- ✔ **Close all running programs.** The more programs you have running, the less memory is available to other programs. Installation programs typically update files and programs; so if you keep other programs running, installation may not work properly.

    Obviously, if you're using an add-on for a Machinima package, you shouldn't close the main package!

- ✔ **Have your local computer store add more RAM to your computer.** This step is, admittedly, drastic and somewhat expensive. However, adding more memory can really help the speed of your computer and allow more programs to run at the same time.

**Customer Care:** If you have trouble with the DVD, please call the Wiley Product Technical Support phone number at (800) 762-2974. Outside the United States, call (317) 572-3994. You can also contact Wiley Product Technical Support at `http://support.wiley.com`. John Wiley & Sons will provide technical support only for installation and other general quality control items. For technical support on the applications themselves, consult the program's vendor or author.

To place additional orders or to request information about other Wiley products, please call (877) 762-2974.

# Index

## • *M* •

## • Q •

## • R •

# Notes

## BUSINESS, CAREERS & PERSONAL FINANCE

0-7645-9847-3

0-7645-2431-3

**Also available:**

- Business Plans Kit For Dummies
  0-7645-9794-9
- Economics For Dummies
  0-7645-5726-2
- Grant Writing For Dummies
  0-7645-8416-2
- Home Buying For Dummies
  0-7645-5331-3
- Managing For Dummies
  0-7645-1771-6
- Marketing For Dummies
  0-7645-5600-2

- Personal Finance For Dummies
  0-7645-2590-5*
- Resumes For Dummies
  0-7645-5471-9
- Selling For Dummies
  0-7645-5363-1
- Six Sigma For Dummies
  0-7645-6798-5
- Small Business Kit For Dummies
  0-7645-5984-2
- Starting an eBay Business For Dummies
  0-7645-6924-4
- Your Dream Career For Dummies
  0-7645-9795-7

## HOME & BUSINESS COMPUTER BASICS

0-470-05432-8

0-471-75421-8

**Also available:**

- Cleaning Windows Vista For Dummies
  0-471-78293-9
- Excel 2007 For Dummies
  0-470-03737-7
- Mac OS X Tiger For Dummies
  0-7645-7675-5
- MacBook For Dummies
  0-470-04859-X
- Macs For Dummies
  0-470-04849-2
- Office 2007 For Dummies
  0-470-00923-3

- Outlook 2007 For Dummies
  0-470-03830-6
- PCs For Dummies
  0-7645-8958-X
- Salesforce.com For Dummies
  0-470-04893-X
- Upgrading & Fixing Laptops For Dummies
  0-7645-8959-8
- Word 2007 For Dummies
  0-470-03658-3
- Quicken 2007 For Dummies
  0-470-04600-7

## FOOD, HOME, GARDEN, HOBBIES, MUSIC & PETS

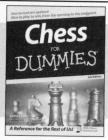

0-7645-8404-9

0-7645-9904-6

**Also available:**

- Candy Making For Dummies
  0-7645-9734-5
- Card Games For Dummies
  0-7645-9910-0
- Crocheting For Dummies
  0-7645-4151-X
- Dog Training For Dummies
  0-7645-8418-9
- Healthy Carb Cookbook For Dummies
  0-7645-8476-6
- Home Maintenance For Dummies
  0-7645-5215-5

- Horses For Dummies
  0-7645-9797-3
- Jewelry Making & Beading For Dummies
  0-7645-2571-9
- Orchids For Dummies
  0-7645-6759-4
- Puppies For Dummies
  0-7645-5255-4
- Rock Guitar For Dummies
  0-7645-5356-9
- Sewing For Dummies
  0-7645-6847-7
- Singing For Dummies
  0-7645-2475-5

## INTERNET & DIGITAL MEDIA

0-470-04529-9

0-470-04894-8

**Also available:**

- Blogging For Dummies
  0-471-77084-1
- Digital Photography For Dummies
  0-7645-9802-3
- Digital Photography All-in-One Desk Reference For Dummies
  0-470-03743-1
- Digital SLR Cameras and Photography For Dummies
  0-7645-9803-1
- eBay Business All-in-One Desk Reference For Dummies
  0-7645-8438-3
- HDTV For Dummies
  0-470-09673-X

- Home Entertainment PCs For Dummies
  0-470-05523-5
- MySpace For Dummies
  0-470-09529-6
- Search Engine Optimization For Dummies
  0-471-97998-8
- Skype For Dummies
  0-470-04891-3
- The Internet For Dummies
  0-7645-8996-2
- Wiring Your Digital Home For Dummies
  0-471-91830-X

* Separate Canadian edition also available
* Separate U.K. edition also available

Available wherever books are sold. For more information or to order direct: U.S. customers visit www.dummies.com or call 1-877-762-2974.
U.K. customers visit www.wileyeurope.com or call 0800 243407. Canadian customers visit www.wiley.ca or call 1-800-567-4797.

**WILEY**

# SPORTS, FITNESS, PARENTING, RELIGION & SPIRITUALITY

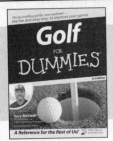

0-471-76871-5

0-7645-7841-3

**Also available:**
- Catholicism For Dummies
0-7645-5391-7
- Exercise Balls For Dummies
0-7645-5623-1
- Fitness For Dummies
0-7645-7851-0
- Football For Dummies
0-7645-3936-1
- Judaism For Dummies
0-7645-5299-6
- Potty Training For Dummies
0-7645-5417-4
- Buddhism For Dummies
0-7645-5359-3

- Pregnancy For Dummies
0-7645-4483-7 †
- Ten Minute Tone-Ups For Dummies
0-7645-7207-5
- NASCAR For Dummies
0-7645-7681-X
- Religion For Dummies
0-7645-5264-3
- Soccer For Dummies
0-7645-5229-5
- Women in the Bible For Dummies
0-7645-8475-8

# TRAVEL

0-7645-7749-2

0-7645-6945-7

**Also available:**
- Alaska For Dummies
0-7645-7746-8
- Cruise Vacations For Dummies
0-7645-6941-4
- England For Dummies
0-7645-4276-1
- Europe For Dummies
0-7645-7529-5
- Germany For Dummies
0-7645-7823-5
- Hawaii For Dummies
0-7645-7402-7

- Italy For Dummies
0-7645-7386-1
- Las Vegas For Dummies
0-7645-7382-9
- London For Dummies
0-7645-4277-X
- Paris For Dummies
0-7645-7630-5
- RV Vacations For Dummies
0-7645-4442-X
- Walt Disney World & Orlando
For Dummies
0-7645-9660-8

# GRAPHICS, DESIGN & WEB DEVELOPMENT

0-7645-8815-X

0-7645-9571-7

**Also available:**
- 3D Game Animation For Dummies
0-7645-8789-7
- AutoCAD 2006 For Dummies
0-7645-8925-3
- Building a Web Site For Dummies
0-7645-7144-3
- Creating Web Pages For Dummies
0-470-08030-2
- Creating Web Pages All-in-One Desk
Reference For Dummies
0-7645-4345-8
- Dreamweaver 8 For Dummies
0-7645-9649-7

- InDesign CS2 For Dummies
0-7645-9572-5
- Macromedia Flash 8 For Dummies
0-7645-9691-8
- Photoshop CS2 and Digital
Photography For Dummies
0-7645-9580-6
- Photoshop Elements 4 For Dummies
0-471-77483-9
- Syndicating Web Sites with RSS Feeds
For Dummies
0-7645-8848-6
- Yahoo! SiteBuilder For Dummies
0-7645-9800-7

# NETWORKING, SECURITY, PROGRAMMING & DATABASES

0-7645-7728-X

0-471-74940-0

**Also available:**
- Access 2007 For Dummies
0-470-04612-0
- ASP.NET 2 For Dummies
0-7645-7907-X
- C# 2005 For Dummies
0-7645-9704-3
- Hacking For Dummies
0-470-05235-X
- Hacking Wireless Networks
For Dummies
0-7645-9730-2
- Java For Dummies
0-470-08716-1

- Microsoft SQL Server 2005 For Dummies
0-7645-7755-7
- Networking All-in-One Desk Reference
For Dummies
0-7645-9939-9
- Preventing Identity Theft For Dummies
0-7645-7336-5
- Telecom For Dummies
0-471-77085-X
- Visual Studio 2005 All-in-One Desk
Reference For Dummies
0-7645-9775-2
- XML For Dummies
0-7645-8845-1

## HEALTH & SELF-HELP

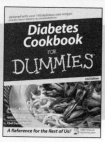

0-7645-8450-2

0-7645-4149-8

**Also available:**
- Bipolar Disorder For Dummies
  0-7645-8451-0
- Chemotherapy and Radiation
  For Dummies
  0-7645-7832-4
- Controlling Cholesterol For Dummies
  0-7645-5440-9
- Diabetes For Dummies
  0-7645-6820-5* †
- Divorce For Dummies
  0-7645-8417-0 †

- Fibromyalgia For Dummies
  0-7645-5441-7
- Low-Calorie Dieting For Dummies
  0-7645-9905-4
- Meditation For Dummies
  0-471-77774-9
- Osteoporosis For Dummies
  0-7645-7621-6
- Overcoming Anxiety For Dummies
  0-7645-5447-6
- Reiki For Dummies
  0-7645-9907-0
- Stress Management For Dummies
  0-7645-5144-2

## EDUCATION, HISTORY, REFERENCE & TEST PREPARATION

0-7645-8381-6

0-7645-9554-7

**Also available:**
- The ACT For Dummies
  0-7645-9652-7
- Algebra For Dummies
  0-7645-5325-9
- Algebra Workbook For Dummies
  0-7645-8467-7
- Astronomy For Dummies
  0-7645-8465-0
- Calculus For Dummies
  0-7645-2498-4
- Chemistry For Dummies
  0-7645-5430-1
- Forensics For Dummies
  0-7645-5580-4

- Freemasons For Dummies
  0-7645-9796-5
- French For Dummies
  0-7645-5193-0
- Geometry For Dummies
  0-7645-5324-0
- Organic Chemistry I For Dummies
  0-7645-6902-3
- The SAT I For Dummies
  0-7645-7193-1
- Spanish For Dummies
  0-7645-5194-9
- Statistics For Dummies
  0-7645-5423-9

# Get smart @ dummies.com®

- **Find a full list of Dummies titles**
- **Look into loads of FREE on-site articles**
- **Sign up for FREE eTips e-mailed to you weekly**
- **See what other products carry the Dummies name**
- **Shop directly from the Dummies bookstore**
- **Enter to win new prizes every month!**

* Separate Canadian edition also available
† Separate U.K. edition also available

Available wherever books are sold. For more information or to order direct: U.S. customers visit www.dummies.com or call 1-877-762-2974.
U.K. customers visit www.wileyeurope.com or call 0800 243407. Canadian customers visit www.wiley.ca or call 1-800-567-4797.

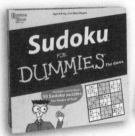